Hermes Pan

Hermes Pan

The Man Who Danced with Fred Astaire

JOHN FRANCESCHINA

OXFORD
UNIVERSITY PRESS

OXFORD
UNIVERSITY PRESS

Oxford University Press, Inc., publishes works that further
Oxford University's objective of excellence
in research, scholarship, and education.

Oxford   New York
Auckland   Cape Town   Dar es Salaam   Hong Kong   Karachi
Kuala Lumpur   Madrid   Melbourne   Mexico City   Nairobi
New Delhi   Shanghai   Taipei   Toronto
With offices in
Argentina   Austria   Brazil   Chile   Czech Republic   France   Greece
Guatemala   Hungary   Italy   Japan   Poland   Portugal   Singapore
South Korea   Switzerland   Thailand   Turkey   Ukraine   Vietnam

Published by Oxford University Press, Inc.
198 Madison Avenue, New York, New York 10016

www.oup.com

Oxford is a registered trademark of Oxford University Press

Library of Congress Cataloging-in-Publication Data
Franceschina, John Charles, 1947-
Hermes Pan: the man who danced with Fred Astaire /John Franceschina.
p.   cm.
Includes bibliographical references.
ISBN 978-0-19-975429-8 (alk. paper)
1. Pan, Hermes, 1909–1990 2. Choreographers—United States—Biography. 3. Dance in motion pictures,
television, etc.—United States—History. I. Title.
GV1785.P2713F73 2012
792.82092—dc23
[B]
2011035538

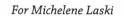

For Michelene Laski

CONTENTS

Foreword   ix

Introduction   3
1. Black Bottom to Broadway   9
2. Try Dancing   21
3. Fifteen Cents a Dance   33
4. The Man Who Danced with Fred Astaire   52
5. Chica Chica Boom Chic   102
6. Red Robins, Bob Whites, and Bluebirds   128
7. Wonderful Nonsense   154
8. He Could Make a Wooden Indian Dance   167
9. The Life of an Elephant   186
10. Star Turns   210
11. Seventy-Five Watusi Witch Doctors   234
12. Help Me Dream   252

Acknowledgments   271
Notes   273
Bibliography   283
Index   291

FOREWORD

When John told me he was preparing a biography of my uncle Hermes, I was surprised and happy—and worried how he might convey Hermes's personality. I'm sure Tio, as we called him, would have been edgy at the prospect; he could be uneasy when he was the center of attention.

Hermes Pan would *love* this book!

For my part, I enjoyed talking to John and sharing the humanizing family details that are frequently missing from the biographies I've read. Tio's sense of humor and his affectionate involvement in our family are not usually evident in the many articles about his dancing career. John, on the other hand, has captured the gentle, kind, and quirky side of the man who to me, my brother, and my two sisters was like a bonus father. I am so grateful.

Michelene Laski

Hermes Pan

Introduction

When you're involved in something that later becomes great,
you never realize it at the time. You just hope it's good.
                    —Hermes Pan to Maureen C. Solomon, 1983

It would satisfy Hermes Pan, who had a unique sense of humor, to begin with a chicken joke, or at least an amusing story. One of his favorites was about the time he joined Cole Porter on a Friday evening for dinner at Henri Soulé's Le Pavillon, fashionably regarded as the finest French restaurant in New York City. Nervously awaiting the arrival of the famous Broadway composer, Hermes spent a good part of an hour drinking martinis—four of them in all—so by the time he and Cole were seated, at a premium table in a dim alcove just off the main dining room, Pan was feeling no pain. Porter was an ebullient host and a felicitous raconteur whose witty topics of conversation were matched by his elegantly prearranged menu selection: caviar, Caesar salad, and a chicken perfectly prepared in a delicate golden sauce. A dinner fit for a king—but not Hermes Pan whose religious beliefs taught him not to eat meat on Fridays. Not wanting to appear dissatisfied with Porter's choice of entrée and order something else, Hermes decided that his best option was to pretend to eat the chicken—the four martinis had done their best to prevent any other solution from entering his mind. Misdirecting Porter through lively conversation, Pan proceeded to take the chicken, a bite at a time, and drop it into the napkin on his lap, interjecting a vegetable into his mouth between the discarded bites—all the time watching Porter's gaze so that the ruse could be completed outside of the composer's line of vision. Hermes had managed to dispose of all the chicken on his plate by the time champagne, dessert, coffee, and brandy were served, and the ruse would have passed unnoticed if not for the busboy clearing the table who grabbed Pan's napkin and let fly the hidden chicken all over the restaurant's rich red carpet—in view of Porter and everyone else seated in the vicinity. Cole said nothing to Pan about the incident, but when he was at dinner with Fred Astaire, a few months later, Porter told him about it, concluding, "Pan's very nice, but you know he's a little *scary.*"

Called the "doyen of Hollywood dance directors,"[1] having the longest career of any choreographer in musical films, the "quiet giant of film dance" who, with Fred Astaire, "created not just a series of film musicals, but a series of icons that permanently etched in the public's mind for generations what film dancing and, indeed, Broadway dancing were supposed to look like,"[2] Hermes Pan is a legendary figure to fans and students of the Hollywood musical, yet all but unknown to the general public. If his career had been limited to the Fred Astaire–Ginger Rogers musicals he choreographed at RKO, his work would be worthy of a full-length study, but given the fact that he went on to choreograph at Twentieth Century-Fox, M-G-M, Paramount, and later for television, winning both the Oscar and the Emmy for best choreography, a book-length study of Pan's eighty-nine films is a necessary addition to the annals of film dance. As dance historian Jerome Delamater wrote in 1979, "Hermes Pan has one of the most extensive careers—extending from 1933 to the present—of any Hollywood dance director,"[3] and yet, except for a handful of articles and interviews published in dance magazines—and most of those keeping him in the shadow of Fred Astaire—he remains an obscure figure.[4] Although Pan did not lead a controversial life—critic John Kobal once described him as "self-effacing to the point of almost vanishing"[5]—writing about Hermes Pan is tracing the history of the Hollywood musical from its golden age. It is a study of the collaboration between a "benevolent perfectionist" who cared as much about the human being as he did about the dancing, and the stars, composers, and directors with whom he worked.

In the early 1980s, David Patrick Columbia and Kenyon Kramer convinced Pan to collaborate with them on an autobiography entitled "Dancin' in the Movies: A Hollywood Life," of which an outline and two sample chapters were completed as of 12 October 1983. No publisher was interested in optioning the prospectus. As a choreographer, Pan was considered old news, and his life deemed too ordinary to be of much interest to readers. Some years later, David Patrick Columbia attempted to stimulate interest in another Pan biography, *The Man Who Danced with Fred Astaire*, and he met with the same disinterest. The response to documenting Pan's life was hardly surprising. Even his niece, Michelene Laski, responded quizzically when I approached her about the present biography. "There's nothing to write about," she insisted. Pan was universally revered as the kindest man in the world. There were no scandals, no hidden agendas, or closeted skeletons. "He led a normal life."

Normalcy is certainly relative particularly when it is applied to the choreographer of eighty-nine films and Fred Astaire's most frequent collaborator. In many ways, Pan lived the American Dream. Armed with only an eighth-grade education, an inexhaustible imagination, and a talent for dancing, Pan rose from the ranks of the Depression's poor to the most prolific and arguably the most successful of Hollywood's film choreographers, supporting his sister and widowed mother along the way, befriended by stars and starlets, princesses, and world and religious leaders. Living comfortably in Beverly Hills, Rome, and Tehran, where he was a frequent guest of the shah of Iran at the Golestan Palace, he spent his retirement in good health and celebrated for his achievements, a beloved and admired figure until his death. To what already appears to be too perfect an existence, Pan added a lifetime friendship and collaboration with Fred Astaire, the greatest dancer of his generation; deeply committed religious beliefs; a genuine concern for everyone he met; an unbounded generosity toward his family and friends; and the humbleness and selflessness of a monk—all of which is supported by factual evidence.

A closer examination of what appears to be a rags-to-riches fairy tale, however, reveals a great many apparent contradictions in Pan's life. Even though he was prolific, he was not a workaholic—far from it. In the words of David Patrick Columbia, "Pan simply fell into choreographing. If he could do what he wanted, he'd stay at home, drink wine, smoke cigarettes, and dance. He wasn't ambitious."[6] And, even though he achieved great fame as a choreographer, he never thought of choreography as his life's work. It was his "day job," an activity he enjoyed but not what he felt defined him. Unlike other major Hollywood choreographers, Jack Cole, Bob Fosse, or Michael Kidd, for example, Pan claimed not to have a characteristic style to his work, preferring to allow the period of the film and the dramatic situation to dictate the style of his choreography. Pan believed that dance was the elevation of real life into fantasy and worked to make his dances fun to perform. Jerry Jackson, Pan's friend and assistant, noted that Pan's genius lay in finding the essence and mood of a number. "Hermes was less interested in steps than the style and theatricality of the movement. He might take suggestions from his dancers or assistants, but he always had a concept of the style and dramatic necessity of the movement."[7] Popular dance forms, special effects, and an ever-present sense of humor were hallmarks of Pan's choreography, all designed to serve the needs of the film rather than create any kind of brand. In many ways, Hermes resembled more the anonymous artisan or monk from the Middle Ages who viewed himself as a conduit of God's inspiration. Devoutly religious, Pan believed that his remarkable abilities were God-given and that he was the vessel through which his talent found fruition in the dancer's movements. Without ambition or inflated ego, Hermes never pushed himself out to be noticed. He honestly believed that his place was in the shadow of the performers.

Similarly, Hermes appeared satisfied to live in the shadows in his personal life. As Jerry Jackson observed, "He led a very private life,"[8] one that was anomalous to his being among the A-list Hollywood personalities always in demand at parties and opening nights. Hermes was grateful to have been accepted into Hollywood society though he was not entirely comfortable in it. He liked people but hated pretense and gossip—the stuff of which he believed Tinseltown was created. Still, he was a devoted friend to many great stars—Ann Miller, Ginger Rogers, Lana Turner, Rita Hayworth, Richard Burton, Elizabeth Taylor, Tyrone Power, Linda Darnell, Katharine Hepburn, to name a few. Pan was an expert listener and confidant but rarely shared the details of his private life even with his closest friends, and in public interviews he was happy to reveal the details of his youth, discuss his work with Fred Astaire, and offer advice to young hopefuls, but he never steered the discussion toward his personal life. As David Patrick Columbia suggested, "Hermes never felt like a big deal." He truly did not believe his life was a subject worth discussing.

It was well known in the film community that Hermes Pan was homosexual but nothing was ever spoken about it in public.[9] There is no record of when he actually realized his preference, but his experience as a chorus boy in Broadway musicals certainly provided him the opportunity to interact with like-minded young men. In Hollywood, Pan's accumulation of gay friends became a problem because, as he told David Patrick Columbia, his mother did not like seeing him entirely in the company of men. It made her uncomfortable—obviously because she sensed the sexual preference of her son. Because Pan adored his mother and always sought to please her, her discomfort caused him to become secretive about his associations—so much so that even some of his associates were unaware of his sexual preferences. Jerry Jackson, for example, told me that "everyone thought he was asexual. I never thought of Hermes in a sexual way with anyone," and even William J. Mann, in *Behind the Screen: How Gays and Lesbians Shaped Hollywood 1910–1969*, cites Pan as a heterosexual dance director (Mann 2001, 278).[10]

As a devout Roman Catholic, Pan was concerned with his sexual preferences since Church doctrine determined that homosexual acts were contrary to the natural law of procreation and therefore sinful. Homosexual desires or attractions, on the other hand, were deemed not sinful in themselves but "disordered" temptations to sin. Pan sought to keep his urges under control even though the contradictions that marked his professional and personal lives were again in evidence. The dilemma of being a good Catholic and homosexual was further confused for Pan when, during one of his trips to New York City, he was contacted by Francis Joseph, Cardinal Spellman, the archbishop of New York inviting him to an all-male party. Whether or not Pan had been aware of Spellman's reputed voracious homosexuality (his affair with a chorus boy from *One Touch of Venus* was well known in Broadway circles),[11] he was surprised and flattered to be included in Spellman's private clique but astounded at what seemed to him to be a flagrantly public display. The incident in no way corrupted Pan's religious fervor, but it did encourage him to be even more perspicacious in his private life. Pan's passion for men and religion found its greatest expression in Italy, which from the 1950s to the end of his life provided him a second home. Rumors of Pan's Italian protégés were rife among studio dancers, but Jerry Jackson, who was with Hermes in Rome, said that there was no public manifestation of this. Even in Italy Pan was circumspect in his behavior. Indeed, as David Patrick Columbia suggests, "Pan's sexuality was a burden for him."[12]

Because he was a famous Hollywood choreographer, Pan could not live his life entirely in the shadows, but whenever he made a public appearance it was always in the company of a famous friend or woman with whom he might spend the evening dancing. Ironically, the person perhaps most responsible for keeping Hermes out of the shadows was Fred Astaire, the dancer in whose shadow Pan spent much of his career. While Hermes modestly counted himself among Astaire's best friends, a group that included Randolph Scott, Bill Self, Jock Whitney, and David Niven (Giles 1988, 149), David Patrick Columbia suggests that Hermes was Astaire's closest friend. "They were soul mates, both with the same sort of odd and childlike sense of humor. Fred always told people that others were his best friends, but Hermes was truly closest to him. Pan felt that he and Astaire had a karmic relationship." For Pan the relationship began in the late 1920s, long before he even met Astaire, when dancers used to comment on their resemblance. During the Broadway run of *Happy* (in which Pan danced in the chorus with his sister, Vasso "Ditty" Pan), Hermes walked over to the Alvin Theatre where Astaire was appearing with his sister Adele in *Funny Face* and took his first look at the great dancer, twenty-nine and balding. The eighteen-year-old Pan was not impressed—a view that was reversed five years later when the two met at RKO studios in Hollywood where Hermes found an artistic soul mate with whom he would develop a symbiotic relationship for the rest of his life. Others would stimulate Pan's other passions, but Astaire helped fuel the fire that burned brightest in Pan's personality—the urge to communicate through dance.

Because he had little ambition or any kind of a master plan, Pan's life appears in retrospect to be a rambling narrative of (often) unrelated activities guided more by luck (or as Pan would suggest, the hand of God) than any kind of self-determination. The first twenty years of his working life were spent supporting his family. That he managed to do it principally through a job he loved was a happy accident. The next thirty years were spent philosophizing and exploring what Pan felt he should be doing with his life. No longer taxed with the simple necessity of earning money, Hermes finally allowed himself to ask, "What do I *really* want to do?" The last twenty years depict Pan as a world traveler, the darling of princes and the elite, and a beloved celebrity, duly honored for his achievements. The journey meanders through family celebrations and religious observances (Hermes was not happy when Astaire wanted to rehearse on Christmas or Easter), Pan's famous pasta dinners, and elaborate Hollywood parties—though always with the underlying need for privacy, or, perhaps better said, a retreat from the public world in which Hermes Pan fell into fame. Like a monk, Hermes needed a retreat where he could experience a spiritual life independent of his work.

Hermes did not dwell on the contradictions or complexities of his day-to-day existence. Instead, he met the ironies of life with a great wide grin. As David Patrick Columbia remarked, "Pan was very serious about life, but handled his life in a way that wasn't serious. He was light hearted, and sunny, and positive. Hermes had a big wide laugh. His head would fall back with a guffaw, tears of joy often streaming down his face." Jerry Jackson recalled working on a Carol Channing special with Pan in the 1960s. They were completing rehearsal for the "Jimmy Dean" number at the CBS studios, when choreographer Michael Kidd entered to work with another star. On his way out, Hermes asked, "Who is that?"

Jerry answered, "Michael Kidd." Hermes nodded in quiet recognition. Jackson ran back to the studio to retrieve a bag that had been left behind and Kidd stopped him to ask, "Who was that?" "Hermes Pan," Jerry replied. Michael Kidd nodded in recognition. When Jerry told Hermes that neither of the two famous film choreographers recognized the other, Pan chortled heartily at the irony.

1

Black Bottom to Broadway

In the spring of 1956 on his way back to the United States from a trip abroad, Hermes Pan took the opportunity to visit the small town of Aigion (or Egion as it is often called) on the northern coast of the Greek Peloponnese to locate the house where his father, Pantelis Panagiotopoulos, was born.[1] Established during the Homeric epoch, replacing a Neolithic settlement, the town was named, according to legend, for the goat that fed Zeus. Accordingly, the community abounded with farms and raisin merchants in its earliest days before it was annexed by Rome, the Byzantine Empire, the Franks, the Ottoman Empire, and the Venetians. The first city to be liberated during the Greek Revolution of 1821, Aigion greeted the nineteenth century with an emergence of powerful middle-class families that prompted the development of a new way of thinking politically and economically in an attempt to create a humanistic modern city out of the over-tilled and eroded farmland. What Hermes found in 1956 was a lively village with fishing boats and sailboats crowding a single long pier that stretched out over the bluest of water. To the east he could see the Gulf of Corinth, and to the south, luxuriant forested mountains. The town proper was dotted with restaurants and shops arranged in a mosaic of miniature town squares inhabited by tourists and genial locals.

If Hermes went to Aigion in search of his ancestry, his was not a difficult task for the Panagiotopoulos (meaning "All Saints" in Greek) family was one of the two most famous, wealthy, and powerful families in the town (the Polychroniadi family was the other). His relatives, Andreas Panagiotopoulos, an early pioneer in the field of learning and minister of education, and Spyros Panagiotopoulos, a popular and innovative mayor of the city, were held in such high regard by the citizens, that, almost as soon as he had arrived, Hermes was treated as a local celebrity. With virtually no effort, he located his cousins, the theatre his ancestors had built (the first to be erected in the city), and the rustic house where his father had lived.

Pantelis Panagiotopoulos, born 1868, and his brother, Alkis (sometimes listed as Ilkis in American documents), born 1875, were trained as confectioners, one of the few nonpolitical family businesses. Alkis doted on his older brother, a habit

Pantelis Panagiotopoulos (Courtesy of the Vasso Pan Meade Collection).

that would create much melodrama in the years to come, not only because of the hero worship so typical between siblings. Pantelis was handsome, educated, and groomed for a political career, and the younger Panagiotopoulos aspired to follow in his brother's footsteps. Life for the Panagiotopoulos brothers loped along un-eventfully until 1895 when the southern American state of Tennessee announced to the world its plans to celebrate one hundred years of statehood in a Tennessee Centennial and International Exposition scheduled to open the following year. Because the site of the exposition was to be the state capital, Nashville, the city decided to build a replica of the Parthenon in Athens as its contribution to the festivities. Nicknamed the "Athens of the South," because of its many educational and cultural opportunities, Nashville not only wanted to sponsor the erection of a replica of a Greek monument, but it also sought to encourage real Greeks to be in attendance at the fair. To that end, the legislature called upon Greek cities to send a representative who would bear the title, "Greek Consul to the South." In Aigion, it was quickly and unanimously decided that the eldest son of the Panagi-otopoulos family should represent the city at the exposition. Pantelis was eager to make the trip across the world, hardly aware that he would never return to his home.

The first mention of Pantelis Panagiotopoulos in the United States occurs in the Nashville City Directory of 1896 in which a misspelled "Panteli Panagioto-pulo"[2] is listed as living at the Commercial Hotel and working for P. Brous and Company, wholesale and retail confectioners. Why would Pantelis need to find a job when his official designation in America was "Consul of Greece, Nashville, Tennessee"? The celebration scheduled for 1896 was delayed by the presidential election and bureaucratic red tape retarding the appropriations necessary for erecting the many structures planned. The exposition would be inaugurated on 1 June 1896 but the public would not pass the gates until 1 May 1897. Certainly, Pantelis was on hand for the inaugural ceremony, which involved marching bands, military units, Confederate veterans, and the ladies from the Daughters of the American Revolution in a parade winding from downtown to the exposition grounds, and a fireworks display spelling out an invitation to "Come to the Centennial Exposition, 1897"; but then there was almost a year to wait until his official duties would begin. What's more, prestigious as the title may appear, the position was essentially an honorary one, designed to elevate the status of the Greek participants at the exposition and encourage the attendance of other Greeks living in America by offering them what appeared to be official representatives from the "old country." With the spring opening of the Tennessee Centennial and International Exposition, Pantelis moved from the Commercial Hotel to 438 North Summer, on the north side of the city across the Cumberland River, where he would reside for the next four years.

By the time the exposition closed on 31 October 1897, 1,676,000 spectators had passed through its gates having paid 50¢ for adults and 25¢ for children to witness new inventions, such as the kinetoscope and X-ray equipment, and ride the giant seesaw, seventy-five feet in the air, or the gondolas on Lake Watauga. On 11 and 12 June, President McKinley visited the event along with representatives from wire services and newspapers in Washington and major northern cities. Pantelis was in attendance at the president's reception on 12 June and stood in line to shake McKinley's hand. On 22 September, he heard Booker T. Washington speak at the Negro Pavilion, and on 8 October, Pantelis was among the large crowd that had gathered to hear William Jennings Bryan.

It is tempting to suggest that the exposure to American politicians, humanitarians, and orators at the exposition (not to mention hearing the Twenty-Second Regiment Band of New York City, conducted by Victor Herbert on a daily basis between 2 August and 8 September) is what inclined Pantelis Panagiotopoulos to remain in the United States. Certainly there was a vitality in Nashville in the late 1890s that would have been difficult to upstage in the Greek Peloponnese. But what ultimately prompted Pantelis to stay in Tennessee was the most basic of human experiences: love.

Her name was Mary Aljeanne Huston (born 14 March 1884), daughter of blacksmith and carriage-maker, Charles Henry Huston, and Edmonia Elizabeth (Betty) Phillips. Pantelis and Mary met in 1900 when she was sixteen and he was

Mary Aljeanne Huston (Courtesy of the Vasso Pan Meade Collection).

thirty-two. At the time, she was living at 411 Main Street with her parents, her seven-year-old sister, Lillian, her maternal grandmother, Mary M. Phillips, and her aunt, Mary L. Phillips. The presence of an extended family within the Huston household is an important detail both in her courtship and subsequent married life, as well as in the lives of her children.

Though not a "Virginia Belle," as contemporary sources suggest, since she was born in Davidson County, Tennessee, Mary embodied all the qualities of southern gentility, and her charms were not lost on the Greek immigrant whose Old World work ethic and cultured sophistication deeply impressed Mary's household. They were married in March 1901 in a Greek Orthodox ceremony (in a 1983 interview for *Cineaste* Hermes noted to Dan Georgakas, "We were always aware of our Greek heritage"), and a year later, on 4 March 1902, the couple's first child was born, a son named Panos. The following year, Pantelis became a U.S. citizen, and on 16 February 1906, a daughter, Vasso Maria, was added to the family. By the time Vasso was born, the Panagiotopoulos family had moved to 1717 Glenwood Place, an upscale address in Memphis, the city where Pantelis's brother Alkis had been working as a confectioner since the turn of the century. Evidently Alkis's endeavors had been profitable, because the 1900 census suggests that he was able to support an eighteen-year-old servant and nineteen-year-old clerk in

The Panagiotopoulos residence at 1717 Glenwood Place (Courtesy of the Vasso Pan Meade Collection).

his household on 349 Main Street, and Pantelis, not one to shun opportunity, saw the move as an opportunity to leave the employ of P. Brous and Company and make good on his own. Soon he would be listed in the city register as president of the Eutrophia Company, the parent company of the Eutrophia Hotel and Café at 10 South Main Street, and the Panagiotopoulos family grew accustomed to the luxury of money and servants.

On 10 December 1909, Hermes Joseph Panagiotopoulos was born at the house on Glenwood Place where day-to-day operations were handled by a staff of four African-American domestics: Mary Williams, cook; Cleveland Callaway, domestic servant; Millie Carley, house maid; and a baby nurse (unnamed in the 1910 census). Panos and Vasso, who had devised nicknames for each other (in family circles, Panos was "Bubber" and Vasso was "Ditty"), immediately christened the baby "Snooks," (unconsciously anticipating a character Fanny Brice would make famous both in vaudeville and on radio), a nickname to which Hermes would answer for the rest of his life.

In 1911 Pantelis, who had grown weary of the hotel business, moved the Panagiotopoulos family to 1511 Compton Street in Nashville to begin a new commercial venture, the Ocean Restaurant for which he was proprietor, head chef, and maitre d'. Not surprisingly, the children saw little of their father, but the business was successful enough to allow the family to take Sundays off in the spring and summer for picnics at Radnor Lake and occasional vacations at the seashore.

Cleveland Callaway, Mary Williams, Millie Carley, baby nurse (Courtesy of the Vasso Pan Meade Collection).

In the absence of a father who was busy with the family business, and a mother who, at twenty-six, was more of a free-spirited big sister than parent, Hermes was raised by an African-American nanny, affectionately called "Aunt Betty," who, un-surprisingly, made a lasting impression on the child. Pan's friend and biographer, David Patrick Columbia, recalled:

> In 1915, when Hermes Pan was six years old, the family mammy, a big black woman who was called Aunt Betty, took the boy home with her one night to her apartment in the black ghetto of Nashville known, as it was in many cities in the American South, as Black Bottom. It was there that the child was first exposed to what was called "gut-bucket" jazz and the shuffles and foot-slapping dancing of the local black Americans. His reaction was an exhilaration which he recalled seventy years later, his eyes still lighting up with joy at the memory, as nothing short of "sen-sual." That was Pan's first exposure to what he knew as "dance." (Colum-bia, May 1991, 759)

As Hermes noted in a syndicated news report in the *North Adams Transcript* (30 January 1935), "Down south there's music in the air where colored people are around. My mother says I took to dancing because my black mammy carried me

Panos and Hermes outside the Compton Street house (Courtesy of the Vasso Pan Meade Collection).

on her hip and she was dancing even when she walked." Later in life, Hermes jovially recalled being six years old and wanting to go to dance class with his sister. After weeks of subtle (and not so subtle) persuasion, he was finally permitted to attend the class. As soon as the instructor demonstrated a combination, Hermes copied it exactly and started to embellish it, to the delight of the rest of the class who stopped dancing to watch the boy perform spontaneously created steps. Not amused by Pan's upstaging, the instructor promptly kicked him out of the class, telling him never to return. It came as no surprise that two years later when Pantelis asked his eight-year-old son what he wanted to be when he grew up, Hermes answered, "A dancer." In a 15 May 1960 news item, Hermes added that his father "never asked me again. I guess he was shocked." Even though he had named his son, Hermes, in honor of the god in Greek mythology with winged feet, business-minded Pantelis could not imagine how his youngest child could support himself as a dancer.

In 1915, Mary's parents and younger sister returned to Nashville after spending nearly ten years in Memphis where they kept a watchful eye over the Panagiotopoulos family. Not uncharacteristically, Mary's relatives moved into

Pantelis, Hermes, Vasso, Mary, and Panos at the seashore (Courtesy of the Vasso Pan Meade Collection).

the Compton Street house and helped out in maintaining the family business. To entertain the children, the grandparents frequently took them to the Knicker-bocker, a first-run silent film theatre, where, unlike his siblings who were fans of Tom Mix and William S. Hart, Hermes developed a fascination for *femme fatale* Theda Bara, nicknamed "The Vamp." The first of her films Pan witnessed was *Cleopatra* (1917) and the boy became mesmerized by her emotive glances and fantastically exotic costumes. He believed all the stories concocted by her publicists that she was the Egyptian-born daughter of an Italian sculptor and his paramour, a French actress, living in the shadow of the Sphinx (only later would Hermes discover that his idol was born Theodosia Burr Goodman in Cincinnati, Ohio). Pan's youthful imagination ran wild as he read about the adventures of "Serpent of the Nile" as Bara was often called, and he wrote to Fox Studios asking for a photograph so that she could be ever close to him. In "The Mortal Goddesses," a chapter from his unpublished autobiography, "Dancin' in the Movies," Pan noted that "A few weeks later, the glossy still arrived in the mail with an actual signature scrawled across the bottom. I was enchanted" (Pan, Columbia, Kramer 1983, 2a).

Aunt Betty with Hermes (Courtesy of the Vasso Pan Meade Collection).

Theda Bara was not the only fantasy the eight-year-old Pan had on his mind. In 1918, young Hermes began having a recurring nightmare about a scary old creature named Aunt Lucy Godfather who would chase him around the house until he awoke in a sweat. One night, Hermes dreamed that he turned around and pushed Aunt Lucy Godfather down the stairs, after which he never dreamed about his pursuer again. Given Pan's homosexuality it is tempting to read more into the conflation of genders in the dream than is merited, for Pan's grandmother died in 1918 and, as Kelly Sullivan Walden suggests, the dream was likely the boy's way of dealing with the loss of a beloved maternal figure (Walden 2006, 44, 83, 317).

Hermes's first experiences as a ballroom dancer occurred in 1920 when his father brought home an old Victrola and a pile of 78 rpm records. Imitating steps he saw performed by Sam Clark, his mammy's son (who was also his father's chauffeur and general houseboy),[3] Hermes and his sister, Ditty, improvised dances to tunes like the "Wabash Rag" for hours on end. Robin Coons's syndicated *Hollywood Notebook* (30 January 1935) notes:

> Sam was his black mammy's boy, a little older than Hermes. He was a genius at mechanics, a superlative chauffeur, a dream of a cook, and a

Sam Clark (Courtesy of the Vasso Pan Meade Collection).

nonpareil at dancing. He was teaching Hermes the "Black Bottom" and the "Charleston" in the Panagiotopoulos kitchen long before those jazz prances had names. His black mammy was always singing, no matter what her frame of mind. When she was sulking, the blue notes were stressed a little more, that was all. The gardener, the handy man, and all the dusky crew kept vocal tom toms beating rhythms.

To his parents, Hermes's dancing was little more than an expression of youthful vitality. To Hermes and his sister, who both would become professional dancers, the experience was life affirming. In an essay called "Let's Dance," in *Memories*, Barbara Leaming adds: "It was in these informal sessions with Clark that Pan developed the lifelong passion for broken rhythms and afterbeats that made him a natural collaborator with Astaire, who had cultivated his own love of black dancing on the vaudeville circuit. While most whites tap-danced on their toes—a style Pan derides as 'tippytoes' and Astaire called 'pussyfooting'—Sam Clark and other black dancers used toe *and* heel, producing a much stronger sound" (Leaming 1990, 2).

In 1920, Hermes was ten years old and breezing through the fifth grade at public school. Vasso, nearly four years older, was a student at the prestigious

Dot, Hermes, Aljeanne, and Vasso in Florida (Courtesy of the Vasso Pan Meade Collection).

Ward-Belmont School for Women located a few short blocks away from the Panagiotopoulos home on Compton Street. Eighteen-year-old Panos was completing high school and acting girl crazy. After several false starts, he would find the love of his life in Dorothy ("Dot") Bainbridge who became his wife before the end of the year.

In the final months of 1920, Pantelis began to feel more fatigued than usual after work. He thought little of that and his loss of appetite until fever, chills, and difficulty breathing were added to the list of symptoms. By the time he found it necessary to see a doctor, he was diagnosed with tuberculosis and advised to move to a climate that was more amenable to the control of the disease. Mary organized a spring trip to Florida for the family including Panos, Dot, and their new baby daughter, Aljeanne, whose appearance not long after the wedding caused quite a stir among the Panagiotopoulos clan. Sam Clark tagged along as family chauffeur for a vacation of sun and fun while the Ocean Restaurant was left in the care of Charles Huston. As David Patrick Columbia noted, Mary was "a fanciful, easy-going spirit who appreciated her children's pleasures" (Columbia, May 1991, 759). By this time, Panos and his wife had shortened the family name to Pan, for the 1922 Nashville City Directory lists them as Panos and Dorothy Pan, living at 807

Fatherland. The trip to Florida had been designed in the hope that the ocean air would be beneficial to Pantelis, but in a short time, it was obvious that what he needed was a dry, warm climate. After much delay, caused by concerns over the day-to-day operation of the restaurant and the financial security of the family, Pantelis moved to a sanitarium in San Antonio where he appeared to be getting stronger.

Early in November, Pantelis took a turn for the worse and, on 10 November 1922, Mary was notified that her husband had passed away. Once again, Mary assembled her family and they boarded a train for San Antonio to retrieve the body. A week later, they returned home and buried Pantelis according to the rites of the Greek Orthodox Church in the Old Cemetery of Nashville. Prior to the funeral, Alkis emerged like a villain out of a nineteenth-century melodrama, drunkenly brandishing a gun, and demanding the body of his deceased sibling. "You'll have my brother's body in life, but not in death!" he threatened. Fortunately, he was easily disarmed and the ceremony proceeded without further incident.

The unexpected death of Pantelis meant more to the members of the Panagiotopoulos family than simply the loss of a father. It signaled the end of life as they knew it. No one was prepared to deal with the repercussions and change of lifestyle, least of all twelve-year-old Hermes. Somehow Mary and her father managed to keep the restaurant going, but after Hermes graduated from the eighth grade (the full extent of his education) in the spring of 1923, Mary decided that she had had enough of Nashville. She was thirty-nine years old and felt she deserved to live a little. On a whim, she sold the Ocean Restaurant and the house on Compton Street, piled her family into a new Ford Model T she purchased, and directed Sam Clark to drive them to New York City, where she idealistically hoped that her family would flourish. Mary resolved that Panagiotopoulos was far too complicated and exotic a name for life in New York City and, following Panos's example, abbreviated it to Pan. From 1923 on, Hermes Panagiotopoulos would become Hermes Pan, god of the winged feet and player of the pipes.

2

Try Dancing

When the Pans arrived in New York in 1923, what they saw was a city of almost endless possibilities. Broadway was singing the music of Irving Berlin, Jerome Kern, Richard Rodgers, Rudolf Friml, Sigmund Romberg, and Vincent Youmans. Speakeasies gave, as their name might suggest, easy access to liquor outlawed by the Volstead Act in 1919. The Harlem Renaissance helped disseminate jazz and African-American dance styles to white audiences and a system of subways and trains enabled inhabitants to travel around the city and from the city to the rest of the country. Mary Pan most likely was unaware when she brought young Hermes to New York how expedient the city would be for her son's career.

Feeling flush from the sale of her property in Tennessee, Mary rented a spacious apartment at 175 West 81st Street, virtually on the corner of Amsterdam Avenue. Panos and his wife and baby shared a bedroom, while Hermes, Vasso, Sam, and Mary each had their own living spaces. The first several months the family spent in New York felt like an extended vacation. No work needed to be done; no school needed to be attended. The Pans lived the booming lives of affluent tourists. Hermes recalled that he and his sister would playfully walk down crowded thoroughfares side by side with locked arms shouting "Pushy, pushy" as they plowed their way through what Pan imagined to be an endless stream of people. Together they saw Al Jolson in *Bombo*, a revival of *Blossom Time*, *The Ziegfeld Follies*, the *George White Scandals*, and *Running Wild*, an African-American musical that made an especially deep impression on young Hermes Pan. It was the show that introduced the most influential song of the era, "Charleston." When not at the theatre, the Pans visited the parks and zoos and museums in what appeared to be a city of infinite delights.

After about six months, however, the delights ended when the money ran out. Mary had never been educated in financial affairs, happy to let her husband handle the business end of the relationship. More like a child, used to getting money but never wondering where it came from, Mary wired to her father in Nashville asking him to send money from her account. The next day, Charles Huston replied that she was penniless. Further investigation revealed that Uncle Alkis, brandishing a bogus partnership agreement with Pantelis (written entirely in Greek), managed to lay claim to the family fortune, leaving the mother and children destitute before vanishing into the night never to be heard from again. What made matters even worse, Sam, characteristically a safe and dependable driver, had taken the family car out for a night on the town and mistook the direction of the traffic around Times Square. Tipsy after a visit to a local speakeasy and trying to avert oncoming cars, Sam drove onto the sidewalk and crashed into a building. Sam stepped out of the Model T with just a scratch, but the car was a total wreck, the Pan's one sellable commodity gone.

Relieved that Sam was unharmed, the family members stoically accepted the fate of the automobile and concluded that if they were to live in New York City, they would have to work for a living. Luckily for the Pans, jobs were relatively plentiful in the city in the mid-1920s and without much ado, Mary, Ditty, and Dot found positions at the Metropolitan, a fashionable women's boutique on Fifth Avenue. As for Snooks, Sam, and Bubber, they divided their time between working as errand boys at Consolidated Edison, the company that provided electricity, natural gas, and steam service throughout Manhattan, and delivering prescriptions for the local drugstore. While at Con Edison, Pan was encouraged to audition for the company's yearly amateur theatricals, an industrial show to benefit the corporation and entertain its employees. Hermes spent a week perfecting a routine borrowed from steps he had learned in Black Bottom and embellished with his own personal flair. When he finally got up the nerve to show it to the director, he was cast immediately and told to report for rehearsals the very next day. At fifteen years old, Hermes was dancing at the Astor Hotel in the chorus of the *Edison Follies*.[1]

Sam was a fervent patron of the night spot that had recently opened its doors as the Cotton Club on 142nd Street and Lenox Avenue in Harlem. There, watching African-American performers dance to the music of Fletcher Henderson, he picked up many of the new dances such as the "Black Bottom" or the "Charleston" and taught them to Hermes during work breaks. Hermes, in turn, became a fan of the establishment, as he explained to Dan Georgakas: "Earlier when I was in New York I loved to go to the Cotton Club in Harlem and the speakeasies. That was an important part of my dance education. I absorbed a lot of ideas there. After I left New York, I didn't see much black dancing anymore" (Georgakas 1983, 28). Barbara Leaming adds that Hermes was not satisfied in simply replicating the steps he saw at the Cotton Club or learned from Sam Clark. "Once he had learned steps from Clark, Pan started inventing new dances on his own. 'The music would tell me what to do,' he says. 'When I listen to music, I visualize something—it's not just a sound. When I hear music, and especially when I like it, I see motion. I don't see people dancing, but I feel it, so that when I get up and dance, I just do what the music tells me to do'" (Leaming 1990, 2). Hermes taught the dance steps—those he had learned and those he had invented—to his sister and, in short order, Hermes and Ditty became an amateur dance team exhibiting the latest dance crazes in their Upper West Side living room. According to David Patrick Columbia, the youthful exhibition dancers quickly turned their living room shenanigans into cash:

> One night a gentleman caller took the widow Pan along with Hermes and Ditty to a speakeasy, *Le Boeuf sur le Toit* on West 52nd Street. The brother and sister danced an impromptu Charleston to the accompaniment of a piano and ukulele and brought the other customers to a standing ovation. The club's proprietor, one Madame Jeanne (who also provided additional entertainment for her male customers on the floor above the cabaret) was so impressed by the Pans' duo that she invited them to appear nightly for tips. So Ditty and Hermes went to work nightly in Madame Jeanne's. Ditty soon tired of the nightclub scene with its rough and ready, boozy customers and the unspoken but obvious activity of all Madame Jeanne's "nieces." But Hermes, now sixteen, had been bitten by the Show Biz bug and stayed on. Good natured with a sunny disposition and quick to laughter, he played the ukulele and did the Charleston to the delighted customers who showered him with tips averaging sixty dollars a week. (Columbia, May 1991, 759)

In the film by Robert Kuperberg and Gérard Paquet *It Just Happened*, Hermes Pan tells the same story but adds that Le Boeuf sur le Toit was also the hangout for many of New York's gangsters. In an interview with Maureen C. Solomon in the *Los Angeles Reader* (11 February 1983), Hermes recalled that the notorious gangster "Legs" Diamond was so impressed by his juvenile hoofing that he tipped him fifty dollars.[2]

On 13 June 1925, Ditty began a journal that would serve as a primary source of information about the Pan family. The first entry reads:

> Living at 175 W. 81st St. New York. Snooks and I were eating dinner alone (had baked beans, rice, bisquits, etc.). We wondered what we'd be doing every June 13 thereafter and planned to keep account of it—so here goes.

The entry for 13 June 1926 indicates a change of accommodations from the Upper West Side to Virginia Court in Jackson Heights, Queens, a less expensive apartment. Snooks, Dot, and Ditty took the subway down to Greenwich Village and visited the Circus Club where a Charleston contest was under way. Dared by her brother and sister-in-law to enter the competition, Ditty competed and won second prize.

Later in the year, Hermes was encouraged to audition for a new operetta about the Civil War composed by Sigmund Romberg for the Shubert Organization. Once he was at the audition, he discovered that the producers were looking for singers not dancers and began to leave. "Where are you going?" asked J. C. Huffman, the director. "I thought this was a dance audition," stammered Pan. "I'm not a singer." Oscar Radin, the musical director stepped in and asked, "Can you sing me a few scales at the piano?" Hermes sang the scales to his satisfaction and, what he believed to be a happy accident, was given a contract for his first Broadway show, *My Maryland*. It was perhaps lucky for Pan that the show required a singing male chorus of sixty voices!

A romantic costume operetta based loosely on the story of Barbara Frietchie, the southern belle who loved a Union officer during the Civil War, *My Maryland* went into rehearsal before Christmas 1926 in preparation for a 24 January out-of-town premiere in Philadelphia. Even though he had been hired for the singing chorus, when the choreographer, Jack Mason, saw that Hermes could move well, he found himself singing *and dancing* in a great many numbers. Pan was delighted that he could support his family performing an activity he considered "fun," but he never thought of it as a career. For Hermes, singing and dancing was simply the most expedient way of keeping food on the table.

My Maryland opened on schedule at the Lyric Theatre in Philadelphia to glowing reviews and remained there for nine months, closing on 29 October, a month beyond its official New York opening on 12 September (with a different cast). The forty-week tryout run broke all records in Philadelphia, easily surpassing the

Hermes Pan (second from right) in the cast of *My Maryland* (Courtesy of the Vasso Pan Meade Collection).

twenty-nine-week run of *Blossom Time*, the previous record holder. Contemporary reviews lavished praise upon the cast, calling the company "one of the best ever assembled of acting and singing artists," and boasting that the sixty-voice male singing ensemble was comprised of "advanced voice students from the leading music studios of New York." Hermes Pan, who never had a singing lesson in his life, must have smiled to have been counted among them. A happy accident and a hit!

Pan left the production in Philadelphia before the end of the run because of family issues. He never expected to be out of town as long as he was, and even though he was homesick, it was the weekly paycheck that kept him on the road. But in the fall, when his brother was diagnosed with stomach cancer, Hermes felt it was important for the family to be together to help support Panos in his fight against the disease. Although the weekly stipend he earned from *My Maryland* had been critical to the family, Hermes felt positive that if he could audition successfully for one show, he could secure another. It is unclear why he did not request a transfer to the Broadway production of *My Maryland* scheduled to open on 13 September—a move that could have sustained his salary and brought him home. Perhaps he had grown tired of the chorus parts and wanted to move on. In any event, Pan was back on the audition block in the fall of 1927.

By 4 October, Hermes and Vasso (who had left the Metropolitan to begin her show business career in a vaudeville act) were in rehearsal for *Happy*, a college musical by Vincent Lawrence and McElbert Moore, with lyrics by Moore and Earle Crooker, and music by Frank Grey. Announced on 9 August in the *New York Times* as *Dancing Dollars* and on 10 August in the *Syracuse Herald* as *Dancing Mothers*, *Happy* was a lighthearted romp about the respective love affairs of a college poet who wants to write a musical comedy and the fair-haired boy of the class who will come into a fortune if he complies with a clause in his late uncle's will. On 7 November, the musical began a monthlong out-of-town tryout in Queens, Brooklyn, and Montreal before opening at the Earl Carroll Theatre on 5 December. The next day, the *New York Times* (6 December 1927) praised the music as "pleasing, if reminiscent," and congratulated the cast for laboring "willingly to perform the tasks in hand" but found the book, "the weakest single item of the show." The dances and ensemble numbers were considered "often well devised," but the reviewer warned that "with the competition which it must face from the many more elaborate musical productions in town, *Happy* will probably find it difficult going."

The review was nothing like the praise lavished upon Hermes's previous show but it was sufficiently positive to guarantee two months' work for the dancers in the Pan family—work that came at a crucial time, for on 9 December, four days after *Happy* opened, Panos died at the age of twenty-five, leaving behind his ex-wife and six-year-old daughter. Dot and Aljeanne remained members of Pan's extended family, living with him for the next thirteen years, in spite of the fact that Panos and Dot had divorced shortly after the move to New York. Naysayers in the family insisted that Dot married Bubber only for his money and once the money ran out, so would she. Instead of separating, however, she and her ex-husband decided to live together as roommates to share the custody and care of their daughter.

During his final days, Panos, who had been raised in the Greek Orthodox religion, found solace in Roman Catholicism and became a Catholic on his deathbed. This event had a profound effect on the Pan family, prompting Mary, Hermes, and Vasso to take instruction in the new faith. Mary would be the first to follow Bubber's example, but by 1930 all three Pans had become Roman Catholics. Like his brother, Hermes found great comfort in the religion and remained a devout practicing Catholic for the rest of his life.

On 21 January 1928 *Happy* closed at the Earl Carroll Theatre only to reopen two weeks later under new management ("Happy Productions") at Daly's Theatre in a desperate attempt to keep the show alive. After three weeks of mediocre business, however, the producers decided to cut their losses and the dancing Pans again found themselves back on the audition circuit. The family moved from Jackson Heights to the Gregorian Hotel in Manhattan, living quarters closer to places of potential employment. By the spring of 1928, Ditty had been hired by the Shubert Organization for *Padlocks of 1928*, a summer topical revue planned as a sequel to the popular *Padlocks of 1927* that featured Texas Guinan, Lillian Roth, and J. C. Flippen. The sequel did not fare as well as the original during its out-of-town tour and closed before it reached Broadway. Hermes was equally unfortunate in finding employment as a singer or dancer on Broadway, but he did manage to secure a contract with the Strand Theatre, a 2,989-seat stage show and movie palace—as an usher.

Since ushering was hardly as lucrative as being in a Broadway show, Hermes continued to audition for chorus work throughout the summer months. Early in September 1928, he found himself back in rehearsal, this time for *Animal Crackers*, the new Marx Brothers musical with a book by George S. Kaufman and Morrie Ryskind and music and lyrics by Bert Kalmar and Harry Ruby. The plot turned the Marx Brothers loose on the fashionable Long Island home of Mrs. Rittenhouse where Groucho (as the indomitable African explorer Captain Spaulding) retrieves a stolen painting (in the midst of tossing out teeth-grinding puns).

In *Animal Crackers*, the chorus was grouped by director Oscar Eagle and choreographer Russell E. Market into the following categories: Showgirls, of which there were eight; Dancing Girls, of which there were sixteen; Sixteen Market Dancers, all women; and Gentlemen, of which there were only twelve. Although barely nineteen and with no formal training, Hermes had sufficient skill to win a place in so small a group. He was proud of his achievement and certainly grateful for the weekly paycheck but somewhat surprised at how little he had to do in the show. He appeared in the opening number and act finales along with everyone else but only provided vocal and movement background for three numbers, including the famous "Hooray for Captain Spaulding." Compared to *My Maryland* and *Happy*, *Animal Crackers* felt to him like a paid vacation. David Patrick Columbia recalled

Hermes Pan in 1928 (Courtesy of the Vasso Pan Meade Collection).

that much later in his career, Hermes saw Groucho walking before him on a street in Los Angeles. To get his attention, Pan sang the first few bars of "Hooray for Captain Spaulding" to which Marx turned and sang "Did someone call me Shnorrer?" without missing a beat. Even after thirty years, Pan still remembered his harmony parts and Groucho never missed his cues.

At the end of September, the show moved out of the rehearsal studio in Manhattan to the Shubert Theatre in Philadelphia where it played to packed houses and excellent reviews for three weeks in October. Once again, Hermes Pan was in a hit in Philadelphia. The New York opening at the Forty-Fourth Street Theatre on 23 October was a gala event with ticket scalpers charging up to $100 for two tickets into the theatre bulging with spectators anxious to see the Marx Brothers. Few were disappointed in what they saw. As the critic from the *New York Times* (24 October 1928) suggested:

> Delivering his mad-cap chronicle of an African exploration, Groucho touches on nearly every topic of the day and makes some of the most insane verbal transitions heard since his last appearance. "I used to know a fellar by the name of Emanuel Ravelli who looked like you," he says to

Chico. "I am Ravelli," says Chico. "No wonder you look like him," Groucho runs on. "I still insist there's a resemblance." Those who heard him last evening turn the title of a popular song into "You Took a Bandage Off Me"; advise a South American traveler, "You go Uruguay and I'll go mine"; dictate a formal note to his attorney in full, "Dear Madame: Regards— that's all"; and reply to a woman who charged him with bigamy, "Of course, it's big of me"—those who heard an evening of such things were shamelessly satisfied.

Unfortunately, even in 1928, puns and tomfoolery were not the essential building blocks of a successful musical. The reviewer found the score to be "workmanlike if not distinguished," and the dances to be "seldom original" although "some of them display the costumes well, and two or three of them are danced with spirit." Even though he admitted that creating a musical for the Marx Brothers was a thankless task at best, the reviewer concluded that *Animal Crackers* was "uncommonly perfunctory as a musical entertainment." Even without the best of notices, the popularity of the Marx Brothers was sufficient to keep the musical alive for 191 performances and Hermes Pan gainfully employed until 6 April 1929.

While Snooks was working on Broadway the Pan family moved again, this time to a small apartment at 87 Barrow Street in Greenwich Village. In her journal for 13 June 1929, Ditty recorded: "Snooks, Dot and I went walking thru [the]

Swedish baron Yuri von Ungern-Sternberg, Russian prince Nelidov, and Hermes Pan (Courtesy of the Vasso Pan Meade Collection).

Village—passed by Circus Club where we were three years before on June 13th."
Pan's mother, Mary, was home babysitting her granddaughter, Aljeanne. During
this period, Hermes's social life was divided between two families: the Pans at
home and his associates in the theatre through whom he developed an active
social life. At weekly theatre parties he would encounter world travelers as diverse
as Yuri, the Swedish baron of the infamous Ungern-Sternberg family; his friend,
Nelidov, a deposed Russian prince; and Harold Sampson, a California golf professional. Soft-spoken, with a lilting southern drawl, Pan could easily establish an
immediate and intimate rapport with everyone he met. His very natural, relaxed
manner was found quite appealing to theatre personalities that trade on adrena-
line and stress, and his graceful movement and tall, athletically lithe body was
the perfect external expression of an artistic temperament, drawing the attention of wealthy socialites of both sexes. He never spoke about himself except
when asked, and then only through stories of his childhood adventures involving
other people. This characteristic would remain with Pan through old age: in his
unfinished autobiography, the focus is on his friends and how they enriched his
life. Hermes was honestly and simply interested in other people and, as a result,
only the very few were uncomfortable in his company.

Harold Sampson and Hermes Pan (Courtesy of the Vasso Pan Meade Collection).

In August, preparations were under way for a national tour of *Animal Crackers*, but Hermes was uninterested in remaining with the show, preferring instead to join the cast of *Murray Anderson's Almanac* starring the riotously popular Jimmy Savo and Trixie Friganza, and opening at Erlanger's Theatre on 14 August. In addition to appearing as a "gentleman in the ensemble" in two production numbers, Pan was cast as one of four "Noblemen" in a pantomime performance of Oscar Wilde's story *The Young King*, and one of ten "Patrons of Automats" in a skyscraper extravaganza called "The New Yorker." Although his characters were little more than glorified chorus roles, to Hermes, *Murray Anderson's Almanac* was more fun than his previous shows since he was given the opportunity to play different characters. Unconsciously, since *My Maryland*, Pan had been following the path of a theatre career, each new show offering him more opportunities to hone his skills as a dancer. Hermes enjoyed the opportunity of mastering new choreography and staging but dreaded the often carelessly repetitive dancing of the chorus during long runs. While some of the chorus appeared to be sleepwalking through the routines, Pan always performed full out—and, in so doing, he sometimes improvised steps and appeared out of sync with the rest of the dancers, a situation most noticeable in his next Broadway assignment, *Top Speed*.

Initially advertised as *The Good Old Summertime*, *Top Speed* had a book by Guy Bolton, and score by Bert Kalmar and Harry Ruby, the songwriting team responsible for *Animal Crackers*. Directed by John Harwood and choreographed by John Boyle and LeRoy Prinz, the musical told the story of two stockbroker clerks who pretend to be men of notable affluence to win the love of two fabulously wealthy women. The complications that arise out of such deception find resolution in a second-act boat race "involving fortunes, honor, and hearts" (*New York Times*, 26 December 1929).

Rehearsals for *Top Speed* began in the middle of October, almost immediately after *Murray Anderson's Almanac* closed, and it was then that Hermes met LeRoy Prinz for the first time. Cast as part of the male singing chorus, he was able to study, from a comfortable distance, the way Prinz worked with dancers. In a 1972 interview with John Kobal, Hermes recalled that "LeRoy Prinz would make some girls hysterical. He would just love to have them in tears. And that seemed to be the thing, to swear at the girls and be nasty" (Kobal 1985, 627). In a later interview with Svetlana McLee Grody, however, Hermes explained how *Top Speed* provided him with a significant dance education:

> I was one of the eight singers and they had eight dancers. I loved dancing. I always loved to dance. I used to dance as a kid, go to contests, but I never did get a chance to study and I never really wanted to be a dancer as a profession. It never occurred to me, it just happened. I got a job in the chorus because I needed the money and it paid more than what I was doing. While I was singing in the show, I learned a little dancing. I said,

"How do you do a time step, how do you do a pirouette?" I was always watching the dancers in the show. It fascinated me, I would try to learn from watching. Sometimes, I'd ask them to show me a step and I'd practice, so I taught myself. (Grody 1996, 9)

It was also during rehearsals that Pan met the young Ginger Rogers, who won the comic soubrette role of Babs Green after Kalmar and Ruby saw her perform in vaudeville. In her memoirs, Ginger records how she welcomed the opportunity of working on a Broadway show:

What a delight it was to be working with musical comedy people. Everyone pulled together for the good of the show. Not only that, the musical comedy schedule was completely different from vaudeville. After two weeks of *Top Speed*, I was convinced that eight shows a week was to my liking. *Top Speed* boasted an impressive cast. Irene Delroy, a lovely young woman with a sweet singing voice, was the leading lady. Paul Frawley, our leading man, had a strong singing voice and a definite masculine appeal. He needed a strong voice, because there were racing speedboats in the background that made a lot of noise. Lester Allen, the comedy man, kept us laughing all through rehearsals. He had a Chaplinesque quality that captivated audiences. They were the stars, yet there was one member of the cast, a chorus boy, who would prove to be a very important person in my life. His name was Hermes Pan, and he and I made our Broadway debuts together. Hermes and I became good friends. Many nights after the show, he would come up to our hotel room and Mother would make delicious hot sandwiches on an electric toaster we had. Nothing cements a friendship more than eating together and chatting about all the odd or interesting things that have happened during the performances. (Rogers 2008, 71–72)

Top Speed began its out-of-town tour in Philadelphia on 11 November 1929 to excellent notices praising the production for being "topical and up-to-the-minute" and having "the most eye-filling choruses that has appeared here. And can they dance!" (*New York Times*, 17 November 1929). While in Philadelphia, Ginger Rogers's mother, Lela, invited Hermes and a group of dancers up to their apartment for a spaghetti dinner. After dinner, Ginger told Hermes about her dream of becoming a movie star. "Oh, really?" Pan replied, surprised. Ever the gentleman, Pan wished her the best of luck, but privately questioned how the seventeen-year-old girl standing next to him could compete with glamorous women like Theda Bara or Gloria Swanson who possessed what Hermes considered the "movie star look." In her version of the event, Maureen C. Solomon suggests that "Pan thought the young singer had as much of a chance to be a star as he had teaching Fred Astaire to dance" (Solomon 1983, 11).

Throughout his career in the Broadway chorus, Hermes was constantly reminded by fellow gypsies of his physical resemblance to Fred Astaire. They even told him that he behaved like Astaire as well. As Arthur Knight suggested, the comparison was apt. Both Astaire and Pan had a similar angular smile, the same thinning hair, the same protruding translucent blue eyes, the same "jaunty walk with the body thrust forward and the feet scuffing lightly on the ground" (Knight 1960, 40). Although he knew about Astaire and his sister, Adele—they were two of the great musical stars of the day—he confessed that he had never seen them perform. He didn't have the money to buy a ticket.

In its final week in Philadelphia, the *New York Times* (9 December 1929) advertised the addition of Irene Delroy (replacing Brenda Bond) and Harland Dixon to the cast of *Top Speed* and announced that the show would play the week of 16 December in Newark before commencing its Broadway run. Finally on Christmas night, at the Forty-Sixth Street Theatre, Hermes was back on Broadway performing in the chorus of seven numbers including the suggestive "Keep Your Undershirt On" and "Hot and Bothered." What's more, he picked up sufficient technique from the dancers in the show during rehearsals that LeRoy Prinz trusted him to perform complex dance combinations. Of the production, the *New York Times* critic wrote:

> Without attempting to be either smart or sensational, the makers of *Top Speed* have managed to be thoroughly enjoyable. Mr. Ruby, whose music likes the ear, has written, "I'd Like to Be Liked" in the interests of romance, "Keep Your Undershirt On" for [Lester] Allen, "Dizzy Feet" for Harland Dixon (whose are) and "Hot and Bothered" for Miss Rogers. The chorus, in whose honor you should polish your spectacles more carefully than usual, dance what seem to be unnecessarily complicated steps with skill and animation, wearing fresh gay costumes. . . . In these and other respects, *Top Speed* provides a pleasant evening under cover. (26 December 1929)

On 10 March 1930, *Top Speed* moved to the Royale Theatre but Hermes Pan was no longer in the cast. He had been fired from the production in February because the stage manager felt he took too many liberties with the staging. Hermes tried to explain that he had changed the steps so that they would suit him better, but the stage manager was adamant. Pan didn't know it at the time, but his career as a choreographer had begun.

Vasso to return with him to Nashville to help him take care of her cousins. Torn between responsibilities to family members on opposite sides of the country, Ditty elected to remain on the West Coast, a choice for which she believed Claude never forgave her. Since none of the California Pans had a full-time job, the care of their grandfather presented many financial challenges, but in the end, the Catholic Church that had offered solace to them during moments of distress and difficulties in the past once again came to the rescue. The Order of the Little Sisters of the Poor on 2700 East First Street in Los Angeles was a Catholic organization that housed and fed the elderly and the sick by going out and begging for the things their residents wanted and needed. The Pans found a room for Charles Huston with the Little Sisters and "Grandpop" remained there happily until his death in 1934.

The blessing of the Little Sisters did not stop with Charles Huston. The Mother Superior of the convent knew that the Pans were destitute so when someone donated $150 to provide for the upkeep of the building (essentially washing windows), she offered Hermes the job. In "Back from Arizona," a chapter from his unpublished memoir, Pan reports that for nearly two months he washed windows— inside and outside—every day of the week. For his efforts he was fed by the nuns and given a basket of food to share with his family. And at the end of every week, he was given $25 as take-home pay. "The windfall kept us fed with a roof over our heads right up until late spring, when once again we were jobless and broke" (Pan, Columbia, Kramer 1983, 10).

By the end of 1930, Hermes had secured a job teaching tap at the Smaroff-Hixon School on Figueroa Street in the Wilshire District. Although Hermes was earning a mere 15¢ a dance lesson, the school had an excellent track record with many of its students finding work in Ziegfeld shows and at RKO Studios. Gregory Smaroff, founder of the Los Angeles Art Center and a well-known performer on the West Coast circuit, was director of the school and ballet instructor, and Hermes taught tap and jazz dance. Pan explained, "I made up steps at night in preparation for the next day's classes partly out of need. I was running out of steps to teach. I found I could make up better steps than those I already knew" (Solomon 1983, 11). Pan's original dance steps for his students were on display in the revue, *Morning, Noon and Night*, advertised at the end of April 1931. The scheduled performances at "clubs and theaters of the Southland" would offer the first public view of Hermes Pan's choreography on the West Coast (*Los Angeles Times*, 26 April 1931).

By June 1931, the Pans had moved into the Bandera Apartments at 2910 West 8th Street in Los Angeles. They had been forced to flee their previous abode under the cover of darkness because of an inability to pay the rent. At the time, rent was on average $20 to $30 monthly and a family could move into an apartment with a $5 deposit and take the rest of the month to earn the balance. If the monthly earnings did not cover the rent, the Pans ensured that they had $5 on hand so that they could put a deposit on another abode and move on the twenty-ninth day of the month, leaving behind a disgruntled landlord. What Hermes was earning from teaching tap was obviously insufficient to help support the family so he was determined to find a better job. Opportunity came knocking in the familiar person of LeRoy Prinz, who invited Hermes to assist him with the choreography for an African-American musical propitiously called *Lucky Day*. Although Pan might have found Prinz's style of working abrasive, he was flattered that the dance director thought enough of his efforts in *Top Speed* to want to work with him again.

Lucky Day was the brainchild of songwriters Leon and Otis Renee and Ben Ellison, famous for "Sleepy Time Down South" as well as the material they composed for stars like Ethel Waters and Bill "Bojangles" Robinson. Their score, said to have been composed in only three weeks, ranged from the blues to the rumba and included provocative titles such as "Sinful Music," "Steppin' High, Wide and Handsome," "You Better Get Religion," as well as many that might be considered politically incorrect today, "When the Jigs Do the Juba," "Shuffle Your Black Feet," "Cleo from the Congo," and "Miss Loada Coal." The thin thread of a plot involved two world wanderers and their broken-down horse named Ludwig whose sad-sack demeanor is perfect for the movies. The horse is given a film contract and its owners begin living the high life. When the horse's option is not renewed, however, the owners fall on hard times and seek other ways of getting the horse to support them. Rehearsals began in the late fall of 1931 and, among the African-American dancers, Hermes was once again in his element, reawakening sensations he had experienced as a child in Nashville at the Black Bottom and in New York at the Cotton Club. Later in Pan's career, Bill Robinson would tell him that he didn't dance like a white man. That quality made Hermes the apt assistant to LeRoy Prinz on an all-black musical. The rehearsal pianist for the production was a young musician by the name of Hal Findlay with whom Hermes developed a long friendship. Both men would work together again in the years ahead at RKO.

Boasting a cast of one hundred African-Americans and thirty dancing girls, *Lucky Day* opened at the Mayan Theatre on 29 December with critics singling out the musical numbers as the highpoints of the evening (even though the "Congo Dance" was considered objectionable because of an offensive overdose of wriggling). On 13 January 1932, the *Los Angeles Times* reported that Jules Murray, head of the Shubert booking department, had contacted the show's producers with an offer to take the production to Chicago and New York. It also noted that a proposed San Francisco engagement had to be postponed indefinitely to allow for a continued run in Los Angeles due to record advance sales. Originally planned for a three-week engagement, the production remained at the Mayan until 7 February 1932, after which it moved to the Pantages Hollywood Theatre on 11 February as a live stage-show accompaniment to a film. A week later, *Lucky Day* moved to the Orpheum, where, in an abbreviated production, it accompanied the film *Ladies of the Jury*. After a week at the Orpheum, the show moved away from Los Angeles to engagements in San Diego and San Francisco.

Hermes Pan received no program credit for his efforts (neither did Hal Findlay), but it did provide him with a salary at a time when he desperately needed money and it did introduce him to the concept of the "Tab Show." In her paper, "A Tab Show: The Stepchild of Musical Comedy," Caroline Schaffner (who performed in Tab Shows between 1922 and 1925) suggests:

> Sometimes called tabloid musical companies, the musical tabloid com-
> panies were referred to in old-time show business lingo as "Tab Shows."
> These companies were a rather special segment of musical theatre in
> America from the early 1900s to the 1930s. Musical tabloid companies
> had several distinguishing features. They always carried a line of girls, a
> chorus line. It could be four or twenty girls, depending on the size of the
> company. They carried no strippers and permitted no bare legs. All
> females in short wardrobe wore opera lengths—and they had better be
> clean.
>
> With some exceptions, most tabloid companies played in picture-
> show theatres, in connection with silent movies. They were the vaude-
> ville between showings of the film. (Loney 1984, 199)

What Schaffner neglected to say was that the Tab Show was almost always a touring show, sometimes playing one night only in any given city. Closely allied to Tab Shows were the musical-dramatic "Prologues" that introduced the screening of a major motion picture. These shared many of the same characteristics with the musical tabloids except for the element of touring. Prologues were typically designed to be presented at a specific theatre before the showing of a specific film and the nontouring factor permitted a more lavish production since the scenery and costumes and orchestra did not have to travel. Financial considerations typically reduced the production values of touring shows.

On 13 June 1932, Ditty wrote in her journal: "Living 1621 North Formosa, Hollywood [the family had moved to yet another apartment]. Night before I just got back from six weeks with Ted Lewis Act. Went to a call at M-G-M. Snooks working in prologue at Chinese. Went to see Marianne (roommate in act) in Andy's Packard [Andy was a boyfriend; Ditty mentions cooking breakfast for him in his apartment in an earlier entry], met her boyfriend and others." Ditty's passing quickly over her brother's participation in the prologue at Grauman's Chinese Theatre does an injustice to the magnitude of the event. The film that was premiering was *Grand Hotel* with Greta Garbo, John and Lionel Barrymore, Joan Crawford, and Wallace Beery, and, according to the *Los Angeles Times* (1 June 1932), there were more than one hundred performers in the cast. Happily for Hermes, the prologue was played not only on the opening night of the film at the end of April but through the entire run that extended through July.

Ditty's brief remarks in her journal regarding Hermes's and her performance work suggest the attitude about Hollywood that she shared with her brother.

Neither was seduced by the glitter of Hollywood. The need to earn a living far outweighed any dreams of stardom. Vasso never recorded her attending the Academy Awards or Hollywood parties with her brother; in fact, in 1938 she even neglected to mention that Hermes won the Oscar for Best Dance Direction. Vasso's daughter, Michelene, noted that Hermes was unimpressed by the trappings of the movie business. "He enjoyed them sometimes, but he didn't obsess over them. He had no patience with the 'show-business' type of people. He would make fun of 'the Dance' and people being too serious about it. He enjoyed simply listening to the music and rhythm and moving to it."

Following the run at the Chinese Theatre, Hermes landed a job touring with a Tab Show operated by Wilbur and Hazel Cushman, actors whose claim to fame was their participation in the Broadway production of *Topsy and Eva*, a musical version of *Uncle Tom's Cabin*. Their Tab Show, often billed as *Cushman's Garden of Glorious Girls*, featured a number of star performers (most often Rudy Wintner and Dale Jackson) and a chorus of eight glorious girls. Contemporary accounts portrayed the Cushmans as a smart and amiable couple who insisted that their company dress well, behave themselves off the stage as well as on, and leave no bad impressions in the community. Pan recalls that Cushman, a "diminutive and somewhat threadbare-looking man with large promises and small follow-up," had promised him $50 a week in addition to room and board, though he rarely received his salary and often not even a meal or a mattress (Pan, Columbia, Kramer 1983, 1). A Cushman Tab Show always featured a comic sketch (usually built around the antics of Rudy Wintner), interpolated songs (sung either by characters in the comedy or featured specialty acts), and dances (always performed by a chorus line of glorious girls). Musical accompaniment was provided by a single musician, usually performing on the theatre organ. During Pan's tenure with the company, Al Berube provided the musical background. Three performances were given on Sundays, at 3:00 p.m., 6:00 p.m., and 9:00 p.m. and two performances on all the other days, at 3:30 p.m. and 8:40 p.m., if the company was fortunate enough to be booked for a full week.

Offering sixty-minute musicals with titles, such as *The Vagabond Lover*, *New Town Murder Case*, *The Million Dollar Doll*, *Little White Lies*, and *Innocent Cheaters*, and advertising exotic and colorful dances like "In an Italian Garden" or "The Incense of Buddha," *Cushman's Garden of Glorious Girls* was the source of many an anecdote for Pan who, in later interviews, would not hesitate to describe his experiences. To Constantine in 1940, Hermes called the operation "a broken-down stock company," for which his responsibilities included dancing in the shows, staging the dances, singing in the male quartet, and designing (and making) the costumes for the entire company. The performers rehearsed one show during the day while performing another at night and traveled in a huge moving van along with the costumes, scenery, and props: "You can well imagine the style and comfort in which we traveled when twenty out of the twenty-five people riding would smoke. Naturally, there were no windows" (Constantine 1945, 6). In an interview with Ronald L. Davis (Ronald L. Davis Oral History Collection No. 245) held at the Margaret Herrick Library, Hermes continued:

> We would play a split week between Phoenix and Bisbee, Arizona. . . . At first we went to Sacramento, and we were stranded there for ten weeks. No, we were supposed to have been there for ten weeks, and we were stranded for two weeks [the money ran out]. And then we got backing and again we would play like one night stands between Modesto, Merced, Visalia. . . . We were stranded in Merced [in another interview, Hermes gives the town as Modesto] and they wouldn't let us out of the hotel [where] the company was staying, and we'd sign [over] our checks. That's the only way we could do it—all stay in the same hotel and sign our checks. At least we could eat and have a place to sleep. So we got a booking in Antioch . . . but still the proprietor of the hotel wouldn't let anybody leave without the bill being paid. [Pan's mother happened to be traveling with the company at the time.] So I got the bright idea that if I left my mother as security, we could go and do the date. (Davis 1983, n. p.)

In the film *Dance Crazy in Hollywood*, Hermes refers to the incident as "the time I hocked my mother in Modesto." Maureen C. Solomon adds that money problems stranded Hermes and company in Tucson, forcing the performers to subsist on donations from more prosperous fellow actors from the East Coast. Even while stranded on the road, Hermes took advantage of every opportunity to watch others dance. In Phoenix, he happened to notice a ten-year-old girl dancing in a production at the Phoenix Little Theatre and suggested to her mother that she try her luck in Hollywood since he believed that she had what it takes to make it in the movies. The girl's name was Martha O'Driscoll, who went on to perform in thirty-seven films before retiring to marry a millionaire at age twenty-four.

On 10 March 1933, when an earthquake emanating from Long Beach shook Los Angeles, Hermes was stranded in Bisbee, Arizona. Since phone service to Southern California had been disrupted by the quake, Hermes felt that the only way he could check on the welfare of his family would be to leave the tour so he gave notice, leaving his employer to remark, "I suppose there must be a lot of work back there in Los Angeles—with all that debris to clean up" (Pan, Columbia, Kramer 1983, 2). In spite of the fact that he claimed to have been stranded all over the West Coast during his almost yearlong tenure with the Cushman company, Pan admitted to Svetlana McLee Grody that the experience taught him an important lesson: "While we were playing one show, we'd be rehearsing for the next one, which gave me great experience in working fast" (Grody 1996, 11).

When Hermes Pan returned to Los Angeles after his stint with the Tab Show, he discovered that the family residence had been condemned by the city and its inhabitants were living out on the sidewalk until they could find available housing that had not been affected by the earthquake. Fortuitously, Hermes found himself and his family a small one-bedroom house at 6092½ Selma Avenue in Hollywood for $27 a month. Typical of the Pans' sleeping arrangements in Los Angeles, Mary and Vasso slept in the bedroom, Dot and Aljeanne took the living room, and Hermes and the dog slept in the kitchen.

Not long after the move, Vasso was called for an audition for the dancing chorus in the *Circus Queen Murder* at Columbia Studios and was hired as one of six dancing girls. The next day when she appeared for work on Stage Six, the assistant director told her and the other five chorines to put their heads together and come up with the choreography for the dance routine they were supposed to perform. Since the six dancers could not agree on any of the steps, Vasso suggested that her brother, a dance director, might be able to help and put in a call to Hermes, suggesting that he report to the studio immediately. Since the Selma Avenue residence was within walking distance of Columbia Pictures, a few blocks away on Sunset and Gower, Pan ran all the way, completely out of breath when the assistant director asked him how much he wanted for choreographing the number. "Whatever seems fair," was Pan's reply, not knowing what to expect, and when he saw that the assistant had written on a scrap of paper what looked like $10, Hermes jumped at the offer. Two days later, the routine was choreographed to the delight of the director and a messenger arrived on the set with Pan's wages in an envelope. Checking to see that he received the full $10 he was promised, Hermes opened the packet to find ten $10 bills—he had misread the assistant's offer. In "Back from Arizona," Pan recalls the experience as "one of the greatest moments in my memory," even surpassing his winning the Academy Award in 1937. Not only had he earned enough money to pay the rent and the electric bill, Hermes was able to stock up on groceries and throw a party for his family and friends who came by to congratulate him on the windfall. Hermes and his family even allowed themselves the luxury of buying toothpaste—a sign of prosperity at a time when salt and baking soda were typically used in oral hygiene (Pan, Columbia, Kramer 1983, 11–12).

After his two-day job with Columbia, which represented Pan's first choreography on film, Hermes continued to look for more permanent employment. He returned to giving dance lessons, this time for Maurice Kosloff, whom he characterized as a charlatan hoping to extort money from starry-eyed parents trying to advance their children's careers in the movies. Pan was paid a measly 75¢ a day for the service so when he found work at the Music Box Theatre preparing for a new revue, he abruptly and happily ended his association with Kosloff. The show was to be called *Nine O'Clock Revue*, the second edition of a popular entertainment that had featured female-impersonator Julian Eltinge in the summer of 1931. For the new edition, Hermes was hired to dance, stage the dances, design the costumes, and stage-manage the production. Though the job description was similar to the Cushman experience, the pay was better and actually forthcoming, and there was no danger of becoming stranded in some California or Arizona town.

of confidence and he left the rehearsal thinking, "If the great Astaire likes it, it mustn't be too bad."

In the days that followed, Hermes was introduced to Thornton Freeland, the director of the film; Mark Sandrich, the second unit director; Max Steiner, the musical director; Van Nest Polglase, the art director; and Hal Borne, a young classically trained pianist who had recently moved to Hollywood. Borne had been hired as a "sideline" pianist (one who is seen but not actually heard by the movie audience) for the band at the Aviator's Club in the film. John Mueller notes that as soon as Fred Astaire heard him play, he exclaimed, "I think we got a piano," and requested his services as rehearsal pianist and musical arranger throughout the 1930s (Mueller 1985, 44).

On Tuesday, 22 August, chorus dancers began rehearsals for the film's three production numbers. Pan devised the choreographic concept for both "The Carioca," and "Flying Down to Rio," and, for the first—and last—time in his career, he actually wrote down the choreography. During rehearsals Hermes was responsible for teaching and cleaning the actual dance steps while it fell to Dave Gould to create the Busby Berkeley–like geometric patterns of movement. Pan spent a great deal of time in seclusion with Fred Astaire minutely working out a dance routine step by step, before the chorus was even called. When they rehearsed a partnered dance (in this case a Fred and Ginger dance), Hermes took the role of Ginger, and when he taught the routine to Ginger, he danced Fred's part. He had to be able to master the steps for both partners.

On the first day of chorus rehearsal, Dolores Del Rio, Fred Astaire, Gene Raymond, Raul Roulien, and thirty-four tango dancers were called from 11:00 a.m. to 7:20 p.m. to work on the tango sequence for "Orchids in the Moonlight." Ginger Rogers joined the rehearsals on 31 August (two days after the *Hollywood Reporter* announced that she was assigned a featured role in RKO's next musical, *Hips, Hips, Hooray*), and "The Carioca" sequence was shot between Saturday, 23 September, and Saturday, 30 September. "Flying Down to Rio," with its big airplane sequence, was rehearsed and shot during the week of 2 October. The rushes for *Rio* were so promising that RKO picked up its options on Fred Astaire and Mark Sandrich for future projects and Dave Gould asked Hermes to assist him with his next assignment, *Hips, Hips, Hooray*.

Hermes was justifiably proud of his contribution to *Flying Down to Rio*. In his unpublished autobiography, he happily recalled the two weeks of twelve-hour days rehearsing "The Carioca" in preparation for a full week of filming the number. While Dave Gould set up the shots and camera angles, Pan meticulously drilled two separate choruses in different styles of dance. A "White Group" performed choreography typical of Busby Berkeley in addition to the "two heads together" step that Hermes had created, while a "Black Group" performed shim shams and jazz steps that gave Pan the opportunity to display what he called "real dancing" on the screen. He seemed particularly proud of the fact that Fred Astaire enjoyed performing his choreography at the climax of the number because it "gave him a chance to really move." Pan concluded that "The Carioca" was the most sensational dance number he had ever seen. "It was, as Fred said to Ginger in the picture, a 'hot" dance number' (Pan, Columbia, Kramer 1983, 24–27).

Hermes noted to John Kobal, "You'll notice that even in *Flying Down to Rio* there was less of the big production type of number with twenty girls and twenty boys, even though they were still doing geometrical designs like the Berkeley thing. I love dancing as such, and I really like to see a few people rather than huge productions where dancing was lost. To me, it wasn't really dancing. . . . It was just a fortunate situation that I did meet Astaire and that he was of the same outlook, feeling and mentality as I was. It sort of blended into a beautiful thing, it worked out very fortunately" (Kobal 1985, 622). Speaking with Ronald L. Davis, Pan elaborated on his similarities with Astaire: "Like his rhythms and my rhythms were just exactly almost—it's almost uncanny that we would do things so much alike. And we even sort of had a little language ourselves. Dancers have a certain language they knew as terms. He'd say, 'Oh, well, that's a real groovy sort of nippy thing.' And say a 'Whap' here, and 'that's sort of zap.' And this is 'Right now.' And so I knew exactly what he meant, and he would know exactly what I meant when I'd say, 'Well, that's it': This says it. This is something—no kidding, no nonsense" (Davis 1983, n. p.).

A 22 November news item in the *Hollywood Reporter* announced that RKO had hired three orchestras to complete the dubbing for the film to ensure its readiness for an opening at Radio City Music Hall during Christmas week. In those days of movie musicals, singing was typically filmed using an orchestra positioned at the other side of the sound stage, about a block away from the singer; the dances were filmed using a piano track and an orchestra was dubbed in later. As Arlene Croce explained, this process worked for everyone but the dancers themselves:

> Cutting a dance sequence to the demands of exact synchronization was a totally unfamiliar task to film editors. The task was lightened if the dance movement was relatively simple in its relationship to the musical track. The technique of post-synchronization freed sound stages from the perils of direct recording, but the separation of picture and sound introduced new perils in the cutting room, where a "down" dance accent would frequently be made to coincide with a musical upbeat. A rhythmically complicated dance presented hideous problems; in desperation, film cutters would cut away to crowd reactions, yapping dogs, gurgling babies— anything to avoid getting sight and sound together. (Croce 1987, 15–16)

In a 1972 interview with John Kobal, Pan noted: "At first, when we started Astaire and Rogers, we had to dance to a piano track, then they'd put in the music later, which was just horrible. And then sometimes they'd try and record the taps at the same time as we were shooting it. Then they finally overcame that and we had playbacks. But for most of those Astaire-Rogers things we didn't have playbacks.

We danced to a piano track for quite a few of them" (Kobal 1985, 631). Arlene Croce credits director Mark Sandrich with developments in the playback system but notes that numbers that simply required singing would continue to be recorded using the orchestra a block away on the set (Croce 1987, 39). The first of Pan's films to use some sort of a playback device was the Sandrich-directed *Cockeyed Cavaliers*, during the filming of which production records note "playback and sound track on set."

Once *Flying Down to Rio* opened, all such perils were forgotten as reviewers and audiences alike praised the dancing in the film. At the preview in Pomona, when Fred and Ginger finished dancing "The Carioca," the audience applauded and the *New York Times* (22 December 1933) paid particular notice to Pan's work:

> An impressive number of scenes are devoted to a dance known as "The Carioca." During this interlude that nimble-toed Fred Astaire and the charming Ginger Rogers give a performance of this Carioca. The music is delightful, and besides Mr. Astaire and Miss Rogers, many other persons dance the extraordinarily rhythmic Carioca, one feature of which happens to be that of the couples pressing their foreheads together as they glide around the floor.
>
> The production seems to get more and more lavish as it continues. In its latter stages it takes to the air again and there are some effective ideas of girls strapped to the wings of flying machines and going through a precision drill. These scenes have all the sensation of the girls being actually in the air.

On 17 October, a week before the "Orchids in the Moonlight" sequence in *Flying Down to Rio* had completed filming, the Wheeler and Woolsey comedy, *Hips, Hips, Hooray* began production under the direction of Mark Sandrich (but with Dorothy Lee instead of the previously advertised Ginger Rogers). Bert Kalmar and Harry Ruby, who had contributed scores for *Animal Crackers* and *Top Speed*, provided the story and songs for this musical romp into the world of cosmetics and cross-country automobile races. Though the film was budgeted at $226,094.92, Dave Gould was paid a flat $150 for the dance direction (as opposed to the $1,500 he received for *Flying Down to Rio*, and the $450 he was paid for *Melody Cruise*), a clear indication of how little dance would figure in the production. Pan's work as Gould's (once again uncredited) assistant involved creating a few dance steps (including a faux ballet routine) with the help of pianist Hal Findlay for the number, "Keep on Doing What You're Doing," which was rehearsed and filmed on Halloween and the day after. He provided a second eye for Gould working with Ruth Etting, Wheeler and Woolsey, and twenty dancing girls during the first half of November but, compared to his efforts with Astaire, Pan considered his work on *Hips, Hips, Hooray* negligible. Although the *Los Angeles Examiner* proclaimed the film "one of [Wheeler and Woolsey's] best in a long time" (25 January 1934), the

Variety critic felt that "the production all around [was] much better than the material provided" (27 February 1934).

Joseph Ignatius Breen, head of the Production Code Administration, the Hollywood watchdog of morality, was troubled by the content of *Hips, Hips, Hooray*. In October 1933, Mark Sandrich had issued a statement affirming emphatically that no nude women would be seen in the film but the Breen office was far from satisfied. The film was subsequently banned in Australia until a series of deletions were made, and only allowed to be shown in New York City if the prolonged view of Wheeler and Woolsey in an automobile with children on their laps in connection with the song "Keep on Doing What You're Doing" was eliminated. Also required to be cut was the line "Why, we haven't any baggage, but I think I could dig up a bag." The double entendre in both instances remains clear even today and it is no surprise that religious leaders—especially Catholic religious leaders—were up in arms. Hermes Pan, a devout Roman Catholic, was often teased about the reaction of the Legion of Decency to his films. Typically, he laughed at the censor's comments, finding them excessive overreactions. "Every day, in real life, people do and say things that are slightly suggestive for the sake of a good joke. What's wrong with putting it on the screen?"

In the middle of February, Hermes was back at the studio supervising the movement for *Strictly Dynamite*, a Jimmy Durante comedy for which Ginger Rogers had been announced as one of the leads (*Hollywood Reporter*, 21 December 1933). As was the case with *Hips, Hips, Hooray*, by the time filming had begun Ginger Rogers was no longer in the cast. Somewhat anticipating *The Dick Van Dyke Show* on television in the 1960s, *Strictly Dynamite* was about a poet who becomes a gagman for a big-time radio comic (Jimmy Durante), falls under the spell of his girlfriend (Lupe Velez), reconciles with his wife (Marian Nixon), and leaves the hustle and bustle of New York for a novelist's career in the country. This harmless nonsense featured songs by Harold Adamson and Burton Lane ("Swing It Sister" and "Oh, Me! Oh, My! Oh, You!"), Irving Kahal and Sammy Fain ("Money in My Clothes"), and Jimmy Durante ("Hot Pattata," and "I'm Putty in Your Hands," in collaboration with Adamson). Also included in the film was Irving Berlin's "Manhattan Madness," though Berlin received no on-screen credit. Merian C. Cooper, who served as executive producer on Hermes Pan's previous assignments, was replaced on this film by Pandro S. Berman, an RKO executive who would figure prominently in Hermes's future.

According to the RKO Production Files, no dance director was listed for *Strictly Dynamite*, but modern sources attribute the staging to Hermes Pan. Rehearsal pianist Hal Findlay was on salary for a mere week and a half in the middle of February, so music and staging rehearsals were not extensive. "Putty in Your Hands" required Jimmy Durante and Lupe Velez to shimmy and sway; "Hot Pattata" necessitated a few simple steps and repetitious turns for the same duo; and for "Oh, Me! Oh, My! Oh, You!" Lupe Velez had to master seductive hand gestures and footwork that was hidden by a long dress. All of this was the kind of movement

Until a dance routine was more or less complete, Pan and Astaire rehearsed in front of mirrors, ten feet high and twenty feet wide, on a guarded stage, permitting no one entrance except for Hal Borne and, when she was available, Ginger Rogers. Producer, director, author, composer—all were forbidden entry until a dance was ready to be shown. In the weeks that preceded the start of filming on 28 June, Pan helped Astaire shape "A Needle in the Haystack," a virtuosic dance filled with humor than seems to emerge naturally from the choreography—a trait that can be found in most, if not all, of Pan's dances with and without Astaire. He danced the Ginger role in "Night and Day," the partner number that Arlene Croce calls "an incomparable dance of seduction" (Croce 1987, 33), while Astaire was perfecting the steps and, again as Ginger, he helped the dancer polish the choreography of "The Table Dance," a difficult and rather dangerous duet stepping on and off furniture originally devised by Carl Randall, the choreographer of the Broadway version. Working closely with Astaire, Hermes began to discover techniques of staging dance for film that influenced the rest of his career. Pan explained:

> My first serious experience with dancing was working with Astaire. The way he moved contributed a lot to my subsequent thinking when I came to choreograph. In all those films I did with him at RKO, we were always conscious of the camera. We'd rehearse in front of those big mirrors, and those were our cameras. If you travel across the screen you get a much better effect of movement than if you come straight down the middle because you don't see that motion. All you get is a figure getting larger. We designed things so that if you had a step that came from the back and you wanted it to [look like it was] coming forward, instead of coming straight down we'd do it diagonally. Then you had motion and speed. (Kobal 1983, 128)

On 13 June, the day Ditty began writing her journal nine years previously, Hermes took the night off to celebrate his new contract with RKO. Hermes, Dot, Ditty, and their friend Frank Lewis visited the free cocktail hour at the White Horse Tavern and managed to smuggle beer out of the bar and up to their home where they continued to drink while they dressed for dinner at a restaurant called the Coco Tree. After dinner, they attended a preview of *Down to Their Last Yacht*, Dave Gould's latest effort starring Mary Boland as the queen of a South Sea Island on which a yacht rented out to the nouveaux riches has run aground. Hermes liked Dave Gould and wished him success, but he was unimpressed by the musical, a reaction shared by reviewers who wrote that "the film is a sorry mélange of Hollywood native dancing, theme-song singing and preposterous comedy" (*New York Times*, 24 September 1934); and "it has no dance like the Carioca to wow 'em, the nearest thing being a kind of Polynesian ceremonial or 'South Sea Bolero,' which is quite without distinction" (*Los Angeles Times*, 27 August 1934).

The next day, 14 June, was Dave Gould's first day at work on *The Gay Divorcee*. Even after a party night, Hermes was up bright and early, heading back to the studio to divide his time between partnering Astaire and assisting Dave Gould on the development of another dance extravaganza—"The Continental." Arlene Croce notes that in the weeks that followed, Hermes would function as a connection between Astaire and producer Pandro S. Berman, director Mark Sandrich, and dance director Gould. He would keep them informed about the lengths of numbers and the amount of extra personnel (audiences, crowds, ensemble dancers, dummy orchestras) that may have been added (or deleted) during the development of the various numbers in the show (Croce 1987, 89). Since Astaire's contract gave him artistic control over the filming of his dance routines, Hermes played an important part in communicating how Fred and he wanted the dances photographed:

> Fred and I had complete artistic control. We more or less told the directors what to do. A lot of directors don't know very much about music so there wasn't much choice. We even told them the angles we wanted, where it should be shot, what had to be cut. We explained how a step looked better from here, not so good from there. The cinematographers were very crucial in all this. They might have a suggestion that we try something different. Or they would explain why what we wanted couldn't be done. I would always consult them. I'd ask them about the lens and if they could pull away, all sorts of technical details. (Georgakas 1983, 26)

Camera operator Joseph Biroc, who had known Hermes Pan from earlier work at the studio, adds in an interview with Leonard Maltin:

> [Astaire] would always rehearse on the rehearsal stage in front of big mirrors, so he could see everything he was doing. Then we would go in there every once in a while, when they had most of the routine down, and you would see it, the music would be playing. Pretty soon you got the music in the back of your head. You couldn't think of anything else. And you would drift right in with it. You knew exactly what he was going to do, when he was going to jump up; you were prepared for it.
>
> The dolly guy would say, "Now when he gets over here on the beat—" He probably didn't know as much as I did, and I didn't know anything. He would say, "On the eighth beat they are going to do this." I would say, "The hell with the eighth beat, touch me when you want it to happen." Or, "Touch me before it happens." So Pan would say, "Watch me when he gets over there and the camera is going to pull back." When the camera pulls back naturally you are going to have more room. So the camera would go back and we'd get him jumping up in the air. And Pan would tap the guys and okay now we are going to do the regular routine. Even today, I don't know one note from another. (Maltin 2008, 234–235)

Filming *The Gay Divorcee*. Hermes Pan, seated, left; Joseph Biroc, behind the camera; Fred Astaire and Ginger Rogers, right of center (Courtesy of the Academy of Motion Picture Arts and Sciences).

Once filming began for *The Gay Divorcee*, it was Pan's responsibility to watch the daily rushes of Fred Astaire's numbers. Before Astaire would take a look at them himself, he quizzed Pan about the quality of the work. "Great," was Pan's typical response. "Are you sure?" Fred inquired. Without waiting for a reply, he continued, "When you described them to me, you seemed to think there was one little step you didn't like." Once Hermes gave his input, Astaire went to watch the rushes on his own, and if he felt that, at any time, the figure on the screen looked even slightly off balance, he and Pan would persuade the director to film the sequence again.[2]

On Saturday, 7 July, a week after *The Gay Divorcee* went before the cameras, Hermes Pan, Mark Sandrich, and Dave Gould auditioned more than five hundred hopefuls for the thirty girl dancers required for "The Continental." Among the girls chosen were Vasso Pan and Angela Blue. "The first time I saw Angie Blue was in the early 1930s in a chorus audition lineup," Hermes remarked in his memoir, "Meeting the Frog Prince." "She was wearing a bikini bathing suit and a live marmoset on her shoulder. Her appearance was so outrageous I hired her just because I thought she'd be fun" (Pan, Columbia, Kramer n.d., 249). Hermes did not know at the time that Angela Blue would become his dear friend and favorite assistant. On Monday, 9 July, the thirty girl dancers were in rehearsal with Dave Gould and Hermes Pan on Stage Ten for "The Continental," joined on the following day by thirty boy dancers, chosen at another audition. The ensemble rehearsed from ten in the morning through early evening for the next two weeks, and then filming began. Astaire and Rogers joined the dancers in more rehearsal on Saturday, 28 July, and Pan finished shooting "The Continental" on the last day of the month.

While supervising the chorus dancers for the sixteen-minute extravaganza "The Continental," which incidentally won the Academy Award for Best Song in 1934, the first year that category was included in the Oscars, Pan was developing

the choreography for "Let's K-nock K-nees," a diverting but undistinguished routine for Betty Grable, Edward Everett Horton, and a chorus of bathing beauties
and beaux inspired by Cole Porter's "Salt Air" number in the original score for *The
Gay Divorce*. Effectively utilizing the terpsichorean strengths of Grable and Horton (or, in the latter case, hiding his weaknesses), Pan's choreography for the principals cleverly combines tap dancing with the requisite "knock-knee" step. When
the dancing chorus appears, the characteristic step is passed from group to group
in a kind of theme-and-variations structure that, in the view of most critics, went
on for too long.

"Let's K-nock K-nees" went before the cameras on the seventh and eighth of
August, and after *The Gay Divorcee* completed filming a week later, Pan took a brief
hiatus from RKO to teach Katharine Hepburn how to tap. Credited with the
famous remark regarding Astaire and Rogers, "He gives her class, she gives him
sex," Hepburn was under contract at RKO and spent much of her free time on the
set of *The Gay Divorcee*, watching Fred and Ginger dance. After the film wrapped
on 13 August, Hepburn approached Hermes Pan for private tap lessons, a request
that impressed Pan since it indicated that she had an appreciation of how movement could help and inform her acting. Even though he came to realize that her
desire to learn tap was for her own recreation, nothing more than a hobby, he
respected Hepburn's fascination with the physical discipline required in tap
dancing and cherished the hours they spent together on Saturdays at her home in
Coldwater Canyon. By the end of October when Hermes went back to work at
RKO, *The Gay Divorcee* had opened throughout the United States to rave reviews
and record attendance, a phenomenon that would be repeated in London and
Paris, where it premiered to the largest cash sale of customers in the history of the
Cinéma Avenue.

Following the New York City preview on 5 October, the Dancing Teachers Association gave a demonstration of "The Continental" at their annual convention in
the Hotel Astor. Attending the event was Mark Sandrich, who found himself
pressed by dance teachers to simplify the dance steps on the screen. Subsequently,
the Dancing Masters of America, Inc., sent a manifesto to RKO Studios arguing
that "the motion pictures have done a great deal in stimulating interest in ballroom dancing, but it is our belief that the dances that are shown in various pictures are too elaborate and too much exhibition dance style. We earnestly urge
that some effort be made in which the next ballroom dance that is shown will be
something that the dancing public could actually do." In an article in the *Los Angeles Times* (6 January 1935), Hermes Pan made known his reply to the association's
request:

> Pan doesn't see why steps should be too simplified. They are made first
> for audiences' amazement; if people want to imitate them, that is their
> own business—especially, he chuckled, if they keep coming back to check
> up on this or that step. He does concede that it is unwise to complicate

aristocratic and courtly dances, providing a colorful and effective counterpoint to the dramatic scenes. Since Pan's name does not appear in the production files for *Becky Sharp*, his specific contribution to the sequence is conjectural. Having assisted Dave Gould and Fred Astaire, Pan was accustomed to helping choreographers realize their vision by suggesting steps and patterns, or simply by teaching the ensemble the combinations. In rehearsals, Pan's cheerful and unflappable demeanor and seemingly endless store of patience made him especially suited to teach dance steps to principal actors who, quite often, were terrified of dancing or had no sense of rhythm.

After a two- or three-day hiatus for work on *Becky Sharp*, Hermes was back to work with Fred Astaire on *Top Hat*. On 15 March their efforts culminated in an "estimate script" in which all the musical numbers developed through the story meetings and dance rehearsals were listed with the approximate footage of film planned for each event. This is an important document since it indicates a running order for the film, implies how far the choreography had progressed (numbers with no footage are obviously less structured at this point), and even indicates material that does not appear in the finished film.

Listed first was a tap dance for Astaire and an African-American boy, eventually unused (83 feet of film); next "Fancy Free," a solo for Astaire in his hotel room, just above that of Ginger Rogers, including a song, a tap dance, and a sand dance (104 feet); "Fancy Free" Reprise (30 feet); "Isn't This a Lovely Day," in which Astaire sings and dances with Rogers (length still undetermined); "Top Hat, White Tie, and Tails," a stage performance designed for Fred and twenty-two boy dancers (length undetermined); an untitled routine on the Lido Beach involving twenty-four girls, unused (length undetermined); "Cheek to Cheek," Fred and Ginger dance (10 feet); "Get Thee Behind Me, Satan," a song for Ginger Rogers, eventually unused (length unspecified); "Piccolino," for Astaire, Rogers, an Italian singer, forty girl and forty boy dancers requiring four days to film (18 feet); and a "Finale Dance," for Astaire and Rogers, heavily abridged in the final film (23 feet).

Of the four numbers that had been more or less choreographed by 15 March, "Piccolino" was the most challenging for Pan because neither he nor Astaire liked the song. Both had wanted the obligatory big production number to be about a dance, like "The Carioca," or "The Continental." What Berlin wrote, however, was about a song not a dance, and neither Pan nor Astaire could convince him to change "Hear the Piccolino" to "Do the Piccolino." Though Berlin felt a particular fondness for the number, Hermes considered it perhaps the least distinguished part of an otherwise remarkable score. As Pan has remarked again and again, "If it's bad music, it's usually bad dancing," and the RKO Production Files chronicle the 125 hours he spent in rehearsal trying to perfect a dance for the "Piccolino." Because of the spinning and whirling involved in the number, Hermes put his dancers on a diet—no candy, cigarettes, or rich foods—and required them to be tested for "spinning sickness" before the extravagantly stylized ribbon dance went before the cameras.

On 5 April, the day *Top Hat* began filming, a syndicated column, "In New York," by Paul Harrison, printed the following item:

> Among your correspondent's correspondence is a gracious little note from Hermes Pan, Mister Hermes Pan. He was not annoyed because I recently expressed amusement at the name of Hermes Pan; he admits that it might remind one of anything from a candy bar to a Grecian goat. But he does take exception to this department's identification of him as a chorus girl [on 22 February 1935]. He is, as a matter of fact, an RKO dance director. . . . An aberration without alibi. To Hermes, son of Zeus and Maia, messenger and herald of the gods, apologies. (*Kokomo Tribune*, 5 April 1935)

Hermes enjoyed a good joke, even when he was the subject of it.

By the beginning of May, "Fancy Free," "Isn't This a Lovely Day," and "Top Hat," had been filmed without incident, each taking two or three days. Universally accepted as one of Astaire's iconic dances, the theatre-performance number "Top Hat" permitted Pan and Astaire to synthesize motifs and routines from the dancer's Broadway career: the focus on top hat and tails from "High Hat" in *Funny Face*

Hermes Pan demonstrating a step on the set of "Cheek to Cheek" (Courtesy of the Academy of Motion Picture Arts and Sciences).

Astaire's dancing. On the first show, accompanied by Lennie Hayton's orchestra, Fred performed his numbers from *Top Hat*, the first time the tunes had been heard anywhere, since the film had yet to be released. Immediately after the broadcast (which arrived on the West Coast at 4:00 p.m., Astaire called Pan for an appraisal. As was their ritual, after Hermes replied that the show was great, Fred continued to pump him about the minutest detail of the performance until Pan came up with a suggestion that Astaire felt would improve his performance on the next broadcast. For the next three weeks, Hermes could expect a phone call from Fred after every show.

On 13 August, the *Hollywood Reporter* reviewed the West Coast opening of *Top Hat* with the caption, "*Top Hat* Grand Example of Top Notch Screen Musical," and proclaimed that " 'Piccolino' is zee beeg numbaire, done in Hollywood's version of the Lido (and it's something the Lido should look into). Hermes Pan and Mark Sandrich give their all to it and their all is something you must see." At the end of the month, the film opened in New York to rhapsodic reviews and an all-time box office record—by 4:00 p.m. on opening day, thirteen thousand people had bought tickets, and by the end of its first week, it grossed $131,200. Originally budgeted at $637,131.05, *Top Hat* earned RKO $1,295,000 in profits. Hermes had another hit on his hands.

Hermes and Vasso Pan at the premiere of *Top Hat* (Courtesy of the Vasso Pan Meade Collection).

Fred Astaire returned to Los Angeles by train on the Super Chief on 4 September 1935, and on the very next day he met with Hermes Pan and Hal Borne to begin brainstorming about what to do with the seven Irving Berlin songs in his next vehicle with Ginger Rogers, *Follow the Fleet*. More closely resembling *Roberta* than *Top Hat*, *Follow the Fleet* cast Astaire as "Bake" Baker, a sailor, and Rogers as Sherry Martin, his former dance partner and girlfriend, who meet up again when his ship docks in San Francisco. She has a sister, Connie (Harriet Hilliard), who is interested in his friend "Bilge" Smith (Randolph Scott), but her ardor scares him into the arms of another woman until the end of the film when he learns of Connie's sacrifices on his behalf. Hermes Pan was guaranteed seventeen weeks of work at $200 a week ($3,400) while Ginger Rogers was paid $2,000 weekly; Astaire received a total of $60,000 and Irving Berlin earned $75,000 plus 10 percent of the profits. For the first week, Pan, Astaire, and Borne met from 9:30 a.m. to 6:00 p.m. daily. Borne played through the score a number of times until either Hermes or Fred would experience a visceral response to a song. When that happened, the trio would focus on that number for the rest of the day, or if inspiration seemed to be running low, Borne would begin playing the other tunes in the event that something would "click." As Pan recalled to Ronald L. Davis in 1983, "We'd start on one or two [numbers] at the same time and then as we went along, we'd maybe break in another idea for another type of number that would come in later."

Hermes Pan, Ginger Rogers, publicity director Eddie Rubin, Fred Astaire, and Hal Borne on the set of *Follow the Fleet* (Courtesy of the Academy of Motion Picture Arts and Sciences).

From 13 September until 24 September, Pan was back to work on *Love Song*, rehearsing and filming the final production number, "I Dream Too Much," with two dozen dancers and six showgirls. Reviews for the film note the similarity between Pan's staging and earlier Astaire-Rogers chorus production numbers and the comparisons are apt. "I Dream Too Much" is a number performed in a theatre, on a three-level set, with stairs on opposite sides joining on the middle level then dividing again to the stage floor. It opens with a dozen men in tails singing to Lily Pons, who is high above them on the third level. The showgirls appear at the top of the staircases wearing evening gowns (as in the fashion-show sequence in *Roberta*) and glide down the stairs posing seductively for the camera. Unlike the mannequins in the earlier film, however, these women are flirting with the camera, not simply modeling dresses. The dancers, partnered into twelve couples, return performing a simplified Astaire-Rogers type routine that ends in a tasteful lift reintroducing Miss Pons. The tempo increases and the dancers swirl around the stage in a bright waltz, finally posing on the staircases as the curtain falls. Perhaps the *Variety* review (4 December 1935) said it best: "Another curious song mistake is just ahead of the finale in the title song. As background for Miss Pons's singing this number, there is a dance routine staged by Hermes Pan which looks suspiciously like a holdover from one of the Fred Astaire pictures. It's good, or could be, in its place, but doesn't belong here." Nevertheless, opening in New York City in December, the film took in $90,000, the best business in the three months since *Top Hat*.

On 25 September, Pan rejoined Fred and Hal, anxious to see what they had come up with in his absence. Among the first steps he was shown was the start of Astaire's routine in "I'd Rather Lead a Band." Pan was of particular assistance to Astaire in the development of the second part of the number, a call-and-response section in which Fred taps choreographic commands to the sailors at attention behind him. When Ginger joined the group on 30 September, work progressed on the dance hall competition dance, "Let Yourself Go," and on "I'm Putting All My Eggs in One Basket," the first true vaudeville duet of the Astaire-Rogers series. In her autobiography, Rogers recalls the number:

> When Fred created routines, he always tried not to repeat steps from other dances. "Eggs in One Basket" was no exception. On the rehearsal stage, we asked Hal Borne to play the number on the piano. Gradually, little by little, a goofy dance began to take shape from the silly things Fred, Hermes, and I were doing to the piano's rhythm. I suggested that it would be funny if I got caught in a step and couldn't come out of it. Fred should try everything to get me to the next step while I ignored him and continued doing what I was doing. Fred liked the idea, and we tried it out a few different ways. As the rhythm of the dance changed from waltz time to fast jazzy time, I suggested that Fred fling me out in a spin and let go of me on the return. I'd end up on the floor, doing an Edgar Kennedy

slow burn as I sat there. Because the two characters we were playing, Sherry and Blake, were not sophisticated, we could get away with this type of nonsensical dance. (Rogers 2008, 179–180)

For the dance contest, "Let Yourself Go," Hermes had the idea to involve the amateur dancers that frequented the ballrooms around Los Angeles. He talked RKO into sponsoring dance contests at the Palomar Ballroom and enlisted the winners—thirteen couples who had both the right look and sufficient technique—for the Paradise Ballroom sequence in the film. He finally settled on Bob Cromer, an eighteen-year-old dishwasher, and Dorothy Fleisman, a twenty-year-old stenographer, as the couple who would compete against Astaire and Rogers. The desire to employ good amateur dancers in *Follow the Fleet* was not a whim for Hermes Pan, who had always been on the lookout for new talent. Don Ackerman, one of the dancers he cast as a sailor, had used the tombstones in the cemetery that abuts the RKO studios as support so that he could climb over the adjoining wall to get an interview with the dance director. Before studio security arrived to escort Ackerman off the premises, he met with Hermes Pan and was hired on the spot. The speed with which Pan hired the dancer may have been less due to his phenomenal talent than to the dearth of available A-list male dancers in Hollywood. In the syndicated column, "Screen Life in Hollywood" (12 December 1935), Hermes lamented that there were only about fifty Grade-A male dancers in Hollywood, another hundred or so that would do, and a further hundred who said they could dance and would do in the back line. In the past, dance auditions typically netted two hundred applicants, from which it was easy to pick twenty-five or more. But for *Follow the Fleet*, only fifty men applied, of whom only ten were hired. The reason for the drop in available dancers: the popularity of the "Top Hat, White Tie, and Tails" number from *Top Hat*. Suddenly, male chorus dancers were in demand, and dancers worth their salt only wanted to work the jobs that guaranteed them the greatest number of weeks. The unfortunate dance director who could only offer two or three weeks of employment was faced with the necessity of giving dance lessons to whatever men happened to be available, even if his name was Hermes Pan and the film starred Fred Astaire and Ginger Rogers.

Ginger's solo reprise of "Let Yourself Go" allowed Hermes the opportunity to create another dance for Rogers on his own, and the differences between the audition tap sequence in *Follow the Fleet* and the "demonstration" tap number he created for *In Person* display Pan's ability to create dances that capture dramatic nuance. In the earlier film, the dancer is a movie star whose problems do not extend to having to convince someone of her talent. The number is relaxed, playful, and ostentatious because the dancer has no doubt of her abilities. In the second film, the dancer is not an established star and is desperate for work. She presents herself more stiffly in the dance, not completing phrases with as much authority as she might under more relaxed circumstances.[4] Both numbers work as entertainment certainly, but for Pan that was never enough: they also had to embody the dramatic situation.

Hermes conceived the Astaire-Rogers adagio "Let's Face the Music and Dance" as a dramatic performance number of greater proportion than what ended up on-screen. According to Henry Sutherland's syndicated column, *Hollywood Sidelights*:

> Most of the [*Follow the Fleet*] routines will be fast and peppery enough to please the warmest warm-sock fan, but there's only one sequence turned over to Hermes for his very own.
>
> In the bit, Fred and Ginger will portray two suicide candidates, turned down by their respective true loves and ready for the river. Idea is they meet on first bounce, and after a conflict of intentions between the sullen waters and a sultry new love affair, call it quits and exit arm in arm. It's all demonstrated in the dancing.
>
> "We can have a chorus of about twelve girls. Won't have room for more because the set is a small stage," Pan said. "The way I see it now, the girls will wear ugly, frowning masks to indicate the attitude of the lost loves, then suddenly slip them [off] to show beautiful smiling faces significant of the new. That's just an idea. We'll have to work it all out."
>
> "The music will be good, contrasting lost hope and new hope, and ending with a gay lift." (*Sandusky Star-Journal*, 31 December 1935)

The RKO Production Files shed little light on when or why the number was reduced to the duet between Astaire and Rogers. The obvious answer is that the dance was so effective that everything else became extraneous, and at 110 minutes, the film had no room for unnecessary bits. In any event, by the time "Let's Face the Music and Dance" went before the cameras, it had become another number about a dress.

On this occasion, Ginger appeared in a beaded gown with heavily beaded sleeves hanging down from her wrists. Every time she made a quick turn, the sleeves would fly in Astaire's direction, causing him to duck or get slapped in the face by a sleeve. After a series of rehearsals, the dancers felt they had mastered the problem and went for a take. All was well for about the first fifteen seconds, before a sudden twist on Ginger's part caused the sleeve to fly directly at Fred, smacking him on the jaw and hitting him in the eye. Since the plan was to film the number in one piece, without cuts, Astaire continued to dance even though he was in something of a daze. Once the routine was over, Fred asked for a second take since, feeling groggy, he had little sense of what he had just performed. After about twenty takes, none of which seemed to please Pan or the performers, they all adjourned for the evening, expecting to continue filming the next day. When they returned to review the rushes the next morning, however, the first take looked terrific; the attack of the beaded sleeve was imperceptible and "Let's Face the Music and Dance" was a wrap.[5]

Hermes Pan and his yellow Buick (Courtesy of the Vasso Pan Meade Collection).

Follow the Fleet was released on 21 February 1936 and, like its predecessors, it became an immediate hit. The *Reporter* (25 February 1936) announced that the film topped all previous Astaire-Rogers musicals, scoring record-breaking draws throughout the country. Radio City Music Hall in New York City wired that the Saturday attendance broke all previous records at that theatre. Although reviewers found imperfections in the book, the musical numbers were universally praised, with *Variety* (26 February 1936) calling them "all honeys," and the *New York Times* (21 February 1936) suggesting that "even though it is not the best of [the Astaire-Rogers] series, it still is good enough to take the head of this year's class in song and dance entertainment." Ultimately, *Follow the Fleet* netted RKO $930,000 in profits.

With the money he earned from the film, Hermes Pan purchased a yellow Buick for $2,500 and paid the down payment on a house at 6310 Rodgerton Drive in Beechwood Canyon under the "Hollywoodland" sign. Pan considered buying the house "one of the great milestones" in his early career: not only did it have a moat leading to the entrance, it had three bedrooms. For the first time since the family moved to Los Angeles, Hermes did not have to sleep with the dog in the kitchen! Just as he was moving his family into their new lodgings, Hermes was notified that his work on *Top Hat* had been nominated for an Academy Award in a brand new category, Best Dance Direction. Since Busby Berkeley, Sammy Lee, LeRoy Prinz, and Dave Gould were also nominated, Pan had no expectations of winning, but at twenty-six years old he was flattered to have been considered. In spite of the fact that his talent and gentle demeanor had won him the respect of the entire film industry, Hermes still viewed choreography as a day job.

At the end of February, he was happily reunited with Katharine Hepburn on the set of *Mary of Scotland*, his next assignment for RKO. The big-budget Scottish

Vasso and Aunt Mamie Purple standing by the moat at 6310 Rodgerton Drive (Courtesy of the Vasso Pan Meade Collection).

costume drama full of bagpipes and battles had a single dance, set in the court of Elizabeth, which Hermes was required to research and teach. Since the script simply indicated "a dance" without any more specificity, Pan and the musical director, Nathaniel Shilkret, spent hours studying the music and dances of the sixteenth century. For the film, they chose to replicate the "coranto," a dance introduced into England by the French and especially popular at Elizabeth's court. Hermes learned that the steps and structure of the dance were not unlike the minuet, except that the partners were arranged opposite one another in lines like the Virginia reel. Pan was given only two days to teach the cast the steps and patterns of the coranto, which, according to Willa Okker's syndicated column, "The Hollywood Parade," subsequently became the latest rage at Hollywood parties (*Times and Daily News Leader*, 12 June 1936).

As soon as he had he completed his work for *Mary of Scotland*, Pan found himself at the Biltmore Hotel in Los Angeles accompanied by his sister for the 1936 Academy Awards. Hosted by director Frank Capra, the gala ceremony this year would mark the first time the statuettes were referred to as "Oscars." Pan watched with childlike delight as Bette Davis won the Best Actress award and Walt Disney

was awarded the trophy for Best Animated Short Film. He applauded enthusiastically when "Lullaby of Broadway" took the award for Best Song, hiding his disappointment that neither "Cheek to Cheek" nor "Lovely to Look At," the only other
nominations, came away the winner. When Dave Gould's name was called in the
category of Best Dance Direction, Hermes was neither surprised nor disappointed.
Among the first to rise and congratulate Gould, Pan believed the honor was
deserved and dismissed the whispers of his friends and fans of the Astaire-Rogers
series, suggesting that he should have won. "For a boy from Tennessee with an
eighth-grade education and who never had a dance lesson," he thought, "just
being invited to the Academy Awards is winning enough."

The week after the awards ceremony, Hermes was at work with dance directors
LeRoy Prinz, Bobby Connolly, Roy Randolph, and Dave Gould planning the first
annual Easter Ball and Pageant of the Screen Dancers' Guild, scheduled for 4 April
at the Fiesta Room of the Ambassador Hotel. Pan enjoyed preparing for parties,
especially when dancing was involved, and he filled his days away from the studio
with a flurry of social activity. A week later, Hermes and his sister were among the
guests of Martha O'Driscoll, the young actress Hermes discovered in Arizona,
throwing a housewarming party with swimming, dining, and dancing at her new
home in Laurel Canyon. The list of invitations read like a "Who's Who in Hollywood," and Pan and Vasso made such an impression at the festivities that they
became in great demand throughout the Hollywood social scene. When 4 April arrived, it was Pan's turn to play host at the Easter Ball to luminaries, such as Bing
Crosby, Myrna Loy, Henry Fonda, Lionel Barrymore, Adolphe Menjou, and Erik
Rhodes, his old friend from the Astaire-Rogers series. For the boy who dreamed
about Theda Bara, Hollywood parties provided a rich fantasy life full of glamour and
excitement, but which Pan felt had nothing to do with reality. He did not want to be
defined as a celebrity or choreographer: he was just Hermes Pan from Tennessee.

By the second week of April, Hermes was back at RKO with Fred Astaire and
Hal Borne, working on a new musical with songs by Jerome Kern and Dorothy
Fields called I Won't Dance (released as Swing Time). This addition to the Astaire-
Rogers canon, budgeted at $881,160.86, cast Fred as John "Lucky" Garnett, a
vaudeville dancer and gambler who needs to earn $25,000 to prove he's worthy of
marrying his fiancée, Margaret Watson (Betty Furness). But by the time he has
the money, he has fallen in love with "Penny" Carrol (Ginger Rogers), a dance instructor who, in turn, is courted by a bandleader, "Ricky" Romero (George
Metaxa). When Penny discovers that Lucky has a fiancée waiting in the wings, she
agrees to marry the bandleader out of spite, but a delay in the wedding services
forces Penny to come to her senses and reunite with Lucky. Hermes was paid
$5,100 for employment guaranteed from April through 15 July and received
screen credit as "Dance Director."

Between the second week of April and 11 May when filming began, Pan,
Astaire, and Borne focused on five numbers: "It's Not in the Cards," designed as a
vaudeville routine for Astaire, Victor Moore (who plays "Pop" Cardetti, Astaire's

Pandro Berman, Hermes Pan, Victor Moore, and George Stevens, on the set of *Swing Time* (Courtesy of the Academy of Motion Picture Arts and Sciences).

vaudeville partner), and a chorus of six boy dancers; "Pick Yourself Up," planned as a duet for Astaire and Rogers; "Waltz in Swing Time," another routine for Astaire and Rogers; "Bojangles of Harlem," designed as a blackface number for Astaire and a chorus of twenty-four girls; and "Never Gonna Dance," the final duet for the couple. According to Nathaniel Shilkret, musical director for the production, "It's Not in the Cards" was the brainchild of Jerome Kern, who had his heart set on beginning the film with a vaudeville act (Shilkret 2005, 172). The number opens on a stage set with Moore failing repeatedly to perform a successful card trick. His partner, Astaire, sings "It's not in the cards for you" while Moore tries to explain why doing the act is so important to him. Fed up by the lack of sympathy shown by Astaire and his six male assistants, Moore leaves the stage free for Astaire and the boys to dance. The number was filmed from 11 May to 13 May but cut after the pre–Labor Day premiere at Radio City Music Hall. According to Hermes Pan, once the number was on film, no one, including himself, thought it was any good.[6]

When Pan and Astaire began working on "Pick Yourself Up," neither of them had any idea what they were going to do with the number.[7] "It's like doodling," Pan suggested. "You start with a blank piece of paper and you say, 'Well, this might be good for a beginning,' and you get one step, and pretty soon you come up with something else. For me, it's a matter of working from step to step. Finally, you get

Hermes Pan in typical rehearsal clothes working with Ginger Rogers (Courtesy of the Academy of Motion Picture Arts and Sciences).

a picture of the overall idea you're trying to convey. So this number is something that happened in progressive stages without any preconceived plan." Once they had the concept, however, Pan recalled that it was "one of the few numbers that sort of came easy." There were few difficulties, even in filming the number. "We rehearsed it in the morning and shot it—it was one of those few numbers that . . . when we got into the dance everything was just clear sailing."

The same could not be said when filming "Never Gonna Dance," the final dance duet and latest working title of the film. Ginger Rogers recalls the number being difficult because they had to dance up eighteen steps to a second level: "Everything that could have gone wrong did during the shooting of the number: an arc light went out; there was a noise in the camera; one of us missed a step in the dance, where Fred was supposed to catch me in the final spins; and once, right at the end of a perfect take, his toupee flipped off" (Rogers 2008, 194). Speaking to Susan Winslow in 1982, Hermes recalled that the trouble really began when the number was down to the last sixteen or so bars. It was late in the evening, beyond the usual quitting time, but everyone felt that sixteen bars shouldn't take all that much time to film. After three or four takes, everyone started to get tense, frustrated that so little bit of dance should create so many problems. George Stevens, the director, sensing the mood, suggested, "Well, Freddie. . . Ginger, don't you want to quit? It's after six." Not wanting to have to return in the morning to film a mere sixteen bars, and feeling so close to the end, the dancers elected to continue filming. But the number seemed jinxed as take after take proved fruitless. Because of the constant dancing, Ginger had developed a blister on her foot that started to bleed. The wardrobe people appeared and patched her up, but no sooner had they solved the problem of one blister when another erupted. Sweaty from all the studio lights and physical exertion, Astaire changed his shirt and collar only to get makeup all over his new collar. It was getting later and later since between takes, the crew had to wipe out the scuff marks on the Bakelite floor, and makeup and lighting had to be checked to preserve continuity to the earlier part of the dance. The director kept offering to quit for the day, but the dancers insisted that they wanted to press on. Finally, on the forty-seventh take, Fred grabbed Ginger and spun her around; she made an elegant exit; he extended his arms to her; and the number was over. Finally, the director called "Cut" and applauded—everyone on the set applauded. It was very late and time to go home. How late was it really? Ginger Rogers, who was dancing, remembers completing the final take at 4:00 a.m. Hermes Pan who was watching, nervously chewing on his black felt hat, claims the perfect shoot occurred around 10:00 p.m.

The "Waltz in Swing Time" was one of the few times Pan and Astaire created a dance before the music had been composed. As Hermes explained to John Kobal:

> We wanted to do a jazz waltz, and we'd be on the rehearsal stage and the pianist would play a waltz beat and we'd do things in rhythm. We were very excited about the idea of doing a swing waltz. So we told Kern about it, and he wrote a swing waltz. But I think it was very difficult for him because he didn't really understand what we meant. I must say that Hal Borne, our rehearsal pianist all that time, had a great deal to do with it, and with adapting Kern's music into a waltz. We used part of "Never Gonna Dance" and paraphrases of other songs, and put them into the thing, so Hal was a tremendous influence. We really couldn't get Kern to write what we wanted. I don't think he really knew what we were talking about. (Kobal 1985, 628)

Robert Russell Bennett, the orchestrator of the film, tells the story differently. In his version, Kern told him, "Go over and see Fred and find out what he wants." After a brief conference with Astaire, Bennett created "Waltz in Swing Time," with so many notes that two pianists had to play it (both Hal Borne and Hal Findlay are cited in the production documents for the film). Bennett notes that Hal Borne added a nice treatment of one of the songs in the show, 'A Fine Romance,' as a sort of middle section, but, in his view, that was the extent of his contribution (Ferencz 1999,159).

Similar difficulties arose with "Bojangles of Harlem." From the very beginning, Astaire and Pan were concerned about the number. It didn't swing, and in spite of their efforts to help Jerome Kern understand the musical style they were trying to achieve, the composer was unable to give them the sound they wanted. As a result, during rehearsals it again fell to Hal Borne to improvise jazz licks and add the kind of syncopation that would loosen up Kern's basically square tune. Much of the music accompanying the dance was based on a musical vamp that continued to modulate to higher and higher keys rather than the actual melody of the song.

Although the earlier portion of the choreography for "Bojangles of Harlem," had been worked out during prefilming rehearsals, the shadow dance sequence was a later development that extended the projected shooting schedule for the film by nine days. Hermes got the idea while he and Hal Borne were on the sound stage waiting for Astaire to arrive for rehearsal. He noticed three lights at the top of the stage that cast three shadows as he moved around. The idea amused him, so when Astaire arrived he pointed to the shadows, suggesting, "Look, three shadows. It's interesting, isn't it? Why couldn't we do something like this?" Ever the worrier, Fred replied, "Well, how are you going to do it?" Hermes, ever the optimist, insisted, "Well, it's certain that somebody has the know-how in a studio this size. If it can be done, it will be interesting. You could dance with your shadows." Pan phoned George Stevens and invited him to the sound stage where they were rehearsing. Hermes demonstrated the shadow effect and expressed his concerns about how it could be achieved. "Well, that's simple," George replied.

Hermes teaching the chorus "Bojangles of Harlem" (Courtesy of the Academy of Motion Picture Arts and Sciences).

"We just go to the special effects department and have 'em work it out. Tell 'em what you want them to do and we'll do it."

Vernon Walker, RKO camera-effects specialist, jumped on board immediately. "All you do is get Astaire in front of a screen and photograph his shadows first. Then we take those shadows and make a split screen, and then we photograph Astaire doing the same routine in front of them." Pan was thrilled that his idea was workable. "It was a cinch for them, you know. And it turned out to be a fantastic number," worth every moment of the three days it took to film. Hermes never ignored the opportunity to mention afterward that "Bojangles of Harlem" is one of the few musical clips in the collection of the Museum of Modern Art in New York City.

Swing Time was a happy experience for Pan. He had a comfortable and creative working relationship with Fred Astaire, Hal Borne, and Ginger Rogers, and a chorus of dancers that adored him. The relaxed atmosphere instilled by director George Stevens also put Pan at his ease and, since he was as committed to the mental and physical health of his dancers as he was to their technique, beach rehearsals were often scheduled. These were, of course, sources of fun and

Hermes Pan surrounded by his girls (Courtesy of the Academy of Motion Picture Arts and Sciences).

relaxation, but for Hermes it was impossible to dance well without a sense of fun and relaxation. He was a strong believer in exercise and demanded that his dancers maintain a high level of physical fitness. Swimming and athletic activities at the beach were some ways of achieving that end. Jumping rope was another activity especially popular with chorus girls, particularly after Hermes demonstrated jump rope techniques that put the girls to shame. Still, the physical regimen was only a small part of Pan's work with his dancers. He was also concerned with their emotional well-being and, as he used to say, their souls. He talked to them; he listened to their romantic problems, their dreams, their complaints. And because he was one of the few dance directors in Hollywood who treated dancers like human beings, they opened up to him.

It was because of this generous interest in people that Hermes continued to foster new talent. Studio publicity reports two new faces discovered by Pan during *Swing Time*. One, a San Francisco–based model named De La Nore, literally tripped over Hermes while he was sunning himself on the beach at Santa Monica. Pan noted that the way she recovered after the fall indicated balance and poise and he hired her on the spot for the RKO chorus. The other was an eighteen-year-old Georgia boy, Blackwell Gunn, whose parents had sent Pan a letter begging him to come to Georgia to tutor their son. When Hermes replied (a personal response, not a letter concocted by the publicity department) that his commitments at the studio made it impossible to get away, the family moved out to Los Angeles.

Hermes Pan and chorus at rehearsal on the beach (Courtesy of the Academy of Motion Picture Arts and Sciences).

Impressed by such persistence and commitment, Hermes auditioned the boy and passed him on to the studio casting department.

Pan's passion for encouraging young talent should not suggest that he was easily impressed. Far from it. He was among the most demanding dance directors in Hollywood. He posted the following requirements when casting the two dozen women dancers in *Swing Time*:

> A girl must be a whirlwind tap dancer who can do every step in a tap routine; she must be not more than five feet, five inches tall, not less than five feet, two. She must have a perfect figure and a face which photographs well. She must have personality that gets over to audiences, and must be able to average 99% in a physical examination—so that she can stand ten-hour days of rehearsal without cracking. Applicants who are brunettes will be given the preference, other things being equal, and if they aren't they'll have to wear wigs.

One thousand and ninety-three dancers appeared at the casting call and immediately 93 were "typed out," eliminated because they did not have the look Pan was seeking. The thousand that remained were divided into groups of 200, each of which was scheduled for a full day's audition. At the end of each subsequent day, 190 dancers were sent home, and, by the end of five days, 50 candidates remained. On the sixth day, Hermes and his assistants began the grueling process of final selection, always a bittersweet time for the dance director since more would leave the audition disappointed than elated. "Some of the girls were the best dancers in Hollywood," Pan admitted sadly, "But they didn't have beauty. Reluctantly, we had to let them go" (*Literary Digest*, 12 December 1936, 21). "I loathed the auditions. They were too painful. There might be eight jobs and a hundred dancers to fill them. . . . The more active I became, the more frequently I would pick the dancers and then leave the room before the try-outs were over, leaving my assistant to spread the mainly unhappy news" (Pan, Columbia, Kramer 1983, 6–7).

Almost immediately after *Swing Time* was completed, Hermes found himself on a train headed south to Dallas, Texas, with Ginger Rogers; her mother, Lela; Louise, her hairdresser; publicity director Eddie Rubin; RKO still-photographer John Miehle; and Ginger's friends Lucille Ball and Florence Lake. Texas governor John Allred had commissioned Ginger an admiral in the Texas navy at the New Year's Ball at the Biltmore Hotel in Los Angeles and invited her to participate in the Texas Centennial Exposition in the summer of 1936. Ginger in turn invited her closest friends (and members of the studio publicity department) to accompany her. When Rogers and company arrived on 7 August, they were greeted by a delegation from the Texas navy, which escorted them to the Hotel Adolphus with panoply typically reserved for royalty. Hermes took note of the precision movement of the color guard and was busy imaging ways that he might integrate it into a production number as they were whisked away to the football stadium filled to capacity with fans cheering the arrival of their favorite star. Pan watched in the hot August sun as Ginger Rogers rode around the stadium in an open Cadillac, the crowd standing and stomping and dripping wet from the heat and humidity. Later in the evening, after an extravagant champagne dinner, Pan and his fellow travelers returned to the hotel only to realize that the hotel was not air-conditioned and in the heat, their rooms more resembled saunas than comfortable bedrooms. Lucille Ball suggested that they wrap themselves in wet sheets and lie directly under the ceiling fan to stay cool through the night. Pan took her advice and quickly went off to sleep dreaming that he was on a train back to California.

When he returned to Hollywood during the second week of August, Hermes was assigned to choreograph the ballroom sequence in *A Woman Rebels*, a Katharine Hepburn film directed by his friend Mark Sandrich. After meeting with Sandrich and Roy Webb, the musical director, Pan determined that two days' work was all that he needed to teach and structure the dancing—yet another waltz—for the ballroom sequence in which the two sisters of the story (played by Katharine Hepburn and Elizabeth Allan) dance and converse with their beaux (Van Heflin and David Manners). The situation was evocative of the ballroom sequence in *Becky Sharp* where the dancing provided a background to the dialogue, and the choreography in *A Woman Rebels* echoes that of the earlier film. As Pan was completing his work on the film, *Swing Time* opened in New York City to healthy crowds and excellent notices, even though the *New York Times* reviewer seemed discontented:

> That was no riot outside the Music Hall yesterday; it was merely the populace storming the Rockefeller's cinema citadel for a glimpse of the screen's nimblest song and dance team, Ginger Rogers and Fred Astaire, in their latest festival, *Swing Time*. Maybe they felt better about it than we did. We left the theatre feeling definitely let down. The picture is good, of course. It would have to be with that dancing, with those Victor Moore, Helen Broderick and Eric Blore. But after *Top Hat*, *Follow the Fleet* and the rest, it is a disappointment. (28 August 1936)

The critic's concerns did not bother Hermes. He knew that comparisons to earlier films would not always be favorable since people wanted to see again what they most enjoyed, and his and Astaire's commitment to freshness—never repeating a routine—might be disappointing to some. He took great pride, however, in the critic's notice of "Bojangles of Harlem," when the shadow dance routine was called "one of the best things [Astaire] has done." In the *Los Angeles Times* (23 September 1936) Edwin S. Schallert, who seemed to enjoy the film more than the New York critic, reiterated that "Fred has his great moment in the shadow number, which is smartly created." *Swing Time* may have earned the studio less profit ($830,000) than *Top Hat* or *Follow the Fleet*, but Hermes Pan felt that for him, it was a much greater artistic success.

By the end of September, Hermes was working again with director George Stevens on *Quality Street*, another vehicle for Katharine Hepburn. Based on a James M. Barrie play, the film depicted the plight of the two Throssel sisters who run a school. To maintain the interest of an old suitor, Valentine Brown (Franchot Tone), plain Phoebe Throssel (Katharine Hepburn) disguised herself as Livvy, her attractive niece, only to realize that it was Phoebe who Valentine really loved. Hermes was paid $300 to arrange the dances for three sequences in the film. The first took place at the children's school where the students, led by Phoebe, were practicing a minuet. The second was a ball during which waltzing couples provided a background for a dialogue scene. The final sequence was another ball at which twenty-four couples arranged in three parallel lines danced a minuet with choreography similar to that at the children's school. Working with rehearsal pianist Hal Findlay, Hermes created, rehearsed, and filmed the dances between 24 September and 21 November. Although in later interviews Pan had few memories of the film (he recalled staging the brief waltz sequence but little else), he did remember that Katharine Hepburn asked him to teach her movement so that she could differentiate the way Phoebe and Livvy behaved.

Even before work on *Quality Street* was completed, Pan was back in rehearsal with Fred Astaire and Hal Borne on the next Astaire-Rogers vehicle. *Stepping Toes* (originally called *Watch Your Step*) attempted to capitalize on the popularity of *On Your Toes*, the successful Rodgers and Hart Broadway musical that combined classical ballet with tap dancing. The plot cast Astaire as Petrov (really Pete P. Peters), an American ballet dancer living in Paris who actually prefers taps to *tendus*. He falls in love with a picture of Linda Keene (Ginger Rogers), an American musical performer, and contrives to be on the same ship when she sails back home. A rumor that they are married causes Linda no little embarrassment since she has a fiancé in New York, and a bogus photograph that appears to provide proof of the marriage forces them to flee reporters and actually get married. But just as a romantic relationship blossoms, Linda finds Petrov with another woman and begins divorce proceedings, until he wins her back in a final dance—this time with a chorus of women wearing Linda Keene face masks.

Because the film traded on an actual corps de ballet, studio brass decided to put two dance directors on the project. Hermes Pan would, of course, work on all of the Fred Astaire–Ginger Rogers material, and Harry Losee, a protégé of modern dancers Ruth St. Denis and Ted Shawn, was imported from Broadway to choreograph the ballets. Director Mark Sandrich had originally approached Léonide Massine, the high-voltage choreographer for the Ballets Russes, to create a ballet for Fred Astaire and Harriet Hoctor, the prima ballerina of the film, but his salary requirements of $5,000 a week for a guaranteed five weeks proved unacceptable to the studio.[8]

Stepping Toes (*On Your Ballet, Stepping Stones, Stepping High, Round the Town, Dance With Me, Let's Dance*, and *Twinkle, Twinkle* were other working titles trying to capture the cadence or gist of *On Your Toes*) was to be a $960,117.07 production, of which George and Ira Gershwin were scheduled to receive $55,000 for the score (less than what Kern or Berlin had been paid). Hermes Pan was guaranteed $7,550 for work extending from 2 November 1936 (when he, Astaire, and Borne began developing the dances) until 10 March 1937. Harry Losee was paid $2,500 and Pan's assistant, unnamed in the RKO Production Files, was budgeted at $225 for three weeks' work.

From the outset, Hermes wondered why Fred wanted to be involved with classical ballet. He knew Astaire didn't like the idea of dancing ballet or "classical stuff" as he called it. What's more, Fred didn't even like ballet dancers; it infuriated him that they had to warm up for at least a half an hour before they could dance. But Astaire, always seeking to do something different, seemed to welcome the opportunity, especially since it allowed him to dance with someone other than Ginger Rogers. As Hermes suggested to John Kobal: "Fred was getting a little tired of being known as a team, and for a long time he was the one who wanted to break away. But the public demanded them. It was like divorcing your wife" (Kobal 1985, 626).

Though the Gershwins had been an institution on Broadway (they had composed two shows for Fred and Adele Astaire: *Lady Be Good!* and *Funny Face*), their recent track record registered fewer hits than in the 1920s, and everyone at the studio, from producer Pandro Berman to Hermes Pan, was anxious to hear the new score hoping that the authors of "Fascinating Rhythm," "'S Wonderful," "Someone to Watch Over Me," "Embraceable You," and "I Got Rhythm" were still at the top of their craft. On the first day he showed up for work, Pan was still dubious. Previous to starting rehearsals he was given a copy of the score, but since he did not read music, he didn't know what any of it sounded like. On the sound stage where he and Fred often rehearsed, he found someone other than Hal Borne at the piano. Thinking that this was a rehearsal pianist for another film, Hermes set down one of the songs on the piano and asked, "Look, would you mind playing this for me. I'm going to start rehearsing on this tomorrow and I haven't heard it yet." As the pianist began to play the number, Pan interrupted, saying, "Well, gee, that's sort of—can you play it a little faster? It's almost like a march, and it has such a strange tempo." The pianist played the song over and over in different styles and in different tempos, but nothing seemed to work for Pan. "Well, you know, Gershwin or no Gershwin, this is not for me. This is not my type of dance feeling," he said. "I don't know what I'm going to do with it." Hermes took the music from the piano and began to walk away. "Thanks anyway. I'll see you later. I've got a meeting. In fact, Gershwin is going to be there. I don't know what I'm going to tell him, but I'm not going to keep my mouth shut." The pianist said goodbye and Pan left for his meeting. When he arrived, Pandro Berman and Fred Astaire were there, and not long after, in came the rehearsal pianist that Hermes had just left. Berman and Astaire stood up and greeted the pianist, "Mr. Gershwin." Pan was mortified and silent for the rest of the meeting. Finally, after Berman and Astaire had left, he apologized to the composer, "Mr. Gershwin, as you might expect, I'm embarrassed and very sorry I said what I did." Instead of being offended, Gershwin simply replied, "Well, you know, maybe you were right."[9] From that day forward, Hermes was an avid Gershwin fan.

Pan's usual pattern of working with Fred Astaire prior to filming was again the rule, a basic 9:30 a.m. to 6:00 p.m. schedule throughout the month of November, except on Tuesdays when they had to knock off early. Fred had signed a contract with Packard, an automobile company, for a series of radio shows called *The Packard Hour*, which aired on Tuesday nights. According to David Patrick Columbia, Astaire insisted that Hermes be present at every broadcast, even though he was not on the payroll and did not have anything to do with the program (Columbia, June 1991, 849). Given their professional relationship and friendship, it was difficult for Hermes to turn Fred down. Besides, he was a little flattered, knowing that Astaire, who danced on a wooden studio floor on the program, didn't want to make a move without him.

"Slap That Bass," Astaire's first song and dance in the film, grew out of a walk around the RKO lot. "Fred and I were walking on the lot one day and there happened to be a cement mixer. They were building something and there were all kinds of chugging rhythms, you know, construction noises. And we just started dancing against them—something dancers automatically do—all the way down

Hermes Pan, Fred Astaire, and Mark Sandrich, seated center among the crew on the set of "Slap That Bass" (Courtesy of the Academy of Motion Picture Arts and Sciences).

the street. That became the basis for the number in the film" (Collura 1983, 11). Studio publicity dated 26 December and published in the *San Antonio Light* (27 December 1936) announced that Hermes Pan had designed the set for the big ensemble dance for *Shall We Dance*. "One of the largest sets constructed at RKO, modern in theme and design, it was approved by producer Pan Berman and director Mark Sandrich." There is no evidence in the production files of Pan's contribution to the set design or to what setting the release refers, but choreographers always have input about the spaces in which dancers are forced to dance, and certainly Hermes would have had much to say to designer Van Nest Polglase about the setting for "Slap That Bass."[10]

"Let's Call the Whole Thing Off," a duet for Astaire and Rogers, had a similar spontaneous genesis during an early rehearsal session. As Ginger Rogers recalled:

> Fred, Hermes, and I got together for our rehearsal of "Let's Call the Whole Thing Off," and we sat around and gabbed a bit. Out of these gabfests came our dances.
>
> "What shall we do this time?"
>
> "The scene is Central Park, New York, so whatever we do must be authentic."
>
> "Let's see, what do people do in the park?"
>
> "They bicycle, jump rope, play volleyball, and what else?"
>
> Hermes murmured, "Say, I'll tell you what I used to do as a kid—"
>
> "Wouldn't it be fun," I jumped in, "to do a number on roller skates? We might be able to do a tap or two with them. . . ."
>
> Fred was hesitant. "Well, let's think about it, but in the meantime get the prop department over here and tell them what we need for us to try. . . ."
>
> The prop department delivered a variety of skates, and the moment I put on a pair, I knew this was right. Soon the room was full of the rumble of rolling metal wheels on a hardwood floor as the three of us whirled around. The creative juices were flowing. Two hours later, after steps had begun to emerge, we concluded that the skates were a good idea. (Rogers 2008, 212–213)

The roller-skating number went before the cameras on Christmas Eve, the first day of shooting for *Shall We Dance* (the musical's new title thanks to a suggestion by director Vincente Minnelli). According to studio records, it took about thirty-four hours of rehearsal, four days of filming, and 150 takes to achieve the number that appeared in the final cut.

"They All Laughed," another Astaire-Rogers dance duet in the film, took seven days to shoot, starting on Tuesday, 9 February. By that date, Hermes had learned that RKO had renewed the option on his contract and that he had, again, been nominated for an Academy Award, this time for the "Bojangles of Harlem" number in *Swing Time*. Although his confidence was riding high, he was not at the moment a happy man. For some time he had been trying to cast the chorus dancers for *The Robber Barons*, an Edward Arnold film set in the Gay Nineties. Because in the period showgirls were voluptuously beefy, Pan needed twelve "well-upholstered" chorines who tipped the scales at 160 to 175 pounds, and who were expert dancers. The search was proving more difficult than he imagined and time was running out, for after "Slap That Bass" went before the cameras at the end of February, Hermes needed to begin the choreography for the next picture. He was still auditioning overweight chorus girls early in March when he joined the Hollywood elite gathered at the Biltmore Hotel for the Ninth Academy Awards, hosted by comedian George Jessel. He watched with excitement as Walter Brennan and Gale Sondergaard were named the winners in a new category, Best Supporting Actor/Actress, and applauded vigorously when "The Way You Look Tonight" from *Swing Time* was named Best Song. For Best Dance Direction, he was up against Bobby Connolly, Busby Berkeley, Dave Gould, and Seymour Felix, but with "Bojangles of Harlem," Pan honestly believed that he might actually deserve the award. When Seymour Felix won for his luxurious staging in *The Great Ziegfeld*, Hermes was a little disappointed. It was the second year that staging rather than dancing brought home the Oscar, and he began to wonder if real dancing would ever be appreciated by the Academy.

Two days later, Pan took a break from casting to attend a skating party at the Rollerdome in Culver City, hosted by Ginger Rogers and her current boyfriend, Alfred Vanderbilt. In attendance were Joan Crawford, Franchot Tone, Kay Francis, Frank Morgan, George and Ira Gershwin, Harold Lloyd, George Murphy, Jack Oakie, Humphrey Bogart, Cary Grant, and Cesar Romero, all wearing casual dress. It was the absence of tuxedos and diamond necklaces that Hermes most enjoyed; he loved being in the company of Hollywood's elite, when they let their hair down, when they acted like real people rather than celebrities. The food table, covering almost one-quarter of the skating rink, reinforced the casual atmosphere of the party with spaghetti, chili, tamales, Boston baked beans, sliced ham, various cheeses, hot dogs, and hamburgers, made to order. Humphrey Bogart proved to be the champion skater of the evening, taking running jumps over chairs and doing tricks. When a failed attempt caused him to hit hard on the skating floor, he told Pan, "I used to travel with a circus and did this for a living. I was pretty good at it then. I just haven't done it in a little while." The party was covered by *Life* magazine in its "*Life* Goes to a Party" column and noted, "Unique among Hollywood parties, this one was so much fun, nobody got drunk."[11]

By the end of the first week of March, Hermes Pan had found his dozen overweight chorus girls and his work was in full swing on *The Robber Barons*, a loose biography of Jim Fisk (Edward Arnold), a peddler, then railroad tycoon, who tried to corner the gold market on the New York Stock Exchange while falling in love with a French chanteuse's beautiful maid, Josie Mansfield (Frances Farmer), whom he catapults to stardom. Of the three songs composed for the film by

Nathaniel Shilkret, a recent collaborator with Hermes on several projects, only two, "Ooh, La, La," and "The Temptation Waltz," required choreography. The first was a performance number at a French musical revue where Fleurique (Thelma Leeds) sang to the patrons in the boxes while twelve overweight chorines dressed in tights, tunics, plumed military hats, and carrying spears performed military drills on stage, prancing offstage when the number was over. Their look recalled the chorus attire of the famous *The Black Crook*, the spectacle that many say popularized the fad for scantily clad chorus girls in the United States.

The "Temptation Waltz" provided the background to *The Twelve Temptations*, a pantomime performance piece for Josie Mansfield set at the Grand Opera House and made up of short vignettes including "Vanity," "Flirtation," "Desire" (a Spanish dance of passion), "Luxury" (an Egyptian pageant), "Revelry" (a Venetian Carnival celebration), "Jealousy" (a melodramatic scene of rape and murder), and "Death." Though each section was brief, Pan's staging exhibited an impressive variety of styles.

A short rehearsal segment, shot from a distance, of chorus girls practicing a cancan on the Opera House stage to the accompaniment of a single piano was Pan's final contribution to the film. Released on 30 July as *The Toast of New York*, the finished product was greeted with mediocre reviews and audiences. According to the American Film Institute, it cost $1,072,000 to make and lost $530,000—RKO's biggest box office failure in 1937.

Back on the set of *Shall We Dance* during the final weeks of March, Hermes Pan assisted Harry Losee and Mark Sandrich in setting up the cameras for the final ballet sequence. Pan never found the number satisfying because of Harriet Hoctor, the vaudeville ballerina who had been hired as Astaire's ballet partner. "There's this long thing," Hermes told John Kobal, "with Harriet Hoctor doing this incredible ungraceful dance with back bends all over the place and splitting her legs. I don't know whether they thought of her as a future partner for Fred, but he was very much opposed to it because she was too big for him, she was too balletic. . . . And Harriet was always on her toes—and when she wasn't on her toes, her head was in between her legs" (Kobal 1985, 628). On 13 April, Pan was back at the studio on Stage Three with the special effects crew, Hal Borne, and five ballet dancers to create the shadow dancing effect for the opening credits of the movie. By the end of the day, Hermes was happy to be done with *Shall We Dance*.[12]

Once the film was completed, Pan drove out to the picturesque B-Bar-H Ranch in Palm Springs to enjoy a weekend of sun and fun in the company of Fred Astaire and his wife Phyllis, Randolph Scott, Joan Crawford, and Franchot Tone. Pan was greatly entertained by Joan Crawford and particularly fond of Astaire's wife. "Phyllis was a lovely lady. She just didn't understand Hollywood informality: She was a New York socialite. She scared the life out of most of the people in Hollywood. All the producers felt ill at ease around her, because she was a little too formal for them. She had a lisp and a funny *r*, so Fred would imitate her saying there was a perfectly *dweadful* man at the door, and it was David Niven, whom she didn't know yet, dropping by after tennis. Later, David Niven was a good friend of hers. . . . She was very proper. She never came on the set, and if she did she would only stay a few minutes. . . . She was a very good friend of mine, and in her social manner she was very down to earth" (Giles 1988, 109).

Pan had just returned from Palm Springs when *Shall We Dance* officially opened on 7 May. Critics enjoyed the film more than *Swing Time*, with the *New York Times* (14 May 1937) calling it "one of the best things the screen's premiere dance team has done." The *Los Angeles Times* (7 May 1937) added, "It is a pip of a picture, at once erasing the frown left by the stars' indifferent *Swing Time* and challenging anything in the song-and-dance line that has preceded it." And in case Hermes still had doubts about why Astaire chose to do the film, *Variety* (12 May 1937) wrote, "For Astaire *Shall We Dance* offers final proof of his being head man as to dancing, just in case there ever was any doubt. Prior to this he has only hinted at the ballet work of which he is capable, mixing it up with those hot breaks. Here he really pours it on and they'll like it." Like *Swing Time*, however, attendance was down for *Shall We Dance*, running at about 76 percent, and the $413,000 profit it earned for RKO was less than half of the profit from *Swing Time*.

Pan spent the month of May moving his family from the San Fernando Valley to Encino where he paid $13,000 for a spacious Spanish hacienda surrounded by an acre of grapefruit and orange trees at 5078 Amestoy, which he nicknamed Pan-Jose. A twenty-five-minute drive from Hollywood through what Pan described as a "countryside of flowers and fragrances," the Spanish contemporary house had three bedrooms, three baths, a den, a living room, a dining room, a breakfast room, and a kitchen, all surrounding an outdoor courtyard. Pan's next-door neighbor was Arthur Treacher, the ubiquitous butler of Hollywood films probably better known today for the chain of seafood restaurants that bear his name. Hermes's family life was in a flurry through the middle of June. Cousins, Tinker and Bubber Horn, were visiting from Tennessee, and his mother had recently entered the hospital because of stomach problems. On 13 June, the whole family plus Father McCoy, their friend and parish priest, piled into Hermes's yellow Buick to visit her, and then returned home for the traditional "Ditty's Diary" party that included actor friends Chet Stratton, Henry Fonda, and Lupe Velez, who drove out to Encino to celebrate Pan's new house.

At the end of the month, Pan was back at the studio to create a dance routine for *Stage Door*, a $971,816 film starring Ginger Rogers and Katharine Hepburn, adapted from the Edna Ferber–George S. Kaufman play about the Footlights Club, the home for aspiring actresses. On the set he was reunited with Phyllis Kennedy, one of the cast members from his touring days with *Cushman's Garden of Glorious Girls*. At a performance during the Denver leg of the tour, she fell and broke her back and her doctors told her that she would never dance again. But through her strong religious beliefs and strength of will, she managed to achieve a complete recovery. Ginger Rogers, a Christian Scientist, was especially impressed by Kennedy's fight back to health and promised to help her career as much as humanly

possible. Pan joined her in that pledge and the name Phyllis Kennedy appears in
many of Pan's films from the 1930s through the 1960s (including *Carefree, Vivacious Lady, Coney Island, Three Little Words, My Fair Lady*, and *Finian's Rainbow*).

Stage Door also provided an important addition to Pan's life with the casting of
fourteen-year-old Ann Miller as Ginger Rogers's dancing partner. Born Johnnie
Lucille Collier in Chireno, Texas, Miller almost didn't get the part because Ginger
Rogers felt that she was too tall, but a good word from Rogers's friend, Lucille Ball,
and Ann's naïvely exuberant suggestion, "Oh, please, Miss Rogers, couldn't you
wear higher heels and a higher top hat and I could wear lower heels and a shorter
top hat," won the day.

The number Hermes Pan choreographed for Ginger and Ann was called "Put
Your Heart into Your Feet and Dance," words and music by Hal Borne, again Pan's
rehearsal pianist, and Mort Greene. The song first appears at a dance class to
which we are introduced by the image of several young women performing a kick
line. Out of this kick line emerge Jean Maitland (Ginger Rogers) and Annie (Ann
Miller), who converse while they perform a tap combination. Since *Stage Door* was
not a musical, director Gregory La Cava was not interested in holding up the action of a scene for a musical number. Ann Miller initially found it difficult to dance
and speak simultaneously but quickly mastered the concept under Pan's patient
dance direction. The song appears a second time as a performance number at the
Club Grotto, where the two women are working as dancers. On this occasion, a
dancing female chorus enters down a short staircase followed by Rogers and
Miller wearing bespangled top hats, black loose-fitting pants-dresses, and carrying canes. The tap number is interspersed with dialogue scenes that cut away
from the dancing so that the movie audience never sees the complete routine.
Although Pan received no on-screen credit for his work on the film, his name does
appear as dance director in the *Stage Door* production files where his salary is
given as $700 for a guaranteed two weeks' work. Although the film received re-
spectable and, in many cases, glowing reviews, it earned a mere $81,000 in profits
for RKO.

By the end of June, Hermes Pan was preparing for the next Fred Astaire film,
A Damsel in Distress, a million-dollar musical with a score by George and Ira Gershwin, in which Jerry Halliday (Astaire), an American musical comedy star, is
mistaken for the American boyfriend of Lady Alyce Marshmorton (Joan Fontaine) and ends up falling in love with her. Pan was promised screen credit as
"Dance Director," and payment of $1,669.73 for preproduction work up to 17
July, and a guaranteed nine and a half weeks at $350 a week after that. For the
first time since *Flying Down to Rio*, Astaire's leading lady would not be Ginger Rogers but a young non-dancer, non-singer, by the name of Joan Fontaine. If Hermes
had questions about Fred's taking on a ballet film with *Shall We Dance*, he was
mystified why the studio cast Fontaine in a dancing role opposite Astaire: "Joan
Fontaine was no dancer at all. . . . The poor girl couldn't even walk. Naturally, she
was terrified, and they really didn't do much dancing. . . . But I think Fred was so

delighted to be on his own that he couldn't have cared less who he danced with" (Kobal 1985, 626). From the end of June through the middle of September, Hermes worked with Joan on the choreography for "Things Are Looking Up," the one dance she was slated to perform with Astaire:

> That's the thing where they walked across—down the path . . . and then do just very simple little walking things, and when I started to work with her I just couldn't believe the stiffness. And I worked and drilled and my sister[13] worked with her and showed her how to move and things, and she would get the steps but it looked like she was stepping on eggs, like she was conscious—which she was—of every move. And I told Fred, you know, and he became very depressed and discouraged, and he said, "Well, just simplify it. Just make it walk, walk, walk." And so I kept on cutting things down just to . . . So it ended up just . . . It actually wasn't too bad, now when you look at it. (Winslow 1982, 16–17)

Joan Fontaine recalled dancing with blisters on her feet and fighting the summer heat. "All those ballet lessons I had taken in my early youth had not prepared me for duet dancing, for the leaps and lifts devised by Astaire and Pan. I tripped over fences and stepping stones to the tune of 'Things Are Looking Up.'. . . I also fell on my face" (Fontaine 1978, 88). Hermes, Angie Blue, and pianist Hal Borne worked privately with Joan on location at the RKO Ranch throughout the month of August to prepare her for rehearsals with Fred Astaire at the beginning of September, and by the middle of the month, the number was ready to be filmed.

More successful, from a terpsichorean point of view, was the casting of George Burns and Gracie Allen, who came to the project with their own choreography, a whisk broom dance they acquired from the surviving member of Evans and Evans, a popular vaudeville team. When they demonstrated the routine for Astaire and Pan, who had final approval of the casting, they so impressed the star and dance director that Pan incorporated the routine into a number with Astaire in the film, "Put Me to the Test." Later George Burns would note the experience with pride that he and Gracie ended up teaching Fred Astaire how to dance. On 26 July, a few days before Pan began filming "Put Me to the Test," he was a guest on the Burns and Allen Radio Show. When he asked Gracie how she felt she rated as a dancer, she replied, "I'd say I'm between the world's best dancer, and the world's worst cluck . . . I have to dance between Fred Astaire and George" (Mueller 1985, 9).

Fred, George, and Gracie also became the centerpiece of Pan's most ambitious choreography yet to be seen in a film, the "Fun House" routine set to the Gershwin song "Stiff Upper Lip." In an interview with Svetlana McLee Grody, Pan explained:

> I was down at the amusement park [Ocean Park Pier, Venice Beach] one night with some kids and we were going through the barrels and the chutes and the rides and the mirrors and I said, "My gosh, this is a natural,

why hasn't somebody done it before?" I was working with Fred at the time and I said, "Fred, I've got it." And he said, "What?" "A number in the fun house." He said, "Fun house—what's that got to do with England in that period?" I said, "Well, they had fun houses in England too, you know." And he said, "But there's no reason." I said, "Let them find a reason." I talked to George Stevens [the director] who was very receptive. They all liked the idea, "Great, let's do it!" So they built a fun house. I said to the set designer [Van Nest Polglase], "Give me everything you've got, give me a turntable, barrels, distorted mirrors, anything you can think of, just put it in. I'll do something with it." He built this wonderful set and I just went in and experimented with dance-ins. When Fred came in later he loved it. (Grody 1996, 5)

The "Fun House" began rehearsals on 23 September and finally went before the cameras on 3 October, completing filming five days later.

From *A Damsel in Distress*, Hermes moved to *Having Wonderful Time*, an expensive Ginger Rogers vehicle in which typist Teddy Shaw (Rogers) finds love at a mountain resort called Kamp Kare-Free in the arms of camp employee Chick Kirkland (Douglas Fairbanks, Jr.). Call sheets for the production indicate that the songs (written by Sam H. Stept and Charles Tobias) "Nighty Night" and "My First Impression of You" were in rehearsal from the end of October through the beginning of November, and "Kare-Free-Kamp," and "The Band Played Out of Tune" were staged during the month of November. Since the completed picture omits these numbers and demonstrates no choreography beyond social dancing that functions as background for dialogue, it is impossible to access Pan's staging for the original numbers in the film.

While Hermes was completing his duties on *Having Wonderful Time*, *A Damsel in Distress* opened to excellent notices. Anticipating a glowing *New York Times* review, *Variety* (24 November 1937) boasted that "Astaire and his vet terp aide, Hermes Pan, have devised four corking dance routines," and added, "Most novel and elaborate dance routine is the fun-house sequence at the county fair, wherein a roller-slide, treadmills, goofy mirrors which distort the dancers into weird elongations or squat torsos, revolving tunnels, etc., have been blended into one of the most arresting dance sequences screened." In spite of good press *A Damsel in Distress* posted a loss of $68,000, the first Fred Astaire movie to lose money.

After spending a quiet Thanksgiving with his family, Hermes began work on *Radio City Revels*, a big-budget ($884,960) musical featuring Kenny Baker, Ann Miller, Bob Burns, Jack Oakie, Victor Moore, Milton Berle, Helen Broderick, and Jane Froman. The thin plot about an Arkansas hillbilly (Bob Burns) who can only write hit songs while he is asleep provided little more than a framework for the songs by Allie Wrubel and Herb Magidson. Pan, who was paid $3,383.09 for nine and two-thirds weeks' guaranteed work, hired Vasso and Bill Brande as his assistants,[14] forty-one chorus dancers, and twenty-four specialty performers. On 3

December, Hermes began rehearsals on Stage Nine for the finale production number, "Speak Your Heart," sung by Jane Froman and danced by Ann Miller and chorus dancers. Five days later, Pan and his dancers were allowed to rehearse on the actual set: "The floor is white, the back wall a series of horizontal stripes verging into blue. At left, Hal Kemp's band plays; at right, a streamlined white stair with no visible support curves up past a succession of illuminated bars (modeled after a New York casino) to a bowl-like platform bulgy with drapes" (*Los Angeles Times*, 15 December 1937). After the song had been sung and Jane Froman's dance double was escorted down the stairs passing men in tails and women in black evening dresses, Ann Miller made her entrance through a trap in the stage floor, tapping as an elevator platform brought her into full view. She continued with an elaborate tap solo that allowed her to whirl around the stage, supported by the entire dancing chorus. Beginning on Saturday, 11 December, Pan filmed the number in three days.

He next turned to "Swingin' in the Corn," a production number set in the fields of Arkansas. Dancers Melissa Mason and Buster West began the dance in a kind of countrified Fred and Ginger routine, followed by Harriet Calloway in a series of comic leg lifts recalling the high kicks made famous by Charlotte Greenwood. Finally, Buster West concluded the section with a humorously acrobatic tap routine peppered with pratfalls and faux ballet moves, Pan's homage to *Shall We Dance*. The Brown Sisters, a quartet of African-American women, followed, singing the tune in a swing arrangement and giving way to a group of African-American dancers behind them doing the Lindy Hop (a structure similar to the African-American section of "The Carioca"). The number demonstrated Pan's characteristic focus on one or two dancers in a crowd. Even though there were as many as forty-one chorus dancers moving throughout the event, the camera consistently drew our attention to a single couple or individual who would function either as representative of, or entertainment for, the group. "Swingin" in the Corn was filmed in three days beginning Friday, 17 December.

In between the two large production numbers, Hermes staged and filmed a solo tap routine for Ann Miller to the tune of "Taking a Shine to You," the opening number of the film sung by Kenny Baker. In this sequence, Miller displayed many of the moves that would become signature steps throughout her career, not the least of which was the "machine-gun" tap routine. More than an expertly devised and performed number, "Taking a Shine to You" also managed to be plot progressive. Kenny Baker, singing the song inside a radio studio, was interrupted by Ann Miller's tapping, drawing the attention and applause of the studio audience away from him and toward her. The moment served as Baker's introduction to Miller (they would, of course, fall in love) and demonstrated her capability to be a featured performer at Radio City, an aspiration weaved throughout the film.[15]

When Hermes left the set of *Radio City Revels*, he walked across the RKO lot to *Vivacious Lady*, another Ginger Rogers vehicle, costarring James Stewart and directed by George Stevens. A nonmusical film, it told the story of Peter Morgan

(Stewart), a botany professor who married a nightclub singer, Francey Morgan (Rogers), after a whirlwind courtship but was afraid to tell his straitlaced parents about it. Pan began the film with a chorus girl routine in the nightclub where Peter encountered Francey performing. Dressed in black leotard-like bodices with feathered tails that managed to find their way on to Peter's lap, the girls shimmy in a kind of bunny dance as a background to a dialogue scene. Next came Francey, singing the one song in the picture, "You'll Be Reminded of Me," written by George Jessel, Jack Meskill, and Ted Shapiro. Although she does not dance in the number, her singing is seductive enough to sweep Peter off his feet and into matrimony.

The next choreographic event in the film occurs at a college party in Old Sharon, New York, where Peter is maneuvered into dancing with his previous fiancée, and Francey is paired with Peter's cousin, Keith (James Ellison). Francey and Keith contrive to exchange partners with the other couple on the crowded dance floor so that Peter and his wife can have a moment together. The choreographic sequence, anticipating "Change Partners" in *Carefree*, functions as a background to the dialogue. Finally, late in the film, Pan is given the opportunity to stage a dance between Ginger Rogers and James Ellison when hot jazz music on the radio inspires them to demonstrate the latest swing dances for Peter's mother (Beulah Bondi), who falls prey to the syncopated rhythms as well. The cheerfully energetic improvisatory dance in an apartment setting owed more to the black Lindy Hoppers than to Fred and Ginger and, with it, Pan demonstrated the ability to capitalize on popular dance forms.

On 10 March, Hermes was back at the Biltmore Hotel for the Academy Awards, this time with his arm around Ann Miller, on a double date with Mr. and Mrs. Walt Disney. Pan appeared at Miller's door wearing a black tuxedo and carrying a gardenia corsage. When Ann's mother opened the door, she nearly fainted, thinking it was Fred Astaire. Ann appeared in a yellow taffeta gown that perfectly matched the corsage, and since her Texas childhood had not prepared her for the scent of gardenias, Miller recalled that the corsage made a deep sensual impression on her. Before the couple left the Miller household, however, Ann noticed an odd expression on Pan's face, and it took her by surprise when her southern-gentleman escort blurted out, "Annie, where in hell did you get that make-up? It's terrible." In her autobiography, Ann Miller relived the incident:

> In those days I wore pancake make-up and I wore it rather thick in my prodigious efforts to look eighteen. For my first date I guess I went a little overboard on the glamour bit. Pale white face, blue eye shadow, coal black lashes, and dark lipstick. Hermes hated it. He made me go in and wash my face, and I had to do my make-up all over with very little lipstick. . . . Through the years Hermes and I have had many a laugh over the "mask" of make-up he made me wash off before he would take me out on that first date. He has always told me he knew I was very young, he guessed somewhere between sixteen and eighteen. "For Pete's sake, with

that mask on your face, how could anyone tell who you really were?" It was several years before I screwed up the courage to tell him that on our first date I wasn't quite fifteen yet. I lacked a month and two days. (Miller 1972, 71–73)

Pan had again been nominated for Best Dance Direction along with Busby Berkeley, Bobby Connolly, Dave Gould, Sammy Lee, and LeRoy Prinz. On this occasion, however, his work on the "Fun House" sequence in *A Damsel in Distress* won him the Oscar, notable because it would be the last time the award was given. His tablemate, Walt Disney, won another award as well, for *The Old Mill*, in the Best Animated Short Film category. Hermes and Ann Miller danced the night away in celebration of his award, the beginning of a professional and social relationship that would continue for fifty years. Pan was shocked when he won the Oscar, but the shock of winning soon transformed into another profound emotion for the choreographer: a feeling of emptiness. In his memoir, "Meeting the Frog Prince," Pan described his reaction as "a deep feeling of lack. It felt like a certain gluttony, as if too much self-satisfaction had turned into nothing. Greed and gluttony—not of appetite, but of the spirit. . . . I began to feel a little guilty about getting too much" (Pan, Columbia, Kramer n.d., 247).

Two weeks after the Academy Awards, Pan was back at work on *Having Wonderful Time*. Unhappy with the film originally under the direction of Alfred Santell, producer Pandro Berman had asked George Stevens to reshoot a few sequences, and Stevens enlisted Pan to enliven a particularly dull dialogue scene with energetically unobtrusive background dancing. Because of his friendship with Walt Disney, Pan was able to borrow "Heigh Ho" from Disney's *Snow White and the Seven Dwarfs*, which had just been released across the United States. Faced with the dilemma of creating movement in a small cabin crowded with people as background to the dramatic action, Hermes staged "Heigh Ho" in a "follow-the-leader" serpentine pattern, the familiar and repetitive nature of which bolstered the energy of the scene while allowing the theatre audience to focus on foreground action.

By 23 April 1938, when he had completed the additions to *Having Wonderful Time*, Pan had already accumulated a salary of $6,916.45 for fifteen weeks of preparatory work on another Irving Berlin film—the newest Fred Astaire musical, *Carefree*, which cast Astaire as Tony Flagg, a psychiatrist who is hired to psychoanalyze his best friend's fiancée, Amanda Cooper, played by Ginger Rogers, returning as Astaire's dancing partner. Pan's contract for the film was extended to 21 July for which he would be paid $450 weekly for a guaranteed twelve and two-thirds weeks. Bill Brande and Vasso Pan were again contracted as Pan's assistants at $55 weekly for a rehearsal period from 25 April through 14 May. Though he received screen credit, "Ensembles staged by Hermes Pan," there was very little ensemble work in the final film, and most of Pan's effort in *Carefree* was functioning as a mirror for Astaire, assisting in the creation of his numbers. Sometimes that involved going to the golf course on hot days with Hal Borne (and a traveling piano) to watch Fred drive balls in preparation for "Since They Turned Loch Lomond into Swing," the first dance to be filmed, in the middle of April, three weeks before shooting was scheduled to begin on the production. For several years Astaire and Pan had been planning a golf dance solo, but until *Carefree* they could never find a suitable spot for it in a film. When they told Mark Sandrich about the idea, the director asked Astaire for a demonstration. They all went to the practice tee at the Bel-Air Country Club and Fred ad-libbed a few steps, hitting the ball while humming to his own accompaniment. Sandrich approved, set up a private driving range at the RKO ranch for rehearsals, and Pan and Astaire began designing the number, often in temperatures that reached 95 degrees or more.

On other occasions, Pan's work consisted in convincing Astaire that certain steps or ideas were possible, as in the end of "The Yam" number, a high-spirited routine for Astaire and Rogers set at the country club. As Pan explained, "He's never been the physical type, he's not very strong. But to lift, there are little tricks always, so there are many things that I've gotten him to do where he said, 'Oh, I can't do that. I will not. Oh, forget it.' And I'd say, 'Just try,' and I'd sort of sneak [it] up on him. There was a thing in 'The Yam' number in *Carefree* where I wanted a finale of him throwing Ginger over his leg over six different tables" (Kobal 1985, 627). Ginger Rogers recalled demonstrating the routine with Pan for Fred and noticing a smile develop on Astaire's face. Once Astaire saw that the steps were possible and aesthetically pleasing, he accepted them without question. Another experiment in the creation of a dance craze ("The Carioca," "The Continental"), "The Yam" was a traveling dance that moved Astaire, Rogers, and a dancing chorus from a country club dance floor to outside the building and back. The complicated number took a full week to film, from Monday, 27 June to Saturday, 2 July.

The obligatory adagio dance in which Astaire seduces Rogers, "Change Partners," began as a scene song and developed into a "Night and Day"–like dance duet in which Astaire hypnotized Rogers into dancing with him. The number took another week to film, beginning on Wednesday, 6 July, followed by a dream sequence, which was originally planned for color processing ("I Used to Be Color Blind"), that went before the cameras in mid-July for the final week of shooting. The RKO Production Files present a synopsis of the sequence that is somewhat at variance with what is seen in the final film:

> Amanda is still asleep. Her bedroom has been transformed into a Macabre Forest, the flowers, mushrooms, etc., of which are gigantic. The crying of a hoot-owl awakens her. As she gets to her feet and walks away wonderingly, we see the Full Size Forest. The thunderous breaking of a twig stops her. She looks off—to see Dr. Flagg, who comes toward her. He is a giant of a man, but normal in proportion to the rest of the Forest. He looks like a typical crazy scientist; there is a mad light in his eyes. In one hand he carries a large magnifying glass. Around his neck is a stethoscope and, under his other arm, he carries a large velvet box. His eyes

open wide with interest, and he utters a menacing sound as he clumps his way toward Amanda.

Amanda, frightened, runs from him, until she is finally forced to stop by the edge of a black abyss. Dr. Flagg grins horribly as he picks her up in his hand. He opens the velvet case, and we see a number of Girls, pinned like butterflies, squirming in the box. From his coat-lapel he removes a large pin, and is about to make a specimen of Amanda, when she leaps off the palm of his hand, swings from the stethoscope which hangs around his neck and, like a trapeze artiste, lands on his shoulder—to deliver a violent kick at Dr. Flagg's chin. When he turns to her, she kisses him on the lips; then jumps on to a giant mushroom, to laugh up at him. A peculiar look comes into Dr. Flagg's eyes: it's love—in a gigantic way—and, as the result of the kiss—which makes all things equal—he becomes her size.

Now, hand in hand, they wander through the Forest until they come to the gorgeous romantic Castle, surrounded by lily-pads the size of dance floors and, in the distance, a Rainbow. Whereupon Dr. Flagg sings "Color Blind," at the conclusion of which they do their dance, utilizing slow motion and the Dunning process. The dance concludes with Dr. Flagg kissing Amanda. The scene dissolves back into Amanda's Bedroom—as she embraces her pillow.

It is not known if the opening section of the dream was actually filmed and cut before the final edit. Another omitted number, "The Night Is Filled with Music," was on the production schedule to be filmed the week of 21 June, even though Ginger Rogers insisted in her autobiography that the "only numbers that were ever done for the film *Carefree* are in the released film" (Rogers 2008, 242).

During the six months Hermes was working on *Carefree*, he built a swimming pool at Pan-Jose and spent weekends out at the Girard Golf Course (now the Woodland Hills Country Club) with Reverend Jim O'Callaghan. Hermes was an able amateur golfer—his earlier association with Harold Sampson had paid off on the golf course—but, with Father Jim, Pan was always more concerned with exploring new ideas about religion or metaphysics than finding the fairways.

By the time *Carefree* had wrapped, Hermes found himself involved in a lawsuit filed against I. C. Overdorff, Edward W. Rose, and W. A. Garrabrant, managers of a dance academy called the National Talent Pictures Corporation, charged with capitalizing fraudulently on the ambitions of mothers desiring film careers for their children. According to police reports, circulars and pamphlets distributed by the "school" displayed the names of Hermes Pan, LeRoy Prinz, and Dave Gould, and represented them as being members of the faculty. On 31 August, Pan and Prinz testified in court that they never consented to the use of their names in connection with the school's promotional advertising and that they had no involvement whatsoever with the company. A week later, Overdorff testified that he had spoken directly with Hermes Pan who, he swore under oath, agreed to be present at the school, and that he "had an understanding" with dance director David Robel that Prinz would appear as one of the guest faculty. On 7 September, the charges against Garrabrant were dismissed since he was proven to be a field representative who had no actual part in the swindle, and Overdorff and Rose were found guilty of fraud and petty theft. Rather than being annoyed with the proceedings, Pan was surprised and somewhat flattered that the guilty parties thought that he was famous enough to draw business and felt compassion for them when the judge passed down a harsh sentence. Firmly devoted to the words of the Christian prayer, "Our Father," "Forgive us our trespasses as we forgive those who trespass against us," Pan wished evil on no one.

A week after the trial, Pan returned to RKO for his next assignment, for which he was contracted from 14 September 1938 to 21 January 1939, a guaranteed eighteen and two-thirds' weeks at $450 per week. The film, *The Story of Vernon and Irene Castle*, was a $1,211,880 bio-musical starring Fred Astaire and Ginger Rogers as the Castles, perhaps the most celebrated dance team in America prior to the First World War. Because the film sought to reproduce the dances made famous by the Castles, Irene Castle served as technical director for the film, more of a curse than a blessing for director H. C. Potter and Ginger Rogers, whom Castle did not want in the role. For Pan, who had seen a print of the Castles' 1915 film *The Whirl of Life* and had studied their instructional manual *Modern Dancing*, it was an excellent opportunity to learn the "Texas Tommy," the "Castle Walk," the "Maxixe," and other period dances from Irene Castle personally. It was also a return to his days as a go-between since Mrs. Castle's professional dislike of Ginger Rogers required him often to function as a mediator between the women.

Irene Castle had wanted a highly publicized search for the actress who would play her in the film, not unlike the search for Scarlett O'Hara in *Gone with the Wind*. What materialized instead was a casting call for "the eight most beautiful girls in Hollywood" for "The Girl on the Magazine Cover" number in the film for which Pan was assigned the enviable duty of choosing eight beauties out of one thousand applicants. Unfortunately, the publicity from the beauty contest failed to appease Irene Castle, and the number was not included in the final print of the film. In addition to searching for beauties, Pan was busy casting chorus dancers for the film, and in that endeavor he noticed a profound change in the film industry. In the syndicated column *Today in Hollywood*, Robbin Coons noted:

> Hermes Pan, a tender-hearted guy, is having his troubles. The big chorus numbers of yesterday are gone from the screen. The other day he had to select sixty steppers for a series of dance shots showing how Castle dancing influenced the world. "Two years ago," he said, "the girls were so busy I couldn't have found sixty. Today I ask for sixty and 500 girls apply. He knows most of the girls, but he has to look through them when he's selecting. He can't hire all of them. It breaks him up. He wishes the "big numbers" would come back, but thinks they won't—not soon. (*Lowell Sun*, 25 November 1938)

Although Pan had little creative input in the choreography for the film, his work pattern was typical of an Astaire-Rogers project. From the middle of September through the end of October, he, Astaire, and Hal Borne sequestered themselves to work out the dance routines—or, in this case, to master the authentic choreography and organize the steps into dances. When Ginger Rogers appeared, Pan taught her the choreography, even though Irene Castle was too often present at those early rehearsals to cavil about minute details. When filming began in November, Hermes was on hand to teach the ensemble the "Castle Walk" and all the other Castle routines that are imitated by dancers throughout the film. He supervised the challenge tap routine for Astaire and Sonny Lamont (with whom Pan had worked on *Old Man Rhythm*), taught Ginger the "Yama Yama Man" routine (after learning it from Irene Castle), choreographed the rehearsal routine for the girl dancers in the sequence set at Papa Aubel's theatre, and by the middle of January 1939, supervised a military routine, "Hello! Hello! Who's Your Lady Friend?" in which Astaire dances with a partner in drag against the background of a unit of soldiers singing and performing a military drill.

In March, Hermes Pan began choreographing the dances for *Little Mother*, a Ginger Rogers vehicle released as *Bachelor Mother*, about Polly Parrish (Rogers), a fired department store clerk who is mistaken as the mother of a foundling. Late in the film, Polly is taken by her boss's playboy son, David Merlin (David Niven), to a New Year's Eve party at a swank café where Rogers proceeds to dance in a variety of styles with four different partners. Casting the four men was particularly difficult for Pan, even though fifty appeared at the call, because the mere mention of dancing with Ginger Rogers was enough to make even the best dancers weak in the knees. After a lengthy callback, during which the finalists got to dance with Rogers (and occasionally step on her feet), Hermes picked Stephen Carruthers to dance the rumba, George Ford to do the waltz, Joseph Bixby to dance the foxtrot, and Reed Hadley, the slow waltz. The montage of dances was rehearsed on Monday, 20 March and filmed on the three following days.

Earlier in the film, Polly is escorted by a coworker, Freddie Miller (Frank Albertson), to a dance hall called the Pink Slipper, where they participate in a swing-dance contest performing choreography recalling Pan's work in *Vivacious Lady* and *Radio City Revels*. They are followed by David Merlin who is forced to enter the dance competition in order to get on the dance floor to shadow Polly. Even though the dance floor is crowded with contestants, Pan keeps a tight focus on Polly's dancing with Freddie and David and his partner so that the action of the scene is never lost. Hermes Pan rehearsed and filmed this sequence in the middle of April and received a total of $500 for his work on *Bachelor Mother* but no screen credit. Two weeks later, *The Story of Vernon and Irene Castle* opened to respectable reviews but less than stellar business. Like *Carefree*, which was released in September 1938, the film posted another loss for RKO.[16]

5

Chica Chica Boom Chic

After *Bachelor Mother*, Hermes Pan found himself unemployed. The poor showing of the last two Astaire-Rogers films convinced RKO that the partnership had run its course: Ginger Rogers would stay on at the studio to do nonmusical films, but Fred Astaire let his contract lapse and moved on to other studios, and for the first time since 1933, RKO did not pick up the option on Pan's contract. In "The Mortal Goddesses," a chapter of his memoir, Pan noted that his confidence in his work as a choreographer had grown significantly during his tenure at RKO and that he was anxious to be off on his own. "I had some complaints that developed during those years that I mainly kept to myself concerning money (too little) and credit (not enough), but these were never sources of potential contention, because I knew at all times that I was a cog in a very, very important wheel; that my days at RKO were a good thing that would pay off for me in the future. Now I really had something to offer" (Pan, Columbia, Kramer 1983, 10a).

In more than one interview, Pan has described himself as a lazy person, one who enjoys not doing anything, so the first few weeks of employment were paradise at Pan-Jose—relaxing by the pool, entertaining Hollywood celebrities, and playing golf with Father Jim. Hermes admitted to enjoying the indolence to such a degree that he began to feel guilty about it, worrying that his life would return to the days of running out on landlords and sleeping in the kitchen. He began to press his agent, Zeppo Marx (of the Marx Brothers), to find him something, anything, to do just so that he could feel secure in the knowledge that he was supporting his mother and sister and sister-in-law and niece. Even though Vasso and Dot were still working, as the man in the family Hermes felt it was his responsibility to be the provider. Eight or nine months passed and Marx was still unable to secure Pan employment and, recalling the career of Luise Rainer who won the Oscar twice and then never worked again, Hermes began to wonder if the stories about the so-called Oscar jinx were true.

Determined to stop sunning himself by the pool, Pan advertised his services as a dance instructor (something he swore to himself he would never do when he left Kosloff), hoping that the Fred-and-Ginger mania that was sweeping the country might send young hopefuls his way. His first students were a teenage brother and sister, the children of a restaurant chain tycoon, who had aspirations of becoming the next Fred Astaire and Ginger Rogers but hardly the talent to realize their dreams. Professional dancers came to him to refine their craft; actors asked Hermes to teach them how to move; and middle-aged housewives came to dance with the man who danced with Fred Astaire. Students offered Pan hundreds of dollars to travel to their hometown so that they could study with him, but not wanting to leave California ("just in case something in pictures came along"), Pan requested exorbitant fees and required all students to come to him. A young Astaire freak from New York took Pan at his word and traveled all the way to California for ten lessons at $75 a lesson.

In the middle of November, while Hermes was developing his student clientele, his mother was diligently arranging the wedding of his sister to Charles Meade, a teller at the Bank of America on Hollywood and Vine where Vasso cashed her pay-checks. Meade always managed to be the teller who waited on her, and a relationship developed to the extent that he took the bus all the way out to Encino to court her. Charles Meade proposed to Vasso under a big oak tree that still stands on the property (even though the house and fruit trees are long gone), and on 18 November 1939, they were married in a small wedding ceremony at Blessed Sacrament Church on Sunset Boulevard. No elaborate party followed, just a simple get-together of relatives and family friends topped off by the place setting of sterling silver Hermes gave her as a wedding gift.

Six months after the wedding, nearly fifteen months since his last film, Hermes Pan received a phone call from Fred Astaire telling him that he was under contract at Paramount to do a film with Artie Shaw and his band and wondered if Hermes might be interested in choreographing. This was the opportunity Pan had been waiting for and, in June 1940, he was back to work on *Second Chorus* in which Danny O'Neill (Fred Astaire), a college-age trumpeter and leader of a band called the Perennials, vies with his friend and fellow-trumpeter, Hank Taylor (Burgess Meredith) for the affections of Ellen Miller (Paulette Goddard) and a place in Artie Shaw's band. Before filming began at the end of July, Pan carried out his typical routine with Fred Astaire and Hal Borne, who was again on board as rehearsal pianist, collaborating on the creation of the dances and acting as Astaire's dance partner. Hermes felt right at home, even though the experience would be a new one for the choreographer since he would actually appear on screen as a clarinetist in Astaire's band.

Pan assisted Astaire in the preparation of four dance segments: "Dig It," written by Hal Borne and Johnny Mercer as a duet for Astaire and Paulette Goddard; a Russian burlesque of "Would You Like to Be the Love of My Life," written by Artie Shaw and Johnny Mercer as a Cossack dance routine for Astaire; "Hoe Down the Bayou," written by Bernard Hanighen and Johnny Mercer for an Astaire tap solo; and "Me and the Ghost Upstairs," written by Hanighen and Mercer as a dance duet for Astaire and Hermes Pan.

Hermes Pan, Paulette Goddard, and Fred Astaire in *Second Chorus* (Courtesy of the Academy of Motion Picture Arts and Sciences).

"Dig It" allowed Astaire to break away from the high-society dances that characterized his work with Ginger Rogers and explore the new generation of swing. Pan, who had integrated the Lindy and jitterbug in many of his films without Astaire, spent five weeks teaching Paulette Goddard the steps to the dance. When it went before the camera in August, it was filmed in a single take, the last of Astaire's full-length duets to be shot all in one take, without cuts (Mueller 1985, 189). In *Paulette: The Adventurous Life of Paulette Goddard*, the actress is quoted as saying of the routine, "I'll never try dancing on the screen again. I was determined that the dance would be good. Imagine me dancing with Astaire. And I guess it was all right. We did it just once, one Saturday morning for the cameras. Just one take. I'm glad it was all right, because I couldn't have done it again. I couldn't possibly ever have done it again" (Morella 1985, 99–100).

The Russian dance permitted Pan and Astaire to explore traditional Cossack steps for comic effect, and the cutaway shots to Paulette Goddard's reactions during the number make it clear that the focus of the event was not the dancing but the humor.

"Hoe Down the Bayou" gave Astaire the opportunity to perform a tap solo while conducting Artie Shaw's band. At first, Astaire's movements appear to be simply synchronously evocative of the music, gliding movements, for example, coinciding with lyrical musical phrases. Gradually, Astaire's gestures become literal representations of what is being played as if his dancing is actually conducting the orchestra with sharp side-kicks producing drum hits and rim shots and the movement of his hands creating drum rolls and dynamics. Finally, Astaire progresses from being a visual representative of the sound (the conductor) to a separate sound-making element (the tap dancer), and he engages in another highly intricate and technically difficult dance, complicated further by having a trumpet in his hand and pretending to play it.

"Me and the Ghost Upstairs" would have been Hermes Pan's dance debut on the screen had it not be deleted from the film. The number was intended for a Halloween party at a country club where Astaire's band had been hired to play. After Astaire sings the song, he is joined by Pan dressed in a sheet tauntingly mirroring his movements before the two engage in an energetic dance duet with jitterbugging, Lindy lifts, and conga routines. Watching Astaire dance with Pan, it is easy to comprehend how easily Hermes functioned as Ginger's surrogate.

When Hermes completed his duties with *Second Chorus*, he found himself again among Hollywood's employed choreographers, moving on to Republic Pictures to complete the choreography for *Hit Parade of 1941*, a half-million-dollar musical about a floundering radio station, featuring Ann Miller, Kenny Baker, Frances Langford, the singing group Six Hits and a Miss, and Borrah Minevich and His Harmonica Rascals. Danny Dare, the choreographer of record, was moved up to codirector in the midst of filming and asked Hermes to complete the dance direction. The exact nature of Pan's contributions to the finished film is not known, though visual evidence suggests that he contributed to Ann Miller's routines, "Swing Low, Sweet Rhythm," and the spectacular production number "Pan American Conga," which completed filming on 6 September. Although the musical received lukewarm reviews, Ann Miller's dancing and Jule Styne's songs (with lyrics by Walter Bullock) were considered the high points, with one of the songs, "Who Am I?," nominated for the Academy Award in the Best Music, Original Song category.

Not long after *Hit Parade* had wrapped, Hermes received a call from Darryl Zanuck's secretary at Twentieth Century-Fox, inviting him to come in for an appointment. Forty years later in his unpublished memoir, Pan recalled the episode vividly. He was ushered into an office so substantial that he felt like he was in the Sistine Chapel. Chomping on a cigar, Zanuck sat behind a gigantic desk, certainly looking the part of a film mogul even though, in reality, he was a small man. Slowly approaching his potential employer, Pan nervously waited for him to speak, all the time wondering who was supposed to break the ice. As Hermes briefly meditated on proper office etiquette, he noticed that when Zanuck took his cigar from his mouth he had a modest set of buck teeth that immediately reminded him of a chipmunk. Pan stifled his customary guffaw at the thought and politely smiled (Pan, Columbia, Kramer 1983, 16a–18a).

Three days later, on 3 October, Hermes Pan signed a contract with Twentieth Century-Fox for a guaranteed eight weeks from 14 October to 8 December at $400 per week. Studio head Darryl Zanuck had long been a fan of Pan's choreography as well as his reputation as a generous and unflappable colleague. Even though he had other celebrated dance directors on staff, such as Nick Castle, Geneva Sawyer, Fanchon, and Oscar-winner Seymour Felix, he was anxious to have Pan, another Academy Award winner, on board. David Patrick Columbia suggests that Astaire's luster had rubbed off on Hermes and that Zanuck's decision was as political as it was professional (Columbia, June 1991, 848). Unlike the conditions under which Pan was used to working at RKO that often made him feel "like somebody's country cousin," Fox provided him with a private bungalow that included an office, a bedroom, a bath, and a shower, as well as two assistants. Even though Hermes was not entirely comfortable with what he called the Fox philosophy of making musicals, "To hell with the story, make 'em happy,"[1] he believed that he could make a difference at the studio, and, if he was able to remain there long enough, even work toward the integrated musical film that he and Astaire and Mark Sandrich had developed at RKO.

The project for which Hermes Pan was hired was *Road to Rio* (also known as *A Latin from Manhattan, Rings on Her Fingers,* and *They Met in Rio*, but released as *That Night in Rio*), starring Alice Faye, Don Ameche, and Carmen Miranda, with a score by Harry Warren and Mack Gordon. The farcical plot cast Don Ameche as Larry Martin, an American entertainer performing in Rio de Janeiro, who is hired to impersonate his look-alike, Baron Manuel Duarte, a well-known investment banker. Since Duarte has a wife (Alice Faye) and Martin a girlfriend (Carmen Miranda), the impersonation creates comic romantic entanglements that find resolution before the final musical number. Casting a dancing chorus was particularly difficult since, to provide an authentic South American look, Hermes wanted only dancers with dark hair. Because of the popularity of musicals with a south-of-the-border setting then in production, the best available dancers were blondes. According to a syndicated news release (8 December 1940), Pan's friend Angie Blue, who had assisted him on *A Damsel in Distress*, and Pearlie May Norton, both blondes and unemployed because of the rash of dark-haired roles, burst into Pan's office and convinced him to reconsider his choice of hair color, arguing that a great blonde dancer in a dark wig is infinitely superior to a brunette with bad technique. As a result, Pan hired both women (as well as a number of other blonde dancers) and asked Angie to assist him with the choreography. According to Larry Billman, after *A Damsel in Distress*, Blue withdrew from dancing to marry Charles DeShon, with whom she had a son, Dennis. When he was hired at Fox, Hermes sought Angie out and persuaded her to return to her professional career starting with the job of assistant choreographer on *That Night in Rio* (Billman 1997, 240). In either case, the collaboration was a fortuitous one for Blue, who remained employed as Betty Grable's dance-in and Pan's assistant through much of the 1940s.

In the weeks between 14 October and 15 November when filming began, Hermes worked with Angie Blue on the staging of two numbers, "Chica Chica Boom Chic," the production number for Carmen Miranda that opens the film, and the musical scene, "The Baron Is in Conference," that immediately follows. Not only was the philosophy at Fox at odds with Hermes's way of thinking, the construction of the film—starting off with the two biggest musical numbers—was antithetical to his taste. When asked by interviewer Svetlana McLee Grody how he might choose the placement of musical numbers in a film, Pan replied, "I would hate for the best thing I was going to do in the picture to be right at the opening. In other words, I would like something developed, so the audience could get interested in the characters and the story. Then your forte would be stronger; than wasted at the beginning of the film. It's a matter of what would be better balance" (Grody 1996, 2).

Despite his concerns over starting "big," for "Chica Chica Boom Chic" Hermes created a production number that he modestly described as "hot." Organically developing from Carmen Miranda's opening solo (backed by the ensemble's subtle shoulder movements and simple swaying), through the entrance of Don Ameche (backed by more complicated and dynamic movements from the ensemble), a formal dance section erupts into a samba with various permutations (including a swing rhythm section) as the background ensemble occupies the dance floor. Particularly interesting is the hesitation step that is added toward the end of the dance just before Carmen Miranda rejoins the number. It not only adds interest by an unexpected variation to the choreographic pattern, but it also prepares the audience for Miranda's return and the big finish to the number. What Pan found especially challenging with the samba was teaching his version of it to Carmen Miranda. "Carmen didn't dance much but she was energetic," Hermes noted. "She danced with her hands and her eyes" (Lewis, Spring 1991, 27).When she demonstrated how she did the dance, Hermes found that it wasn't very violent, and violent was his word for the way he performed it. "In Brazil," Pan noted, "they do the Samba in 6/8 time, but in America it has to be done to 4/4 time. That's faster—like swing. And nothing you've ever seen before." Once the dancing chorus arrived for rehearsals prior to filming, Hermes taught the sixteen couples involved in the dance the American way of doing the samba, and seeing them perform it on the dance floor he proclaimed, "It's going to catch on. It's going to be the next dance fad. If you can waltz, you can samba."[2]

Hermes began the musical scene, "The Baron Is in Conference," as a dialogue between four secretaries and four businessmen with the simplest of staging to give focus to the lyrics of the song. The secretaries break into a samba step momentarily, but that is the extent of the dancing in the first part of the number. The second part discovers Don Ameche impersonating Baron Duarte in a setting that is cluttered with showgirls who pose and preen and walk. Once the chorus had been assembled to learn the number, Hermes and Angie Blue had only eight days of rehearsal (eight or nine hours a day) to perfect it. To make their job more interesting, the studio had imported six New York models with little or no dance experience and required Pan to include them in the routine. On the second day of rehearsal, the models complained that they were having trouble with the choreography, objecting, "It makes us feel clumsy, and sort of off balance." Hermes solved the problem by adding lead oversoles weighing three pounds to each of the girl's shoes. The girls were forced to wear the weights for the entire rehearsal, doing the steps in rhythm and in tempo, in spite of their complaints that it was impossible to move with lead in their shoes. On the third day, Hermes had the weights removed and the six models, Lillian Eggers, Marian Rosamond, Roseanne Murray, Bunny Hartley, Mary Joyce Walsh, and Bettye Avery, performed the routine like Hollywood dancers.

In December, shortly before filming ended for the holidays, Pan, who never considered himself "political," issued a syndicated press release offering an explanation for the recent routing of Mussolini's forces by the Greek army: "Every man in the Greek army is a male Isadora Duncan who has spent long hours practicing the twists and the pirouettes of the classic dance. And so he can handle a bayonet like no other soldier in the world. He leaps from crag to crag with all the sure-footedness of a goat, and thanks to his training in the dance, he never makes a lost motion. I am surprised that the experts who try to interpret the war never realized the truth. I thought it was obvious. The Italians haven't a chance; nobody has a chance against a Greek soldier except maybe another ballet dancer" (*New York Times*, 15 December 1940).[3] Even before the United States entered the Second World War, Hermes attempted to enlist to add the support of another Greek soldier-dancer to the fight against the Axis Powers, but as he was the sole support of his mother the army refused him.

During the filming of *That Night in Rio*, Hermes, Carmen Miranda, and Betty Grable became good friends, and on Sunday afternoons, Betty and Carmen would visit Pan at Pan-Jose with the Banda da Lua, Miranda's personal orchestra. Carmen would entertain, performing Latin-American songs, and everyone would dance, drink wine, and enjoy what would become known as "Pan's famous pasta dinners." After hours, Hermes was fond of dancing with Carmen at the Palladium and Band Box where he was also seen jitterbugging into the early hours of the morning with Ann Miller. He and Ann attended Dorothy Lamour's New Year's party at the Band Box where they joined other Hollywood celebrities to greet 1941 playing gin rummy, checkers, backgammon, darts, blocks, solitaire, and a variety of other indoor sports. So often were they spied together that Jimmy Fiddler's "In Hollywood" column for 3 February 1941 warned readers: "Stand by for elopement news from Ann Miller and dance director Hermes Pan." Miller, of course, was well aware of Pan's homosexual preference but enjoyed the dancing and reveled in all the attention from the press.

On 15 January, four days after filming was completed for *That Night in Rio*, Hermes was signed to a six-month contract with Fox at a weekly salary of $500 with an option to extend for another six months at $750 per week. Pan was

immediately assigned to collaborate with Geneva Sawyer, another of Fox's choreographers, on the dances for *Blood and Sand*, a bull-fighting epic directed by
Rouben Mamoulian and starring Tyrone Power, Linda Darnell, and Rita Hayworth. Without receiving screen credit, Pan and Sawyer designed three choreographic events for the film: an explosive flamenco dance at a café; a celebratory
fiesta sequence in which the townspeople dance a traditional *sevillana* when matador Juan Gallardo (Tyrone Power) returns to Seville; and a seductive *el torero*
dance for Juan's mistress, Dona Sol (Rita Hayworth), as she flirts with matador
Manolo de Palma (Anthony Quinn). The first two events added to the atmosphere
and rhythm of the film while the third was integral to the dramatic action. As Pan
remarked to John Kobal:

> Sol didn't have to be a dancer. But there was something which was meant
> to be seductive, just moving around the room pretending to be a bull-
> fighter. Mamoulian told me he didn't want it to look like a dance number,
> just an impromptu sort of thing where somebody is being seductive. He
> worked very closely with me the way he does with everybody on his
> films because he had an overall feeling for what he wanted. I'd never
> seen Rita dance before, as a matter of fact I don't think I'd ever heard of
> her before then. We used to have lunch together and talk, and we became
> very good friends. Of course I found out about her family, and that she
> was an accomplished dancer. . . . On the film things went smoothly.
> Mamoulian is a fine director. At the time I thought it would be Tyrone
> Power and Linda Darnell's movie, 'cause he was the star and Linda was
> under contract at Fox, but when Rita came on she was just dynamite.
> You couldn't believe the excitement when we saw the rushes. Not that
> she was conscious of the impression she was making, but the studio was.
> (Kobal 1977, 121–123)

Pan's lunches at the studio with Rita Hayworth developed into pasta dinners for
two at Pan-Jose and a lifelong friendship in which Hermes became Rita's confidant.[4] "She would sort of confide in me. I guess she knew that I wasn't after anything and that she could talk to me without me talking to other people. She was
always a little suspicious of people. We became very close because she trusted me"
(Leaming 1989, 55). In *Blood and Sand*, Pan was fortunate that Rita was an expert
Spanish dancer. Unlike Ginger Rogers, she was uncomfortable making suggestions, preferring, like Betty Grable, to be told what to do. "She was the type of
person who, when you told her to do something, she did it. She was amiable and
childlike, nothing like the sensual women she usually portrayed" (Lewis, Spring
1991, 27–28).

On 29 January, while Pan was working on *Blood and Sand*, his mother died
from appendicitis at their home in Encino. She was only fifty-seven years old and
her death was a severe blow to Hermes: "I was alone for the first time in my life

and without an immediate purpose other than my work" (Pan, Columbia, Kramer n.d., 248). After the burial in early February, Hermes soberly returned to the studio to supervise the dances for *The Great American Broadcast*, a fictional history of the early days of radio, with a score by Harry Warren and Mack Gordon, and featuring Alice Faye, Jack Oakie, John Payne, Cesar Romero, and specialty acts: the Four Ink Spots, the Nicholas Brothers, and the Wiere Brothers. Since the specialty performers created their own routines, Pan's responsibilities consisted in staging Jack Oakie's performance of "Give My Regards to Broadway," arranging extras in scenes that involved social dancing, and choreographing the singing chorus down a staircase in "The Great American Broadcast" number. Because of the small amount of work required, Pan received no screen credit for dance direction. Although modern sources attribute the choreography to Nick Castle, who was under contract to Universal when the film was being made at Fox, film reviewers at the time who mentioned the dance direction attributed the work to Hermes Pan.[5]

Around the middle of February, Pan was in preparation for *Miami* (released as *Moon over Miami*), the next Betty Grable vehicle at Fox. Budgeted at $950,000, the film cast Miss Grable as Kay Latimer who travels to Miami with her sister Barbara (Carole Landis) and aunt (Charlotte Greenwood) in hopes of finding a millionaire husband. She falls in love with Phil McNeil (Don Ameche), but when she discovers that he is penniless, she leaves him to marry his wealthy friend, Jeffrey Bolton (Robert Cummings), with whom her sister is in love. Before the concluding medley of musical numbers, however, the sisters are reunited with the men they love.

Again Pan was working with Angie Blue who, in addition to assisting the dance director, would function as Betty Grable's dance-in at rehearsals and at setups. Hermes made no secret of the fact that Angie Blue was one of his favorite assistants: "She was a person who was a marvelous dancer yet she was pliable and I could grab her by the hand and throw her into position and she'd just do it, you know? I could turn her around and whip her like a piece of clay and she would fall into things. She was like putty" (Grody 1996, 8). David Patrick Columbia recalled that Blue had a "quirky gaminesque" quality that interested Pan. "When he worked out a number, Angie would 'be Grable' the same way he would 'be Ginger' with Fred. Betty Grable was then instructed by Pan to 'do Angie.' The famous Grable itty-bitty walk as well as the bathing suit, hands on hips, over-the-shoulder pinup of the 1940s was simply her 'doing Angie' " (Columbia, June 1991, 848).

Partially because of a feeling of loneliness, but mostly because there were so many unanswered questions in Pan's mind about what he actually wanted to do with his life, during the production of *Miami*, Hermes organized a discussion group that met once a week during lunch at the lake on the Fox back lot to discuss philosophical questions. In his memoir Pan explained that he had developed a passion for philosophy, particularly that of Thomas Aquinas, Immanuel Kant, and David Hume. He quickly discovered that a small number of his dancers shared his interests and Hermes recommended that they meet regularly to discuss one specific topic. The first meeting examined one of Pan's most burning issues: the question, "What is certitude? How do you know anything with certainty?" (Pan, Columbia, Kramer n.d., 248).

Angie Blue became one of the core participants of Pan's discussion group. Blue had a lifelong ambition to become a nun, a dream she fulfilled in 1962 when she entered the Carmelite Monastery in Carmel, California. Other dancers and even some of the principal players such as June Haver participated in Pan's discussions, creating an experience for Pan that he found mentally challenging, spiritually enlivening, and highly stimulating for his creative imagination. Following each discussion, he would return to rehearsals with a charismatic energy that co-workers found inspiring and exhilarating.

Pan felt more at home working on *Miami* than he had on *That Night in Rio*. The weekly discussions were having a positive effect on him, and the fact that the studio liked his work enough to offer him a renewable contract bolstered his confidence to the point where he became comfortable offering suggestions at story conferences in Darryl Zanuck's office. Often Pan's observations about musical structure were taken to heart, for certainly the musical program for *Miami* created by songwriters Leo Robin and Ralph Rainger felt more idiomatic to Pan than what he considered the lopsided structure of the previous film. It began with a short musical scene, "What Can I Do for You," that established Kay and Barbara Latimer as working girls who also sing and dance. "O Me, O Mi-Ami," sung by an invisible chorus while location shots of Miami whirled across the screen, not only established the atmosphere and location of the dramatic action but also prepared the theatre audience for the chorus as accompaniment for other numbers in the score. Like all of Pan's previous musicals, *Miami* was set in an environment that welcomed social dancing. Orchestras were always playing somewhere and a piano was always available to accompany a spontaneous burst of song. The first such burst in this film was called "You Started Something," sung first by Robert Cummings, then by Betty Grable, and finally by Don Ameche. Before Ameche's chorus, however, Grable does a tap routine with the Condos Brothers that begins subtly in a seated position and develops organically into a full-out number. Pan felt that Grable was not much of dancer: "She really was not a good tap dancer, and she couldn't do ballet. . . . She could move, and she had very beautiful legs; her color was beautiful; she was pleasant to watch, and when she was on the screen she had a certain magnetism" (Kobal 1983, 183). It was Pan's responsibility to create movement for Grable that would maximize her talents and disguise her faults. As Stephen Harvey, associate curator of the Museum of Modern Art in New York City noted, "When you see a Grable musical choreographed by Hermes Pan, you're never aware of her limitations. You're simply won over by her charm" (Lewis, Spring 1991, 27).

Pan particularly enjoyed working on "Is That Good," a novelty duet sung and danced by Charlotte Greenwood, the comedienne with the idiosyncratic leg lifts, and Jack Haley, the Tin Man from *The Wizard of Oz*, who happened to worship at the Church of the Good Shepherd in Beverly Hills where Hermes attended mass. Like many of the numbers Pan helped create for Astaire and Rogers, the song develops out of the reality of a dialogue scene, explodes into the fantasy of a light swing dance, and returns to the reality of the initial situation, which in this case involves the couple's falling on to a sofa.

"The Kindergarten Conga," sung by Grable encircled by ensemble dancers, was another of Pan's Latin production numbers where the percussive rhythms of the music are expressed in physical accents with the body. When, in rehearsal, no male dancer looked as good doing the steps as Hermes Pan did when he demonstrated them, Betty Grable went to Darryl Zanuck's office and suggested that Hermes do the number with her, claiming that she wouldn't be satisfied with anyone else. When he got wind of the idea, Pan went to the producer to object, explaining that it would be impossible for him to supervise the filming of the sequence if he were dancing in it. Pan's protests went unheeded and *Moon over Miami* marks his film debut as a dancer. The tap routine he performs with Betty Grable takes into account her limitations without becoming uninteresting. In many instances, it looks like a simplified Astaire-Rogers duet, underscoring a comment Pan made to John Kobal in 1972, "I'm sure that I absorbed a lot from [Fred Astaire], subconsciously even, and from his style" (Kobal 1985, 627). Studio publicity noted that during rehearsals for "The Kindergarten Conga" advertised as "one of the most difficult terpsichorean efforts seen on the screen in some years," Betty Grable collapsed from exhaustion.

The final production number, "Solitary Seminole," was designed to feature the tapping Condos Brothers as well as Jack Cole and his dancers, Florence Lessing and Anna Austin. To make the number as authentic as possible, Pan had requested that the studio hire Cole because of his background in ethnic dancing. Cole had little respect for Pan's work and even less patience with the studio system. At every turn he felt his art was being compromised. Instead of dancing to music that evoked repetitive drumbeats and mournful cries of a reed flute—characteristics of authentic Seminole Indian music—he was forced to deal with a swing tune tenuously masquerading as Indian music. He was also unhappy with the choreography for the background dancers that would frame his number. He voiced his concerns to Hermes Pan, and Pan replied by adapting the choreography to Cole's needs. Ever the diplomat, Pan knew that the music for "Solitary Seminole" was not what Cole had in mind when he accepted the job and he tried to accommodate the dancer in every way possible, given the nature of the music, the number of chorus dancers on hand, and the fact that he had to integrate the Condos Brothers' tapping routine into the number as well.

According to Cole's biographer, Glenn Loney, by the time the number was filmed, Cole had managed to be cited for four major Production Code violations, causing the studio to edit down Cole's dance sequence to next to nothing. And, even with the reduced screen time, Cole's choreography was seen in only four states once the film was released because it was considered too erotic by the Hays

Office (Will H. Hays was the president of the Motion Picture Producers and Distributors of America, the organization that implemented the Production Code).[6] Neither the *New York Times* nor *Variety* mentions Cole's contribution in a review, and notices throughout the country that do mention Cole's name erroneously attribute the sixty backup dancers as his company. Not surprisingly, Pan fared much better in reviews, both as a dancer and dance director.

"I loved working with Betty," Hermes gushed to Constantine in a 1945 interview. "She has a wonderful sense of humor and making that picture was one big round of fun. One day we decided to give up smoking, and the penalty for breaking down was to have a gooey pie pushed in the face. After a few days Betty slipped. I knew it, but couldn't catch her at it. At an Academy dinner, I happened to sit several tables away from Betty. I strained my neck trying to look casually in her direction. Sure enough, she picked up a cigarette and with the first puff, she spied me looking at her. What a shriek she let out! . . . Next day on the set, I had a lush cocoanut [sic] pie awaiting. Betty approached gingerly on the scene. I let loose and scored a direct hit, right on the beam! Boy, those Keystone Kops had nothing on me that day" (Constantine 1945, 7).

Even before *Moon over Miami* wrapped on 21 April, Pan was at work with Geneva Sawyer on the next Fox musical, *Passport to Life* (also known as *Passport to Love* and *Sun Valley*, but released as *Sun Valley Serenade*), with a score by Harry Warren and Mack Gordon, and starring Olympic ice-skating champion Sonja Henie, John Payne, Dorothy Dandridge, the Nicholas Brothers, and Glenn Miller and his orchestra. Ann Miller was also considered for a role in the film, as she noted in her autobiography, *Miller's High Life*:

> I went to Twentieth Century-Fox for a screen test for a role in a Sonja Henie film. The role was that of a sophisticated woman, so again I smeared my face with heavy make-up—only to find Hermes Pan on the sound stage. Much to my embarrassment he ordered me in front of everyone to go and wash my face before he would permit me to go in front of the cameras for my test. I didn't get that role. The reason given— I looked too young. I have always jokingly blamed Hermes for causing me to lose that role. (Miller 1972, 73)

Passport to Life cast Sonja Henie as Karen Benson, a refugee who falls in love with a big-band pianist (John Payne) during an engagement at the Idaho ski resort. Henie had two dance routines, one with John Payne off the ice, and the other with Harrison Thompson in a skating ballet. According to studio publicity, "The Kiss Polka" was the first dance number Henie had ever performed off the ice and Hermes spent hours training the skater to relax into the steps. To disguise the star's inexperience, Pan took the focus off the feet in the number and put it on weaving arm movements, causing Milton Berle, cast as the band's agent, to refer to the routine as a "pretzel dance." Finding six couples to add to the dance was an additional challenge. When the casting call was posted, Hermes expected at least fifty applicants, but no one showed up at the audition. Because so many musicals were being filmed at the time, all the top chorus dancers of both sexes happened to be working. As a result, Pan had to work with less able dancers, forcing him to simplify the choreography, which, given the inexperience of his star, may have been a blessing.

The challenges Hermes faced in arranging a dance for Sonja Henie were magnified when he had to create the ice-skating ballet. He had never choreographed on ice before and, though he felt confident in his ability to arrange dance patterns, he knew that, being a medium different than a solid wood floor, ice would force him to make concessions. He put on a pair of ice skates and experimented on the rink on Stage Fifteen, discovering what a skater might be able to do easily in a dance routine. He learned that the principal difference between dancing and skating was space. "If this were done by ordinary dancers," he explained, demonstrating a step, "this move should bring the dancers three feet further down stage, and I would have to figure further movement accordingly. But because they are on skates, and figuring the amount of momentum that went before, they will have advanced fifteen feet instead of three." The only real concern Pan expressed working on ice was that it might spoil him for dance routines on a hard floor afterward. His excitement over this new challenge quickly turned to dread once filming began:

> I had this idea that I would like a reflection of black and white, so I got together with the set man [Richard Day] and he said, "Well, we'll get that effect by flooding it with nicosin dye." So there was about half an inch of water on the ice. Anyway, Henie was very difficult to work with. She wouldn't listen to you, and she would rather do what she wanted to do. Anytime she got into a good spin, she would stay in it for 5,000 years. So, this day I was at the microphone and she got into a beautiful sit spin, and she was supposed to leave at the count of eight, and just get off, because there are sixteen boys coming down the ice on their cue and if she doesn't move it's going to be a straight collision. I was counting, and the cue came, and she was still doing her spin, and, there was nothing anybody could have done about it, and they hit her, and she was down in the nicosin dye. She was black. Her face was covered in it.
>
> She was furious. She said she refused to work like this and walked out. That was in the morning. Zanuck called me into his office and said, "Tell Sonja Henie that if she doesn't finish the number tonight, that's it, there will be no finish to the number." I think that everybody thought that her real reason for stalling was that the next day we would be going into overtime and she was already getting a fortune, and this way she'd get even more. . . . I told her what Zanuck had said and she flew into a storm. She and her mother used to swear in Norwegian, screaming and hollering.

She said, "I won't come back." In the end she changed her mind and we did a few more shots, just to tidy it up. The next day the picture was closed down. (Kobal 1983, 186–190)

The lushly orchestrated background to the ice-skating ballet was derived from two of the film's melodies, the ballad "I Know Why," and "The Kiss Polka," and introduces a bluesy waltz motïf that would reappear as "At Last," a duple rhythm ballad in the film *Orchestra Wives*.

In spite of the production problems, Sonja and Hermes became good friends who continued to socialize after the film was completed. Pan recalled being invited to a formal dinner party at Hénie's white brick mansion in Holmby Hills. In "The Mortal Goddesses" Pan noted that "her house bore witness to her business acumen, as did she. There was already a large collection of art on the walls and Sonja herself was resplendent in what I gather was only part of no small collection of jewels" (Pan, Columbia, Kramer 1983, 30a). For Pan, Henie—the terror at work—was a charming companion after hours who later wrote that Karen Benson was the favorite role of her career.

On the movie set, however, more enjoyable than the ice-skating ballet was Pan's experience with "Chattanooga Choo Choo," where he could sit back and enjoy the Nicholas Brothers working with Dorothy Dandridge. Although Hermes had learned to dance from watching African-American dancers and felt comfortable in the idiom, Pan did not presume to choreograph a number for the Nicholas Brothers. Since working with Astaire taught him when it was wise to make suggestions and when to give the artist complete creative control, Pan let the Nicholas Brothers stage "Chattanooga Choo Choo." According to Kevin Lewis, Hermes believed it was one of the most outstanding dance numbers with which he had been associated but refused to take any credit for its success (Lewis, Spring 1991, 27). Pan modestly sought to facilitate the realization of the Nicholas Brothers' choreography, no more, no less.[7]

After *Sun Valley Serenade* wrapped in May, Pan sold Pan-Jose in Encino and moved with his sister, her husband, and her six-month-old daughter, Michelene, to 11839 Hesby Street in North Hollywood, three blocks east of Laurel Canyon Boulevard. Dot and her twenty-year-old daughter Aljeanne moved less than three miles away to 4173½ Arch Drive, the home Vasso and her family had recently vacated in their move to Hesby Street. No sooner had Hermes moved into his new home when he was called back to Fox to work on the next Harry Warren–Mack Gordon musical, *Caribbean Cruise* (released as *Week-End in Havana*), with Alice Faye, Carmen Miranda, John Payne, Cesar Romero, and forty-eight chorus dancers. For this film about a Macy's salesclerk (Alice Faye) looking for love and adventure in pre-Castro Havana, Hermes Pan promised "two hundred gorgeous feminine Zombies and Carmen Miranda in a voodoo jive"—his description of the climactic production number, "The Nango." Hyperbole notwithstanding, Pan advertised that "in excitement it will outdo anything previously seen on the screen. . . . It will make the average jitterbug feel that he's been doing slow motion for half of his life." According to Harry Brand, Fox publicity director, the original script indicated the following scenario for the dance:

> Alice Faye and John Payne had just finished having a spat. Miss Faye goes to a famed Havana casino, and while she is tailing a Conga line, Payne suddenly returns. The pair make up their differences with a heavy embrace and kiss. And then Cesar Romero and Carmen Miranda, who are just ahead of [Faye] and Payne, follow suit by kissing. The routine likewise called for all the others in the Conga line to kiss.

Hermes Pan and Charles Friedman, imported from Broadway to design production numbers at Fox, planned a lavish spectacle involving forty-eight chorus dancers, the four principal actors, and innumerable extras. However, when Ernesto Piedra, technical adviser to the film, saw what was going on, he requested that the number be revised to eliminate the collective kissing sequence at the end. He pointed out that in Cuba, when unmarried couples go out on the town, they are customarily chaperoned by a duenna, the mother of one of the girls in the party. According to Piedra, the duenna would never permit kissing among unmarried couples. As a result, Pan altered the choreography from a conga to a samba and limited the kissing to John Payne, Alice Faye, Cesar Romero, and Carmen Miranda.

Hermes was forced into another compromise in an earlier nightclub routine, "Rebola Bola," for Carmen Miranda and company when the members of Miranda's Banda da Lua refused to perform his choreography. During a rehearsal Aloysio Oliveira, the leader of the band, balked at the dance director's attempt to teach the musicians a dance step: "I am sorry," he began in his most dignified manner, "but we are musicians, not dancers. It is impossible. We will play. But dance—no, it cannot be done." With characteristic tact and diplomacy, Hermes replied that he appreciated the musicians' concerns. "I'll tell you what we'll do," he promised. "We won't start the routine until after you've taken your seats. So if you will walk to the orchestra seats in this way," Pan demonstrated a series of steps, "everybody will be satisfied." "Okay," nodded Aloysio, with a knowing grin. "We'll do the dance if it's not a dance. If you call the dance a walk, it's all right." "What do you mean?" inquired the dance director. The bandleader smiled. "That's just doubletalk. Sure— we're anxious to cooperate." Pan's original concept was more complicated than what was seen in the completed film—walking down staircases, crossing to opposite sides of the stage, and backing up to reveal Carmen Miranda—but Hermes made the most with what he had and managed to integrate dance-challenged musicians into a complex palette of movement at the beginning of the number.

On 26 June, Twentieth Century-Fox extended Pan's contract for another six months beginning on 15 July, at a salary of $750 per week. As a result, when *Week-End in Havana* completed shooting on 6 August, almost immediately Hermes was preparing the dances for a college football musical, *Rise and Shine*, with songs by Leo Robin and Ralph Rainger, and starring Jack Oakie, Linda Darnell, Milton Berle, Walter Brennan, and dancer George Murphy. In a 1980 interview, Pan recalled his trepidation at having to discuss the choreography for the film at story conferences in Darryl Zanuck's office.

> I must say, it's always been one of the bugaboos of my career, of never being prepared. I go into a meeting with panic inside because I have absolutely no ideas whatsoever. I feel like a complete idiot when they ask me a question because I have nothing much to say. I remember we used to have meetings with Darryl Zanuck, he would always have a story-music conference and he'd have the director, myself, composers, and so forth in, having all read the script, and he would say, "Hermes, what are you going to do here?" I'd say, "Darryl, I haven't the slightest idea. I'm sorry. I'll have to talk to you about it later." He'd say, "Okay, all right, all right—." So it got to be almost a gag that I never knew what I was going to do. Fortunately something usually developed and he got so that he would trust me. He would say, "I know you don't know what you're going to do but I hope you'll do something good." I'd say, "Okay, thanks, I'll try." (Grody 1996, 3)[8]

On 10 September, after nearly a monthlong search for a large female dancing chorus, Hermes finalized the casting of Claire James, Violet Church, Virginia Maples, Edna Mae Jones, and Mary Scott, formerly a dancer at Ciro's in Los Angeles. What the women essentially had to do in the film was look beautiful and behave as cheerleaders, and in the opening number, "Hail to Bolenciewicz," each received a showgirl close-up as she paraded toward the camera carrying a baton. Somewhat more taxing was the "Men of Clayton" fight song in which the seated cheerleaders were choreographed to gesticulate with their arms and legs enthusiastically (and seductively) in support of the football team. Most complex of all was the "Get Thee Behind Me, Clayton" production number in which a large crowd of people—some carrying banners and placards—gathers underneath the window of football star Jack Oakie and demonstrates support with swaying, dynamic gesticulation, serpentine lines, and finally the jitterbugging of two front couples. A final cheerleading "Rah!" movement ends the number and the crowd silently marches away concluding what was more of an exercise in crowd control than choreography, more characteristic of Busby Berkeley than Hermes Pan.

In George Murphy's numbers, however, Pan returned to his idiosyncratic style. "Central Two, Two, Oh, Oh" was a swing nightclub solo for Murphy, who performs an extended tap routine filmed without cutaways. The only cuts used were those changing the camera angle on the performer to focus more clearly on his interaction with patrons. One such interaction involved his pulling the tablecloth out from under a pile of dishes and then using it as a kind of toreador cape in the dance. The use of props in this and another tap routine to the reprise of "I'm Making a Play for You" later in the film recalled Pan's earlier work at RKO with Fred Astaire, and the ingenious novelty duets Hermes created for Astaire and Rogers were evoked when Murphy sings "I'm Making a Play for You" to Linda Darnell while they are riding bicycles. Pan transforms the song into a kind of bicycle ballet, during which they perform arabesques and other simple dance movements while riding. And for Walter Brennan, cast as a woman-chasing grandpa, who believes the Civil War is still going on, and Ruth Donnelly, Mame Bacon, a racketeer's accomplice, Hermes Pan embellished a comical seduction scene with another one of his trademark Latin dances. Two songs were advertised for the film but did not appear in the final cut, "It All Depends on Thee," and "Dance It Off." It is not known if Pan choreographed the last named before it was dropped from the picture.

From the gridiron, Pan moved to the Hawaiian island of Ahmi-Oni, the setting for *Song of the Islands*, the Betty Grable, Victor Mature, Jack Oakie feature that went into production as soon as *Rise and Shine* closed. With a score by Mack Gordon and Harry Owens, the musical told the story of Eileen O'Brien (Betty Grable), daughter of the blatantly Irish proprietor of beachfront property, who falls in love with Jefferson Harper (Victor Mature), son of the owner of the adjacent cattle ranch who wants to buy the O'Brien's property. The opposing sides manage to reach an agreement in business and in romance at the big Saint Patrick's Day luau. In a 6 May 1941 story-conference memo, Darryl Zanuck noted that he wanted a "*Philadelphia Story* type of picture . . . in a Hawaiian setting."

For the dancing and local-color segments of the film, Pan and the casting department sought twenty-five chorus girls and three hundred Polynesian types. While many of the dancing girls were cast from among the stable of Hermes Pan's dancers, the ethnic types were more difficult to cast, particularly in such large numbers. A publicity release dated 12 December 1941 reports that technical adviser John Reasin had to approach a chief on a remote Hawaiian island about sending extras over for the filming. The chief replied that his men were too busy with the cane harvest and suggested, "You say your business is now moving pictures. They must be very heavy pictures that you need our help in moving them. Why can't you leave them where they are?"

With Angie Blue again on board as his assistant and Grable's dance-in, Hermes created a series of hula-inspired dances that maximized the amount of cellophane available to the prop department in November and December 1941. As the studio explained, "Hula dancers wore shimmering skirts of cellophane, which shed as they rehearsed. After each rehearsal janitor crews push-broomed the scattered cellophane and retrieved [it]. There might not be any more after this is gone." Dark wigs were also an endangered commodity since they were made of real hair typically imported from China and Yugoslavia. With Europe and Asia at war, the usual trade routes for such commodities were cut off.

Pan begins the film with a hula danced to the music of the popular "Hawaiian War Chant," reprising a favorite device of placing a single dancer at the center of a circle of dancers. The musical event is less of a number than a series of establishing shots providing local color and setting the choreographic style of the film. "Down on Ami Ami Oni Oni Island," the first production number of the film, presents Betty Grable in a grass skirt singing and performing the hula, followed by Hilo Hattie singing and dancing in a highly exaggerated series of gesticulations and butt thrusts. At the end of the singing, Hermes Pan staged Grable and chorus girls wearing grass skirts in a Hawaiian-inspired dance combining motifs from the Charleston, tap, and swing dance with the hula, as a kind of foreshadowing of the production number at the Saint Patrick's Day luau, "O'Brien Has Gone Hawaiian," in which the hula is first interrupted by, and then combined with, the Irish jig. Pan's choreography for the "O'Brien" dance is especially notable for its purely percussive section (reminiscent of many of Astaire's solo dances) where the orchestra becomes silent and the dancers are accompanied only by the beating of drums or the sounds created by their feet. After a section of pseudo-native dancing, the percussive sounds are interrupted by an orchestral statement of Balfe's "Killarney," and Pan begins to infuse the native dancing with the steps of an Irish jig. The music next changes to swing, and the addition of a short tap routine for Betty Grable drives the hula-jig to a spirited conclusion.

On 6 December, the day before the Japanese attacked Pearl Harbor in the Hawaiian Islands, *Song of the Islands* completed filming. On the same day, Ginger Rogers finished shooting *Roxie Hart*, a nonmusical satire about a Chicago dancer (Rogers) who confesses to a murder committed by her husband in order to attract publicity. Although the film was not technically a musical, Rogers did dance in two sequences for which she requested Hermes Pan to provide the choreography. The first dance, called the "Black Hula," was designed as entertainment for reporters who came to interview the alleged murderess. To the music of the "Black Bottom," Hermes staged a seductive solo dance for Rogers employing many of the characteristic steps of popular dances of the 1920s. The solo became a duet for Rogers and reporter Homer Howard (George Montgomery) and then opened up to include all the reporters in a Charleston-like free-for-all. The second choreographic event was a seductive tap dance up a metal staircase at the top of which Rogers engaged in a kind of rhythmic dialogue between tap sounds and hand claps that climaxed with a pelvic thrust directed at George Montgomery, watching her from the bottom of the stairs. In her autobiography, Ginger Rogers commented:

Since Roxie was supposed to be a dancer, I thought I should work a little tap routine into the proceedings and found a perfect spot for it. Roxie is in jail and I wanted to do my dance on metal stairs. Truly, I'd always wanted to do taps on a metal staircase, because I knew the taps would have a good, resounding sound. Twentieth Century-Fox didn't have a metal staircase on hand and had to go to a good deal of trouble to locate one. It was finally found in the wreckage from a demolished building in downtown Los Angeles. It was worth the effort; the tap sequence was a pure joy to do and, I'm happy to say, a pure joy to watch. . . . Years later, when *Roxie Hart* was turned into the stage musical *Chicago*, Gwen Verdon told me how sad she was that she was not going to be able to dance on a metal staircase. (Rogers 2008, 287–288)

While Hermes Pan was working on *Song of the Islands* and *Roxie Hart*, Twentieth Century-Fox extended his contract for one year, beginning 15 January 1942, and raised his salary to $750 weekly.

The first project under Pan's new contract was *My Gal Sal*, a biographical musical about composer Paul Dresser, starring Victor Mature as Dresser and Rita Hayworth as his gal Sal. Because there were five production numbers in the film and only a two-month production schedule, Hermes asked the studio to assign Russian-born choreographer Val Raset, with whom he worked on the *Shim Sham Revue*, as co-dance director. Working again with Rita Hayworth was an especially happy experience for Pan. In a 1982 interview, he told Ray Nielsen that "Rita was a wonderful dancer. She'd been in a dance team before she even went into films and she was a very, very hard worker who would come in always on time and work hard and never complain. She was sort of the ideal person for a choreographer to work with. She was no trouble at all." When Nielsen asked how he went about creating the dances for the film, Hermes replied, "I would read the script. The score was all written because it was a period picture. So I would just figure out the type of number I would like to do in that particular spot in the story. Of course, it had to be of the period and something that would be plausible in the spot it was in. Then I would discuss it with the director [Irving Cummings] and producer and then I would be pretty much on my own to do whatever I wanted. Of course, I would naturally discuss it with Rita who was always very agreeable as she always seemed to have a lot of confidence in my judgment" (Nielsen 1982, 42–43).

Pan began the "Belles of Broadway" ("On the Gay White Way") sequence with a stage filled with high-kicking couples (the women performing skirt-tossing steps reminiscent of the cancan) in preparation for Rita Hayworth's entrance (in a horse-drawn cab) and song, backed by the male chorus whose choreography shadows her as she crosses the stage. After a cutaway to a reaction scene, the number goes into a duet adagio for Hayworth and her partner, Hermes Pan—once again pressed into on-screen service—accompanied first by a foxtrot arrangement of the tune, then a rhythmic Latin variation, and finally a lilting waltz. The tempo increases as the high-stepping chorus reenters, and after a series of turns by the solo couple, the number builds to a spirited climax. In his syndicated "Behind the Scenes in Hollywood" (8 January 1942), Harrison Carroll noted that early January Rita Hayworth was knocked cold during the rehearsal of "On the Gay White Way" when she and Hermes Pan bumped their heads together.

Drawing upon theatrical images of the period, Hermes positioned a male chorus dressed in blue tails on opposite sides of a staircase, down which Rita Hayworth enters and sings "Come Tell Me What's Your Answer, Yes or No" to the men who walk and pose with her. When waltz music begins, she dances with the men, first, two at a time, then individually, before exiting at the top of the stairs. Gower Champion clearly recalled Pan's staging when he choreographed the title number in *Hello, Dolly!* on Broadway.

Pan introduced another of his trompe l'oeil effects in "On the Banks of the Wabash" with Rita singing against a painted background, and walking among dancers posed as part of the painted picture (not unlike the device used in the Sondheim-Lapine musical *Sunday in the Park with George*). The chorus suddenly comes alive performing realistic tasks like walking or riding a bicycle as a kind of prelude to the tap and clog steps of Rita and her partner, inspiring the entire group to break into a square dance, followed by a polka, then a bright gallop to complete the festive number.

Once again relying on period images, Hermes opened the bathing beauty number "Me and My Fella" on a beach stage set with shots of beach umbrellas out from which dancers' legs are extended and couples emerge singing. Rita enters sexily twirling her umbrella before going into a "sand dance." Suddenly, she gets the idea for a train, and she and the men form a line across the stage, moving their arms in locomotion as twirling umbrellas (one at the head of the line, the other at the rear) function as the wheels. The operetta tradition of the nineteenth century inspired Pan to choreograph "My Gal Sal," the final production number, with eight men in top hats and tails and eight women in evening gowns swirling around the stage as an introduction to Rita Hayworth, who enters glamorously and simply sings the song accompanied by the dancing chorus. The elegant simplicity of Pan's staging reveals the soul of Paul Dresser's most famous song.

My Gal Sal completed filming on 27 February 1942, a few days before the *Hollywood Reporter* (3 March 1942) announced: "Ginger Rogers and Fred Astaire may be reunited for the first time since the team was broken up several years ago at RKO in Paramount's *Lady in the Dark*. Miss Rogers will play the title role and negotiations have been started with Astaire. If the deal jells, Rogers and Astaire will present at least one dance routine together." Although speculation was buzzing that Hermes Pan would choreograph the film, he had just signed a new contract with Twentieth Century-Fox, a studio uninterested in lending out its top dance director to a rival studio, and when *Lady in the Dark* began filming later in the year, neither Astaire nor Pan was involved with the production.

On 9 March, Hermes began production on *Strictly Dynamite*, a musical about a boxing champion (Victor Mature) who agrees to star in a Broadway musical and falls in love with a chorus girl (Betty Grable) who happens to be married to his sparring partner (John Payne). Released as *Footlight Serenade*, the film featured songs by Leo Robin and Ralph Rainger, with whom Pan worked on *Moon over Miami* and *Rise and Shine*, and includes the least favorite of Pan's choreographic creations:

There's only one number that stands out in my mind from that time, because I was very unhappy about it. It was a number I did with Betty Grable. It was the worst number that I've done, that Grable's ever done, that anybody has ever done! It was one of those horrible things which is just forced on you because of the song. It was during the war and it was called, "I'll be [sic] Marching to a Love Song," and it was just the most awful number. (Kobal 1983, 191–192)

Evidently Fox agreed with Pan for only the final moments of the number, with the obligatory close-up on Betty Grable, Victor Mature, and John Payne, were included in the final print of the film.

According to studio publicity for *Footlight Serenade*, when filming began, Hermes Pan was not only the dance director off camera but also the Broadway dance director cast in the picture. However, as Pan's choreographic responsibilities left him little time to play a role in addition to partnering Betty Grable in a tap-jitterbug routine, Hermes relinquished the role to George Dobbs. Although studio documents suggested that Pan was unable to learn his lines for the role—a highly suspect excuse since the character had little to say in the film—the fact of the matter was that for nearly a decade he had been waging a fight with film studios to stay off camera. He really did not want to perform in films.

Again with Angie Blue as his assistant and dance-in for Betty Grable, and the help of Geneva Sawyer, with whom he had collaborated on *Blood and Sand* and *Sun Valley Serenade*, Pan created a variety of dance sequences to capitalize on the talents and legs of his star: an energetic audition tap routine for Grable to the tune of "Are You Kiddin'?"; a spectacular jitterbugging tap duet (performed with Pan) to the boogie-woogie accompaniment of "Land on Your Feet";[9] and a "Boxing Number" ("I Heard the Birdies Sing") in which Grable dances with her shadow, not unlike the "Bojangles of Harlem" sequence from *Swing Time*. Unlike the Astaire number, however, the shadow in the "Boxing Number" descends from the screen, challenges Grable to a boxing match in front of the theatre curtain, and wins! It is important to note that in both shadow numbers, Pan proceeds from a perception of reality into fantasy: what is initially believed to be the image of the performer suddenly takes on a life of its own. Pan managed to teach his star her routines with little difficulty. "Betty Grable hated to rehearse and admitted it," Pan explained. "She'd say, 'Oh, just show it to me and I'll do it.'" Unlike working with Fred Astaire, which Pan considered a collaborative experience, working with Betty Grable involved Pan and Angie Blue creating complete routines ahead of time and teaching them to her, much in the same way they might work with a dancing chorus.

The problem number in the film (other than the uninspired military drill in "I'll Be Marching to a Love Song") was a short waltz rehearsal sequence between Grable and Mature during which he lifts her to shoulder height and catches her around the waist as she drops to the floor. At one rehearsal, Mature, not an expert dancer, caught her in an awkward way and Grable ended up with torn abdominal muscles, causing a delay in the filming of all of her musical numbers in the film until her muscles had healed. While he was waiting for Betty to recover, Pan set about cleaning the musical sequences in which the dancing chorus appeared as well as teaching Mature better dance technique and a few flashy tap steps that he would employ briefly in a dialogue sequence. In his studio biography, Hermes Pan recalled having staged "a swell fight between Betty and Jane Wyman" in the picture but it does not appear in the final print.

For *Footlight Serenade* Hermes Pan asked the scenic artists to add powdered Carborundum to their glossy paint to save dancers from falling on the glassy surfaces of movie dance floors. In addition, he ordered several of his chorus girls to gain weight because wartime musicals were restoring the public's interest in buxom chorus girls. By way of explanation, his assistant, Geneva Sawyer, noted that "when the world's at war, the public wants stability wherever it can get it and the chorus line is one thing that should definitely cater to the public." As a result, Sawyer prophesied that the average weight of Hollywood chorus girls would rise to 122 pounds before the war was over, a prediction that was enthusiastically welcomed by dancers who felt that any respite from dieting was a step in the right direction.

After his work *Footlight Serenade* was completed, Hermes Pan moved on to the next Sonja Henie vehicle, *Iceland*, a patriotic musical about an Icelandic girl (Henie) who pretends to be married to an American soldier (John Payne) so that her younger sister can marry the man she loves and, by the final ice-skating spectacle, finds love and marriage with the same soldier. Harry Warren and Mack Gordon provided the tunes played by Sammy Kaye and his orchestra throughout the film. Hermes and his dance assistant, Kenny Williams, received no on-screen credit for their efforts; instead, James Gonzales was alone credited for "Skating Ensembles." The two big ice spectacles in the film are profoundly different from the ballet in Henie's previous film in that there is no interrelation between Sonja and the chorus skaters. Once the chorus has done its routine, typically an establishing shot of the event's motif, it stands in the back or to the side while Henie performs, enjoying complete control over her movement. Although Pan was involved in the planning stages of the ice spectacles, suggesting patterns and shapes to Gonzales, he did not attend rehearsals or approach Sonja Henie while she was on the ice. According to contemporary newspaper reports, the ten minutes of ice show in the film cost $511,000.

Hermes was pleased to work with the skater off the ice, however, in a brief section of social dancing when she and John Payne dance to the tune of "There Will Never Be Another You" and in the one chorus production number, "Lover's Knot," a folklike polka routine reminiscent of "The Kiss Polka" in Henie's previous film. Unlike "The Kiss Polka," which is a partnered dance throughout, "Lover's Knot" invests more time in the separation of the sexes, in the style of a square dance; like the earlier number, however, the choreography relies on dynamic arm movements with a final intertwining of arms before the partners kiss. In his continual attempt at creating new dance crazes, Pan designed the basic pattern for the dance in such a way that anyone could perform it, and to help in its execution, Pan worked with lyricist Mack Gordon to ensure that the words of the song would give step-by-step instructions for the dance. Studio publicity announced that "Lover's Knot" had the potential of overtaking the popularity of "The Lambeth Walk" in dance halls across the country but, although the number was well received in the film, the dance never achieved the celebrity of Pan's earlier dances for Astaire and Rogers.

By the middle of June, when the ice routines were being filmed for *Iceland*, Hermes and Vasso were happily moved into their new homes at 4332 Gentry Street in North Hollywood. Hermes had bought a house at that address for his sister and her new family and built himself a bachelor pad on the adjoining lot. "With a living room, bedroom, kitchenette and a bath, it was all that I needed. It also removed the problems of worrying about mortgage payments" (Pan, Columbia, Kramer 1983, 246). On 13 June, Pan rushed over to Vasso's house in a panic at 8:30 a.m. thinking it was 11:30 a.m. and that he was late for work on the set of *Springtime in the Rockies*, scheduled to begin shooting on the fifteenth. Featuring songs by Harry Warren and Mack Gordon, the musical cast Betty Grable as Vicky Lane, a Broadway dancer who reunites with a former partner Victor Prince (Cesar Romero) because of the womanizing of her partner-boyfriend Dan Christy (John Payne). In an attempt to get her to appear in his next Broadway show, Dan follows Vicky and Victor up to Lake Louise where they are appearing with Harry James and his Music Makers. And with the help of his valet (Edward Everett Horton) and secretary (Carmen Miranda), Dan manages to win Vicky back, professionally and romantically as well.

Again assisted by Angie Blue, Pan created three major choreographic events for the film. Set on a Broadway stage, "Run Little Raindrop, Run," was a typical Hermes Pan routine, beginning with dancers performing normal everyday actions—in this case, people getting caught in the rain. Within the simple structure of the dance steps (which appear to be merely heightened walking patterns) a pantomime scene of conflict is played between Grable and Payne—he tugs at her too aggressively during a dance step, she attempts to trip him on another. The number succeeds as both entertainment and plot development and exemplifies dance critics' estimation that Hermes Pan was a genius at turning simple movements into glorious dance (Zona 2008, 15).

"A Poem Set to Music," a ballroom adagio Pan created for Betty Grable and Cesar Romeo to a Latin instrumental played by Harry James and the orchestra, was the focus of much attention from the Fox publicity department. A multitude of press releases advertised the number as "the first time that this dance form has been employed in 'narrative dancing,' that is, a dance which attempts to tell a poetic story, in keeping with the lyrics of the piece." Evidently the publicist neglected to notice the absence of lyrics on the sound track and never witnessed any of the Astaire-Rogers adagios, all of which were intrinsically narrative and not coincidentally cocreated by Hermes Pan. In addition, like many of the Astaire-Rogers duets, "A Poem Set to Music" was about a dress, this time a twenty-five-pound creation with beading made out of lead. According to studio reports, Grable rehearsed the routine in dance clothes and only wore the costume for the camera, although the weight of the dress and complexity of the dance necessitated frequent rest periods and multiple takes (Hulse 1996, 125).

Hermes opened the production number finale, "Pan-American Jubilee," with Betty Grable and John Payne in front of the grand drape on the stage of a theatre, singing and dancing a simple samba with a hesitation step that permitted Pan to incorporate swing-dance motifs into their movement. The curtain opens to reveal dozens of dancers in colorful costumes swirling around in a variety of partnered steps before Carmen Miranda appears, backed by the male dancing chorus. Cesar Romero enters to jitterbug with her and Betty Grable (again with the hesitation step) followed by Charlotte Greenwood, performing her idiosyncratic leg lifts, and Edward Everett Horton, who had danced eight years earlier with Betty Grable in *Gay Divorcee*, finally joining in the dancing. The multitude of chorus dancers separate to allow the principals entrance up the center, and the entire company engages in a series of snappy turns as the colorful number comes to an end.[10]

Although the *New York Times* called the film "just a second-rate song and dance," the *Hollywood Reporter* judged it "an hour-and-a-half of sparkling diversion," and *Variety* reviewed it as "solid entertainment, aiming for hefty grosses all along the line." The yeas outweighed the nays and *Springtime in the Rockies* earned over $2,000,000 at the box office, making it one of the top-grossing films of 1942.

Even before *Springtime in the Rockies* had completed filming on 1 August 1942, Hermes Pan was at work on the dances for *Coney Island*, a turn-of-the-century musical about saloon singer Kate Farley (Betty Grable) who is transformed into a Broadway star by promoter Eddie Johnson (George Montgomery), and who is loved by her manager Joe Rocco (Cesar Romero) whose attempts to stifle her affections for Eddie are unsuccessful. Again assisted by Angie Blue, Pan prepared a series of colorful period numbers for the film under the supervision of Fanchon, the celebrated dance director, costume designer, producer, and authority on fin de siècle period style. Notable among Pan's creations were "By the Sea," a montage of the various kinds of entertainment available at Coney Island; "Beautiful Coney Island," a number establishing the interior of Joe Rocco's Ocean Garden saloon; "Put Your Arms around Me, Honey," a saucy performance routine for Betty Grable and eight high-kicking chorus girls; "In My Harem," an oriental number with Phil Silvers, solo dancer, Carmen D'Antonio, and eight harem girls; and a "Winter" ("Pretty Baby") sequence that begins with chorus dancers playing in the snow and throwing snowballs, then moves into a dance that simulates ice skating, and ends with Betty Grable waltzing with two dancers costumed as the front and back ends of a horse. Lifelike behavior elevated to fantasy through comedy, props, and waltzing—the stock-in-trade of Hermes Pan.

Two other routines were singled out by critics as especially noteworthy: the "Miss Lulu from Louisville" number in which Grable wearing dark makeup and a black wig does a strutting tap routine with six male dancers in similar makeup, and the lavish out-of-this-world-except-in-Hollywood film finale "There's Danger in a Dance," which begins with Grable dancing with a chorus line of men, followed by minstrel-show tap dancers, and women in antebellum gowns swaying to the tune of "Wait 'Til the Sun Shines, Nellie." When no suitable candidate appeared to partner Grable in a climactic schottische tap routine, a waltz, and a Latin-inspired dance, Pan was drafted again.[11] He consented to dance with her only on the condition that he receive no billing for the role. "I'm a dance director and if I blossomed out as an actor suddenly," he explained, "I might have trouble convincing people my real ambition is to be a dance director, not an actor." In any case, Fox payroll records (dated 16 February 1943, a month after *Coney Island* completed filming) indicate that Hermes was paid a flat $750 for dancing with Betty Grable in addition to his guaranteed weekly salary. Hedda Hopper in her syndicated column, "Hollywood," noted that "There's Danger in a Dance" was the most expensive dance sequence ever put on the screen. It cost the studio $187,000, topping "A Pretty Girl Is Like a Melody" from *The Great Ziegfeld* by $38,000 (*Salt Lake Tribune*, 11 January 1943).

Twentieth Century-Fox spent $1,620,000 and three and a half months on *Coney Island* and though the reviewers were quick to argue that "it isn't Coney

Hermes Pan and Betty Grable in *Coney Island* (Courtesy of the Academy of Motion Picture Arts and Sciences).

Island—not even fictitiously" and point out the historical inaccuracies in the film, the musical earned almost $3,500,000 in the United States alone. While Pan was working on *Coney Island*, he also contributed choreography to *Hello Frisco, Hello*, a turn-of-the-century musical about performers in San Francisco's Barbary Coast that was in production at the same time. Alice Faye, John Payne, Jack Oakie, and June Havoc were the singing and dancing stars of the film, and Val Raset was the attributed dance director, also under the supervision of period expert Fanchon. Although it is impossible to verify precisely what dance direction Hermes contributed to the film, it is clear that the roller-skating routine incorporated in the "It's Tulip Time in Holland" number owes its inspiration to Pan's roller-skating choreography for "Let's Call the Whole Thing Off" in *Shall We Dance*.

In December 1942, while Pan was working on films set on opposite coasts, Fox renewed his contract for another year, providing forty weeks' guaranteed employment at $750 per week. This was an amendment to his contract the year before that stipulated a weekly salary of $850 should the option be renewed. Never one to haggle over finances, Hermes was happy to have consistent employment in a job that he considered fun. Recalling his days with Twentieth Century-Fox, Pan sounded a bit like a child in a candy store:

> For me this time at Fox was a nice era. Because they had very glamorous sets, and wonderful color, which we didn't have at RKO. Also the music had become much easier to record and I had much more money and much more freedom at Fox because the directors I worked with . . . weren't what I'd call especially musical—Walter Lang, . . . Irving Cummings[12]— these weren't great ideas men and they left that pretty much up to me so long as it didn't hurt anything.
>
> The numbers I did for Betty were just things I dreamt up—pretty much the way I dreamt up the "Fun House" number. . . . The story just told you what you needed, and you went ahead and thought, "Wouldn't this be fun to do in dance form," or, "Nobody has ever done that, I wonder why?" and so I'd try it. As long as the director and the studio felt what you were doing didn't harm the characterization, you could do pretty much what you wanted to do. And those girls weren't any trouble to work with—not Rita, or Carmen who was a wonderfully funny gal to work with, and Betty was easy. . . . You just had to bear in mind what she couldn't do. (Kobal 183, 190–191)

6

Red Robins, Bob Whites, and Bluebirds

Sweet Rosie O'Grady (also called *Police Gazette Man, Police Gazette Girl,* and *The Girl on the Police Gazette* during production) was the first new project for Hermes Pan in 1943, preproduction rehearsals and conferences beginning as soon as *Coney Island* and *Hello Frisco, Hello* completed filming in January. For this Gay Nineties film about musical comedy star Madge Marlowe (Betty Grable) who falls in love with Sam Magee (Robert Young), the reporter from *The Police Gazette* who reveals her humble beginnings as Rosie O'Grady, Hermes Pan—again assisted by Angie Blue and supervised by Fanchon—created four production numbers inspired by late nineteenth-century styles of dance, period songs, and the highly evocative original score by Harry Warren and Mack Gordon.

In "Waiting at the Church," a performance number in Madge Marlowe's musical, *The Belle of Bond Street*, Pan re-created the atmosphere and production techniques of 1890s musical theatre even down to the use of gas-burning footlights. Betty Grable in a wedding dress, surrounded by chorus dancers in bridesmaid costumes, choirboys, and even the minister, has all that she needs for a wedding except for the groom. Characteristically, Pan transforms the normal physical activities pertaining to the dramatic situation—pacing, chatting, consoling the bride—into choreography that is organic and entertaining, yet idiomatic to the period, particularly in the way the staging emphasizes the comic movement of women's bustles.

For "The Wishing Waltz," a performance number in Marlowe's musical, *Sweet Lady*, Pan created an elegant waltz adagio routine punctuated with spins and turns that climaxed in a series of over-the-leg lifts reminiscent of his work with Astaire and Rogers. Because of the dearth of available male dancers, Hermes Pan was again drafted as Grable's waltzing partner, and again he received an additional $750 for his on-screen appearance. For "Goin' to the County Fair," a novelty number accompanied in part by a harmonica band, Pan reprised the period bustle walk and gave Betty Grable the opportunity to strut and tap in the old-fashioned clog style.

Hermes hired the Robert Mitchell Boy Choir for the "Sweet Rosie O'Grady" number, dressing them as paper boys hawking the *Police Gazette*. Founded in

1934, the boy choir comprised twenty boys between the ages of eight and fourteen and had a repertoire of songs in nine languages. Although Pan's staging made few demands on the boys' abilities, it was considerably more animated than their accustomed concert-style presentation. After the boys complete an angelic hymn-like version of "Sweet Rosie O'Grady," a tabloid photograph of Rosie (Grable) comes to life besieged by eight reporters angling for a story. She slips behind a screen to change into a seductive black translucent robe that easily reveals her million-dollar legs, and then she performs a variation of the cancan with sixteen male dancers to music evocative of Offenbach. Two of the dancers lift her to their shoulders and the rest give her the ends of ribbons and circle around her as in a maypole dance. Unexpectedly, the circle becomes a phalanx and Betty uses the ribbons as reins and the men as horses pausing for a final pose in which she falls into the men's arms. During the filming of this number, Betty pulled a knee tendon, an injury that forced the picture to close down for seven weeks while she recovered.[1]

Sweet Rosie O'Grady completed filming on 4 May 1943. It cost $1,185,000 to make and, in spite of the *New York Times* calling it "pretty as a bowl of wax fruit and just as dull" (21 October 1943), the filmed earned $5,900,000 in worldwide distribution.

After production had wrapped on *Sweet Rosie O'Grady*, Pan went on vacation to New York City, the first trip he had taken since he joined Twentieth Century-Fox. Fred Astaire's wife Phyllis had told Cole Porter about the trip, and Porter wired Pan asking him to call on him when he arrived in the city. Hermes knew Cole socially as well as professionally since they were both frequent visitors at the Astaire home, so he expected little more than a few drinks and a friendly chat. Instead, he discovered that Porter wanted him to choreograph his next Broadway musical, *Mexican Hayride*, a lavish south-of-the-border spectacle with a book by Herbert and Dorothy Fields and a cast of eighty-nine performers led by Bobby Clark, Gypsy Rose Lee's sister June Havoc, and the precocious hoofer Bill Callahan. Rehearsals were to begin in the fall with a Boston premiere scheduled for the end of December. Pan was flattered to have been invited to choreograph *Mexican Hayride* even after he heard the score, which he found uninspired except for the ballad "I Love You." But his commitment to his next assignment at Fox, *Pin Up Girl*, extended through 23 October 1943, and even though Fred Astaire tried to convince him that the projects did not overlap and that he had enough time to prepare for the musical, Hermes decided that he "just didn't feel like going to New York" and passed on his first opportunity to choreograph a Broadway show. In his place, a Danish dancer named Paul Haakon, a specialty dancer in the production, was put in charge of the dance direction—his first choreographic assignment for a Broadway musical.[2] Fred Astaire could not understand Pan's reluctance to take advantage of the opportunity and began to lecture him, like an older brother, on how to manage his career. Hermes appreciated Astaire's concern, but he was not interested in building a career. In "Meeting the Frog Prince," Pan explained that all of his material success in Hollywood had left him with a feeling of spiritual "emptiness" and the belief that "there must be more important contributions to be made in life." As a result, he began to offer up in prayer each of his dances as it went before the cameras in the hope that his material effort might be accepted as his spiritual contribution. "Why I began to have these thoughts, I could not determine. Perhaps it was partly because since my father's death, I had not even had the time or luxury of considering what it was that I wanted *to do*" (Pan, Columbia, Kramer n.d., 247–248).

Hermes was back in Los Angeles for the annual 13 June celebration with his sister and the rest of the family, and on this occasion Sperry Brown, a childhood friend of Pan's in Nashville visited, bringing with him steak and shrimp for broiling out on the patio. Vasso provided an apple pie and salad, and Dot and her daughter Aljeanne brought a pot of home baked beans. Father Jim appeared to congratulate the Pans on another fine year and remained for dinner, after which Hermes passed around photographs while the guests toasted their hosts with champagne and beer. Pan had barely recovered from the champagne the next day when he was called to the studio for preproduction meetings about *Imagine Us* (released as *Pin Up Girl*) with Angie Blue, his assistant, and Fanchon, once again the "supervisor of musical numbers."[3] The plot about Lorry Jones (Betty Grable), a stenographer-USO hostess who pretends to be a Broadway star to impress war hero Tommy Dooley (John Harvey), allowed Grable ample opportunity to sing and dance to the tunes of James V. Monaco and Mack Gordon in unabashed performance situations unobstructed by the loosely threaded story. Because the star of the film was pregnant, her production numbers had to be filmed early in the process rather than at the end as was the usual procedure, after all or most of the dialogue scenes had been shot. Pan had little time to waste and spent the rest of June and all of July choreographing the numbers. The first two numbers to go before the cameras were "The Story of the Very Merry Widow," the intended finale of the film, and "Once Too Often," a New Orleans–flavored performance number at the Club Diplomacy in Washington, D.C.

Pan opens the "Merry Widow" routine with ten couples waltzing to a traditional arrangement of Franz Lehár's "Merry Widow Waltz." Betty Grable appears in a seductive black dress and sings a swing update to the "Merry Widow" story accompanied by a Latin dance routine (a Pan staple at Twentieth Century-Fox) allowing her to pose seductively and show her legs. If working with Ginger Rogers was often about a dress, working with Betty Grable was always about her legs, and Pan managed to show them to their best advantage. Next, Hermes staged "Once Too Often" as an apache blues number introduced by trumpeter Charlie Spivak and his orchestra while a tattooed and surly-looking dancer (Hermes Pan in another film performance, this time working against type) dances with Angie Blue, a rare moment when Pan and Blue are captured together on film. Betty Grable appears on the balcony above them and laments the infidelity of her man before joining him in a "tough-love" tap routine. As in the past, Pan was paid $750 for his on-screen dance.

Betty Grable and Hermes Pan dance "Once Too Often" (Courtesy of the author's collection).

Next to go before the cameras was "This Is It," a simple, swaying performance routine at the Club Chartreuse for Grable and a male quartet (the Stardusters). After the studio brass saw the rushes for the number, it was speedily replaced by "Don't Carry Tales Out of School," a sauntering, hip-swaying tap number, a reprise of which, sung by Grable in a different costume (without the backup chorus and tap routine), was also filmed. Then came the title song "Pin Up Girl," sung by Grable at a USO canteen in Missoula, Missouri, and danced by the Condos Brothers with a tap routine idiosyncratically starting from a seated position, not unlike their tap sequence in "You Started Something," from *Moon over Miami*. Hermes filmed the Condos Brothers' dance in full body shots with no cutaways for dialogue or outside reactions.

Club singer Molly McKay (played by comedienne Martha Raye) was given two lively novelty routines, the first of which, "Red Robins, Bob Whites and Bluebirds," was accompanied by the undisguised patriotism of an extended roller-skating spectacle performed by Gloria Nord (looking a lot like Sonja Henie) and the Skating Vanities in luxuriant red, white, and blue plumed costumes. According to the *Hollywood Reporter* (29 June 1943), Hermes had been scheduled to choreograph the roller-skating routine but since he was taxed with finishing all of Betty Grable's numbers first, the studio brought in Gae Foster, who had a popular chorus line of girls in vaudeville, nightclubs, and film shorts, to collaborate with Pan on the skating sequence. Hermes was so impressed with Foster's work that he insisted she receive on-screen credit for the number even though much of the choreography was actually his.

In the second of Martha Raye's routines, "Yankee Doodle Hayride," Pan gave her a comic tap routine with a pratfall and provided the Condos Brothers with yet another opportunity to impress spectators with their agility. For Hermes Pan, working with the Condos Brothers was like working with Fred Astaire or the Nicholas Brothers. He was present with suggestions whenever they needed them but he allowed them the full extent of their creativity. In Robert Kuperberg's film *Dance Crazy in Hollywood* (1994), Pan explained, "I don't like to choreograph with a heavy hand. I think it's good for people to have fun and enjoy what they're doing. We would have coffee time and make up little games to relax the tension. It shows up on the screen that people enjoy what they're doing. Sometimes the choreography gets heavy, but I always try to keep it light." Even though Pan preferred a relaxed atmosphere when working, he would not permit any dancer to relax in performance: "I don't like what I call 'pussyfoot dancing.' If you do a thing, you do it! We used to have an expression 'right now.' If you step or turn, you really do it without kidding around. You do it RIGHT NOW" (DeMarco 2010, 180).[4]

Pan's original plan to end the film with "The Story of the Very Merry Widow" proved unsatisfactory to the studio for, according to Grable's biographer Tom McGee, her pregnancy was deemed too obvious in the sultry black costume worn in the number and her legs appeared rather heavy (McGee 1995, 117). After much discussion, producer William LeBaron suggested a military drill in which Betty would put a regiment of chorus girls through their paces. Director H. Bruce Humberstone thought it was a good idea but Pan was unconvinced. He reminded the studio brass that the last time Betty Grable donned a military outfit ("I'll Be Marching to a Love Song") the result had been a choreographic disaster. Dismissing Pan's objections, the studio hired Alice Sullivan, a precision dance expert who had staged lavish production numbers at the Roxy Theatre in New York City, to create the drill, which ultimately turned out to be an unfulfilling ending to a musical film because the star was not even permitted to be on-screen with her leading man. Betty Grable noted that "to hide my by-now obvious pregnancy, they wrapped me in a Sam Brown belt—I looked so tough. I was very unhappy with that routine" (McGee 1995, 117). The reviewer for the *New York Times* (11 May 1944) was unhappy as well: "It might also be added that this picture comes to the most abrupt and pointless end you ever saw. Could it be that this is the musical which really scraped the bottom of the barrel?" Pan's doubts had been confirmed.

Throughout the filming of *Pin Up Girl*, Hermes continued to be unsettled with what he felt he was doing with his life. "I really thought very seriously of retiring altogether and going into a completely different and more spiritual sort of world. It had always been in the back of my mind, so now I thought, 'Oh, well, it doesn't matter. I've had my little fling'" (Kobal 1985, 631). He decided to quit the studio, sell his house and automobile, and join a monastic order where he could escape what he considered the "shallow, hurly-burly values" of Hollywood life. He spoke to Father Jim O'Callaghan about his decision and the priest advised him to visit a monastery and stay there for a few days, just to see what it was like. Hermes began contacting various monastic houses throughout the United States, hoping to find an order with the spiritual environment he was looking for, and he finally decided on the Abbey of Our Lady of Gethsemani, a Trappist Monastery located near Bardstown, Kentucky. Founded 21 December 1848, the Abbey of Our Lady was considered the "mother house" of all Trappist monasteries in the United States. Built on two thousand acres of farmland, the monastery also had a secular division called Gethsemani Farms that sold Port Salut cheese, fruitcake, and Bourbon fudge. To join the order there, he would have to undergo a lengthy and rigorous screening process—a psychological evaluation, six months as a postulant, two years as a novice monk, and three years as a junior professed monk—before being allowed to take his final vows. Pan was impressed by so careful and strict a discipline and contacted the abbey, requesting permission to visit the site as a guest.

At the end of August, Pan took a train to Nashville to visit friends before moving on to Bardstown. Hermes spent three days at the monastery guest house learning about the Cistercian Order. His room was furnished with a plain wooden bed, a small wooden desk, and a straight-back wooden chair. The mattress on the bed was little more than two inches thick and lay across wooden slats without a box spring. A large crucifix hung over the bed, symbolizing both the sacrifice required to be a good Catholic monk and the austerity of the lifestyle at the monastery. In "Meeting the Frog Prince," Pan recalled that on his first night, he was awakened by a Brother tapping at his door at 2:30 a.m. inviting him to participate in Matins, the morning prayers. Even though Hermes had expected an early morning call, he was completely unprepared "to have to get up in the middle of the night and behave as if it's morning" (Pan, Columbia, Kramer n.d., 260).

After a weekend without food, conversation, music, and access to a dance floor, he admitted that, no matter how strong his religious fervor, he was completely unsuited for a cloistered monastic life. Hermes slowly began to realize that his life was where it should be—dancing.

On 17 September, as soon as Pan returned to Hollywood, he signed a two-year agreement with Fox, beginning 15 January 1944, with forty weeks of employment at $750 per week guaranteed, and an option to extend for two years at $850 weekly, or for one year at $1,000. With the execution of the contract, Pan was bound to "devote his services exclusively to the producer in directing, conceiving and creating stage effects, ensembles, dances and dancing, and the rehearsals for the same, and . . . otherwise assisting in the production and creation of motion pictures." The agreement also stipulated that rules of conduct must be observed and that the contract may be suspended due to an act of God or terminated on one week's notice if the artist engages in what the studio deems immoral behavior. The standard "morals clause" was hardly an issue for Pan, who was accustomed to guarding the privacy of all of his personal affairs.

Not having an immediate assignment at the studio, Pan took a train up to San Francisco to spend a few quiet days at the Palace Hotel where, by complete coincidence, Paulette Goddard was staying as well. One morning Pan ran into her in the lobby and she invited him to join her and her friend Diego Rivera, the renowned Mexican muralist, for drinks the following afternoon. Without hesitation Hermes accepted the invitation, anxious to meet the artistic genius who was outspoken in his commitment to Marxism, materialism, and atheism, philosophies diametrically opposed to Pan's way of thinking. Hermes did not know quite what to expect at the appointed hour, but the man he found in Goddard's company charmed him immediately, and by the third round of drinks, Hermes had Rivera's card in his hand and an invitation to visit him at his studio in San Angel near Mexico City. Returning to Los Angeles a few days later, Pan was assigned to create a jitterbug sequence for *Home in Indiana*, a nonmusical about harness racing that had begun production early in September with two of Pan's old friends, Walter Brennan and Charlotte Greenwood in the leads, and Jeanne Crain and June Haver in their first featured roles. Just as he began developing the choreography for the scene specified in the script: "Interior ballroom: men in dark jackets and flannel trousers, girls in light swirling dresses giving out with all the modern jitterbug or samba steps," Pan was taken off the picture, replaced by Geneva Sawyer, and reassigned to *When Irish Eyes Are Smiling*, another turn-of-the-century musical scheduled to go into production after the New Year. Since he suddenly had time on his hands, Pan decided to take Diego Rivera up on his invitation and boarded a train from Los Angeles through to Mexico City.

When Hermes arrived, Diego asked him to lunch at the San Angel Inn across the street from the modern, boxlike, two-house complex that constituted Rivera's studio and that of his wife Frida Kahlo. Over a meat-and-potatoes lunch and several bottles of wine, Rivera explained to Pan his plans for experimenting with new techniques for depicting motion on canvas and concluded by asking the choreographer to pose for him. Pan was flabbergasted, never having expected anything like this and, even though he had planned to stay in Mexico for only a few days, he agreed immediately. Rivera told him to come to the studio the next morning wearing something he would feel comfortable in. Fearing the heat of the Mexican midday sun, Hermes chose shorts and a tee shirt and appeared at the appointed hour. "What do you want me to do?" he asked the painter. "I want you to dance," was the reply. "Just a few steps." Pan continued to dance and pose as the artist created charcoal sketches of him, twelve in all. For the painting, Rivera selected the sketch of Pan performing a pirouette, stopping in a three-quarter position—what Hermes referred to as his "Astaire pose."

For the next two weeks, Hermes came to the studio every morning, typically armed with a bottle of tequila to warm him up—although he knew that the midday sun could be excessively hot, he grew to realize that the studio in the early morning was always terribly cold. The routine was always the same: he would pirouette then pose, then pirouette and pose again ad infinitum until the artist instructed him to stop. Between pirouettes, Pan took a swig of tequila to keep warm and as the morning wore on, after several swigs of tequila, the pirouettes got more and more difficult to perform.

The sessions typically ended by lunchtime when the two men crossed the street to the San Angel Inn where they ate, drank wine, and discussed philosophy. Rivera claimed that beauty was his god and that he believed only in what could be perceived through the senses. In his recollection of the conversation in "Meeting the Frog Prince," Pan noted that the concept of certitude—the issue with which he had struggled much of his life—was again in play. Because Rivera claimed to be governed by his senses, Hermes asked him to explain what his god, beauty, tasted like and sounded like. Although he was unable to answer Pan's queries, Rivera seemed impressed by the dancer's philosophical acuity and, for days after the conversation, "he would mention the questions, always pensively. How does it taste? How does it sound? What does it feel like?" (Pan, Columbia, Kramer n.d., 267–268).

Just as Hermes was ready to return to Los Angeles, Rivera's five-by-four-foot portrait of the dancer was completed. Pan was amazed by what he saw. Choosing the blue and white color scheme of the Greek flag to honor Pan's Greek origins, Rivera painted Hermes dressed in tight blue shorts and a turtleneck T-shirt. Around his waist is a cloth belt with a design that suggests an ancient Greek pattern in cream and tan, reflecting the skin tones used in the painting (and also evoking the tie that Hermes typically wore around his waist when rehearsing). Pan's bare feet and expressive hands are slightly exaggerated in size, drawing attention to the fact that his work lies in dance steps and gestures. Hermes holds his right arm straight (though lifted slightly) by his side, while his left arm is bent back allowing his left thumb to touch his waist. His tautly muscular legs are apart, his weight resting on his right foot as if he is ready to modulate to another pose. The confidently masculine athletic figure of the dancer evokes images of Greek statues and vase paintings, most specifically the late archaic *Hermes*, by the Berlin Painter in the Museo Gregoriano Etrusco Vaticano, Vatican City, who is captured in a strikingly similar pose. Also in keeping with the Berlin Painter's *Hermes*, Rivera painted Pan's body in semiprofile and painted the head almost entirely in profile so that the body and head are facing slightly different directions. Pan's eyes appear to be directed to an unseen focal point that dancers use to spot themselves when performing. The concentrated stare also suggests that the dancer may be creating the next movement in a dance combination. The kinetic portrait this creates is emphasized by the billowing blue-and-white background that appears to emanate like an aura from his body. At first glance, the background shapes seem to be simple replications of the main figure but on closer examination, arms and legs in different positions appear, and suddenly the background suggests different movements made by the main figure prior to the pose captured by the painter—as if the painting were a photograph made with a slow aperture—and the viewer sees the entire combination of shapes at one time and in one space.

Pan was so overwhelmed by the work that Rivera offered it to him as a gift, but Pan was only willing to accept it if he could give something to the painter in return. Needing materials for new projects, Diego asked for $50 worth of paint, nothing more. Though the painting Hermes carried with him on the train back to Los Angeles was a great treasure, he cherished even more the friendship of the Mexican artist whom he initially thought he would certainly dislike, if only because of his ideas. Later Pan realized that he had somehow had a profound effect on Rivera's beliefs when the artist, shortly before he died, painted over the words "Dio Non Existi" (God does not exist) on the mural he created for the Reformer Hotel in Mexico City.

Pan found life in Hollywood even more superficial and insignificant after his return from San Angel and buried himself in the preparations for his next film while keeping his eyes on the trade papers to stay up-to-date on the progress of the new Cole Porter musical. On 28 January 1944, *Mexican Hayride* opened at the Winter Garden Theatre in New York City to a huge advance sale ($300,000) and good-to-rave reviews. To acknowledge the occasion, Hermes sent Cole a telegram wishing him and his new musical much success. Two weeks later, on Valentine's Day, Porter wrote to Hermes in care of Twentieth Century-Fox:

> Dear Hermes,
>
> Thank you so much for the opening night wire. I only received it today as it was sent to the Winter Garden. You have not yet been forgiven for not doing the dancing for *Mexican Hayride*. The result of your refusal was that we had to have different dance directors before we finished, and the entire result is that the dances are all completely mediocre.[5]
>
> I shall be in Hollywood toward the end of February and hope to see you.
>
> Again my thanks and all my best wishes,
>
> > Sincerely yours,
> > Cole Porter

Porter's letter confided in Pan few of the real difficulties surrounding the production during the out-of-town previews. The son of the producer, Mike Todd, Jr., recalled:

> During the rehearsals in New York, the individual elements of *Mexican Hayride* seemed wonderful. When the show was put together in Boston

for its opening, nothing meshed. . . . Bobby Clark who had not done a
book musical for many years, seemed inhibited and overcome by the
large and complicated production. . . . The dancing, now confined by the
big sets and a large cast, lost the verve it had had in the bare New York
rehearsal halls.

The point was sadly and emphatically made when the trouble-ridden
first rehearsal in Boston was suspended to give the cast a breather. Todd
called for the first complete run-through of the music by the entire
orchestra assembled on the stage. . . . It was such a large orchestra that
some of the string section spilled over into the adjacent box at the right
of the stage. Before the overture was completed, a cello player seated in
the stage-box fell over backwards. I was sitting in the middle of the
house, near Cole Porter's and Hassard Short's "nephews." As the problems connected with the staging of the show became apparent, the
nephews had begun to snicker at the proceedings. When the cellist keeled
over they started to giggle, and in a stage whisper one of them said,
"What's next?" Todd, who was sitting in the third row, next to Porter and
Short, immediately jumped up and ran to the box. It was soon obvious
that the cellist had suffered a stroke. Sammy Lambert, the stage manager, phoned for an ambulance. That evening we heard that the man had
died on the way to the hospital.[6] (Todd 1983, 111)

Pan received Porter's note while he was at the studio choreographing a fictional-
ized musical biography about the life and loves of composer Ernest R. Ball, *When
Irish Eyes Are Smiling* (released as *Irish Eyes Are Smiling*). Set in an era reminiscent
of *The Toast of New York* when being voluptuous was more highly regarded than
being thin, the film again required Hermes to cast chorus girls of a slightly larger
size than usual. "We don't want slim chicks for this number," producer Damon
Runyon warned, "but young females of fetching avoirdupois, solid substance and
well-rounded curves." As a result, the eight beauties in Pan's burlesque line aver-
aged five feet four inches without heels and weighed in at 120 pounds or more.
"The current movie ideal of feminine pulchritude," Pan explained, "is entirely hay-
wire. It is due to the vagaries of the motion picture camera that makes small girls
look just right and the just-right girls look like giantesses. My research reveals
that in the Gay Nineties, girls who pranced on the stage were not considered eli-
gible unless they weighed in at around 150 pounds. Our burlesque octet in *Irish
Eyes*, although averaging only 120, will look like 135 in the picture. I suspect that
if you look around in real life, most of the full-grown women who attract the male
eye are not too far off that figure."[7]

In addition to the buxom burlesque routine, "Be My Little Baby Bumblebee,"
Pan created three spectacular production numbers for *Irish Eyes Are Smiling*: "Strut
Miss Lizzie," a hot minstrel show number for Mary "Irish" O'Neill (June Haver),
the chorus girl beloved of Ernest Ball (Dick Haymes), and chorus dancers—all in

dark makeup; "My Album of Memories," a medley of Ball's greatest hits presented as living pictures framed by chorus dancing, beginning with an Irish jig and ending with a grand waltz accompanied not surprisingly by "When Irish Eyes Are Smiling," and "Let the Rest of the World Go By"; and "Bessie in a Bustle," an original ragtime routine composed by Mack Gordon and James V. Monaco in period style, featuring June Haver and Kenny Williams.

Pan conceived "Bessie in a Bustle" in three parts: the first depicts the male chorus, dressed in light blue suits, sauntering with a popcorn vendor in the park while a barbershop quartet sings about Bessie's charms. Kenny Williams, dressed in an Irish green suit, appears and changes the idyllic mood of the quartet to that of a hot ragtime, singing and dancing about what Bessie looks like in a bustle. In the second part, June Haver appears as Bessie in a large bustled dress, cut away in front to display her legs. She struts and jigs in front of the male chorus before the chorus women, also wearing large bustled dresses, enter and pair up with the men. In part three, using the magic of film editing, Pan once again transforms reality into fantasy, this time amusing the audience through gender reversal. Dressed in male attire, June Haver enters behind the crowd, which the audience quickly discovers is not comprised of the men and women of the previous scene but of men dressed in the women's costumes. After a comic ballet routine by the men (accompanied by corps de ballet music from *Swan Lake*), Haver and Williams (both cross-dressed) conclude the number with a nimble duet for which Pan borrowed elements of soft-shoe, clog steps, and cakewalk. Studio publicity noted that "Bessie in a Bustle" took nearly a week to film.

June Haver and Chorus performing "Bessie in a Bustle" (Courtesy of the author's collection).

Shortly after *Irish Eyes Are Smiling* finished shooting, Hermes was in negotiations with producers Vincent Morey and Arthur Sulgrave to choreograph a new ballet for Patricia Bowman, the prima ballerina of a fledgling dance company called the Manhattan Ballet in New York City. Pan spent much of the month of May conceptualizing a jazz ballet for Bowman in preparation for rehearsals scheduled to begin on 1 June, only to learn near the end of the month that the Manhattan Ballet season had been postponed indefinitely due to lack of funding. At the same time Hermes was frustrated in his hopes of choreographing for a venue other than film, the *Hollywood Reporter* (23 May 1944) announced that Pan's next dance chore at Fox would be *Where Do We Go from Here?*, the Kurt Weill–Ira Gershwin musical about 4-F Bill Morgan who finds himself, through the machinations of a genie, taking part in key moments of American history. Hermes spent the months of June and July alternating between preproduction meetings at the studio and driving down to Long Beach to go swimming with Father Jim. In the middle of the summer, Pan was taken off the project and assigned to the next Betty Grable film, *Billy Rose's Diamond Horseshoe*. Although *Pin Up Girl* had opened to bad reviews, box office business was so good that it became Twentieth Century-Fox's highest-grossing film of 1944 and the studio wanted to strike while Grable was hot.

Diamond Horseshoe, with a score by Harry Warren and Mack Gordon, told the story of Joe Davis, Jr. (Dick Haymes), a medical student who wants to go into show business over the objections of his father (William Gaxton), a performer at the Diamond Horseshoe engaged to Claire Williams (Beatrice Kay) who also works at the club. Her roommate Bonnie Collins (Betty Grable) is enticed by the promise of a mink coat to pretend to fall in love with Joe and then dump him so that he will leave the nightclub, but Bonnie and Joe fall in love for real, elope, and he returns to medical school. The film's budget of $2,500,000 was an indication that no expense was to be spared in creating a replica of Billy Rose's New York nightclub or in realizing the most lavish production numbers, one of which was planned as a dream sequence with cartoon and live action in an attempt to compete with the synthesis of live action and animation that Disney was exploring in *The Three Caballeros* and Gene Kelly's dancing with Jerry the mouse in *Anchors Aweigh* at M-G-M. Studio publicity announced:

> The cartoon strip, brand-new innovation in *musicomedy* films, will be a feature of Betty Grable's main number in *Billy Rose's Diamond Horseshoe* now in production at Twentieth Century-Fox.
>
> Hermes Pan will stage the unique number which brings the cartoon play into the Grable picture. Betty, as Bonnie Collins, is a singer whose legs bring record attendance to the Diamond Horseshoe, but don't bring in enough salary to buy their owner a mink coat. To the frustrated Bonnie, a mink coat is a symbol of success. She dreams of her ambition, to be swathed in priceless mink, in a lavish setting with music by Mack

Gordon and Harry Warren. The minks in question are lively cartoon figures who cavort through their part while Betty . . . sings and dances.

For financial reasons, the number never materialized,[8] and Hermes Pan ended up
having to create an entirely live-action cartoon in which Bonnie dreams of wearing
a mink coat that will gain her admittance to elite clubs (the Stork Club, Twenty-
One) and a fashionable salon (Elizabeth Arden). She arrives at the exclusive New-
port residence of Mrs. Sylvester Standish (Margaret Dumont) and sees a sign that
reads "Peddlers, solicitors, and all women without mink coats, kindly use the service entrance." She rings the bell, and four footmen in dark makeup appear carrying fanfare trumpets. A red carpet is rolled out for her and she strolls down it
with her fingers outstretched (as if she is waiting for her nails to dry after her trip
to Elizabeth Arden). She is announced to wealthy Mrs. Standish who sings a
greeting to her and introduces her to other bespangled guests, who sport comic
book names such as "Major Catastrophe," "Lady Be Good," "Duke of Duchess,"
"Lady Your-Slip-Is-Showing," and "Sir How-Dare-You." Bonnie receives a call from
a maharajah that coincides with the phone ringing in her bedroom and she
awakens from her dream. For Pan, what began as an experiment in new technology, synchronizing live action with animation, became a disappointing exercise in stylized movement with little actual choreography.

At the beginning of August, three weeks before production was scheduled to
begin for *Diamond Horseshoe*, Hermes Pan and his assistant, Angie Blue, began
dance rehearsals.[9] The first numbers they worked on were "Play Me an Old Fashioned Melody," sung by Beatrice Kay, and "A Nickel's Worth of Jive," performed by
Betty Grable, establishing the parameters of the age-old dispute between old and
new styles of music. To validate their respective points of view, Kay and Grable
engage in a singing contest, first with ballads, next with lullabies. Finally the chorus enters the dispute, with the men preferring the old songs and the women
praising the new, and William Gaxton proclaims both Kay and Grable the winners
of the novelty duel. It was the creation of this number that inspired Hermes Pan
and Angie Blue to stage a bogus argument on the set, and over the next several
months of work, Pan and Blue pretended to feud to entertain themselves and
their coworkers. Since their feuding typically resulted in either or both of them
getting a custard pie in the face, the game kept the atmosphere of the picture light
and jovial.

For the opening number of the film, "Welcome to the Diamond Horseshoe,"
Pan staged a spectacular showgirl routine, complete with close-ups and Ziegfeld-
inspired poses, to suggest the style of lavish entertainment available at the club.
The next number, "Cooking Up a Show," extended the showgirl conceit by intro-
ducing the girls as ingredients ("Sugar," "Paprika," "Tabasco," "French Dressing,"
"Relish," etc.) in a meal that is completed by Betty Grable, presented as a fish sur-
rounded by chorus girls in green makeup to suggest algae or seaweed. This Busby
Berkeley kind of number was followed by one of Pan's signature Latin routines,

"In Acapulco," beginning with six sleeping figures on stage—the audience sees only ponchos and hats. Entering in a quite revealing grass-skirt-like costume, Betty Grable awakens the men beneath the hats, and a parade follows of showgirls wearing extravagant headgear and exotic costumes (again evoking Ziegfeld). Grable and the six male dancers return and eclipse the showgirl routine with a spirited flamenco-styled dance that incorporates swing and tap steps before the chorus falls back to sleep. A humorous element is added to the routine in the shape of a lonely seventh figure on stage who appears to sleep through the entire number.

Pan's interest in combining choreography with special effects inspired the William Gaxton–Beatrice Kay duet, "Carrie Marry Harry," for which Hermes devised a strutting soft-shoe routine embellished with trick photography by Fred Sersen, in charge of special effects. Reminded of the elongated images created by funhouse mirrors in *A Damsel in Distress*, Pan had the idea to present the head and torso of the dancer at the top of the screen and the moving legs at the bottom, creating the illusion of long thin figures. Separating the torso from the legs was a white picket fence that disguises the use of a split-screen device in the number. Like the relationship between Astaire and his shadows in "Bojangles of Harlem," the upper and lower images are synchronous until the very end of the number when they begin to behave independently of one another, informing the audience of the trick.

Pan returned to the Busby Berkeley–like aesthetic of "Cooking Up a Show" in the finale of the movie, with Betty Grable introducing various desserts on the menu depicted as showgirls, among whom we find "French Pastries," "Baked Alaska," "Pistachio Parfait," "Cherries Jubilee," and "Jell-O." Once again Betty is denied a final caress with her leading man, for Dick Haymes is offstage singing one of the film's most memorable ballads, "The More I See You," through a microphone as she and the cast at the Diamond Horseshoe take their final bows.

When Hermes had completed the staging the numbers in *Billy Rose's Diamond Horseshoe*, he moved briefly over to another Fox film in production, the nonmusical thriller *Hangover Square*, to coach Linda Darnell on the dance and movement required for her role as a music hall trollop, Netta Longdon. A close friend of Ann Miller, Linda Darnell was, in Pan's words, "a very loveable, sweet girl," nothing at all like the role she was preparing. In the film, she seduces composer George Harvey Bone (Laird Cregar) into composing songs for her but is strangled by him during one of his "black moods" after he discovers that she is engaged to a theatrical producer. Early in the movie, Netta performs "Have You Seen Joe?," a saucy period ditty composed by Lionel Newman with lyrics by Charles Henderson. Hermes staged the number with animated gestures, seductive walking, and percussive kicks, drawing attention to Darnell's legs. A shameless tease of an onscreen audience of men, the number succeeded without Darnell having to master a complicated dance routine. For Pan, the most difficult assignment was teaching her to kick in rhythm and to gesture on specific beats.

In early October when *Diamond Horseshoe* and *Hangover Square* were filming, Hermes was approached by Mike Todd to choreograph the Sigmund Romberg–Herbert and Dorothy Fields musical *Up in Central Park*, scheduled for a Christmas opening in Boston. Todd had been the producer of *Mexican Hayride* and was not anxious to repeat the choreographic nightmare that Pan's refusal had caused for the previous show. Once again Hermes seriously considered the offer and again refused, explaining that the two films on which he was working were not scheduled to wrap until the middle of November, certainly not time enough for him to prepare for a late December opening. Pan did not tell the producer the real reason for his refusal: he wanted to spend Christmas with his family in the sunshine of California, not alone in a Boston winter.

Hermes believed the winter holidays were intimate family celebrations made every year more special by a new arrival in his sister's household. First he had her daughter Michelene to spoil, then came Mary Anne, and the youngest, Patrick. At Christmastime, Pan doted on Vasso's children as if they were his own. Michelene recalls that "Hermes spent Thanksgiving at our house. He went to Mass by himself at the Church of the Good Shepherd on Christmas Day, then spent the day with us. . . . He was generous at Christmas, gave us bikes and ice skates. He didn't cook on those days, but he would have spontaneous dinner parties for any reason. He often made corned beef and cabbage on St. Patrick's Day."

When he wasn't spending time with family and friends during the holidays, Hermes began to prepare for his next assignment, *State Fair*, the only musical Richard Rodgers and Oscar Hammerstein II wrote directly for the movies. The film told the story of the Frake family and their trip to the Iowa State Fair where Margy Frake (Jeanne Crain) finds romance with a newspaperman (Dana Andrews); her brother Wayne (Dick Haymes) falls for a singer, Emily Edwards (Vivian Blaine), who is married but neglects to tell him; and Papa and Mama (Charles Winninger and Fay Bainter) win blue ribbons at the fair. Pan was impressed with the score and script of the film, especially the way the musical numbers flowed in and out of the dramatic action, and he looked forward to exploring new ways of making choreography appear as natural and organic as everyday activity on a farm in Iowa. Unlike many artists who draw from personal experiences to make their work organic, Pan drew only from his imagination, choosing to keep his personal life quite separate from his work. When Svetlana McLee Grody asked, in a 1980 interview, how Pan's background influenced his work, Hermes replied: "You mean is it a part of my life? No, it's always been a part of my imagination. Nothing ever occurs to me because I feel it is a part of my background. No" (Grody 1996, 9). As a result, Pan felt that he had no real style or trademark in his choreography other than allowing his imagination to process what was in the script. Certain patterns and combinations might be repeated, but he felt that it was imagination that allowed him to feel as comfortable at a state fair in Iowa as he did in a fun house in London.

Immediately after the New Year, production began on *State Fair*, with the opening number "Our State Fair," sung by characters performing simple farm chores, scheduled for filming on 3 January 1945. Sequences that required dance or patterned movement on a larger scale were shot in February and early March so that Pan and his assistant, Dave Robel, had sufficient opportunity for rehearsal. Vivian Blaine's "That's For Me" and Dick Haymes's "It's a Grand Night for Singing" were shot during the last week of February using hundreds of extras and forty dancers. Both numbers make ample use of social dancing in the performance pavilion, but "Grand Night" also opens up to include rides at the fair, allowing it to become a spectacle without violating the probability of movement. Pan enjoyed transforming natural behavior into dance in his previous work; here, natural activity at the fair is the dance, and Pan manages to structure it with interest and variety without making it appear artificial.

Hermes shot the one self-conscious production number in the film, "All I Owe Iowa," on the first three days of March, again with forty dancers, hundreds of extras, and a backup ensemble of harmonicas, an idea Pan borrowed from the "Goin' to the County Fair" number in *Sweet Rosie O'Grady*. Initially sung by Marty (William Marshall), another performer at the fair, Emily takes the number down to the audience where the spectators are encouraged to join in, and once they do, the entire assembly joins forces for a celebratory square dance, interrupted momentarily by a young couple's jitterbugging. The crowd surrounds Marty and Emily in four concentric circles, each moving in opposite directions, and the number ends with a percussive spelling of the state's name (highly reminiscent of the ending to "Oklahoma!" which occurs in the same structural position in the musical *Oklahoma!*). Again the movement is natural and effortless and even the spontaneous manifestation of the circle routine is plausible as a natural extension of the Virginia reel. Although the reviewer for the *New York Times* (31 August 1945) quipped, "Someone could do a great musical about a gay, noisy, pungent State Fair. Rodgers and Hammerstein could do it. But they didn't do it this time," Pan wrote of the experience, "Beautiful score and a very happy picture."

On 3 April, shortly after his work on *State Fair* was completed and Twentieth Century-Fox put him on "Laid-off" status, Pan was in Brooklyn at the Three Hierarchs Greek Orthodox Church on Avenue P for the opening of the first canteen designed particularly for American servicemen of Greek origin. In addition to signing autographs, he danced as part of the entertainment for the troops on a bill that included film actress Katina Paxinou and Broadway soprano Joan Dexter. So often were Hermes Pan and Joan Dexter seen together while he was on the East Coast that gossip columnists began to anticipate a budding romance. In Dorothy Kilgallen's syndicated column dated 12 May 1945, she wrote that "Hermes Pan and Joan Dexter, the coloratura, are a *heartillery* barrage." So circumspect was Pan's behavior that his true romantic inclinations continued to remain hidden from the gossip columnists.

Six days later, Hermes was back in Los Angeles where Fox had just completed negotiations for the loan of Pan and Angie Blue to Paramount Studios for the production of *Blue Skies*, another Irving Berlin musical, for which Hermes would be paid $1,000 per week for a guaranteed twenty weeks. When Pan and Blue began rehearsals at Paramount on 21 May, the stars of the film were Bing Crosby playing the role of Johnny Adams, a crooner and nightclub entrepreneur who can't seem to settle down, and Paul Draper in the role of Jed Potter, the dancer who loves Mary O'Hara (Joan Caulfield) who is actually in love with Johnny. Pan's first order of business was the casting of the chorus and, according to studio publicity, he auditioned the Goldwyn Girls, the Cover Girls from Columbia Studios, and the Diamond Horseshoe girls with whom he had recently worked at Fox. Hermes decided to use a few dancers from each group rather than hire any group as a whole since no single group of beauties had precisely the look he wanted.

After seven weeks of dance rehearsals and recording the vocal tracks for the film, *Blue Skies* went before the cameras on 16 July and by the end of the month, Bing Crosby succeeded in having Paul Draper replaced with Fred Astaire. Draper, an expert dancer, had dared to complain about the limited dancing ability of Miss Caulfield (a particular favorite of Bing Crosby) and because the film was designed as a vehicle for Crosby (Paramount publicity announced that half of the film's running time would be devoted to Crosby's singing), it came as no surprise to Pan when Draper was replaced.[10] He knew that the dancer was right in his estimation of Caulfield's abilities and sought to make whatever she did look polished, comfortable, and professional. Hermes was, of course, delighted when Astaire appeared on the set and pleased to work again with Dave Robel, Astaire's assistant, who would help Hermes develop the spectacular "Puttin' on the Ritz" tap routine.

Called by *Life* magazine "the most stupendous tap dance of all time," "Puttin on the Ritz" took Pan, Astaire, and Robel five weeks to assemble and was filmed after the rest of *Blue Skies* had been completed. Astaire begins the number simply, interweaving his vocal lines with rhythmical tap phrases that mirror the musical interludes. The virtuosic tap dance that follows incorporates slow-motion camera work, a trick device that allows his cane to leap from the floor into his hand, and a split-screen effect that allows Astaire to dance with eight images of himself much in the same way that he danced with his shadows in the "Bojangles of Harlem" number in *Swing Time*.[11] Although Astaire's biographers characteristically attribute the concept and choreography for the routine to Astaire, "Puttin' on the Ritz" was truly a collaborative effort. As Pan noted to Ronald L. Davis, "With Fred Astaire, he was doing most of his own stuff, but then he kept relying more and more on me. . . . I used to do—well, I would say fifty-sixty percent of the choreography" (Davis 1983, n.p.).

The other showcase routine that Pan designed for Astaire was "Heat Wave," the number that Jed (Astaire) is warned against performing when inebriated because of a dangerous climactic dance routine on a shallow bridge unit high above the dance floor. Of course, he drinks too much when Mary (Caulfield) calls off their wedding and dances the number anyway, first with Nita (Olga San Juan) in a sensual Latin dance punctuated by heavy drumbeats, then in a boogie solo accompanied by music Astaire composed for the sequence. In both of these sections, Jed exhibits no obvious symptoms of inebriation—in fact his footwork is as crisp and secure as anyone on the stage, and no one appears concerned about his performance. However, when the music returns to percussive Latin rhythms and Jed and Nita head for the stairs, suddenly a sense of fear is built into the number with reaction shots of characters expressing concern. Twirling chorus dancers, punctuating the percussive rhythms with physical accents, provide a spirited background to the dancing couple and, as expected, the bridge routine proves too dangerous for Jed to negotiate safely and he falls to the floor, forcing Pan's narrative dance to end abruptly.[12]

Unlike the virtuoso routines Hermes created for Fred Astaire, Bing Crosby's numbers were staged simply to maximize the performer's charm and hide his limited dancing ability. Like Betty Grable, Crosby hated to rehearse, so Pan gave him steps that could be easily assimilated and quickly mastered. Contrary to his typical practice of working from the lyrics of a number, Pan assigned very little dance movement to Crosby in "Everybody Step," for example, preferring to create motion and interest through the undulations of the chorus whose movements, gestures, and facial expressions are conducted by Bing as he sings the song. Pan's choreography for "I'll See You in C-U-B-A," sung by Crosby with Olga San Juan, is reminiscent of the strutting "Carrie Marry Harry" routine from *Diamond Horseshoe* without the lively special effects—simple, corny movements that he knew both could sell. The challenge for Hermes in "A Couple of Song and Dance Men" was giving Crosby and Astaire steps that would not accentuate how much poorer a dancer Bing was than Fred. Pan decided that, rather than try to disguise Crosby's limited abilities, he should emphasize them and make a joke of his ineptness. In his assessment of the dance, however, John Mueller found Pan's decision to be ultimately unsatisfying:

> [Crosby] jumps in desperately on some of the steps in the beginning but soon gets stuck in the wrong phrase. Later Astaire tries to help him out—for example, by turning him in a parody of a ballet promenade. Finally, Crosby essentially gives up, faking dance steps while Astaire frolics. There is nothing inherently very funny—or even interesting—in demonstrating that Fred Astaire is a better dancer than Bing Crosby. There is comedy inherent in having one dancer calculatedly out of coordination with the other, but Crosby would have to work harder, and the dance would have to be far more intricately choreographed, for that to happen. As it is, the dance mostly seems a commentary on Crosby's famous laziness about rehearsals. (Mueller 1985, 270–271)

Blue Skies cost around $3,000,000 to produce and easily made a profit, earning more than any other Astaire film, before or after. On 7 September, Twentieth Century-Fox wrote to Paramount, "Please be advised that our plans and schedules necessitate our commencing the use of the services of Hermes Pan not later than October 8, 1945. Will you, therefore, plan to return the artist to us not later than October 7, 1945, so that he may commence his services for us on October 8, 1945."

The project for which Hermes was required was *The Shocking Miss Pilgrim*, a rather unusual Betty Grable vehicle with a score assembled from George Gershwin's trunk by Kay Swift and Ira Gershwin who also provided the lyrics. The film, set in 1874, told the story of Cynthia Pilgrim (Betty Grable), a graduate of Packard's Business College in New York, who secures a job as a type writer with the Pritchard Shipping Company in Boston, becomes a spokeswoman for women's rights, and marries her boss John Pritchard (Dick Haymes). It afforded Betty few opportunities to display her legs or dance and provided, for Hermes Pan and his assistant, Angie Blue, a challenge similar to that of *State Fair*—all of the choreography had to appear to be normal daily activity. Not having the luxury of performance contexts, and faced with a film set in late nineteenth-century Boston, Hermes was forced to use movement even more sparingly than he had in some nonmusical films. Neither Grable nor Pan was happy with the prospect. She objected to the lack of opportunities in the film to do what she was known for— wear revealing costumes, display her legs, and dance. A momentary scene in which she lifts her skirt believing herself alone (but actually witnessed by Dick Haymes) was, in her view, insufficient for her fans. Hermes was not fond of the score, commenting, "Music from the Gershwin trunk should have stayed there except for 'For You, For Me, Forevermore.'"

"One, Two, Three," a waltz song danced by guests at a Back Bay party, offered Pan the only opportunity for an actual dance routine, but it is less a choreographed number than the kind of patterned social dancing that appears in almost all of Pan's movies. Other numbers involved movement and the use of props or costumes, but nothing that could be considered dancing. In "Changing My Tune," for example, Hermes staged Grable exploring her room at the boarding house, posing in the mirror, fixing her hair, walking down the staircase—all natural activities while she is performing the number. Similarly, in "The Back Bay Polka" Pan gave the boarders who are singing to Betty behaviors idiomatic to their characters and, when it was her turn to sing, he staged her dressing to go to the party. Hermes choreographed an ensemble number, "Demon Rum," as a pep rally sung by Prohibitionists and designed "Tour of the Town" as a simple walking duet for Dick Haymes and Betty Grable. Both numbers were filmed but not included in the final cut. A "Welcome Song," sung by Dick Haymes and the store clerks on the occasion of Grable's arrival, was written for the film, but it is not known if Pan rehearsed the number before it was dropped.

The Shocking Miss Pilgrim cost $2,595,000 to make and earned $2,734,000 in domestic ticket sales.[13] Although her fans remained loyal, the attempt at breaking the established formula of a Betty Grable picture was not a success. The *New York Times* (12 February 1947), for example, concluded that "there is no more voltage in *The Shocking Miss Pilgrim* than in a badly used dry cell."

On 11 December, Hermes received notice from Fox that his contract would be renewed for a period of two years, beginning on 15 January 1946, when his salary would be raised from $750 to $850 per week. But after *The Shocking Miss Pilgrim* wrapped in the middle of February 1946, Pan was laid off. Modern sources, such as IMDB, suggest that during the period of his layoff, he worked on *Till the Clouds Roll By*, the Jerome Kern bio-musical at M-G-M that had been in production intermittently since 8 October. Pan's exclusive contract with Fox did permit the studio to lend out his services but did not allow him to act as a free agent during layoff periods since he could be called back to work at any point. Since no contract between Fox and M-G-M exists regarding the use of Pan's services, it is unlikely that his participation, if any, on the Kern film was for pay. Pan, of course, enjoyed the layoffs; gardening, golfing, swimming, or visiting Fred Astaire at his ranch in Escondido where he and Fred would join Clark Gable and David Niven, horseback riding or hunting for quail.

On 27 May, Pan was called back to Twentieth Century-Fox to begin work on a new project, a turn-of-the-century bio-musical film about composer Joseph E. Howard called *Hello, My Baby* (released as *I Wonder Who's Kissing Her Now*). Starring Mark Stevens as the composer and June Haver as Katie McCullem, the girl who loves him, the film presented Pan and his assistant Evelyn Eager with a wealth of choreographic possibilities denied him on his last effort. Because Stevens had undergone a recent spinal operation, his doctor ordered him to begin dance rehearsals early so that he could ease into the choreography gradually rather than be required to learn it in stretches of eight- or ten-hour rehearsals. As a result, the first number Pan put into rehearsal was a minstrel-show-like cakewalk performed to "Good Bye My Lady Love," with Stevens dressed in light-colored top hat and tails like a southern gentleman and June Haver in dark makeup with a straw hat and cane. The cakewalk steps were sufficiently complicated for Haver to sprain her ankle during rehearsal and cause a three-week delay in production. Not to be outdone, Stevens contracted viral pneumonia—his immune system was not up to the challenge of rigorous dance rehearsals—and delayed production yet another week.

Pan had an especial fondness for June Haver and was profoundly influential in her life, personally and professionally. Like Angie Blue, she was a core member of Pan's philosophical luncheon discussion group on the Fox studio back lot and, like Blue, she entered a convent for a short time (in 1953). During dance rehearsals for *Hello, My Baby*, Pan and Haver were often seen together dining and dancing in Hollywood, giving rise to the typical gossip of a romantic attachment. Like Rita Hayworth, June Haver found Hermes a good listener and a perfect gentleman and theirs was a magical working relationship inspiring Pan to craft dances for her that display much of Haver's best work on-screen.[14]

In *I Wonder Who's Kissing Her Now* Pan created two extravagant production numbers for June Haver as Katie McCullem. In the first, a dream ballet during the production of Joe Howard's stage musical *The Girl in the Moon*, the star Fritzi

Barrington (Lenore Aubert) sings "What's the Use of Dreaming" while, watching in the wings, Katie daydreams of taking her place in the number. Pan begins the dream sequence with a ballet-inspired solo for Katie when suddenly a chorus of men appear, offering her expensive gifts. The music changes to "The Glow Worm" and a tap routine follows, with Katie going from man to man in an attempt to find a partner. She decides on Tommy Vale (Gene Nelson in his film debut), who partners her in an elegant adagio filled with beautifully designed leaps, lifts, and turns before Katie awakens from her daydream and Fritzi takes a bow. The number is plot progressive, demonstrating Katie's ambitions and her ability to achieve them, and anticipates the end of the film where she is the featured performer in a musical. The device (evocative of the dream ballet from *Oklahoma!* with "Dream Laurie" and "Dream Curley" replacing the singing actors in the dance) also enabled Pan to choreograph a production number without being burdened with nondancers (such as Lenore Aubert).

The second of Pan's creations, "I Wonder Who's Kissing Her Now," was divided into three principal events, each portraying Katie as a woman of great desire and coquetry. The first casts her as Madame du Barry (the mistress of French king Louis XV); in the second, she portrays Catherine the Great, Empress of Russia; and in the third, she appears as Lillian Russell, the popular fin de siècle American singing actress. As Madame du Barry, wearing a voluminous hoop skirt with a circumference of nineteen feet, Katie sings a chorus of "I Wonder Who's Kissing Her Now" while moving among eight girls in similar costumes; she dances the minuet with Tommy Vale and exits with him coquettishly, leaving King Louis (Dewey Robinson) alone to "wonder who's kissing her now." Eight men dressed as Cossack guards leap upon the scene to introduce Katie as Catherine the Great, wearing a short black fur dress and Russian fur hat. She threatens to send one of her guardsmen (Gene Nelson) to Siberia for missing a date with her but after singing a chorus of "I Wonder Who's Kissing Her Now" in Russian, she forgives him and the couple performs a Cossack dance in celebration. The third section opens at the St. Louis World's Fair where the chorus is dancing the waltz (by now a Pan trademark), and President Theodore Roosevelt (John Merton) is on hand to meet Katie who appears as Lillian Russell wearing a $8,500 gown of white Chantilly lace embroidered with 1,500,000 pearls and rhinestones. She dances with Roosevelt until Tommy cuts in, and the number concludes as the ensemble sings "I Wonder Who's Kissing Her Now" while Katie and Tommy waltz. Hermes spoke repeatedly of how much he enjoyed working with June Haver and Gene Nelson and predicted that as a team, they would become the successors of Fred Astaire and Ginger Rogers, a prophecy that unfortunately never materialized.

In addition to the large production sequences he designed for June Haver, Hermes created two effective numbers for Martha Stewart, cast as Lulu, a vaudeville star: "Hello! Ma Baby" with its bawdy cancan movements and "Be Sweet to Me Kid" in which Lulu throws candy from a basket and swings out over the audience in a routine similar to the "How'd You Like to Spoon with Me" number in *Till the Clouds Roll By*.[15] In an attempt to train Martha and the rest of the chorus to have good posture, Hermes and the girls invented a game: whoever is discovered slouching has to pay the person who saw them a nickel. As a result, everyone on the set of the film became on the lookout for bad posture. Martha complained that "Hermes Pan is making lots of money off us, but he isn't playing fair. He sneaks around peeking in our dressing room windows so he can catch us slumping off guard" (*Daily News*, 15 October 1946).

In a midproduction interview, Hermes noted, "The trouble with a job like this is that you've always got to be topping yourself, and there's nothing tougher than that. I never take my job home with me at night, though. When I get finished at the studio I forget about it until the next day. If I got thinking about it at nights, I'd probably go crazy" (*Doylestown Daily Intelligencer*, 6 August 1946). In spite of lackluster reviews, *I Wonder Who's Kissing Her Now* earned over $3,000,000 at the box office and was one of the top Hollywood moneymakers for 1947.

Studio records show that on 22 October, Pan was assigned to *Captain from Castile*, a Tyrone Power epic about Hernán Cortés and the conquest of Mexico, for which Hermes was responsible for teaching Power and his costar, Jean Peters, the *zarabanda*, a licentious Spanish folk dance. In the film, the dance occurs the evening after a servant girl named Catana Perez (Jean Peters) secures what she believes is a magic ring from a charlatan (Alan Mowbray) to make the aristocratic Pedro de Vargas (Tyrone Power) fall in love with her. Following a violently passionate dance around a campfire, Pedro proclaims his love and insists that they marry immediately. For two hours a day for a solid month, the performers worked with Hermes Pan and his assistant Antonia Morales on the dance sequence. In studio publicity, Jean Peters revealed that dancing with Tyrone Power was her most difficult scene. "He is a marvelous dancer, extremely graceful, but I never learned to dance a bit in Ohio. Even after rehearsing the dance for a month I was worried for fear I would make mistakes." Pan found her quite clumsy as a dancer and decided to shoot the sequence from the waist up so Peters's expressive looks and hand gestures would not be upstaged by her awkward footwork.

Pan began the sensually seductive dance with rhythmic poses and sinewy hand gestures that established the unstated passion between Catana and Pedro. The staccato, stop-time poses of the opening give way to more fluid motion as Catana leads her partner in a chase around the campfire circle. Pedro catches her and draws her to him, winding their arms together into an embrace (a favorite Pan device) as the percussive intensity of the music forces them to erupt into flamenco poses climaxing with spins that drive the couple to the ground and into a final passionate kiss. Pan's staging of the *zarabanda* gave credence to Juan de Mariana's 1609 condemnation of the form: "A dance and song, so lascivious in its words, so ugly in its movements, that it is enough to inflame even very honest people."

At the end of January 1947, Hermes and Antonia Morales joined Tyrone Power and Jean Peters in Acapulco for the final rehearsals and filming of the number. During the second week of filming, Lana Turner, who was having an affair with Power at the time, appeared in Acapulco, creating quite a stir. Hermes and his assistant were highly amused by the idiosyncrasies of the stars whose use of baby talk when addressing one another publicly afforded an ironic counterpoint to their superstar mystique.

Hermes had been friends with Lana Turner for many years, ever since he turned her down at a dance audition, and suggested that she find another means of work. In Acapulco, dancing again with her at a birthday party thrown for her by Tyrone Power, Hermes realized that Lana was a much better dancer than he had imagined. In "The Mortal Goddesses" he recalled that when he and Lana went back to their seats, they found a lovely young woman—Linda Christian—in Lana's chair, ostensibly flirting with Tyrone Power. Seeing Turner approach, the young lady remarked demurely, "Oh, excuse me, I've taken your place," and got up and walked away. Not long after, Lana left to go to the ladies' room and Tyrone took the opportunity to join Linda on the dance floor, a move that did not escape Turner's notice when she returned to the table. To prevent what he feared might be a scene reminiscent of one of her lurid film melodramas, Hermes asked Lana to dance again, and dance they did throughout the night, stopping intermittently to drink tequila.

As the night passed and the couple became more affected by the alcohol, their dancing grew more complex to include the over-the-leg lift Pan had created for "The Yam" number in *Carefree*. "I'd put my foot up on the table and throw Lana over my leg," Hermes recalled. "She loved it and we did it again and again, although out antics were getting so much attention it was almost embarrassing." After that night, Pan saw neither Lana Turner nor Linda Christian in Acapulco again, though in Hollywood he did often run into Linda at parties when she was the guest of Tyrone Power. Sometime later, after learning that the couple had been married at the church of San Francesco a Ripa in Rome, Hermes received a postcard from Switzerland signed, "Love, Linda and Tyrone." Evidently, the couple had fallen in love while Pan and Lana were dancing "The Yam" in Acapulco (Pan, Columbia, Kramer 1983, 41a–44a).

Hermes was again on the layoff lists in April but he welcomed the respite since he was moving into what he considered his "dream house" at 9435 Lloyd Crest Drive in Beverly Hills. Hermes wanted "Panorama," as he called his new home, to be a combination of classical and modern elements with all the beauty and simplicity of a true classical line but, as Pan observed, "with all the doo-dads knocked off." A huge stone terrace with modern iron and chalk-line furniture in red and white, along with a modern adaptation of an old-fashioned hammock, gave Pan the facilities for outdoor living on a grand scale. The location on the second crest of Coldwater Canyon afforded him a view in every direction—"on a clear day," he observed, "you can see Catalina."

For the interior design Hermes requested function without fantasy, modern but not modernistic and, above all, "nothing cute." The motifs and colorings were all designed to evoke classical Greece. Combed off-white plywood was used for the walls of the foyer and living room and, facing the terrace, floor-to-ceiling windows, framed by off-white draperies with a large philodendron pattern borrowed from the plants growing in the stonework and corrugated glass divisions between the living and dining rooms. Wall-to-wall carpet in Pompeian green was complemented by tones of Greek red and amber used in the fabric of the chairs and lampshades. On one wall of the living room hung his Diego Rivera portrait, installed in such a way that it could be turned around and used as a projection screen. On the same wall, wood paneling concealed cabinets for radios, phonographs, and recordings.

A paneled passageway with windows facing the terrace opened into Pan's master bedroom, where the walls were painted a warm brown. The fabric of the headboard and bedspread mirrored the color, appliquéd in a classical Greek design with off-white felt. Across from the bed was a large bleached mahogany desk over which a Fra Angelico portrait of the Madonna was hung. The blue hues of the portrait were repeated in the lampshades throughout the room, accented in terra cotta. Hermes's dressing room had tweed wallpaper on the ceiling and one wall with enormous closets built out of cedar and Washington fir, and it opened into a three-sectioned bathroom with a shower considered especially large for the late 1940s.

The dining room was circular with wood-paneled walls glazed a deep green. A frieze of the nine classic muses adorned the top of the circle while large convex glass overlooking the terrace occupied nearly one-third of the room. The built-in dining chairs were upholstered in a mango color suggested by the blossoms of the tree growing outside the window, and the circular dining table in bleached mahogany was able to drop down to cocktail or coffee-table height for after-dinner socializing.

To the right of the dining room was a medium-size functional kitchen painted maroon and cream, with multicolored plaid wallpaper on the ceiling and black marbleized asphalt on the floor. The kitchen in turn led to the guest room painted in a deep greenish blue and lemon yellow with a large closet and bathroom in blue and cream tile. In the spring of 1948, a renowned Greek scholar was a guest at Panorama and, after a tour of the house, remarked, "You know, Hermes, the ancient Greeks would have loved this." "Yes, sir," Pan replied, "and I know one modern Greek who likes it too!"[16]

Documents in Twentieth Century-Fox's legal files indicate that Pan's layoff period was completed on 22 May 1947, though he is not assigned to another film until 8 September when his name appears in connection with the Lubitsch A-528 picture *Lady in Ermine* (also known as *This Is the Moment* and released as *That Lady in Ermine*), designed by producer-director Ernst Lubitsch as a costume operetta set in southeastern Europe in 1861, with a score by Leo Robin and Frederick Hollander. On the night of the wedding of Angelina (Betty Grable), countess of the small duchy of Bergamo, to Mario (Cesar Romero), a childhood friend, her castle is held siege by militant Hungarians led by Colonel Ladislas Karoly Teglash (Douglas Fairbanks, Jr.). Mario, now the Count of Bergamo by marriage, escapes to gather reinforcements to overcome the Hungarians. An element of fantasy is present throughout the film since Angelina and Ladislas are the exact replicas of their forebears, Countess Francesca and a tyrannical duke who laid siege to the territory three hundred years earlier. Their portraits, as well as those of other members of the family tree, hang on the castle walls and come alive as a kind of Gilbert and Sullivan operetta chorus when the occasion suits them (similarities to *Ruddigore* should not go unnoticed). In typical operetta fashion, Angelina and Ladislas fall in love and marry after she has her one-day nonconsummated union with Mario annulled.

Hermes and his assistant Angie Blue began rehearsals for the musical numbers early in September, about a month before shooting was scheduled to start. Pan's obvious challenge was developing choreography that would not only fit the style and dramatic situation but also suit both Betty Grable and Douglas Fairbanks, Jr., since the picture was an obvious departure for both performers and the stars felt miscast in their roles (Irene Dunne and Charles Boyer had been announced as the stars in 1942 when the studio originally purchased the property upon which the film was based—a German operetta called *Die Frau im Hermelin*). To solve the problem, Hermes created a dream sequence, "There's Something about Midnight," that allowed Grable the opportunity to sing a romantic ballad called "This Is the Moment," waltz, lift her skirts, and flaunt her legs with cancan steps to the music of "Ooh! What I'll Do" sung by an onstage band high up in the gallery. In addition, the number offered Fairbanks the chance to look like a dancer with leaps and lifts and turns, in a nimble routine that focused more on the electricity of romance than the precise execution of complicated dance steps. And, as a nod to the old Astaire-Rogers convention, Pan ends the dancing with the couple retiring to a couch. After a month of dance rehearsals, two hours a day, Fairbanks noted in an interview, "My wife will be very happy that I've achieved a passable waltz" (*Long Beach Press-Telegram*, 14 August 1948). Hermes Pan was even more impressed with Fairbanks's progress as a dancer, noting to friends that the actor displayed an innate sense of grace and rhythm—qualities that are impossible to teach.

Pan staged the first number of the film "What a Crisis," sung by the portraits of Angelina's ancestors when they come to life, with simple natural movement—as a musical scene establishing the operetta convention of the chorus repeating whatever the soloist says. In the only slightly more choreographed number that followed, "Ooh! What I'll Do (to That Wild Hungarian)," sung by Betty Grable and the chorus, Hermes taught the ensemble to prance in rhythm in a kind of serpentine parade through the castle. Even though training the actors to step jauntily around pillars was the most complicated part of the process, the number took a week to rehearse. Unfortunately, Pan's lyrical staging for "It's Always a Beautiful Day," composed by Lubitsch to Leo Robin's lyrics, and a second elaborately choreographed dream sequence were lost when Otto Preminger took over as director on 5 December 1947, the day after Ernst Lubitsch was buried at Forest Lawn. Many felt that after Lubitsch's death on 30 November, the project should have been shelved, but since Twentieth Century-Fox had spent $2,485,000 on the production, studio executives wanted to finish the movie.

According to Hermes Pan, the lighthearted atmosphere created by a director who actually believed the jokes were funny was replaced by a kind of hopelessness. Preminger, brilliant in work that suited his personality, found little to like in the script or cast and, feeling under pressure to complete the work within budget and on schedule, he cut much of the gaiety from the musical as well as two choreographed routines that had already been filmed. On 5 January 1948, the ordeal was over and none of the cast or crew, least of all Hermes Pan, was hesitant to put it behind them. *That Lady in Ermine* opened to surprisingly good reviews with the *New York Times* (25 August 1948) calling it "a bright and beguiling swatch of nonsense cut straight from the rich gold-braided cloth of best-grade *Graustarkian* romance and done in a nimble, playful style." Although *Variety* (10 July 1948) boasted "*That Lady in Ermine* has all the trappings of a box-office winner," the film earned only $1,500,000 in domestic rentals, nearly a million dollars less than it cost to make.

While completing his duties on the film, Hermes received a communication from Twentieth Century-Fox by way of his new agent at MCA Artists, Ltd. Dated 15 December, the memo tersely stated:

> Please be advised that by reason of the failure of the Corporation to exercise the option contained in your contract of employment with us, dated September 17, 1943, to continue the term of your employment under said contract beyond January 14, 1948, the term of your employment thereunder will expire on January 14, 1948, or upon completion of the services which we require you to render for the production in connection with which you may be engaged in rendering your services on January 14, 1948, under the terms and conditions of your aforementioned contract of employment with us, whichever shall be the later date.

After seven years at Fox, Pan was again a free agent.

7

Wonderful Nonsense

Pan was not out of work long. In spring of 1948, he was hired at Metro-Goldwyn-Mayer Studios to choreograph *You Made Me Love You* (released as *The Barkleys of Broadway*), a $2,325,420 blockbuster starring Fred Astaire and Judy Garland as a bickering husband and wife musical comedy team. On 13 June, the night before he was scheduled to begin his contract (guaranteeing him ten weeks of employment at $1,000 weekly), Pan was a dinner guest at the Astaire home where he and Fred could not stop talking about the idea he had for a number in the film called "Shoes with Wings On." Hermes reminded Astaire of Paul Dukas's musical fantasy, "The Sorcerer's Apprentice," based on a story by Goethe (and used to great advantage in Walt Disney's 1940 cartoon feature *Fantasia*) in which an apprentice inadvertently brings to life a broom that runs amok pouring buckets of water into a basin in the sorcerer's laboratory. The boy's attempt to stop the broom ends up creating more brooms and more buckets of water, making the situation worse and worse. Pan suggested that something similar might be possible if Fred played the role of a cobbler who was given a pair of dancing shoes to mend and, after trying them on, suddenly found himself dancing uncontrollably among the shoes in his shop, all with a life of their own. Fred loved the idea, and after dinner he and Hermes drove back to the choreographer's house where they listened to a recording of the music and began working out a structure for the dance. In subsequent discussions with special effects director Irving G. Reis, it was decided that the background for the number would be photographed against black velvet before which the chorus would dance, dressed completely in black except for white shoes. The shots would then be integrated into Astaire's portion of the routine, creating the illusion that he was dancing with shoes that were alive.[1]

For Pan, who was again assisted by Angie Blue and Dave Robel, rehearsals with Astaire were creative, collaborative, and felicitous. The same could not be said for his work with Judy Garland, who proved difficult and uncooperative from the outset. It seemed clear to Hermes that she did not want him on the film. He believed that, because he had never worked with her, she didn't trust him even though she certainly knew of his work at RKO and Twentieth Century-Fox. He also expected that she did not wish to be cast as another Ginger Rogers and feared that having the choreographer for all the Astaire-Rogers films on board would only invite unfavorable comparisons. In addition, Fred Astaire remarked that Garland had originally wanted Chuck Walters, the director of the film, to choreograph since he had previously designed dances for her. In any event, Pan was let go in July once his work on "Shoes with Wings On" was completed and replaced with Robert Alton, a choreographer familiar with Garland's work and idiosyncrasies, and someone she trusted. Garland, in turn, was removed from the film in the middle of July and replaced by Ginger Rogers. With Garland out of the picture, M-G-M attempted to rehire Hermes Pan as choreographer but found that he had committed his services to a project on the East Coast and was no longer available.

Just about the same time Hermes was completing the "Shoes with Wings On" number, producer Mike Todd was in Hollywood convincing songwriters Jimmy McHugh and Harold Adamson to compose the score for *As the Girls Go*, his new Broadway musical about the first woman president and her rambunctious, philandering husband—the "First Gentleman of the Land." Bobby Clark, the producer's favorite comic leading man, was contracted to star, but Todd was reluctant to approach his usual librettists Herbert and Dorothy Fields to write the book since he still owed them royalties from *Up in Central Park*. As a replacement Clark suggested William Roos, who had assisted him with the script for *The Would-Be-Gentleman*, the Molière play Todd had produced in 1946. Since he was virtually bankrupt at the time, the producer welcomed the idea of using friends of friends, a practice that would be both a blessing and a curse.

With the libretto and score under way, Todd approached another friend, Fred Astaire, and asked him "Who's the best choreographer around?" Without missing a beat Astaire replied, "Hermes Pan," and, according to Mike Todd, Jr., Pan was hired that very day (Todd, 1983 176). Obviously, Hermes was not unknown to Mike Todd who had tried to hire him on two previous shows. Fortuitously, Pan had recently been released from *The Barkleys of Broadway* and finally found himself free to accept the producer's offer.

As the summer began, the creative team for *As the Girls Go* was joined by celebrated theatre designer Howard Bay, who was signed to direct as well as design the production. A famous newspaper columnist named Cholly Knickerbocker (a pseudonym for Igor Cassini) had a brother named Oleg who was making a name for himself in the fashion industry and had recently become popular with the paparazzi by marrying Gene Tierney. Never one to turn down free publicity, Todd hired Oleg Cassini to design the costumes for the show. As Mike Todd, Jr., explained: "Years later, Bill Roos pointed out that Todd had hired a book writer who had never done a musical, a musical team and choreographer who had worked almost exclusively in pictures, a scenic designer to direct and a costume designer who had never before done a show. They were all as anxious as Todd to prove themselves, and not likely to be aggressive about money" (Todd 1983, 176).

On the Fourth of July 1948, the production team was invited to the East Coast to spend the holiday with Mike Todd and his new bride, actress Joan Blondell.

Todd chartered two forty-foot cabin cruisers for a thirty-mile excursion up the Hudson River from New York City to Todd's Irvington estate where the boats were anchored. Hermes, Jimmy McHugh, and Harold Adamson went for a swim while a buffet luncheon was being prepared. With Mike Todd acting like a cruise director, everyone sampled Joan's potato salad and the lox, sturgeon, and Nova Scotia salmon that he had imported from Barney Greengrass's delicatessen earlier that day. Later, after an afternoon of sunbathing and sipping martinis and scotch, Hermes and the songwriters discussed the score on the terrace of the mansion, watching the sun set across the Hudson River. Harold Adamson recalled:

> Joan, Michael junior, Hermes Pan, Jimmy and I were having a drink and enjoying the view when we heard Mike roll up. He came running around the corner of the house and said, "Get that whiskey off the table and get out the vodka. I've got Madame Karinska with me."[2] Mike had a $50 tin of caviar with him, and he started spreading it out bountifully to all of us. Suddenly he turned to Michael junior and said, "Do you want to try a little caviar, Michael?" Junior replied, "Gee, Dad, I don't know whether I like caviar or not." So Mike put a speck on a cracker and said, "Here, try half a buck's worth." (Todd 1983, 178)

On 1 August preproduction work began in earnest on *As the Girls Go*. Hermes Pan, Jimmy McHugh, and Harold Adamson, all coming from the West Coast, were given impressive living quarters in Mike Todd's guest house at Irvington. Members of the production team from New York City either commuted or were housed in one of the two spacious apartments above Todd's six-car garage. Work on the show proceeded wherever the production team happened to be: on the terrace, by the river, in the guest house, or in the sparsely furnished dining room of the main house that provided Hermes with a makeshift dance studio. Here, just off the kitchen area, Pan began working out the steps for his first Broadway choreography.

The first song he tackled was the eponymous opening number. Anticipating in melodic contour and harmony Jerry Herman's "There's No Tune like a Show Tune," and "It's Today," Jimmy McHugh's "As the Girls Go" was a bright, syncopated, two-beat quickstep in the Broadway tradition of "Fine and Dandy" and "There's No Business like Show Business." Adamson's lyrics, while not the most profound feminist statement of the era, certainly anticipated Frank Loesser's "Guys and Dolls" two years later:

> A little touch of femininity can set the world aglow
> In art or science or in industry, it's the girls who run the show.
> AS THE GIRLS GO, so goes all creation,
> AS THE GIRLS GO, so goes all the nation.
> Why do men go out and dig ditches, try to climb the ladder of fame,

Going broke or piling up riches, what's behind it? It's a dame.
AS THE GIRLS GO, gentlemen and scholars
Watch the girls blow all their hard earned dollars.
From the rocky coasts of New England
To the mountains out in Cheyenne,
It's the same cry, it's the dame cry, it's that old primeval yen:
AS THE GIRLS GO, so go the men.[3]

Since Hermes seldom wrote anything down, it is impossible to chronicle the step-by-step development of his choreography for the number from inception to opening night. What combinations he discovered, moving to the music in the dining room at Irvington, were certainly embellished when he was joined by his assistant Carmina Cansino when rehearsals began and amplified by a cast of thirty-four dancers—sixteen women, ten men, and eight showgirls. When "As the Girls Go" debuted in New York, the number was set at the Roxy Theatre, the movie palace also known for its spectacular stage shows and Hermes, recalling his earlier career with David Gould and LeRoy Prinz, staged the number as the ultimate extravaganza evoking the most lavish production values of the *Ziegfeld Follies* and Busby Berkeley films.

Work was interrupted by afternoon swims and dinner parties catered by the ever-charming Joan Blondell, and by the commute into Manhattan for auditions. In addition to Bobby Clark, two other leads had already been cast: Irene Rich, a famous radio personality and movie actress, as Madame President, and Bill Callahan, whom Todd had hired in two of his previous musicals, as Skip, the principal male dancer. But with thirty-two roles and a singing and dancing chorus to be cast, the team had its work cut out. For Hermes Pan, female chorus candidates had to adhere to six basic principles:

1. Be yourself and don't imitate anyone else, even if she may be a successful star.
2. Don't get a "cute" complex, unless those pink fluffy ruffles and baby talk fit your personality.
3. Look your best when you go to work, and don't save all that beauty for a date with the boyfriend that night.
4. Learn what poise is, and keep it at all times.
5. Watch your diet.
6. Don't toot your own horn, but don't be afraid to show your talent.

Pan explained:

Often I've wondered why it is that girls who had individuality and personality, submerge these assets by becoming stereotypes in their actions, dress and even personality. Perhaps it is due to the natural fear of being different. And yet, girls should be different, in that they should be individuals, yet at the same time, they should not attempt freakishness. For example, it is a mistake for all girls to wear the same type of rehearsal outfits, regardless of whether they are cute little blondes or tall, sophisticated brunettes. All too often a girl with a blasé and sophisticated personality wears a pink puff outfit with bows in the hair, which more properly might be worn by some girl who happened to be actually diminutive and cute.

Very often girls will pay more attention to their evening dates and what they'll wear then, than they do to appearing their best at the job. Since many of them hope for stardom or for acting parts, I can't figure out how they can hope to put themselves across when they come to work with their hair done up in wave-holders or what-nots, with a bandana slapped over the mess to conceal it. Many of the girls fail to realize that poise is something more than merely looking graceful when the cameras are grinding. They should spend their time developing an unconscious poise, which will be operative at all times, so that they will be graceful when walking, talking or sitting.[4]

By the beginning of September, As the Girls Go was cast and ready to go into rehearsal. Among those hired for the chorus were Abbe Lane, who would later marry band leader Xavier Cugat; Gregg Sherwood, who married the heir of the Dodge fortune; and Jo Sullivan, who would one day become the wife of composer Frank Loesser. When rehearsals officially began on 7 September, no one on the creative team knew that Mike Todd was broke and that by the time the show

Hermes Pan at auditions for As The Girls Go (Courtesy of the author's collection).

opened in Boston he would be personally in debt for over $750,000. Elaborate sets and costumes were under construction; the Winter Garden was leased for the New York premiere;[5] production values and spirits were high. Bobby Clark had initially expressed concern that there was too much book to the show but seemed to relax as vaudeville routines and comic props like the mechanical horse once constructed for President Calvin Coolidge gave him more than enough opportunities to play with and around the text.

Hermes was back on Broadway but, as he explained in a 1983 interview, he felt somewhat out of his element:

> I'd been on the stage so it was not new to me—to choreograph a Broadway show was new. After working so long in pictures, I found it very limiting. And I used to think, "Well, gee, if I could cut and then—" Because I'd become attuned to the film so long and I'd say, "Well, gosh, we've got to go through this whole thing without a stop, without a breath." And it was tough. To get a stage show finished and all the numbers—it's a tough thing. It takes an awfully long while because you've got to really work—because in film you can cut and say, "Alright, we'll come back tomorrow and finish the number" if necessary. In stage [work], when you're on, you've got to finish it. Once it's open, that's it. So it makes you very tense to get everything before opening night—to have everything you want right. (Davis 1983, n.p.)

For five weeks—three weeks less than his usual rehearsal schedule for a film—Pan and his assistant built and rebuilt choreography with the twenty-six dancers and eight showgirls as Howard Bay staged the book scenes and conductor Max Meth trained the singers. In such a stressful environment, Hermes actually flourished. "I like to know that I have unlimited time, but strangely enough, I've done some of my best work under pressure. If I know I have to do a certain thing then I make myself, force myself, to do it. Whereas if I know I have a lot of time, I fool away a lot of time and maybe change things and just play" (Grody 1996, 7). Although working with *Cushman's Garden of Glorious Girls* had taught Pan to think on his feet, the amount and variety of dancing in his Broadway project required him to have the imagination of a comic poet and the precision of a drill sergeant.

The title song featuring a chorus of female dancers and showgirls was followed a brief two scenes later by another production number, "Brighten Up and Be a Little Sunbeam," in which Bobby Clark, getting a haircut by a comic White House barber, is accosted by members of a children's bugle corps. Clark grabs a bugle, blows a series of bubbles through it, and leads the boys and girls in a military tap number. The very next number was a spirited dance duet for Bill Callahan and principal female dancer Kathryn Lee, entitled "Rock, Rock, Rock!," and introducing the motif of modern music and contemporary dancing—perhaps the

"Brighten Up and Be a Little Sunbeam" (Courtesy of the author's collection).

earliest evocation of what became the rock-and-roll idiom on Broadway. Although it does not employ the electronic instruments that characterize the rock numbers of later musicals such as *Bye, Bye, Birdie*, the music to "Rock, Rock, Rock!" imitates the pop music of its era in exactly the same way. Later in the act, "It's More Fun than a Picnic" gave Pan the opportunity to choreograph one of his trademark waltz ensembles, a buoyant routine for the president's daughter (Betty Lou Barto) and her friends on the White House grounds; and in the first act finale, "Holiday in the Country," Hermes anticipated Stephen Sondheim's "A Weekend in the Country" with the staging of the First Family and their entourage preparing for a trip out of town.

Opening the second act was a sultry beguine, "There's No Getting Away from You," set in Washington's Union Station, for which Hermes designed a fluid partner dance featuring Kathryn Lee and Bill Callahan, backed by the chorus dressed as passengers and redcaps. Although the steps were new—Pan rarely repeated his choreography verbatim—the number was highly reminiscent of his work on "The Carioca" and "The "Continental," his earliest collaborations with Fred Astaire. "There's No Getting Away from You" was originally Pan's only production number in the act. Numbers that followed, such as "Father's Day," a sprightly ditty for the First Family; "Lucky in the Rain," a ballad sung by the president's son and his girlfriend; and Bobby Clark's comic patter "It Takes a Woman to Take a Man," required staging rather than actual dance combinations.

When the company arrived in Boston to prepare for the 13 October premiere, only the costumes for the opening and closing numbers were completed, with the clothes for the rest of the show in various stages of development—in some cases, whole scenes were undressed because the money ran out. In his autobiography,

Hermes Pan and Betty Lou Barto rehearsing "It's More Fun than a Picnic" (Courtesy of the author's collection).

In My Own Fashion, Oleg Cassini remarked, "I did something rather creative for one number. I sent an assistant out and bought fleece, the material that is used for sweat suits, and made warm-up outfits dyed in different colors, thus predicting the athletic look of the 1980s (it seemed rather strange in 1948 though, especially in the opulent context of that show)" (Cassini 1987, 201). Even though the material was relatively inexpensive, it did not facilitate the construction of the costumes, and by dress rehearsal the clothes were not ready. According to Cassini, Mike Todd read him the riot act in front of a hundred people, screaming, "Cassini, you son of a bitch, you don't know your work! You're going to ruin me! Where are the costumes?" After the costume designer threatened to quit, Todd apologized, explaining that he didn't want the cast to know that the money had run out so he needed a scapegoat. Todd found money and the costumes were finished, though Cassini regretted that he was never able to complete the designs as originally planned.

As the Girls Go opened in Boston on 13 October to a disastrous reception. Forty minutes too long, the musical was blasted by every critic in attendance with Elliott Norton prophesying that "Miss Rich [Irene Rich who played Madame

President] has as much chance of getting to Broadway with this turkey as she has of going to the White House. Or, for that matter, as much as Harry S. Truman has of remaining in the White House after next Tuesday's election."[6] Bookies in New York gave Thomas E. Dewey twenty-to-one odds over Truman and a thousand-to-one odds against *As the Girls Go* opening in New York. A disconsolate production staff was called into Mike Todd's hotel room and listened as he ordered changes in the show.

The first to go were the romantic leads. Harvey Collins, who had been cast as the president's son, and Beverly Janis, his girlfriend, were replaced by Bill Callahan, moving up from the role of principal male dancer, and Betty Jane Watson, one of the replacements for the character Laurey in the original run of *Oklahoma!* The next thing to go was the book. It had attempted to be a political satire along the lines of the Pulitzer Prize–winning *Of Thee, I Sing* but missed the mark at every turn. All that seemed to remain of the satire was a short scene in which Madame President, confronted by a depleted defense budget and a national emergency, attempts to win a new battleship on a radio quiz program. The rest of the musical became a ribald sex farce set in the White House. Thumbing through his bound copy of the script, Todd frowned and suggested that not enough time was given to the girls in the show. After all, he had hired sixteen beautiful dancers and eight voluptuous showgirls, but the script offered them little opportunity to showcase their extramusical "talents." Pan suggested that there ought to be a beach number in the show to justify putting the girls in bathing suits, and Harold Adamson jumped in with a title, something he said he'd like to play with, "American Cannes." The very next day the song was written and Oleg Cassini began sketching the costumes: brief bikini-like bathing suits worn under beach robes of flimsy diaphanous fabric. Hermes went off to play with beach balls, and the production number was born. An extended comedy scene was added to the second act in which a gaggle of girls try to get the First Gentleman in a compromising position in order to embarrass Madame President, and a song called "I've Got the President's Ear," originally staged for Bobby Clark and several character actors playing hack politicians, was redesigned for Bobby and the eight showgirls. The character actors were released in Boston.

"American Cannes" (Courtesy of the author's collection).

In the second act, "Lucky in the Rain" and "Father's Day" exchanged places in the running order, and an adagio duet was added to the ballad for Kathryn Lee and Bill Callahan in the sweeping ballroom tradition of Astaire and Rogers. The song, a standard foxtrot with a simple, scalelike melody recalled for Hermes the soaring ballads by Irving Berlin, Jerome Kern, and George Gershwin that he had staged in the past. And having two classically trained dancers at his disposal inspired his choreographic imagination in ways that often more resembled the ballets of Agnes de Mille than his work with Fred Astaire. Hermes had long insisted that his dances were only as good as the songs he choreographed and, partial to the sentiment of the song, he viewed "Lucky in the Rain" among his favorite creations:

> I got lucky in the rain, one day when I had nothing to do for an hour,
> I walked around in a shower,
> I had reason to complain, one moment I was sadly in need of a song,
> Next moment you came along.
> Then the heavens smiled at me.
> My heart said, "How lucky can you be?"
> Things like this you can't explain
> I only know that I met the love of my life
> When I got lucky in the rain.[7]

Kathryn Lee and Bill Callahan performing "Lucky in the Rain" (Courtesy of Photofest).

The chaos of restructuring the show during the day and performing it at night was heightened by the fact that no one was coming to see it. The reviews had scared audiences away so neither the performers nor the creative team could tell whether or not the changes were working. William Roos, the author of the heavily edited book observed:

> The situation was frightening—we were doing absolutely no business and Mike needed money to make the changes. While he was restructuring the show, he would take off to New York in the middle of the night or early in the morning. He'd come back in time for the conferences and the rehearsals. He'd be there when we tried out the new material and then go right out looking for more money. . . . He looked worse, but the show started looking a little better. We tried everything. Somebody thought up a joke and Mike wanted to try it, but it involved hiring a dog act. I don't know where he found an act with twelve dogs overnight, but he brought it in, and we had one rehearsal, and it went into the show that night. It turned out not to be a very good joke, and the dogs were out after their first performance. The show seemed better, but we couldn't really tell, playing to so many empty seats. (Todd 1983, 182)

Director Howard Bay placed much of the blame for the Boston disaster on Hermes Pan's lack of experience with stage musicals. He claimed that "Pan, a very nice and talented guy, had never choreographed a number for more than two dancers—and one of those two was always Fred Astaire. At the beginning he was lost, trying to move around a stage full of people." While it is fair to cite Pan's inexperience as a Broadway choreographer, it is not true that he only staged partner dances in film. Sequences like "The Piccolino" from *Top Hat*, or "There's Danger in a Dance" from *Coney Island*, or "Bessie in a Bustle" from *Irish Eyes Are Smiling*, certainly suggest otherwise and as Jerome Delamater argued in his study, *Dance in the Hollywood Musical*, even though Hermes may have preferred working with only two or three dancers, the principal focus of Pan's film work was the creation of large production numbers rather than intimate duets (Delamater 1981, 94). It is interesting to note that in placing blame, Howard Bay failed to note that he had never directed a show anywhere prior to tackling *As the Girls Go* on Broadway. Many years later in a conversation with the author, Bay admitted that during the rehearsal process he felt overwhelmed as well.

Producer Lee Shubert saw the revamped show in Boston and offered his theatre in New Haven for a week to break in the new material. Mike Todd had hoped to open the show at the Winter Garden on Election Day, 2 November, but postponed the New York premiere to the thirteenth to take the opportunity to play in a new city with new critics and unbiased audiences. On 30 October, the production team left Boston for New Haven and set up headquarters in the Taft Hotel. The refurbished material, still untested with audiences, seemed better and, if nothing else, brighter and shorter than the original. And after weeks of choreographing, rechoreographing, cleaning, and recleaning musical numbers, Hermes Pan had whipped his corps of dancers into an enviable precision. The cast may have been exhausted and looking forward to that first day off after the show was finally "frozen," but moving to New Haven, there was more than the excitement of previewing in a new theatre; there was the honest belief that the show might actually be a hit.

On Election Night, six hours before the show was scheduled to open at the Shubert Theatre in New Haven, the sheriff appeared at the stage door and impounded all the costumes and scenery, promising to release them only if and when the producer would pay the bills he held in his hand. Evidently, Mike Todd was so short of cash that he had made only down payments on all the new scenery and costumes, and the bills were now coming due. To make matters worse, the sheriff demanded cash. Todd made a frantic phone call to Bill Richardson, the Boston investment counselor who had sunk much of his clients' money in the show, and Hermes Pan went to the Saint Thomas Moore Catholic Chapel at Yale to pray. Four hours later, Richardson appeared with a suitcase full of money and the show was allowed to open as scheduled. The cast called it a miracle, though no one, including Mike Todd, seemed to understand how it came about.

The first-night audience in New Haven had a wonderful time with the show—the complete antithesis of the Boston experience. After eavesdropping on audience reactions, the authors, designers, director, and choreographer assembled in the back of the auditorium for a postproduction conference. Mike Todd pronounced the show a hit and told everyone to take the rest of the night off. The next day, the unimaginable had happened: Truman had been reelected and critics called *As the Girls Go* a whopping success. The *Evening Register* (3 November 1948) wrote: "*As the Girls Go* is loaded with laughs and boasts a fabulous collection of beautiful show girls. . . . On Broadway it will undoubtedly go—in a big way!" and the *Journal Courier* (3 November 1948) called it "a typical Mike Todd production, big and expensive and a full evening's entertainment."

Few changes were made to the musical during the week in New Haven, and the cast enjoyed the comfort of performing before packed and appreciative houses. Money issues continued to hound the production and Mike Todd's decision to charge $7.20 for every performance when the show moved to the Winter Garden, the highest ticket price to date for a Broadway show, motivated bookies to continue to lay odds against the show's ever opening in New York.

Whether it was because of Mike Todd's fast-talking deals with backers and ticket agencies or Hermes Pan's daily attendance at Mass in the Yale Chapel, *As the Girls Go* opened on 13 November at the Winter Garden to nearly unanimous raves, the finest reviews a Mike Todd production had received in New York. Brooks Atkinson, writing in the *New York Times* (15 November 1948), spoke for the majority when he called it "a bountiful and uproarious musical show . . . , a gay and rowdy Broadway entertainment with a full cornucopia of music-hall pretties."

Even critics who lamented the unsubstantial book and absence of real satire in the show applauded Bobby Clark's "wonderful nonsense" and Hermes Pan's "whirlwind" choreography. As a first-time Broadway choreographer, Pan was justifiably proud of his reviews.

John Chapman in the *Daily News* remarked that Bill Callahan and "the pretty, long-legged Kathryn Lee" did a "very nice dance," and that the "chorus, well trained by Hermes Pan, dances frequently and violently." William Hawkins of the *New York World-Telegram* singled out "Rock, Rock, Rock!" as the "most solid and effective choreography in the show," and John Lardner in the *New York Star* singled out the military tap of "Brighten Up and Be a Little Sunbeam." Praising a return to old-fashion show business, Richard Watts, Jr., in the *New York Post* observed, "When it gets down to its dancing, the new show is perfectly content to give us fast and uninhibited stepping of the pre-de Mille-Robbins school. Although it has, in the graceful and winning person of Kathryn Lee, a dancer who knows her pirouettes with the best of them, it isn't much concerned with the ballet sort of affair. But Miss Lee and Bill Callahan . . . [dance] delightfully and the chorus girls seem beautifully undisturbed by recent trends in the more serious-minded terpsichorean art forms." Finally, Robert Coleman of the *Daily Mirror* noted that "Bill Callahan and Kathryn Lee stopped the show on several occasions with some of the most exciting dancing seen on the stage in several semesters," and concluded his review, "If you're looking for laughs, *As the Girls Go* is the answer to your problem. If you're looking for scads of beautiful girls, you'll find them at the Winter Garden. You will have to be as stolid as the Sphinx and as grouchy as Scrooge not to have the time of your life at Mahatma Todd's irrepressible new gloom chaser."[8]

As the Girls Go enjoyed a run of 420 performances in spite of an ASCAP strike that hampered the dissemination of the music and the illness of its star that interrupted the run. *As the Girls Go* and Hermes Pan had finally *arrived* on Broadway.

8

He Could Make a Wooden Indian Dance

While he was in New York working on *As the Girls Go*, Hermes sold his Greek-inspired dream house in Beverly Hills. Even before he left Hollywood to do the Broadway show, Pan had decided to sell the property when, accordion to David Patrick Columbia, he discovered that Ginger Rogers could look down into his backyard from her home on the Appian Way, so concerned was he about his privacy (Columbia, June 1991, 849). It might have been difficult for Rogers to spy on Hermes since their homes were over a mile apart, but Columbia's suggestion is not without merit since it is a reminder of Pan's discomfort with the Hollywood scene. He would enjoy being part of it from time to time so long as he could escape from it. When he discovered that living on Lloyd Crest offered him no retreat Pan began the search for a new home.

After he returned to Los Angeles in late November 1948, he found a property quietly huddled in the Coldwater Canyon at 9550 Cherokee Lane, and once he moved in during the summer of 1949, he remained there for the rest of his life. Michelene Laski recalled that "the Cherokee Lane house was modern and warm. The fireplace wall was Bouquet Canyon stone, a soft turquoise color. The whole wall toward the pool and the hills was glass. The entry area featured antique mirrors and a wall fountain from Rome. The bar was mirrored and had a leather banquette, a sleek crystal chandelier, and a black table with eight leather chairs. There was a small guest room." Pan's close friend, dancer Frank Radcliffe, built the bar adjacent to the wall on which Hermes hung movie memorabilia, including one of Irving Berlin's original paintings, and dozens of autographed film stills. Phyllis Astaire helped Pan design the house and paint the fireplace. "She said it was a perfectly *dweadful* fireplace and that it had to be painted black. She came up here in Levi's with a paintbrush and painted the inside of the fireplace for me" (Giles 1988, 109). In her autobiography, dancer Ann Miller recalled with fondness the addition of a tree house on the property:

> [Hermes] had it built in a big old oak tree at his place in Coldwater Canyon, and he actually uses it himself as a retreat when he wants to get away from people, or when he wants to get rid of them. You may have

heard about our Hollywood parties, how they go on and on. Not at
Hermes Pan's house. When he decides the party has gone on long enough,
he just takes his pitcher of martinis and goes up in his tree house and
stays there, and eventually his guests discover he's gone. They know
where he is and they know that's their signal to go home, the party's
over.[1] (Miller 1972, 224–225)

With the change in residence came a change in political affiliation. Until the 1950
census, Pan had been listed as a Democrat in California. As of 1950, Pan joined his
friends Fred Astaire, Ginger Rogers, and George Murphy as a member of the Hollywood Republican Committee. Since Pan insisted that he was uninterested in
politics, the change of parties appears to have been prompted more by friendship
than ideology.

Just after Hermes had moved into his new house, he was introduced by the
pastor of the Church of the Good Shepherd to two Iranian women, Shams Pahlbod
and her mother, who happened to be visiting her. Shams's recent conversion to
Catholicism was of particular interest to Pan, who promptly invited the women
over to his home for a pasta dinner. When they arrived, Hermes was running a
little late and, never one to stand on ceremony, he asked if they would mind setting out the silverware and getting the table ready for dinner. The women stared
blankly at him in reply, and he apologized thinking that he had, perhaps, insulted
them by his request. They said that they were not offended in any way but did not
understand what he wanted them to do. Amused by what he thought was simply
a cultural misunderstanding, he demonstrated the way to set a table and everyone
sat down to dinner and chatted amiably about life in California and the movie
business. After the meal, when the women asked if there was anything they could
do to help, Hermes said that they could help him wash and dry the dishes. They
followed him into the kitchen and appeared somewhat disoriented with the
process so Pan proceeded to teach them what to do. Once the dishes were done, he
offered his guests after-dinner drinks and cigarettes (both tobacco and marijuana)
and, appreciative of the way Hermes welcomed them into his home and made
them feel a part of his family, the women wanted to share some of their background with him. Remarking that Pan had such a lovely house, they took out a
photograph of what they referred to as their home in Iran—the Golestan Palace
in Tehran. The pastor had neglected to tell Hermes that the mother was the dowager Queen Mother of Iran, and that Shams was the older sister of the shah.
Hermes turned crimson, completely embarrassed by his behavior toward royalty,
but the princess was so impressed by Pan's lack of affectation that she immediately adopted him into her circle of close friends. Thereafter, every Monday night
Hermes had an open invitation to dine with her and her family.

Settled again in California, it took Pan little time to secure more film work. In
the early spring of 1949, at Fred Astaire's request, Paramount Studios signed him
at $1,000 a week for a guaranteed ten weeks to choreograph Astaire's latest

vehicle, known by a dozen suggested titles (*Little Boy Blue, Close Harmony, Footloose, Dancing Shoes, I'm in a Dancing Mood, Music to My Ears, Heavenly Days, Footloose and Fancy Free, The Feeling Is Mutual, Highly Desirable, Stepping Along, Music to My Feet*) but released as *Let's Dance*. The $2,000,000 musical costarred Betty Hutton (whose name appeared before Fred Astaire's in the screen credits since she was one of Paramount's featured stars) and introduced songs by Frank Loesser, who won the Oscar for Best Song, "Baby It's Cold Outside," at the 1949 Academy Awards. The plot cast Hutton as Kitty McNeil who breaks up a performance partnership (and a once-romantic relationship) with Donald Elwood (Astaire) when she marries an American flyer during the Second World War. Six years later, when Kitty is a widow trying to maintain custody of her son (over the objections of the child's great grandmother) and Donald is an unsuccessful New York investment broker moonlighting as a performer at a nightclub, the two are reunited and together they succeed in securing custody of the child and falling back in love.

According to studio documents, Pan and Astaire began working out the dance routines in March, with Betty Hutton joining the rehearsals on 18 April and production scheduled to begin on 15 May. Because of script issues filming was postponed until 15 July, though Pan and Astaire continued to work on the dances during the month of June. Hermes found Betty Hutton extremely difficult to work with. "Betty Hutton was never the partner for Astaire, but on the set of *Let's Dance* she was on the verge of a nervous breakdown," he told Kevin Lewis shortly before his death. "She was a difficult person and she was a bad dancer. Once, when she had to do a back bend with Fred, she had her palm up. I said, 'Betty, don't keep your palm up, turn it down. It's a better line.' She started to cry, ran off the set and wouldn't come back. Fred said, 'That woman! That woman!'" (Lewis, Winter 1991, 29). In conversation with John Mueller, Hermes added, "[Betty] said, 'Oh, you think I'm clumsy. I know you think I can't dance.' I said, 'I didn't say anything.' It was a very difficult period" (Mueller 1985, 313).

Pan and his three assistants, Virginia Sanctos, Dave Robel, and Peggy Carroll,[2] learned to work around Hutton's insecurities, though he admitted that he was never able to get her to perform anything in a subtle manner, making it difficult to find choreography for duets that would suit the personalities of both stars. Critics argue that he was most successful in capitalizing on their talents with the creation of the comedy routine "Oh Them Dudes" in which Astaire and Hutton impersonate swaggering cowboys getting progressively drunker in a Wild West saloon. Filled with props and sight gags—false moustaches, a bowlegged burlesque of the way cowboys walk, twirling cowboy hats on the tips of their six-shooters, slipping on imaginary horse dung and wiping it off—the number draws upon square dances, Mexican hat dances, vaudeville, children's games, and Hutton's trademark hip swings, and permits both Astaire and Hutton the freedom to be unrestrained in their physical expression. Although the number was successful on film, the props and physical business made it difficult and often dangerous in rehearsal. In *Puttin' on the Ritz*, Peter J. Levinson reports that Hutton broke the second finger of her left hand when a prop gun fell out of Astaire's hand and hit hers (Levinson 2009, 172).

Hermes felt that the opening duet, "Can't Stop Talking," was less successful for, even though the jitterbug-inspired choreography was designed to maintain high energy, Hutton's inveterate over-the-top performance often made it appear that she and Astaire were dancing certainly in different styles if not in different numbers. Pan noted to Tony Thomas in *That's Dancing!*, "It was a case of very bad casting. I don't think Fred should have been subjected to a partner who would limit him" (Thomas 1984a, 100). Hermes managed to draw twenty-five seconds of elegance from Betty Hutton in an adagio with Astaire to the tune of "Why Fight the Feeling," the film's big ballad and a song of which Astaire was especially fond. However, Pan believed that the number worked because Astaire spent most of the routine dancing with an absent partner rather than his leading lady whose aggressive strutting style may have been appropriate in the energetic finale "Tunnel of Love," especially when supported by an ebullient dancing chorus, but hardly acceptable in an extended lyrical adagio routine. In spite of how he felt about Betty Hutton's abilities in private, Hermes was nothing but supportive of the star's efforts in public. It is in part due to Pan's gentle mentoring and patience that in her autobiography Hutton made no mention of any problems during the filming of *Let's Dance*. Ever the diplomat, in his studio biography written nearly twenty years later, Hermes wrote that "Betty Hutton turned out to be one of the best of Fred's partners."

Pan's most inventive choreography for the film appears, not surprisingly, in Astaire's solo "Piano Dance," initially accompanied by a single grand piano played by Tom (Tommy) Chambers, Astaire's real-life accompanist (Hal Borne having moved on to become a band leader). Hermes staged the routine with Astaire dancing on, inside, and around a grand piano, tapping on the strings, using the lid at one point as a slide and then as a percussion instrument. Pan's choreography begins with Astaire performing characteristic ballet movements using the piano as a kind of bar. With a change of music, Astaire begins to dance with the grand piano, exploring all the possible angles and percussive sounds that the two of them can make in tandem. Abruptly he moves to an upright piano and begins playing a boogie (which Astaire composed), after which he uses that piano's hammer device as a percussion instrument and performs a tap dance on the lid slapping the keys with his foot. Satisfied with the result of that experiment, he moves to the grand piano and, accompanied by the tune of "Tiger Rag," he plays a glissando on the piano keys with his foot (imitating the sound of cats walking over a piano keyboard) while physically performing an impersonation of a cat that climaxes in a number of cats jumping out of the piano and running off camera. According to Pan, "It came to me that it would be very funny . . . if suddenly he'd open the piano and cats would fly out. There was a great deal of 'Oh, you can't do that,' and I said, 'Well why can't you? Just get ten cats and put them in the piano and open it and they'll scatter.' . . . There was no difficulty. . . . You can imagine the poor cats, and this noise, inside a piano—whuumpp. . . . He'd open the thing and the cats flew out. Nobody has seen one of them since" (Mueller 1985, 316).

Both Pan and Astaire were happy with the routine as it had developed up to that point, but they were still in search of the "wow" finish that would elevate the number to another level. In her article, "Let's Dance," Barbara Leaming described how the ending was created:

> In search of an exit gimmick for the Piano Dance, Pan began—as he often did—"noodling around," randomly, dreamily playing with everyday objects, in this case a couple of chairs in his house. With his left foot he raised himself onto the seat, and with his right he gently pressed against the back, shifting his weight until the chair began to tip over. After several tries—and one or two stumbles—Pan discovered that if his left foot exerted just enough pressure on the seat, he could control the speed at which the chair tipped over. What looked like a hazardous stunt— walking over the backs of chairs—was actually the safest thing in the world, if you knew how.[3] . . .
>
> Pan suspected that the hardest part of staging the chair exit would be persuading Fred to try it. . . . "I was always very cautious about making suggestions. . . . I used to call it 'sneaking up on him.' " As a rule, Pan would introduce a new idea with a "maybe something like this would be nice," briefly demonstrating what he had in mind. But the chair exit looked dangerous. "I can't do it," Fred declared. "I'll break a leg. I'm not gonna do it." Part of this was play, of course. Astaire and his choreographer enjoyed their roles: Astaire was the worrier, Pan the assurer. "Look, just *try* it," said Pan, getting on the chair to demonstrate. After going over the chair two or three times, Pan extended his hand to Astaire. "Hold my hand and just try it." Whereupon Astaire climbed on the chair and did as he had been told—perfectly. "Awww, that's simple!" Fred exclaimed in the familiar blithe tone of his on-screen character. (Leaming 1990, 1)

Of the "Piano Dance," the critic from the *New York Times* (30 November 1950) gushed, "Mr. Astaire, who is the greatest dancer on the screen, does a solo exhibition of terpsichorean gymnastics in a night club sequence that is just incredible. With effortless grace he glides all over a piano and over the backs of chairs."

Early in September, after Pan had completed filming "Ming Toy," an oriental production number cut from the final edit of *Let's Dance*, he was named dramatic supervisor of an historic religious pageant, *El Camino Real de la Cruz*, commemorating the arrival in California of Fra Junipero Serra and the Franciscan missionaries. Pan's staging of the event, presented at the Los Angeles Memorial Coliseum at 8:00 p.m. on 18 September 1949, began with a procession depicting Franciscans carrying a large white cross, Spanish soldiers, and California natives in their journey from San Gabriel, which Junipero Serra had founded in 1771, to establish the Catholic mission of Los Angeles. Actor Pedro de Cordoba, filmdom's favorite priest, delivered a history of the city and of the early days of California, followed by members of Blessed Sacrament Parish in Hollywood enacting the fourteen living Stations of the Cross on a high platform, illuminated only by footlights, and narrated by Catholic actors Regis Toomey, George Murphy, Stephen McNally, Gene Lockhart, Macdonald Carey, and J. Carrol Naish. The presentation of the Blessed Sacrament in a monstrance given to Father Serra in 1777 by the viceroy of Spain introduced the sixty-voice Roger Wagner Chorale performing "Salve Regina," and "Stabat Mater." And with the singing of the "Star Spangled Banner" and "Holy God" by the crowd of more than thirty thousand people, Pan's three-hour pageant came to an end.[4] Hermes took great pride in his work on the spectacle for, even though it was a single-performance, mostly amateur event, it provided the rare opportunity for his talents to serve his beliefs.

A month later, Hermes was hired at Metro-Goldwyn-Mayer by Louis B. Mayer's nephew, producer Jack Cummings to choreograph *Three Little Words*, a musical biography of songwriters Bert Kalmar (Fred Astaire), Harry Ruby (Red Skelton), and their wives, Jessie Brown (Vera-Ellen), and Eileen Percy (Arlene Dahl).[5] Hermes enjoyed the move to M-G-M: "Money was much freer. And you could practically get anything you wanted. It was a wonderful feeling. And they'd say, 'How much time do you need?' You'd just tell them. Instead of [them] saying, 'No, we have to shoot this next week,' you'd say, 'Oh, this will take three weeks. I'm sorry I can't get it ready until then. So they'd say, 'Okay.' It was wonderful" (Davis 1983, n.p.).

For Astaire and his newest dancing partner, Vera-Ellen Westmeier Rohe, a Major Bowes competition winner from Cincinnati (who sensibly dropped the Westmeier Rohe from her stage name), Pan conceived a variety of entertaining numbers, his favorite of which was a narrative dance called "Mr. and Mrs. Hoofer at Home," a performance number (at Keith's Theatre in Washington, D.C.) displaying the way dancers might communicate to one another in a domestic situation. Vera-Ellen begins the routine in a solo that combines acrobatics, ballet, and tap, waiting for Astaire to arrive. When he appears, he gives her flowers, and the two tap happily until his desire to read the newspaper or talk on the telephone meets with her disapproval, forcing a quarrelsome tap dance. A reconciliation soon follows in a brief adagio duet that leads the couple to the dinner table where various food props and a toaster catapulting toast into the air come into play. After clearing the table, Fred and Vera-Ellen tap on the table itself before the music accelerates, inspiring them to play football with a baby, to circle the stage performing over-the-leg lifts, and finally to break through the wall of the set rather than using the front door as an exit. "I remember one number I liked very much [that] I choreographed for Fred and Vera," Pan told Ronald Davis, "It was 'Two Dancers at Home' . . . and it was one of those zany numbers so it was fun doing it" (Davis 1983, n.p.).

Fred Astaire and Vera-Ellen in "Mr. and Mrs. Hoofer at Home" (Courtesy of the author's collection).

Hermes staged the opening number of the film, "Where Did You Get That Girl?" as a bright vaudeville routine with both Astaire and Vera-Ellen wearing top hats, pants, and tails, and carrying canes. Noting that the number evokes the choreographic idiosyncrasies of a classic vaudeville routine, John Mueller suggests that the number is unusual for Astaire in the use of knee falls and particularly in the way the choreographic and musical phrases are perfectly synchronous, "quite different from Astaire's usual, more musically complex, approach to choreography" (Mueller 1985, 305). By the 1950s, Pan was no longer the silent partner when it came to choreographing Astaire and, rather than preserving the dancer's particular style, Hermes was more interested in maintaining the period integrity of the dance in which movement was determined by the musical phrase, not in counterpoint.

Pan designed two other duets for Astaire and Vera-Ellen: "Nevertheless," a performance piece, with an easy soft-shoe; and "Thinking of You," the by now obligatory romantic adagio, this time dancing over furniture as well as on the floor. More interesting, however, were numbers created for the dancers individually. In an early scene in the film, Astaire sustained a knee injury that resulted in his inability to dance. "Test Solo," a virtuosic tap routine that Mueller calls "unsurpassed by anything in his film career" (Mueller 1985, 307), was Fred's attempt to monitor his recovery. Happy with the results of the tap-and-cane experiment, Astaire attempts to dance the end of the "Where Did You Get That Girl?" routine with the choreographed knee drops. As he falls to the floor, wincing in pain again, he does not get up, and Red Skelton, who had been watching Astaire dance, runs to his side. The sensitive moment that the two of them share is followed immediately by a Parisian-style vaudeville number, "Come On, Papa," in which Vera-Ellen sings seductively to a group of American sailors who proceed to prance and cancan and fling her through the air. With lifts and splits and leaps, the routine is gymnastic and balletic, capitalizing on Vera-Ellen's strengths. Even not juxtaposed with Astaire's poignant routine, "Come On, Papa" is a silly display and demonstrates how clearly Pan differentiates choreography designed for a vaudeville audience and that created for a real-time dramatic situation.[6]

On 10 February 1950, two days after *Three Little Words* completed filming, Hedda Hopper announced that Hermes Pan turned down two jobs—the new James Cagney movie, *The West Point Story*, at Warner Brothers and Astaire's next at M-G-M, *Royal Wedding*—so that he might be free to take a three-month vacation in Europe. Even if he did not choreograph *Royal Wedding*, Pan did originate the idea of Astaire's dancing with a clothes tree as his partner. In a 1980 interview Pan explained: "[Astaire] said, 'How can you dance with a hat rack?' I said, 'Instead of Ginger!' He said, 'Well you can't lift it.' I explained to him, 'You don't have to lift it much. It can be weighted so you can bend it over, it will flip back and you can go around it.' Finally he got sold on the idea and loved it. We had started rehearsing but I had to leave the picture because I had a previous commitment and couldn't finish the number. He went ahead and did it. It turned out great" (Grody 1996, 5). On his first trip abroad, Hermes planned to make his headquarters in Rome and stop at the Royal Palace in Tehran as a guest of Princess Shams. Hermes indicated that even though his European itinerary was all set, "If I'm having fun, I'll stay until it gets dull." Before he was scheduled to leave, however, Pan signed a contract with Twentieth Century-Fox at $1,000 a week to choreograph a number for *I'll Get By*, a musical about song-pluggers during the Second World War for his friend June Haver, costarring William Lundigan, Gloria DeHaven, Dennis Day, and Harry James.

In early March, while Pan was working on *I'll Get By*, he was spotted at a party hosted by Tyrone Power and his wife, Linda, dancing with columnist Hedda Hopper, who noted that Hermes was so nimble and graceful, "he could make a wooden Indian dance." One of Pan's staunchest supporters, Hopper may have been hyperbolic in her assessment but her sentiment echoed that of the entire film community, which firmly believed Hermes could make anyone look good on the dance floor. A week later on 13 March, Pan's contract with Fox was closed when the number he had been developing for June Haver was cut from the film. Instead of heading off to Europe, Pan remained in Hollywood to choreograph a short rumba routine for Lana Turner in *A Life of Her Own* at M-G-M. In the film, Lily Brannel James (Lana Turner), a successful model, finds herself over-whelmed by success and her love for a man (Ray Milland) married to an invalid. When he misses the birthday party she throws for him to be with his wife, Lily drinks too much and dances far too seductively with someone she picks up at the party (Hermes Pan) who leads her playfully in turns and lifts and spins. Lana instructed Hermes to choreograph a dance similar to the one they enjoyed at her birthday party in Acapulco: "I want to do the same thing in this picture that we did that night—you know, drinking and dancing—and I want you to dance with me. Do anything you like so long as it recaptures the mood" (Pan, Columbia, Kramer 1983, 44a). Hermes re-created that night in Acapulco, re-prising every step they improvised—including "The Yam" lifts—and considered his final product "dramatically effective."

As soon as his work was done on *A Life of Her Own*, Hermes Pan and Father Jim O'Callaghan hopped a train headed east in order to catch the *Queen Elizabeth II* sailing for Europe where they would spend the next three months touring through Italy and visiting Rita Hayworth and her new husband Prince Aly Khan in Cannes, and Princess Shams and the shah of Iran in Tehran. A brief undated handwritten note posted to Hedda Hopper gives a snapshot of Pan's itinerary:

Dear Hedda—

Here is the note I promised to write you. Arrived here in Persia several days ago after passing thru Cannes where I visited Rita and Aly at the Chateau de la Horizon. She looks grand and doesn't *seem* to be at all homesick.

Hermes Pan dancing with Lana Turner in *A Life of Her Own* (Courtesy of the author's collection).

The Imperial Palace where I am staying is something out of *Schehe-razade* or *Arabian Nights*. You wouldn't believe it. The Shah is arranging to have some Persian dancers and singers for me to see tomorrow night.

Best Regards,
Hermes

P.S. Will tell you more when I see you in U.S.A.

Hermes and Father Jim returned to New York on the Ile de France, arriving on 26 June 1950. As soon as he was back in Hollywood, Hermes, assisted once again by Angie Blue, was put back to work at Twentieth Century-Fox where he was hired at a flat fee of $2,000 to create a rumba sequence for the Clifton Webb film *For Heaven's Sake*, costarring Joan Bennett and Pan's friends Joan Blondell and Robert Cummings. Playing the role of an angel who is responsible for connecting unborn children with the parents they have chosen, Clifton Webb materializes as a rich westerner and finds himself enjoying the creature comforts of being human. Pan choreographed a nightclub sequence beginning with couples dancing the rumba to the tune of "Temptation" as background to a dialogue scene. The music changes to a foxtrot arrangement of Tchaikovsky's love theme from the *Romeo and Juliet Overture* during which Clifton Webb and Joan Blondell dance in a jerky, comically awkward fashion (the angel obviously doesn't know how to dance), in contrast to Robert Cummings and Joan Bennett who move elegantly on the dance floor. After a brief dialogue scene, Cummings and Bennett leave the club and the music changes to Duke Ellington's "Do Nothing 'Til You Hear From Me." Dancers continue to crowd the floor as the scene changes.

Music for the film was provided by Alfred Newman, a resident musical director at the studio with whom Hermes was well acquainted.[7] "We used to have trouble with Al," Pan observed. "We used to laugh about it because he would never let us have the beat. We liked drums, rhythm, and we used to say, 'Oh, wouldn't it have been great if we'd had some real rock electric music to dance to.' Al would say, 'We can't overshoot,' and he'd turn down the drums. We said, 'What about the drums? What about the beat? When we accent something we don't hear the accent.' And he would say, 'Well, you can't do that—overshoot' " (Davis 1983, n.p.).

After *For Heaven's Sake*,[8] Pan's contract at M-G-M was extended, and he began working on the dances for *Horseless Carriage* (released as *Excuse My Dust*), a turn-of-the-century vehicle for Red Skelton who plays Joe Belden, an inventor whose belief in the future of the "gasmobile" is ridiculed by Cyrus Random, Jr. (Macdonald Carey), who has eyes on Joe's girlfriend Liz (Sally Forrest). Assisted by his jazz-loving friend Ben (Guy Anderson), Joe wins a cross-country race and the girl. With music by Arthur Schwartz and lyrics by Dorothy Fields, *Excuse My Dust* marked the first time Pan received the screen credit "Choreography by Hermes Pan."

Pan devoted most of his time to the "Waterfront Ballet," a dream sequence that materializes out of Macdonald Carey's daydreams of how Sally Forrest might look in the future when people wear fewer clothes. The dance begins as Liz moves seductively among a group of boy dancers lounging on a loading dock. She dances with one, then another, and soon she finds herself surrounded by men whose bodies are pulsating rhythmically with the music. As another boy leaps to his knees in front of her, a variant of the mating ritual, she responds by climbing up a spiral staircase, followed by the dancers who cling to the metal structure. She decides to dance with her pursuer in a sensual, bluesy adagio with steps drawn from the choreographic palette of modern dance. Abruptly the music becomes more animated and accented, and the change is reflected in the couple's movements. When the other boys appear, her partner leaps from one carton to another until he has reached the highest point. She joins him only to fall into the waiting arms of the boys below who lift her back up to their rival. After an interlude of primitive drum rhythms, Liz and her partner slide down the loading ramp and she begins a long exit, flirting with each of the boys as she crosses and coyly stealing a sailor cap from one of them before she exits. Of the routine the *Hollywood Reporter* (23 May 1951) wrote: "Sally Forrest, known briefly as a capable dramatic actress, reveals an entirely new personality in *Excuse My Dust*—several personalities actually—thanks to a wonderful dance number, beautifully conceived by choreographer Hermes Pan. In the transition from demure small town girl to sultry beauty, Miss Forrest is frankly a wow." In a 1983 interview, Pan expressed his excitement about the number:

> I believe that if you develop your characters you have the battle won because you have the attention of the audience. People are not dumb. They are captivated by mystery. What is this couple doing? Why? How do they feel? Why is he so sad? Only the medium is dance. In dance your imagination is free. You can imagine things that you can't if you hear words because then you know what they are saying or thinking. In dance, you're not sure. You can surmise.
>
> There's a wonderful number in *Excuse My Dust*. . . . It's the turn of the century. In [Macdonald Carey's] mind, he sees a girl in a very old-fashioned dress. As she moves, the skirt comes off, the blouse comes off, and she has on a completely different outfit. The music goes from rinky-tink to heavy blues and then she's in a waterfront ballet and then it goes into reverse and the clothes come back and she ends as the demure little girl he was looking at to begin with. All this happens in his mind. (Georgakas 1983, 28–29)

Pan's other responsibilities for the film included two sassy strutting numbers for Monica Lewis in the role of the flirty Daisy Lou Shultzer, "Lorelei Brown" and "That's for Children," both of which involved staging more than actual choreography. "Goin' Steady" was a sit-on-the-hay-wagon-and-sing number, and "Get a Horse," a musical scene for Macdonald Carey and William Demarest ridiculing Red Skelton's "gasmobile," allowed the ensemble to frolic without actually having to dance. In addition, Pan staged a picnic sequence, "One More You," that was cut from the final film.

Excuse My Dust completed filming around Thanksgiving leaving Hermes free for the holidays with Vasso, her husband, and their children, Michelene (10), Mary Anne (8), Christa (5), and Rock (3).[9] Just after the New Year, Hermes was back at M-G-M working with Ann Miller on her numbers for *The Carnival Story* (released as *Texas Carnival*), in which she plays Sunshine, the irrepressible daughter of the local sheriff who falls for Connie Quinell (Red Skelton), a carnival bum who is mistaken for a Texas cattle and oil tycoon. Connie's partner Debbie Talfont (Esther Williams) who falls in love with Slim Shelby (Howard Keel), the tycoon's foreman, is erroneously believed to be the millionaire's sister.

Pan staged Ann Miller's entrance number, "It's Dynamite" (music by Harry Warren, lyrics by Dorothy Fields), as an exuberant seduction accompanied by an on-screen band (and the six-shooters Miller fires for emphasis). The dance makes clever use of a set of vibraphone keys on the floor in front of a real vibes player; as Miller taps notes on the keys, the musician imitates her movements with real pitches on his instrument. The early part of the number in which she taps out notes and rhythms and kicks a bass drum recalls Astaire's drum set routine in *A Damsel in Distress* and his orchestra-conducting dance in *Second Chorus*. The male chorus dancers enter carrying bongos, and as each passes by her, she plays on his drum before dancing to the accompaniment of the handheld percussion. After partnering with two of the dancers, she moves from table to table tapping until she lands on the lid of a grand piano where she continues tapping behind the bemused figure of Red Skelton. Red ducks nervously when she begins shooting off her pistols as the boys leap over him from the back of the piano and, after she discharges a series of rhythmical gunshots in time with the final accents in the music, she poses behind Skelton in a posture of triumph.[10]

Miller's next routine, "Deep in the Heart of Texas," was another one of Pan's three-part inventions. The first part begins with ensemble singing and a serpentine line (a favorite shape in Pan's staging) led by Esther Williams and Howard Keel, who spontaneously becomes the caller of a square dance. In the second part, accompanied by the music and lyrics of "Clap Your Hands" (music by David Rose, the musical director for the film, lyrics by Hermes Pan and Earl K. Brent), the company performs a square dance, moving appropriately to the instructions sung to them. In the last part of the number, accompanied by two male dancers, Miller performs a bravura tap dance during which she leaps over the dancers and taps through a series of fouetté turns.

When he was not engaged with Ann Miller, Hermes was at work on an underwater dream ballet for Esther Williams, who described it as a "rather sexy underwater fantasy sequence, which began with Howard Keel asleep and dreaming of me. He was lying on his bed when, thanks to a process shot, I came swimming into his room through what looked like midair, weaving my body over and around his bed. I was wearing a diaphanous white negligee with a flesh-colored bathing suit underneath" (Williams 2000, 194–195). The sequence took weeks to rehearse and three days to shoot but was ultimately cut from the film.[11]

Texas Carnival finished shooting at the end of March 1951 and premiered in Los Angeles on 6 September to excellent reviews. *Variety* (11 September 1951) reported, "Plenty of laugh diversion, dressed up to treat the eye and ear, is offered in *Texas Carnival*. Returns in the general market should be good," and the *Hollywood Reporter* (11 September 1951) announced that "[Ann Miller's] dynamic dance number, 'It's Dynamite,' is excellently done, staged with great vigor by Hermes Pan." According to studio records, the film earned a profit of nearly $700,000.

Hermes returned to M-G-M early in June to begin dance rehearsals for *Lovely to Look At*, a remake of *Roberta*, scheduled to go into production in late September with Kathryn Grayson (Stephanie), Red Skelton (Al Wodzscyngkic), Howard Keel (Tony Naylor), Ann Miller (Bubbles Cassidy), and Marge (Clarisse) and Gower Champion (Jerry Ralby). In this version of the musical, Broadway producers Tony and Jerry want their partner Al to sell his half of Roberta's (the Parisian dress salon) to finance their new musical. When they discover the salon is virtually bankrupt, they offer to revitalize it with a Broadway-style fashion show and in the process fall in love with Roberta's adopted nieces, Stephanie and Clarisse, sisters who own the other half of the shop. The character of Countess Scharwenka, played by Ginger Rogers in the RKO version, becomes Bubbles Cassidy, still a club singer, but without the Russian pretensions and a dance partner, and the characters of Clarisse and Jerry, played by Marge and Gower Champion, replaced Fred and Ginger as the dancing couple.

For Ann Miller, Hermes and his assistant Walton Walker[12] devised a saucy tap routine, "I'll Be Hard to Handle," performed at the Club Sirocco with a chorus of male dancers wearing dog masks that, without any subtlety, reveal their predatory nature. Rather than being prey to their gymnastic display, Miller controls the pack with her tapping to such a degree that by the end of the routine, the men, completely tamed, submissively allow her to ride their backs. While the number is energetic and exciting—typical of Pan's designs for Ann Miller—the high point in his choreography for the film is achieved in his work with the Champions who, like other established dance teams with whom Pan collaborated, had much to offer by way of suggestions. In their first number, "I Won't Dance," Pan made elegant use of the props available to the dancers in the dress-construction area of a fashion boutique. He refashioned the idea he gave Astaire about dancing with a clothes tree into Gower Champion's dancing with a dress mannequin, so charmingly and gracefully that he manages to sweep Marge out of a chair and into a vigorous and jazzy dance. Their second routine, a romantic adagio danced to the tune of "Smoke Gets in Your Eyes," was staged on a star-studded set with floor and cyclorama painted blue. Highly evocative of the Astaire-Rogers adagios, the number even ends like Pan's work with Astaire, on a low key, with the couple walking hand in hand into the stars. Typically, Pan worked with his director on the filming of musical numbers to ensure that the camera angles and lighting properly sculpted the dancers. In the case of "Smoke Gets in Your Eyes," however, the director of the film, Mervyn LeRoy, gave Pan complete control over the filming.

In response to the static fashion show described in the script dated 10 September 1951, Hermes Pan typed a page of ideas for the routine at the end of the film. These notes represent one of the very rare occasions when Pan's ideas were actually written down.

10-15-51
From: Hermes Pan
Notes on *Lovely to Look At*
After the three men who open (Red, Gower, and Howard), we open up to the first three girls coming through the garden door, stage center.
From there we go into the modern room with hostess gowns.
Then three more girls who lead us into the bathing group, finishing up with Marge and Gower Champion, who lead us into the four girls in black dresses with the paper men.

From that we go into the street group, coming out of entrance on stage right to the park set (wire horse) into the finale.

Not untypically, the fashion show on-screen bears little resemblance to Pan's original outline. Unhappy with Pan's simple conception, producer Jack Cummings hired Vincente Minnelli to reconceive the fashion show and Tony Duquette to design the set. Originally scheduled for a three-day shoot, the fashion show now took three weeks to rehearse and film, and Pan adapted all of his original choreography to suit Minnelli's new concept. "Adrian had designed over forty costumes, at a cost of $100,000," Minnelli explained. "They deserved as extravagant a mounting as we could give them" (Minnelli 1990, 251).

The new fashion show begins with a fanfare of trumpets leading to an introduction spoken by Red Skelton while masked dancers swirl across the stage with bolts of fabric and pylons as the models appear displaying Roberta's gowns. Skelton appears again introducing swimwear, with the change of scenery—the fabric now represents water—comically getting in his way. Leisure wear follows, and Ann Miller appears in a blue creation, dancing subtly as she removes the outer layers of the garment, much to the consternation of Red Skelton, who pushes her offstage before she removes any more of her clothing. He attempts to introduce morning clothes, but the setting abruptly becomes flooded with red light and the music gets hot with a musical motif that anticipates Pan's "Garden of Eden" ballet in *Can-Can*. The dancers now appear as red devils wearing skulls with antlers leading to the appearance of Gower Champion dressed in black but for a red T-shirt, playing a kind of cat burglar accompanied by a jazzy vamp. He encounters Marge wearing a sensuous red dress and sporting a huge bracelet. He steals it, she retrieves it, and the pair performs a seductive adagio to the tune of "Yesterdays," before she disappears into a corridor illuminated with red light. He follows her into the corridor and encounters a series of arms wearing bracelets. He finally succeeds in finding Marge and dances with her to heavily percussive music, spinning while holding her in a perpendicular position, and carrying her off in a triumphant lift. After the Champions complete their dance the music changes to a waltz, and a grandiloquent setting illuminated by candles appears with a moving canopy under which the models continue to display the clothes. Kathryn Grayson enters to sing, "The Touch of Your Hand," followed by Howard Keel, who adds his voice to the number. Suddenly all the principals are on stage dancing to a reprise of "Lovely to Look At," and the fashion show and film come to an end.

While he was completing work on the new fashion show early in November, Hermes spent much of his free time with Rita Hayworth, who two months previously had filed for divorce from Prince Aly Khan. Pan knew that the marriage had not been an entirely happy one (he always felt that the playboy Khan had been a little too free with Rita's money), and he was pleased to reprise his role as her confidant and dance partner. As the holidays drew near, the couple was regularly seen dancing the night away at the Mocambo. As the years went by, Hermes would remain Hayworth's most faithful and trusted friend, and, according to Michelene Laski, the man Rita would call for help when one or another of her husbands abused her.

Later in the spring of 1952, Hermes began to work with Cyd Charisse on her dance in *Mexican Village* (released as *Sombrero*), a nonmusical in which she plays Lola de Torrano, the sister of a superstitious gypsy matador, Gitanillo de Torrano (José Greco) who believes that he will die if his sister ever marries. Hopelessly in love with Rubén (Rick Jason), Lola acquires a voodoo doll and throws it into the ring during one of her brother's bull fights, resulting in his being gored to death by the bull. Tormented by Gitanillo's death, Lola finds solace on a lonely mountaintop where she overcomes her guilt in a dance of purification. In a 1980 interview, Hermes Pan described the creation of the dance:

> I did a number with Cyd Charisse. It was done on a mountaintop. Actually it turned out to be one of my favorite numbers. She was an Aztec Indian woman doing a ritualistic dance. But I had no music for it. It had to end with her dancing on the mountain in the rain. It was sort of dramatic. So, [Saul] Chaplin [assistant to the production] came down to the set and just wrote along as I started to move with Cyd. . . . I told him I had in mind a dance of purification. The character was alone on the mountain and I wanted her to be dancing in a storm, starting very strong and slow. The first note of music in my mind was her throwing a sword into the ground. [Saul] and I worked out the first section of the dance together and then I had a drummer come in to add percussion and rhythm. I had an idea with a sapling tree. I wanted Cyd to be bent in the wind, right down to the ground and then be catapulted into a big grand jeté. Very effective. I had the prop man working a long time to get this crazy tree to be on a spring so it could bend over and be strong enough, without knocking her out. I finally got that and showed the step to [Saul]. He made a wonderful feeling of the wind, her dancing around the tree, pushing it back and over. It was just a pattern of music that came out of the dance. This was fun, this is the type of thing I like to do. (Grody 1996, 3–4)

Following more than a month of dance rehearsals, during which time Hermes and Cyd saw one another socially, *Sombrero* began filming on 16 June, moving to Mexico at the end of the month for ten days of location shooting in Mexico City followed by stops in Cuernavaca, Tetecala, and Tepoztlán before returning to the studio. In his syndicated column, "Behind the Scenes in Hollywood," Harrison Carroll described the filming of Charisse's number:

> I go out to the *Sombrero* set this week to watch Cyd do a wild gypsy dance before an Aztec temple high in the mountains of Mexico. The scene is

lonely and sinister. The ancient temple, perched at the top of many tiers of stairs, stands out in weird relief against scudding storm clouds and dark, majestic peaks. Cyd, a somber figure in a black dress, is standing barefooted in the dirt at the foot of the stairs leading up to the temple. The dance is about to begin.

"Okay," shouts dance director Hermes Pan. "Wind! Lightning!" The blast of air plasters Cyd's skirt around her slender legs. There is a crackling hiss, a momentary glare as the lightning machine illumines the set. Music is in the air now—an insistent, unearthly beat. Cyd is dancing. She whirls madly to the rhythm of the music. Her whipping skirt is seen to be lined with a rich purple.

Suddenly, she careens away from the stairway, makes a series of spins and hurls herself to the dirt at the edge of a small pool. The violence of the lunge throws her purple-lined skirt up over her waist. She is wearing trunks but Pan yells, "Cut! Sorry, we have to do that again. The skirt came up too high." Cyd gets easily to her feet. "How come she didn't get the breath knocked out of her?" I ask. "She took an awful header to the ground." "That ground is padded," volunteered a grip. "There are mattresses under the dirt." (*Lethbridge Herald*, 14 July 1952)

When the film opened in April 1953, the *New York Times* found only a few things to enjoy about it, one of which was Charisse's dance. *Variety* (24 February 1953) was less impressed with the number, calling it "weirdly staged by Hermes Pan with a 'Night on [Bald] Mountain' effect that is slightly ludicrous despite Miss Charisse's terp talents." In *That's Dancing*, Tony Thomas notes that Cyd Charisse found Pan delightful to work with and credits her association with Pan, who was in the process of helping Fred Astaire work through choreographic ideas for *The Band Wagon*, as a reason why she was hired as Astaire's next leading lady (Thomas 1984a, 153). Even though Michael Kidd was the "official" choreographer for *The Band Wagon*, it was not unusual for Astaire to seek Pan's advice or assistance with a routine, and Hermes never refused to help. Cyd Charisse notes that while rehearsing for *Sombrero* in Studio C, Astaire dropped by to watch her work in the mirror. Twenty minutes after he left, the phone rang. It was Arthur Freed inviting her to do *The Band Wagon* (Thomas 1984, 222–224).

From *Sombrero* Hermes moved directly to *The Student Prince*, an assignment he looked forward to since he was anxious to choreograph for Mario Lanza, whose singing voice he highly regarded. He knew Lanza was temperamental and difficult to work with but he felt confident that, given the nature of the story, the beauty of Sigmund Romberg's music, and the artistry of the singer, he could create movement that would be both appropriate to the action and pleasing to the star. As Hermes commented to Constantine in 1945, "Whenever a situation arises that seems impossible, I always say to myself, 'This is like the beginning and that wasn't easy. I must go on.' It always works" (Constantine 1945, 7). What Pan didn't count on was Lanza walking out on the production because of a dispute with director Curtis Bernhardt over his interpretation of "Beloved," a song composed by Nicholas Brodszky and Paul Francis Webster and interpolated into Romberg's score. After a number of heated exchanges between studio and star during the months of July and August, *The Student Prince* was officially taken off production on 4 September 1952 and Hermes was moved to *Dream Wife*, a nonmusical comedy starring Cary Grant as Clemson Reade, an American salesman, who becomes engaged to the khan of Bukistan's daughter, the princess Tarji (Betta St. John), who has been trained since birth to devote her life to pleasing her husband. When she arrives in New York, however, she is educated by Clemson's former fiancée Effie (Deborah Kerr) in the ways of the liberated woman and breaks off the match.

One of Pan's responsibilities in the film was teaching Cary Grant to dance in three different styles: a jazzy kind of jitterbug, a rumba, and a waltz. Through the months of September and October, Hermes patiently trained the actor for an hour or two every day to prepare him for the brief scene in which he dances solo to the music on his phonograph while waiting for his ex-fiancée to arrive at his apartment. Hermes spoke highly of his work with Cary Grant, considering it an entirely enjoyable experience. Pan found that, even though the actor was not a natural dancer, he was a lively and entertaining student.

More challenging was the second part of Pan's assignment, the creation of the Persian dance sequences in the film, of which there were three. Pan's first effort was a brief routine for an ensemble of dancing girls establishing the local color of Bukistan—not unlike the way the "Hawaiian War Chant" established local color in *Song of the Islands*. The second was the dance that Hermes spent most of his time rehearsing: a sensuous solo for the princess designed to entertain Clemson Reade while he is a guest of the khan of Bakistan. Commencing with the use of finger cymbals, Pan's choreography combines Eastern folk elements with modern dance (not an unusual pairing) and, characteristic of his work, uses a table as a locus for movement. The dance is supplicating and commanding, suggestive of the virgin-whore dichotomy that is a central theme of the film. Subtle, sensuous movements are contrasted with rhythmic punctuations from the hips or fingers, and before the dance builds to a climax of celebratory lifted arms and leaps, the dancer invades Clemson's space, shortening the aesthetic distance between her seductive movements and his involuntary response. With her arms flung down to her sides, the princess ends the dance with a triumphant pose and a final beat of the finger cymbal. The dance has worked its magic on Reade for, later in the film, he decides against marrying his American fiancée in favor of an engagement to the princess. Pan's final effort was a generic nautch dance performed by the princess's dancing girls in their hotel room in New York City. Like the first sequence, it was brief and colorful, entirely unobtrusive to the action and dialogue surrounding it.

Following *Dream Wife*, Pan went off studio to choreograph a nightclub act for Sally Forrest and six male dancers. It is unclear how far the project developed because by the end of the month of November, Forrest had moved to New York to host the new *Playhouse of the Stars* series, and Hermes Pan was back at M-G-M teaching Jean Simmons period style for the film *Years Ago* (also called *Fame and Fortune* and *Father and the Actress*, but released as *The Actress*) in which she portrays the young Ruth Gordon in 1913, anxious to pursue a career as an actress. The film opens on stage at the Colonial Theatre in Boston with a performance of *The Pink Lady* featuring its most famous number "Beautiful Lady," sung by the star Hazel Dawn (Kay Williams) and a male chorus that harmonizes, walks, and sways with her. Pan's staging of the routine is quite faithful to photographs of the original production, and the melody of "Beautiful Lady" and the mystique of Hazel Dawn become motifs that carry through the film. Ruth and her boyfriend Fred Whitmarsh (Anthony Perkins in his film debut) go dancing—the seemingly obligatory social dancing sequence in a Hermes Pan film—in which they waltz while she hums the melody of "Beautiful Lady." Later, Ruth and her girlfriends (Norma Jean Nilsson and Dawn Bender) play at performing in her bedroom, a sequence for which Hermes provided a staging somewhat reminiscent of the "Kiss Polka" from *Sun Valley Serenade* in its use of intertwining arms. Following an evening encounter with Fred, during which they dance to the humming of a jaunty syncopated tune, Ruth reprises "Beautiful Lady" again as she turns off the lights and goes up the stairs, allowing her body to move subtly to the musical phrases. Finally, in an attempt to prove her talent as a performer to her parents, she gives an impromptu performance choreographed with excessive gesticulation, full of passion but little technique. Pan's staging in the film is so organic to the characters that it is impossible to determine how much of the movement was actually preordained by the choreographer and how much grew out of the period improvisations that Pan developed with the actors during rehearsals. As a result, reviews praised the period authenticity of the film with the *New York Times* (13 October 1953) noting that "the flavor of the era is imparted in a tasteful production," and *Variety* (4 August 1953) complimenting the cast for "engagingly putting over the characters that were taken from real life, as well as the feel of the early 1900 period in which the plot is laid." *The Actress* completed filming in January 1953 and almost immediately, Pan was at work choreographing his favorite Cole Porter score, *Kiss Me Kate*.

9

The Life of an Elephant

The film adaptation of *Kiss Me Kate*, the Sam and Bella Spewack–Cole Porter back-stage musical about a production of Shakespeare's *The Taming of the Shrew*, offered Hermes Pan his first opportunity of working with the 3-D process and, given his interest in using special effects in his choreography, he was initially stimulated by the challenge. The film was shot for 3-D and 2-D widescreen; the 3-D shot was taken first, and then the set would be relit for the two-dimensional version.[1] "If something was thrown forward, you would think it was hitting you in the face," Pan explained. "You had to be conscious that everything would be coming at you. The director and the cameraman tried so hard to create these effects that eventually it became boring" (Lewis, Spring 1991, 28). What did not become boring for Pan was working with an ensemble of top-notch dancers that included Ann Miller, Tommy Rall, Carol Haney, Jeanne Coyne, Bobby Van, and a newcomer named Bob Fosse.

Today, much of the attention paid to the film is devoted to the forty-eight seconds of choreography Fosse contributed to the final production number, "From This Moment On." Early on in rehearsals, Fosse had expressed a desire to choreograph one of his own numbers in the film. Since his role as Hortensio, one of Ann Miller's (Bianca) suitors, was small, it was a challenge to find a number where Fosse could be featured rather than Tommy Rall (Lucentio), the suitor whom Bianca favors. Ever interested in promoting young talent, Hermes and music director Saul Chaplin solved the problem by interpolating "From This Moment On" from Porter's musical *Out of This World* and dividing the number into three individual dance duets, the first for Ann Miller and Tommy Rall, the second for Jeanne Coyne and Bobby Van (Gremio), and the third—in the featured position—for Carol Haney and Bob Fosse. During rehearsals Pan grew to admire Fosse's unique style of jazz dancing (they both had a fondness for knee drops) and believed that Fosse's special talent and ambition should be rewarded with an opportunity—even though he knew very little about Fosse except that he idolized Astaire. Saul Chaplin once saw Fosse walking behind Astaire and mimicking the dancer's every movement. Astaire sidestepped a nail that was sticking out of a board and nimbly kicked it out. Fosse immediately tried to copy the routine, and as Martin Gottfried notes, "When Astaire disappeared around a corner, Fosse remained to rehearse and repeat the sudden sidewise step—skirting the nail and then kicking it—until he got it right" (Gottfried 1990, 72). Pan created an opportunity for Fosse to be impressive, and impressive he was. "My big break—and the turning point of my career—came when the studio let me choreograph a little dance for myself and Carol Haney in the film *Kiss Me Kate*," Fosse explained. "It only lasted forty-eight seconds, but it changed my life" (Grubb 1989, 30).

During the rehearsals for "From This Moment On" the shah of Iran contacted Pan to ask for a favor. The shah was interested in dating Ann Miller but since she had stood him up on a previous occasion when he was in California (because of a misunderstanding over a misquoted newspaper story), he felt that Hermes might have better luck in persuading the star to meet with him—this time at the royal palace in Tehran. Hermes delivered the invitation to Ann, saying that the shah and the entire royal family very much wanted her to be their guest for a week and suggested that she ask director George Sidney for the time off. Used to delays because of actors' illnesses or injuries, Pan saw no immediate problem with Ann being gone for a week. The director, however, was of a different mind and replied that shooting around her would waste millions of dollars, an exaggeration certainly, but Hermes had to report to the shah that Ann was again unavailable.

"From This Moment On" was only one of several spectacular dance routines created by Hermes Pan and his assistant Alex Romero for *Kiss Me Kate*. Interestingly, all of Pan's dance numbers in the film, with the exception of the comic "Brush Up Your Shakespeare," and the "Padua Street Song" that was eventually cut, involve Ann Miller. Pan staged her entrance number, "Too Darn Hot," as a vigorous tour de force starting with an impressive tap routine atop a coffee table then moving throughout the space with a kind of perpetual-motion nervous tap step. As the dance becomes more heated, Pan staged a modest 3-D striptease with Miller throwing items of clothing right at the camera. Because of the amount of light necessary for 3-D filming, the temperature grew to 130 degrees on the set during the number and, according to Howard Keel (Petruchio) in his memoir *Only Make Believe*, "They took shammy skins, dipped them in eau de cologne, and whirled them around until they cooled, then patted your face down to help you keep as cool as possible. It was a long, tough film" (Keel 2005, 152).

"Why Can't You Behave?" coupled Miller with Tommy Rall, a dancer who seems at ease in every style of movement. The number capitalizes on Pan's sense of humor and affection for props (a newspaper, false eyes, trick deck of cards, clothes on a clothesline), and gives Rall an opportunity to demonstrate his gymnastic ability, particularly in the use of an unseen trampoline. A tap argument between the dancers is quite evocative of "Mr. and Mrs. Hoofer at Home" in *Three Little Words*, and the use of the slide, after Rall flies toward the camera on a rope to justify the use of 3-D, recalls the "Waterfront Ballet" in *Excuse My Dust*.

In "Tom, Dick, or Harry," Pan depicted Bianca's three suitors vying for her attentions in another energetic tap routine interrupted by brief solos for each man seeking to impress her. Bianca chases the suitors around a central fountain, comically trying to catch them with a butterfly net even though they are trapped in a kind of perpetual motion recalling Gracie Allen's staging in the "Fun House" routine in *A Damsel in Distress*. Each in his turn, the men leap over Bianca and the number ends with moving trenches and the dancers tapping out the vaudeville rhythm of "Shave and a haircut, two bits."

Pan staged "We Open in Venice" with Miller, Rall, Keel, and Kathryn Grayson (Kate) stylishly prancing on a treadmill in front of a map-scrolling backdrop and designed Miller and Rall's duet "Always True to You in My Fashion" with the focus on Porter's lyrics rather than on fancy footwork. He even added himself to the routine, making another on-screen appearance as a sailor at the very end of the sequence, prompted by the lyric "Anchors Aweigh" to provide one last temptation for Ann Miller before the number ends.

"Brush Up Your Shakespeare," performed by nondancers Keenan Wynn and James Whitmore as the gangsters Lippy and Slug, was choreographed as a corny vaudeville routine with clog-like tapping and clowning, reminiscent of the "Put Me to the Test" number in *A Damsel in Distress*. Because Hermes was so busy working with Wynn and Whitmore on the number, Howard Keel asked Pan to lend him Alex Romero for help on staging his individual numbers, particularly "Where Is the Life That Late I Led?" In his memoir, Keel also notes that he and dancer Carol Haney basically devised the movement for "Wunderbar."[2]

After *Kiss Me Kate* had wrapped in July, M-G-M announced that plans were under way for resuming production of *The Student Prince* in the fall and that Edmund Purdom would star as Prince Karl Franz. Earlier in April, the studio had settled its dispute with Mario Lanza over the film, and, as part of the settlement, the singer agreed to allow the studio to use his recordings for the filming of the musical without him.[3] With Angie Blue again serving as his assistant, Pan began dance rehearsals for *The Student Prince* in the middle of October 1953 beginning with a complicated masque ball sequence that appears late in the film. Since the principals Prince Karl (Edmund Purdom) and Kathie (Ann Blyth) were heavily involved in the number, Pan and Blue wanted to give them sufficient time to learn, absorb, and perfect the movement. Like Betty Grable's entrance in "Sweet Rosie O'Grady," the festive masked ball begins with a picture coming to life—a costumed woman in midair, ready to be caught by the men beneath her. After the falling woman is safely in the arms of the dancers below, masked couples in colorful costumes do a polka and a spirited side step accompanied by the music of Jacques Offenbach before cancan girls appear with skirts lifted, kicking high into the air. Tumblers and other trick dancers punctuate the proceedings as balloons fly and streamers fall before the ensemble begins an extended follow-the-leader pattern (recalling Pan's characteristic serpentine lines) and the prince and Kathie dance into a corridor where a dialogue scene continues. This fairly brief but highly energetic bit of spectacle took Pan four weeks of rehearsal to perfect.

Edmund Purdom and Ann Blyth at the "Masked Ball" in *The Student Prince* (Courtesy of the author's collection).

With the exception of a grand waltz during which the prince and his fiancée (Betta St. John) dance briefly, and a simple lift during Prince Karl and Kathie's singing of "Deep in My Heart," the rest of Pan's staging for the film is virtually devoid of dance steps, accounting, perhaps, for his screen credit, "Musical numbers staged by Hermes Pan." Again Hermes was in his element, raising normal day-to-day experience to another more aesthetically organized level of behavior that appears spontaneous and natural both for the actor and for the viewer. No sooner did *The Student Prince* complete filming on 16 January 1954 than Pan was at work in script conferences for another period spectacle, an ancient Roman affair called *Jupiter's Darling* with a score by Burton Lane and Harold Adamson, a friend of Pan's since *As the Girls Go*, and starring Esther Williams.

The story conferences between Hermes Pan, Esther Williams, director George Sidney, producer George Wells, and writer Dorothy Kingsley focused on creating reasonable opportunities for the star to swim in a film set in 216 B.C. Since research indicated that Roman women swam naked and only in the privacy of their huge baths, it was immediately decided that dramatic license should be taken to allow Williams to swim clothed and in public. After much discussion, three (evidently the magic number in Pan's musicals) swimming sequences were chosen. The first was to occur at a bath luxuriantly ornamented with statuary. Above the water the Roman girl Amytis (Esther Williams) would sing "I Have a

Dream" and then dive into the water whereupon the statuary comes to life and swims with her. For the second sequence, Dorothy Kingsley suggested that Amytis might swim with Hannibal (Howard Keel), though through several meetings no one could come up with a viable reason why they should swim together since they were enemies. As the creators dug deeper into research, they discovered that Hannibal could not swim and decided that swimming with Hannibal could be justified if Amytis was trying to save his life (giving rise to a romantic relationship between them). The third sequence developed into a unique opportunity for Esther Williams since it would become her first truly dramatic swim on film. Fleeing on horseback from Hannibal's army, Amytis and her horse dive off a cliff and into the water where she is chased through caverns and submerged ships before finally eluding her captors.

Hermes staged the first routine in a swimming pool filled with six hundred thousand gallons of water. Standing in the pool are statues of mythological figures including two cherubic cupids—whom Pan cast from the Crystal Scarborough School of Swimming in West Los Angeles—that come to life after Esther enters the water. The routine involved seventy-five actors and technicians, five weeks of rehearsal, and a five-day shoot. Unlike earlier swim routines that were filmed through a glass window on the side of a large pool, at Pan's request, the cameras shooting the sequence would actually be in the water moving with the swimmers. Pan's greatest concern was how long the swimmers could remain underwater. It was determined that the comfortable limit was fifty seconds so Hermes had to break up the routine into fifty-second intervals. This presented a significant challenge in coordinating the music for the sequence as each section had to be timed to the second. Hermes explained:

> It's strange how we worked. You can hear under water. They'd put the microphone somewhere floating and you could talk on the microphone and you could hear clearly in the water. And even the music . . . would carry. At first, I used to use a mask and dive down and try certain moves. You know, [you can] stay down [for only] so many seconds . . . and change angles, and say, "Well, if you come around . . . this one boy, and then up and out of the picture, then see a hand grab her and then cut." Then you pick it up from there so it looks like a continuous thing where she's dancing with all these statues. We had to have the boys in cleats to keep them under, or otherwise they'd rise, you know. So they have plastic cleats to put their feet in to hold them down if they struck a pose like a statue. And then you'd have to go down and dive and get [into] your positions, [and] turn the camera first. You wouldn't have time to say, "Well, turn the camera now. Movement." You had to be shooting so that when they finally got the position and did what they were supposed to do, you were [shooting] it because they had to come up for air. It was very tricky. (Davis 1983, n.p.)

takes its inspiration from the finale of *Pin Up Girl* and the "I'd Rather Lead a Band" number from *Follow the Fleet*. Like Betty Grable in charge of running the drill, Ann stands before a seemingly endless body of military personnel. Like Astaire, she gives orders through her taps and engages in a call-and-response routine. When speaking of numbers owing their inspiration to earlier work by Pan, one must put the "Devil's Funhouse" at the top of the list since it uses virtually the same devices as the "Funhouse" in *A Damsel in Distress*. Although the later routine is essentially a duet for Russ Tamblyn and Debbie Reynolds with brief appearances for a red devil, a skeleton, and a witch, the use of treadmills going in opposite directions, fun house mirrors, the revolving cylinder, and the slide down to a revolving stage are too evocative of the earlier award-winning number to discourage comparison.

Once the large numbers were created, Hermes had the time to supervise the staging of the individual songs. For "Sometimes I'm Happy," he provided Jane Powell with simple, though liltingly seductive, choreography; for "I Know That You Know," he created a hide-and-seek game, replacing a formal dance break with playful natural movement, simple walking steps, and an easily manipulated lift; and, in "Ciribiribin," he introduced couples dancing a waltz, a staple of Pan's movie musicals.

Before the Easter holidays while Hermes was in rehearsal for *Jupiter's Darling*, Fred's wife Phyllis had been diagnosed with lung cancer and needed surgery. The first operation occurred on Good Friday at Saint John's Hospital in Santa Monica. Hermes Pan and David Niven waited with Fred through the five-hour procedure that was considered successful. Although she appeared to be recovering, Phyllis experienced a relapse and found herself back in the hospital three months later for more surgery. Hermes maintained a prayer vigil at the Good Shepherd Church for her recovery but the doctors offered little hope, and on 13 September, while *Hit the Deck* was shooting, Phyllis Astaire passed away. As soon as he heard the news, Hermes drove to the Astaire home to console Fred. There he was joined by Fred's sister Adele, producer Sam Goldwyn, and Astaire's close friends Randolph Scott and David Niven, none of whom were able to lessen his grief. Over the next several months, Pan lit a candle at every Sunday mass in Phyllis's memory and continued a prayer vigil for the emotional recovery of his friend Fred.

Sublimating his sadness and concern over Astaire's well-being, Pan went back to work, replacing Ann Miller's "Loo Loo" routine with a number entitled "Lady from the Bayou," a significant departure for Miller since she performs without tap shoes on a set designed to represent row houses at night in the French Quarter of New Orleans. Columnist Harrison Carroll visited the set on an autumn afternoon and witnessed the filming of the number:

> "I call this my evil dress," [Ann Miller] tells me, and, look, I'm going to dance barefooted. I've never done that before on the screen. In fact, Hermes tells me he doesn't want to see a thing in this mambo that

reminds him of Ann Miller." She rushes up on the stage and starts doing kicks to tone up her muscles. Pan orders a rehearsal. It's a wild thing. Everybody leaps and gyrates. At points the [six] boys toss Ann around as if she was an adagio dancer. At the finish, Ann is panting. "Can't I smile just a little," she pleads, "when the boys pick me up and carry me toward the camera? Won't it be all right if I make it an evil smile?"

"No," rejects Pan firmly, "no smile." Giving no time for argument, he orders another rehearsal. This time, things go well until one of the boys leaps up on the porch, grabs a pillar and swings around by it. The pillar suddenly pulls loose at the top. "Cut!" calls Pan. "Oh, murder!" cries Ann impatiently. "I knew we were going to have trouble with this bit." In less than a minute, though, she is ready for another take. This one goes all the way to the finish with Ann whirling and dancing on the steps and into the door of the house. "That was fine!" applauds Pan. But, like all top dancers, Ann is a perfectionist. She hurries to the front of the stage. She has to call for a towel to wipe her brow, but she is protesting, even as she tries to get her breath back. "No, Pan, please. I can do it better," she begs. "I wasn't evil. I could sense it. I went back there like Shirley Temple." (*Lethbridge Herald*, 10 January 1955)

Normally, Hermes would have wandered onto the stage to discuss the matter with his star, but during rehearsals of the mambo sequence he injured his back and was confined to a wheelchair during much of the shooting schedule, leaving the leg work to his two assistants.

By April 1955, Pan was back to normal, regularly leading the dancing at celebrity cocktail parties and preparing for his next assignment at M-G-M, *Weekend at Las Vegas* (also known as *Viva Las Vegas* but released as *Meet Me in Las Vegas*). Pan had already begun rehearsing the production numbers for the film when he hosted another 13 June celebration at his home for his entire family with fried chicken on the menu and home movies of his nieces and nephews as the after-dinner entertainment. As a joke, Vasso's daughter Michelene wrote a letter to him, signing it "Elizabeth Hatfield," a girl who went to school with Hermes in Nashville. It was brought to him special delivery just as the party was breaking up. A very private person—and quite touched that someone from his youth would contact him—Pan refused to read the letter until everyone had left; but as soon as the last car sped away, he gently opened it and began to read. Once Vasso and her family arrived at their home, Michelene phoned Hermes to inquire about the letter. He would not give her any details but he admitted to being deeply moved by a communication from an old friend. When his niece told him that she had written it, he did not believe her, so convinced was he that the letter was authentic. Gradually persuaded that it was all Michelene's doing, Hermes laughed heartily, surprised and thrilled that she would go to so much trouble to fool him and fool him so well. As Vasso noted in her journal, "It was a good gag, and went over big."

Meet Me in Las Vegas starred Dan Dailey as Chuck Rodwell, a successful rancher who spent his profits gambling unsuccessfully at the Sands Hotel and Casino until he encountered Maria Corvier (Cyd Charisse), a prima ballerina performing there. Believing her to be his lucky charm, he requests her presence at the gambling tables, and while they appear to be on a lucky streak they fall in love. The original songs were by Nicholas Brodszky and Sammy Cahn, and Pan, assisted by Pat Denise and Walton Walker, shared the choreographic responsibilities with Eugene Loring, who choreographed two ballet routines for Cyd Charisse and company. Though Hermes shared duties with Loring, their salaries were highly disproportionate: Loring earned $4,875 for the film while Pan was paid $47,042. There was no question as to who was considered the star dance director. The usual happy spirit surrounding the production of a musical film choreographed by Hermes Pan was severely dampened by the presence of Dore Schary, who had replaced Louis B. Mayer as the head of Metro-Goldwyn-Mayer. Cyd Charisse was completely candid about the situation:

> Dore Schary didn't know what he was doing. Please quote me. *He didn't know what he was doing!* He was the biggest mistake they ever made—the beginning of the end. As an example, we were doing a musical called *Meet Me in Las Vegas*, and he was concerned with whether or not he should make this picture, which was already in rehearsal. So he called for a reading of the script. A reading of the script! As if that tells you anything about a musical! So we all had to go in there and read the book, except for Dan Dailey, who flatly refused. Then he said he wanted to see a production number. Hermes Pan and I had been knocking ourselves out on a "Frankie and Johnny" number. Schary wanted to see it from beginning to end. So we did it, and it was a long number that wasn't designed to be done all at once and I got sick—a dizzy thing in my inner ear. Schary pretended he knew what he was doing, but he didn't have a clue. (Eyman 2005, 462–463)

"Frankie and Johnny," sung by Sammy Davis, Jr., offscreen, was, according to Pan, one of his most successful creations. A performance number at the Copa Room of the Sands Hotel, it had a dance arrangement composed by Johnny Green, who Pan noted was "very, very hip for dancers," and focused on three performers, Cyd Charisse (Frankie), John Brascia (Johnny), and Liliane Montevecchi (Nell). "I like to tell a story," Pan explained. "It makes it much more interesting. You don't see much storytelling in dance today. It's just steps. You rarely see something that has a little fantasy, no matter how simple" (Georgakas 1983, 28).

Pan's interpretation of the "Frankie and Johnny" legend begins with a pas de deux for the eponymous couple, a seductive jazz ballet in which Johnny aggressively drags Frankie across the floor before pulling her into a lift as an expression of dominance. Sashaying down the stairs of a barroom where a number of patrons are sitting motionless, the couple begins to perform a vigorous jitterbug-like dance, interrupted by the entrance of Nell who captures Johnny's attention. Frankie exits to powder her nose and Nell and Johnny dance, with Nell dragging Johnny across the floor in another expression of dominance. When Frankie discovers them together, she attacks Nell and a choreographed fight ensues during which the women rip off jewelry and various parts of clothing before Frankie steals a gun and discharges a shot that suddenly brings the other patrons to life. The music changes from a sultry jazz idiom to the rinky-tink sound of a piano in a Wild West saloon, and Frankie goes on a shooting spree, chasing Johnny around the bar, as the ensemble, finally joining the dance, moves subtly behind her in a desperate attempt to escape. When at length a bullet finds Johnny, he is given an exaggerated balletic death, comically punctuated by the music, before Frankie is taken by the sheriff who cuffs her in diamond bracelets. They dance and her seduction of yet another man begins. Universally regarded as one of Pan's masterpieces, the "Frankie and Johnny" ballet took over a month to rehearse and a full week to film.

In addition to the ballet, Pan choreographed two other plot-connected dance routines for Cyd Charisse. The first to appear in the film occurs when she is dining with Dan Dailey at the Silver Slipper and notices his appreciation of low-class burlesque entertainment. When comedian Jerry Colonna appears singing "My Lucky Charm" with chorus girls wearing headdresses representing clover, dice, and rabbit ears, the slightly inebriated Miss Charisse invades the number to demonstrate to her date that, even though she is a prima ballerina, she can shimmy and bump and grind in burlesque fashion. The other plot-connected dance occurs when Dan Dailey takes Cyd to his ranch to determine how amenable she would be to a country lifestyle. When he and the farmhands sing "The Gal with the Yaller Shoes," the men perform down-home choreography, often suggesting horses prancing, and Cyd joins in the jaunty dance with the grace of a ballerina and the ebullience of a folk dancer.

In addition to the multistyled dances designed for Cyd Charisse, Pan created a simple and playful soft-shoe routine for Dan Dailey and Mitsuko Sawamura singing "My Lucky Charm"; a bit of seductive staging using props (sheet music, a picture frame, a rose, and a pink boa) for Cara Williams performing "I Refuse to Rock 'n' Roll"; and sensuous background choreography for four girl dancers in tight red body suits with headdresses comprised of large red tassels, while Frankie Laine sings "Hell Hath No Fury." Hermes also staged two numbers that were on the shooting schedule but not included in the finished film: "It's Fun to Be in Love," sung by Dan Dailey, George Chakiris, and Betty Lynn; and a "Hoofers' Number," designed for the Slate Brothers, whose name appears on the casting sheet but not on the credits in the final cut. With the release of *Meet Me in Las Vegas*, Hermes Pan received some of the finest reviews in his career. The *New York Times* (14 March 1956) argued that "the best thing by far, is the finale—a gaudy satiric ballet, done to the old "Frankie and Johnny" ballad, as arranged by Johnny

Green. . . . It's crazy, man! And cool!" and *Variety* (3 February 1956) called Pan's choreography, "nothing short of terrific."

By the end of October 1955 when his duties at Metro-Goldwyn-Mayer had been completed, Hermes was off on a Caribbean vacation with Ann Miller, who was studying to become a Roman Catholic; Bob Considine's wife Millie; celebrity publicist Earl Blackwell;[6] and Linda Darnell, who had just opened and closed in a Broadway play, *Harbor Lights*. "I got to know Linda Darnell," Pan explained, "when I went on a junket tour with Ann Miller. We went to the Hilton Hotel ground-breaking in Trinidad or something. Ann was allowed to take a guest—an escort. . . . We would go to Barbados, Trinidad, Bermuda—sort of island hopping—a very hectic two weeks . . . but we had lots of fun, and I got to know Linda just from that, more than I did working with her. And she was a . . . very lovable, sweet girl" (Davis 1983, n.p.). Ann Miller had dated Conrad Hilton in the early 1950s and, as a result, had a free pass to his entire hotel chain around the world. The group flew back to New York on 6 November and, after a week in the city, dancing in night-clubs and visiting friends, Hermes boarded a train back to Los Angeles to spend the holidays with his family. Pan did not enjoying flying and avoided airplanes whenever possible. His trips abroad were invariably on ocean liners, and cross-country travel was always by train.

After the New Year, Hermes staged a nightclub act for Tita Purdom, the recently divorced wife of the actor who played Prince Karl Franz in *The Student Prince*. In his syndicated column (12 April 1956), Jim Mahoney reported that the act was scheduled to open at Johnny Walsh's supper club before leaving for a six-week tour of Europe, playing clubs in London, Paris, Berlin, and Rome. When rehearsals for the act were finished in the early spring, Hermes assisted Fred Astaire in the creation of the "Clap Yo' Hands" number in *Funny Face*, even though Eugene Loring had been assigned to choreograph the film. Loring's assistant Bruce Hoy recalled that Astaire, unhappy with the original choreography, brought in Pan at his own expense with the result that "there was friction back and forth between the two choreographers and Fred" (Irvin 2010, 252). Audrey Hepburn, who costarred with Astaire in the film, recalled meeting Pan when she first arrived for rehearsals: "I met [Astaire] when I got to Paramount, on the big, big stage, where there was just a piano and a darling choreographer named Hermes Pan. Hermes was terribly like Fred; it's unbelievable how much of Fred rubbed off on Hermes, and perhaps of Hermes on Fred" (Giles 1988, 10).

While Tita Purdom was traveling around the continent performing, Hermes and his sister bought a beach house in Carpinteria as a retreat for the entire family. Shortly after Hermes had completed the purchase, he was invited by Tadj ol-Molouk, the dowager Queen Mother of Iran, to revisit the Imperial Palace in Tehran at her expense. His earlier excursion in 1950, at the behest of Princess Shams Pahlavi, had so endeared Hermes to the royal family that his presence was eagerly anticipated. On the first visit, Hermes was awestruck with the splendor of his surroundings. On this trip, though no less impressed by his accommodations,

Hermes found himself the center of attention because of a simple gift he brought for Princess Shams: flea powder. Having noticed that her dogs, infested with fleas, had scratched their fur into a bloody pulp, Hermes thought to bring flea powder with him in an attempt to provide some comfort to the beasts. Evidently, no one at the Imperial Palace had seen or experienced the results of the medicine, and Hermes was hailed as a magician and ever beloved by the princess's dogs. At the end of May, Pan visited his cousins in Aigion before traveling to Paris where he spent a week assisting Astaire on the dances for *Funny Face*, rehearsing through-out the night in Fred's room at the Hôtel Raphaël. Sam Irvin notes that Astaire's room was directly above that of producer Roger Edens who, like Ginger Rogers in *Top Hat*, was kept awake at night because of Pan and Astaire's dancing (Irvin 2010, 255). Though Pan's presence was supposed to be a secret, he was recognized leaving the hotel early one morning by one of the dancers in the cast who imme-diately spread the rumor that Hermes was in Paris to rechoreograph the film. To dispel the rumors, Astaire concocted the story that Pan's presence was entirely coincidental:

> One night during an all-night session in a section of the Left Bank we were on a complicated dialogue sequence. It was about 3:30 a.m. and I spotted Hermes Pan in the crowd of visitors on the sidelines. Hermes had just arrived for a holiday in Paris and said he couldn't find his hotel. He happened to see our lights blaring out in the darkness a few blocks away and wandered over to find out what was going on. He spent the rest of the early-morning hours in an adjacent bistro, which we used as shel-ter, delighted that he had got lost. We then explained to the lost Pan where he lived. (Astaire 2000, 316)

Hermes left Paris on 7 June and headed for London where he was entertained by British productions of American musicals in the West End. He saw *Kismet* at the Stoll Theatre, *The Pajama Game* at the Coliseum, and *Plain and Fancy* at the Theatre Royal before boarding the *Franconia*, sailing from Liverpool on 16 June, and relax-ing in first-class accommodations on the return to New York. There he spent a few days at the Waldorf-Astoria visiting Cole Porter before taking the train back to Los Angeles to begin work on *Silk Stockings*, the film version of Cole Porter's Broadway musical.

Fred Astaire was cast as Steve Canfield, an American producer in Paris, collab-orating with a Russian composer Peter Ilyitch Boroff (Wim Sonneveld) on the score for his film *War and Peace* featuring Peggy Dayton (Janis Paige), an American swimming star in her first serious role. Ninotchka Yoschenko (Cyd Charisse) is sent from Moscow to retrieve the composer and the three Soviet commissars keeping an eye on him, but in the performance of her duties she meets Steve and falls in love. Eugene Loring, the choreographer of the Broadway version, had ini-tially been asked to choreograph the film but, after having worked with Astaire on several films, he was not inclined to work with him again: "He's very difficult to work with," Loring explained. "By that I mean it's hard to create for him and get something new and fresh that also pleases him. He's very set in his ways" (Mueller 1985, 390). A compromise was reached with the studio in which Hermes Pan would choreograph every number involving Fred Astaire and Eugene Loring would be responsible for everything else. For his contribution to the film, Pan was paid $35,600 while Loring received $15,000. Rehearsals for Astaire's numbers began in September 1956, nearly two months before the film was scheduled to go into production, and assisting Pan were the familiar faces of Angie Blue, Pat Denise, and Dave Robel.[7]

Hermes choreographed the celebratory opening number "Too Bad" as a musical scene depicting Astaire's success in convincing the three Russian commissars to remain in Paris and enjoy the pleasures of the city. The pleasures, of course, include women, and Astaire dances with two of them, Tybee Afra and Betty Uitti, before passing them on to Bibinski (Jules Munshin) and Ivanov (Joseph Buloff). A third woman, Barrie Chase, who was Jack Cole's assistant on *Les Girls* in rehearsal on a stage nearby, was borrowed to become Astaire's partner in a pseudo cha-cha routine, while the third commissar Brankov (Peter Lorre) performed a folklike dance between two chairs. At the first rehearsal, Lorre approached Pan and confessed, "I'm not a dancer," and Hermes promised not to assign him any movement that would make him uncomfortable. Lorre further explained that just because he couldn't dance did not mean that he would not try to dance. Hermes was quoted in a later interview, saying that Lorre "was sort of elated by doing these dances. He had a lot of inspirational things that he would suggest to make it funny. He said, 'Okay, I'm going to hold on to the chair and I'll do a kazatski.' And I said, 'Great.' I don't like to impose on people and try to make them do things they can't do, so he came up with these ideas and I think it was wonderful" (Youngkin 2005, 392). Balanced between a table and a chair, with a butter knife in his teeth, Lorre resolutely executed the Ukrainian folk dance, comically continuing to dance even after all of the others had finished.

"Stereophonic Sound," a duet for Fred Astaire and Janis Paige, began as a satire of Hollywood's infatuation with new and improved technological devices. A verse specifically dealing with dancing styles was added at Pan's request early in October by Leonard Gershe, one of the authors of the screenplay. Since Janis Paige was not a strong dancer, Hermes watched her closely for the first few rehearsals in order to design a routine that played to her strengths. He discovered that Paige was a fine comedienne and assigned her comic business rather than complicated footwork. There is little subtlety in the staging or in the technical effects that embellish the number. When sung, the lyric "Stereophonic Sound" is processed with reverberation; Astaire and Paige sing into a grand piano to create a "stereophonic" effect; they go to opposite sides of a long conference table to emphasize the wide-angle cinemascope process; and they satirize the various dances mentioned in the added lyric: Russian ballet, English ballet, Chinese ballet, Hindu ballet, and

Bali ballet. During filming, Paige noted that Astaire had difficulty with part of the routine: "The more he tried, the more he went blank. He got so frustrated he walked off the set. 'I'll be back in a few minutes. I've just got to get myself together'" (Levinson 2009, 222). After a few words with Hermes Pan, Astaire returned and performed perfectly. As talent agent Irving "Swifty" Lazar remarked, "Hermes Pan was the only person [Astaire] could talk to when he was doing routines. He believed in Hermes. Hermes could say anything and it would be acceptable to Fred" (Giles 1988, 9).

In "All of You," Fred Astaire manages to convince Cyd Charisse to let go of her Soviet severity and to relax and dance with him. In Pan's staging, Astaire begins by dancing briefly with a chair as his partner, as if to break the ice. At just the right moment he pulls Charisse out to the floor and directs her body around the room. When she unconsciously falls into ballet movements, he understands who she really is and pursues the dance more vigorously. After the obligatory reticence is eradicated, they join in an adagio that ends as the dancers melt onto the floor. According to Peter J. Levinson, the number belongs in the realm of Astaire's most romantic film dancing and was, reportedly, Cyd Charisse's favorite dance number on film (Levinson 2009, 221).

Pan choreographed "Fated to Be Mated," one of two new songs Cole Porter composed for the film, as an exhilarating romantic duet for Astaire and Charisse set on a sound stage at a film studio. Hermes returned to the cantilevered hip lift that he used in Carefree and Three Little Words to propel the couple into a Spanish set, where he staged a Latin-inspired duet to the music of "Paris Loves Lovers." Pan noted in an undated recorded interview with Hugh Fordin that his concept was to set the dance to the percussive Latin rhythms in counterpoint to the soaring melody of the tune. Another hip lift leads the couple on to a waterfront set where they dance to a jazz-inspired arrangement of "All of You" ending with a rather acrobatic routine on the horizontal bars. In an interview, Pan explained, "The 'Fated to Be Mated' was one of my favorites. In fact, I choreographed that number with my assistant when Fred and Cyd were doing dialogue [scenes], and Fred, which was always unusual for him, did the whole thing as I had set [it]. And he made one or two changes, but he let me just practically do anything I wanted on that. The one he thing he objected to [was] catching Cyd in that number, but he finally did" (Davis 1983, n.p.). Astaire added, "I had a couple of things where I had to lift her and catch her and do things, and it worked out. . . . But I had one thing where she was up on a platform, and she had to leap down into my arms. Pan was the choreographer on that, and if it hadn't been for Pan, I don't think I ever would have done it. . . . He showed me a kind of a way to do it. And I did it. I got her and was so pleased. He always used to beat me down and get me to do something that I thought I couldn't do, which I was grateful for" (Levinson 2009, 221). Mueller reports that as another of Pan's practical jokes, he and his assistants created a version of "Fated to Be Mated" that was to be danced entirely on the floor without the use of levels. They performed that version for director Rouben Mamoulian, explaining that they had "a different idea." The director was greatly amused and expressed the wish that he had filmed it, calling it an "extraordinary achievement" (Mueller 1985, 396).

Wanting what he called a "sock" solo in the film, Astaire had asked Porter for a number that would capitalize on the current popularity of rock music but with a twist. The composer responded with the sardonically sassy, "The Ritz Roll and Rock." Announcing the demise of rock and roll because it has been taken over by the elite, the song required Astaire to dance with his top hat, tails, and cane, a comic idea when juxtaposed with rock-and-roll rhythms. Pan and Astaire had worked privately on the solo part of the routine while Eugene Loring's numbers were being shot so that Pan could create the ensemble background for the dance while Fred was involved with filming dialogue sequences. Harvey Evans, one of the dancers in the number, recalled the process: "I picked up the mood of the other dancers. It seemed like Hermes worked very slowly. He was sort of vague about what he wanted. Astaire did not come in much. He would come in a few hours each day. He looked older than I thought he would be. As the number progressed, it was not going to be any kind of great dance number. It was just going to be more Fred Astaire. Fred kept saying, 'Can't the boys be lower?' so a lot of the time we were on the floor. He was impatient but not to the point of annoyance." When it came to filming the routine, however, Evans noted that "Fred suddenly became younger, more boy than the old Astaire. Pan would design something, but it came alive when Fred stepped in. It was a work process that was so brilliant I could not believe it" (Levinson 2009, 223–224).[8]

Even though the number drew good reviews, Pan was not pleased with the final result of the dance. The effect of Astaire ascending into the air with one half of his body reflected in a mirror seemed forced and unnecessary, the very thing that in the past Pan and Astaire had struggled to avoid. The final gesture of the dance was perhaps the most important, if only symbolically: as Astaire fell to the floor, completely by accident his top hat fell off his head. On the last beat of the routine, as if punctuating an end to a style of work that a generation earlier was fresh and reactionary, Astaire smashed his hat.

After the January 1957 completion of *Silk Stockings*, which earned Pan excellent reviews, Hermes left M-G-M to pursue a freelance career. Twenty years of studio contract work had taken its toll. "It was too much of a rat race to have to do everything they shove in your lap," Hermes exclaimed. "It ruins your creativity when you are forced to do one thing after another. You get so sick, you honestly lose all interest" (DeMarco 2010, 179). As in the past, work found him quickly, and before winter was over, Pan was contacted by director George Sidney, with whom he had collaborated on *Kiss Me Kate* and *Jupiter's Darling*, to create the dances for *Pal Joey*, a Columbia Pictures adaptation of the Rodgers and Hart 1940 musical, starring Frank Sinatra as Joey, a womanizing nightclub singer who dreams of having his own club; Rita Hayworth as Vera Simpson, a former stripper, now a wealthy widow who supports Joey and his dream; and Kim Novak as Linda

English, a chorus girl in whom Joey has more than a passing interest. In the transition from stage musical to film, Joey, originally a dancing role, was changed to a singing role to suit Sinatra, creating little opportunity for extended dance routines that involved the principal male character, the antithesis of what Pan had been accustomed to working with Astaire. Even though he was limited in what he could accomplish choreographically in the film, Hermes approached the project with gusto and not merely because he was working again with Rita Hayworth, one of his closest friends.

Pan's choreography begins with a brief segment of social dancing at the Barbary Coast Club, one of several strip clubs in San Francisco's North Beach neighborhood that feature low-class entertainment such as "That Terrific Rainbow," the routine that follows with six low-grade gum-chewing chorus girls strutting their stuff. As the spotlight changes color according to their lyrics ("red hot mama," "blue for you," "green with envy," "orange flame"), the camera cuts away to Joey's unimpressed reactions. Linda enters and the six girls go into a dance staged by Pan with mechanical kicks and lifelessly extended arms, while the camera cuts away to dialogue through the remainder of the routine. Joey is hired at the club and joins the chorus girls in the finale of their act, "Great Big Town," a fragment of a hat and cane number in which, like Russ Tamblyn in *Hit the Deck*, he improvises steps and ends up dead center in a final pose. Although the routine is undistinguished choreographically, it tells us a great deal about how (and where) Joey works and demonstrates once again Pan's ability to focus dancing dramatically.

The social dancing that follows is more sophisticated since it occurs at an upscale charity event where Joey challenges Vera to do one of her old strip routines to raise money. She responds with "Zip," a highly intellectual exercise in which she strips to thoughts of Schopenhauer and other heady pursuits. In preparation for the routine—in the middle of April, about the time filming began on location in San Francisco—Rita and Hermes went to the Arabian Club to watch strippers perform. They caused something of a stir at the club not simply because they were celebrities, but because they arrived in a police car. A half hour earlier, they had just finished dinner together at Fisherman's Wharf and tried to flag down a cab. After about a quarter of an hour, a policeman who had been cruising the area with his partner recognized Rita Hayworth and stopped to ask if there was anything the police could do for her. She asked him to call for a cab, and when he did he discovered that there were no cabs available in the vicinity, so he offered to take her wherever she wanted to go. She explained that she and Hermes were doing research for a new movie role and asked to be taken to the Arabian Club. When the police dropped her and Hermes off, they arranged for a policeman to remain with them until after the show in case the room got rowdy. The visit certainly paid off, for Pan's staging of "Zip" is elegantly subtle, allowing Rita to execute a whole battery of stripper movements without taking off more than her gloves.

Hermes Pan and Rita Hayworth (Courtesy of the author's collection).

Later at the Barbary Coast Club, Joey performs "I Could Write a Book" and spontaneously drags Linda from the wings to join him in an impromptu dance, a simply staged event that results in her turning in to him as he sings a second chorus. The lack of complicated choreography is appropriate in this and the previous number, since both are supposed to be improvisational. Later, Joey and Vera dance to an instrumental version of "Lady Is a Tramp" on the Barbary Coast Club stage after hours. Unlike the romantic adagios Pan created with Astaire, this dance is little more than a box step, but it is quite effective dramatically in showing the chemistry between Joey and Vera. Equally dramatic is Pan's staging of "Bewitched, Bothered, and Bewildered." Although there are no dance steps in the number, the event moves like a dance and evokes Pan's staging of "Changing My Tune" in *The Shocking Miss Pilgrim*. Rita begins the verse lying sensuously in bed. The first statement of the melody leads her to the window, the second to her mirror after putting on her robe. She brushes her hair during the release and sits down to coffee as the first chorus comes to an end. A return to the release takes her to the bathroom where she begins to shower as the number ends. Pan's staging is so organic that the carefully choreographed gestures and subtle movements appear spontaneous, much like Pan's work on *State Fair*.

Frank Sinatra, Rita Hayworth, Hermes Pan, and chorus in a scene from *Pal Joey* (Courtesy of Photofest).

As the opening of Joey's nightclub "Chez Joey" draws near, Hermes Pan makes another brief on-screen appearance as a choreographer leading a group of chorus girls in a simple routine to the tune of "You Mustn't Kick it Around." Linda next appears in a rehearsal for a strip routine wearing an elaborate hooped gown and attended by two fluffily dressed maids who perform ballet movements using Linda's gown as a bar, to a waltz arrangement of "I Could Write a Book." When they begin unwrapping Linda's dress the music changes to a jazzed-up arrangement of Boccherini's "Minuet" that serves as the accompaniment to the striptease. Pan explained to a syndicated columnist why Kim Novak was stripping in such a fashion: "With an eighteenth-century gown, there are so many things you can take off without revealing real nudity. By using the two girls to help her undress, we also appease the censors. On the screen, you can't do much of a strip where the girl takes her own clothes off. But, up to a point, a lady disrobing with the assistance of two maids is permissible" (*Vidette-Messenger*, 22 June 1957).

After Chez Joey is closed, Joey returns for one last look at the place. He plunks out a few notes on the piano that prompt him to recall past events, and a dream ballet (by now a fairly ubiquitous and moribund device) begins to the tune of "What Do I Care for a Dame?" Through broken glass, images of Vera and Linda alternate before Joey appears in black and white on a set with three angled wings on either side of him (very reminiscent of the fashion-show set in *Lovely to Look At*), surrounded by six women, holding on to the wings. In the ensuing ballet, Pan is mundanely literal in his staging. When Joey sings about the police, two policemen enter and lift him. Each time he sings about skirts, a dancer crosses in front of him, turning so that her skirt will billow. When Joey mentions a nightclub, two men and a woman, dressed in sophisticated evening clothes, enter and cross off camera before personnel from Chez Joey appear to present him, now in color, wearing a top hat and tails, and carrying a cane. After Joey arrives as a sophisticate, Vera and Linda appear in midair, hugging the upstage flats on either side of him. They slide down the flats as the music changes to a Latin arrangement of "Bewitched, Bothered, and Bewildered," and the women perform a sinewy dance around Joey, who functions as little more than a maypole for them. He pockets one of Vera's earrings before turning his attention to Linda as the number fades back to reality.

In *Sinatra in Hollywood*, Tom Santopietro echoed many when he suggested that in the dream ballet, "nothing is explained, no insight is gained, and at ballet's end, the only audience reaction is one of bafflement" (Santopietro 2008, 238). What's more, the routine appears perfunctory in setting and choreography, returning to the images of the truncated routines at the Barbary Coast Club that began the film. In an interview with Kevin Lewis, Hermes explained, "Kim [Novak] was a beautiful actress who moved well, but she wasn't a great dancer." When dealing with untrained dancers, Pan subscribed to this philosophy: "You try to see what they can and can't do. You never ask them to do anything that will make them feel inadequate. If they feel easy doing one thing, let them do that. Keep it simple and let them do the simple things well" (Lewis, Spring 1991, 28). In *Pal Joey* his attempt to remain within the comfort zone of his performers resulted in a disappointing ballet.

The cast and crew of *Pal Joey* returned to Hollywood after Easter Sunday, 21 April, a week earlier than planned because the weather in San Francisco had been inappropriate for filming and delays were costing the production $13,000 a day.[9] Back at Cherokee Lane, Pan hosted the traditional "June 13th Journal Party" at his home. In addition to the usual family members, in attendance were Rita Hayworth's two daughters, Rebecca and Yasmin (Rita was too tired from filming to come), and Hernán Belmonte, one of Pan's favorite dancers, an old-timer who had danced with Josephine Baker. Belmonte's native language was Spanish, and he spoke English in a kind of "Spanglish" that was always entertaining to hear. He was terribly vain about his age so he did not have a driver's license or any other form of identification with his birth date. Belmonte and another Pan favorite, Walton Walker, were frequent guests at Pan's home. "When they came over to Hermes's," Michelene Laski remarked, "it was tons of fun and laughs."

In the summer after *Pal Joey* had wrapped, Hermes and his nieces Michelene and Mary Anne traveled to Rome where he began preproduction work on an Italian musical comedy called *Un Paio d'Ali* (*A Pair of Wings*), scheduled to open in

Milan at the Teatro Lirico on 18 September 1957. Pan and company traveled by train to New York and spent the night at the Waldorf-Astoria where the teenage girls delighted in playing tricks on their uncle because he always fell for their pranks. They ordered room service to bring him hot milk saying, "Mr. Pan is very tired," and watched from their room as Hermes opened the door, laughed heartily, and sent the milk across the hall to his nieces' room. The next day, the Pan party boarded the *Ile de France*, and the practical jokes continued as the ocean liner made its way across the Atlantic. One evening, the girls told Hermes that he had been invited to a "Bridge Party" on the bridge of the ship. Dressing nattily for the occasion, Pan took the stairs to the top of the ship, only to be told by a bemused crewman that there was no such party on board. When Hermes and his nieces arrived in Rome, the practical jokes ceased when they checked into the Grand Hotel, the opulent establishment built in 1894 by César Ritz and once owned in partnership with English composer Arthur Sullivan and operetta impresario Richard D'Oyly Carte. When Pan was called away to Paris for a few days to work with Bob Hope on a concert appearance, he left the girls at the hotel with bookings for tours throughout the Eternal City. Instead of hopping on a tour bus, Michelene and Mary Anne chose to remain in the ornate hotel lobby where they made friends with fellow tourists and enjoyed Campari and soda with Rock Hudson, who was filming *A Farewell to Arms* at Cinecittà Studios.

Un Paio d'Ali tells the story of a shy elementary school teacher, Renato Tuzzi (Renato Rascel), who feels like a failure. Deeply in debt and unable to pay his rent, he tries to kill himself by turning on the gas line but because he did not pay his gas bill his attempt is unsuccessful. His landlord's daughter, Sgargamella (Giovanna Ralli), who wants to be an actress, secretly gives him money and emotional support, and in return he offers to give her elocution lessons since she speaks in a rough vulgar dialect. Gradually the landlord, Hannibal (Mario Carotenuto), grows to like Renato and gives him advice on how to get ahead in life: find the weaknesses in other people and exploit them to his advantage. Renato takes the lesson to heart and finds himself able to control his unruly students and foil a blackmail plot. When Sgargamella finally auditions for the film company, she is told that she speaks too well for the role, which was written in a rough vulgar dialect, but Renato finds the courage to express his love for her, and Hannibal agrees to let them marry. *Un Paio d'Ali* had music by Gorni Kramer and a libretto by Pietro Garinei and Sandro Giovannini, who would also direct, assisted by Lina Wertmüller, who later became an important film director. The dancing chorus would be comprised of twelve Italian men called "I 12 Solisti," and the "Charley Ballet," twelve women of various nationalities ranging in age from sixteen to twenty.

In addition to staging solo numbers, Pan and his assistant Valerio Brocca were responsible for four production numbers and a comic duet, highly reminiscent of "Let's Call the Whole Thing Off" from *Shall We Dance* both in musical shape and dramatic situation. Called the "Italian Lesson," the song was a bouncy musical scene in which the professor attempts to teach Sgargamella how to speak proper

Hermes Pan in rehearsal for *Un Paio d'Ali* (Courtesy of the author's collection).

Italian, interrupted by a dance interlude that triggers a romantic interest between them. The score in general was very evocative of American musical film music of the 1930s and 1940s but few of the other songs were imitations as obvious as this duet. The first production number "The Pool, and the School of Life," featuring the twelve male dancers, was set to a heavy Latin rhythm evocative of Carmen Miranda's material in *That Night in Rio*. The second, "The Sgargamella," introduced Giovanna Ralli singing and dancing to a jaunty bebop-flavored ditty accompanied by the men. "A Pair of Wings," sung by Renato Rascel and the male and female chorus, was a ballad cut from the same mold as Harry Warren's "My Heart Tells Me" from *Sweet Rosie O'Grady* and countless other songs for which Pan provided choreography at RKO and Twentieth Century-Fox. The lyrics, "Every man possesses wings, every man is made to soar; . . . Fortunately, your wings are fashioned from reality and dreams. . . . Once you leave the ground and take flight, you'll find everything is a walk in the blue," inspired Hermes to stage the number as an adagio dream ballet in which Renato might experience in fantasy the kind of life he had denied himself in reality. The world was suddenly a vast blue sky filled with ballroom dancing and ballet movements with choreographed lifts that permitted everyone to fly.

Janice Patrick, a member of the Charley Ballet, rehearsing with Hermes Pan (Courtesy of the author's collection).

The last large ensemble number "Extras of the Movie Studio" was a virtuoso routine for the male dancing chorus in which the dancers depict through choreography a variety of supernumerary roles in the movies. The number is constructed like the "Twelve Days of Christmas" so that whenever a new role is mentioned, the dancers are forced to repeat all the previous choreography. To music that is quite brisk in tempo, Pan choreographed a Spanish dance, a Russian dance, a Polynesian dance, a jazz gangster ballet, an American Indian ceremony, a cowboy "Virginia reel," a schottische soft-shoe, and finally, an eighteenth-century minuet. In an interview with Charles Witbeck in 1961, Hermes noted that he created "Extras of the Movie Studio" under pressure. "I was doing a show in Rome and had to come up with a number in twenty-four hours," he explained. "I fiddled around and found an idea. It was the biggest number in the show . . . and one of my very favorites" (*Hartford Courant*, 15 February 1961). In addition, Pan staged two other showstopping novelty numbers in the score, "Homemade Calypso," and "Euripides Rock and Blues," an Italian take on 1950s rock and roll, musically evocative of Joe Garland and Andy Razaf's "In the Mood." Michelene recalled that, since she and her sister spent most of their time in the rehearsal hall, Hermes asked them what they thought of his choreography for "Euripides Rock and Blues." "We told him he had the beat wrong—the emphasis should be on the downbeat—and he changed it, then told people we had choreographed that number!"

Following two weeks of production work and rehearsals in Rome, the company along with Hermes and his nieces boarded a train for Milan where they spent the next month living in an apartment not far from the Duomo, Milan's spectacular

Gothic cathedral within walking distance of the Teatro Lirico where *Un Paio d'Ali* was scheduled to open. The theatre, dating back to 1779 and built in a horseshoe shape, with four tiers of boxes and a balcony, was first used as an opera house (the premieres of Donizetti's popular *L'elisir d'amore* and Cilea's *Adriana Lecouvreur* occurred there) but in the 1920s, the building began being used for public assemblies featuring, among other things, the speeches of Benito Mussolini. After the Second World War, the eighteenth-century building returned to producing theatrical entertainment.

During rehearsals, the members of the Charley Ballet were especially friendly to Pan's nieces since Michelene and Mary Anne were teenage girls, not far from the age of the dancers; one of them, Janice Patrick, called herself Mary Anne's "Mother in Europe." Michelene explained, "There were always lunches and dinners with the dancers, everyone liked to go out in a group and we could tell they were so fond of [Hermes]. He always watched to see that we didn't drink too much wine! He often sent us home after dinner, and the adults would stay out late. A favorite memory: Renato Rascel wrote 'Arrivederci Roma.' One evening at the rehearsal hall, he was at the piano (everyone else was gone or upstairs in the dressing rooms). It was still and quiet and the hall was almost dark. He called us over and played and sang it to us. Of course it brought us to tears and I'll never forget that moment."

If the girls were well taken care of by the company, Hermes was as well, for one of the dancers in "I 12 Solisti" became an intimate friend—a romantic relationship that would last for the next five years. The dancer, Gino Malerba, was handsome, talented, and ambitious, and saw in Hermes an opportunity to step up his career. Always anxious to help and befriend a dancer, Hermes welcomed Gino's attention and fell in love, though it is impossible to document the full extent of his attachment because Pan would allow the fulfillment of his same-sex desires only in the shadows. Jerry Jackson, Pan's assistant, who often saw the couple together, told me that he never sensed Hermes and Gino were lovers. "Gino was very butch. I thought they were just good friends." Letters from Juliet Prowse and Fred Astaire to Pan, however, mention Gino in ways that suggest a more intimate involvement and Pan's friend and biographer, David Patrick Columbia, seems confident that it was a sexual relationship.[10]

After the opening of *Un Paio d'Ali* on 18 September,[11] Pan and his nieces traveled around Italy for the rest of the month before returning to California. As soon as he arrived, Pan was back to work at Universal-International Pictures on a James Cagney film, *The Devil's Hornpipe* (released as *Never Steal Anything Small*).

Star Turns

Never Steal Anything Small was based on the unproduced play *The Devil's Hornpipe* by Pulitzer Prize–winning author Maxwell Anderson and director Rouben Mamoulian. With music by Allie Wrubel, the composer of "Zip-A-Dee-Doo-Dah" from *Song of the South*, the film chronicled the political machinations of Jack MacIllaney (James Cagney) in an attempt to win the presidency of the New York Stevedores' Union. Along the way he commits grand larceny and tries to steal his lawyer's wife Linda (Shirley Jones) by forcing a confederate named Winnipeg (Cara Williams) to make a play for her husband (Roger Smith). The film sought to combine a gritty indictment of graft and corruption with satire, romance, and musical comedy. Always anxious to tackle something new and unusual, Pan was enlivened by the challenge and thrilled to be working with James Cagney whom he knew from his earliest days at RKO when Cagney used to drop by the set to watch Astaire dance.

In addition to the ubiquitous social dance staging, Hermes Pan and his assistants Barrie Chase and Frank Radcliffe were responsible for choreographing five numbers for Cagney, another five for Shirley Jones, and two for Cara Williams. Of the twelve routines Pan rehearsed, only five were retained in the final film. "Helping Our Neighbors" was performed by the chorus marching to a political rally; "Never Steal Anything Small" was sung by Cagney and chorus during the credits and briefly at the end of the film. Cagney was said to have dusted off his dancing shoes for the production, but the dance sequences in the two numbers were cut to give his character a greater sense of realism.

"I Haven't Got a Thing to Wear" is a waltz sung by Shirley Jones (and overheard by James Cagney) as she prepares for a date with her husband. Staged realistically, using a great many costume props, the number begins with her choosing a dress and ends with her waltzing around like a child playing dress up. As in the case of Cagney's numbers, choreographic fantasy was replaced with natural movement, and Pan found himself returning to the aesthetic of *State Fair* rather than breaking new ground.

Hermes set "I'm Sorry, I Want a Ferrari" in an automobile showroom where Cagney bribes Cara Williams with the promise of a new car if she agrees to make a play for Linda's husband. The props in this number are full-size automobiles, not the least of which is a red Ferrari on a treadmill in front of a scrolling background. Cagney performs his signature straight-leg walk and Williams a few grapevine-like steps but no extended dance break occurs. Cutaway shots to three attractive young chorus women (and the fact that the routine took four days to film) suggest that there was more to the number than what appears in the final edit.

For the ersatz commercial "It Takes Love to Make a Home," Hermes designed a comic ballet for Linda and four boy dancers as an advertisement for "Love" products commencing with a waltz routine selling "Love Soap." The music changes to a jazz beat and the choreography becomes playfully literal as the dancers sweep the set with brooms, not unlike the sailor routine for "Hallelujah" in *Hit the Deck*. An off-television-camera grip throws the brooms to the dancers in an attempt to make the number appear more realistically as "live television" as does a cutaway shot of Cagney watching the number on a television monitor. The one extended dance sequence in the film and an obvious satire of television commercials, "It Takes Love to Make a Home" was supervised by Betty Furness, queen of the TV commercial in the 1950s.

Although filming for *Never Steal Anything Small* was completed at the end of January 1958, the musical was not released until February 1959 due to extensive previews and reediting. The *New York Times* (12 February 1959) called the film "a medium grade musical" with the sum hardly equal to the parts, and Hermes dubbed it a "valiant attempt to do something 'different.' 'Difference' turned out to be one of the few musicals that bombed—but good."

In spring 1958, Hermes returned to Italy to visit Gino and after spending a month in the Tuscan sun, he and Gino returned together to Los Angeles in the middle of May. Hearing about producer Samuel Goldwyn's search for a choreographer for his production of *Porgy and Bess* (directed by Pan's friend Rouben Mamoulian), Hermes sent him a telegram on 15 May: "Dear Mr. Goldwyn, Just returned from Europe. If there is any choreography in your picture *Porgy and Bess* I would love to have the opportunity to be of service." Goldwyn had already considered Jerome Robbins and Onna White, whose dances in *The Music Man* on Broadway had made her a hot property, and at the time he received Pan's telegram he was in negotiations with Peter Gennaro, who had assisted Robbins on *West Side Story*. Over a month passed and Pan received no response from Goldwyn. With no immediate project at hand, Hermes and Gino went on a short vacation to Laguna where they were joined at various times by Father Jim and members of Hollywood's elite film community. Pan enjoyed the beach and the companionship. Gino thrived on the connections he was making, giving him free access to the Hollywood film industry.

Late in July, Pan was finally hired as choreographer for *Porgy and Bess*. His contract guaranteed screen credit, "Choreography by Hermes Pan," and a modest weekly salary of $750 from 6 August through 29 August, during which time he would render his services exclusively to the Goldwyn Company. Between 29 August and 20 October, when he was committed to choreographing *An Evening with Fred Astaire*, Pan was required to work on *Porgy and Bess* only "at such times as you and we may be able to agree upon," and after 20 October, he was again committed exclusively to Goldwyn. A week after Pan signed his contract, Mamoulian was fired and replaced with Otto Preminger, the director who succeeded Lubitsch on *That Lady in Ermine.*

Before rehearsals began, Goldwyn had determined that only two numbers in the film would require choreography and staging: "Oh, I Can't Sit Down," sung by the denizens of Catfish Row on their way to a church picnic, and "It Ain't Necessarily So," sung by Sportin' Life (Sammy Davis, Jr.) and the ensemble at the picnic. Pan begins the first routine with an African-American band marching and prancing through Catfish Row leading the ensemble singing and cakewalking out to the levee, with Sportin' Life acting as a kind of major domo. The choreography leans more toward realism than stylization, sustaining the dramatic situation but never elevating it to the dimension of fantasy. The same can be said for "It Ain't Necessarily So," though it is unclear how much Hermes actually contributed to Sportin' Life's choreography since Sammy Davis, Jr., was uncomfortable with Pan's original staging and brought in his own choreographer, Hal Loman, with whom he had worked on *Mr. Wonderful*, his 1956 Broadway musical. Even though he didn't like Pan's choreography, Sammy certainly enjoyed his company. When he wasn't working, Davis hung out with Hermes and the chorus dancers. Nichelle Nichols, one of the dancers, now best known as Uhura on *Star Trek*, recalled that "he and Hermes would tap together, would do challenges. And they would fall all over each other laughing" (Fishgall 2003, 129). With Loman in charge of Sammy's moves, Pan staged the ensemble that encircles the performer when he narrates the story, imitates his gestures during the call-and-response section, and concludes the number with a free-form dance of jubilation. All of Pan's choreography in *Porgy and Bess* is what he considered to be authentic African-American movement—steps and routines taught to him by his mammy Aunt Betty forty-five years earlier. The opportunity of returning to his southern roots choreographically was a major factor in Pan's pursuing the job even at a relatively low pay scale. Another factor was Goldwyn's decision to shoot the movie with Todd-AO, a widescreen process that opens up the screen to over three times its previous dimensions. Always interested in new technology, Pan embraced the challenge of creating novel and exciting choreographic patterns to fill the wider screen.

Both numbers were rehearsed in the middle of September and filmed first on Venice Island near Stockton, California, for "Oh, I Can't Sit Down," and later on Tule Island for "It Ain't Necessarily So," which, Sammy Davis, Jr., is said to have boasted, took "only a couple of takes to finish" (Fujiwara 2008, 226). Although Otto Preminger's contract permitted him to ban Samuel Goldwyn from the set while rehearsing and shooting, Pan's contract did not and, as a result, for the first time in his career, Hermes had to endure the experience of a producer telling him what to do. In an interview with Kevin Lewis, Pan noted that he—like Mamoulian

and Preminger—was at odds with Goldwyn over interpretation: "I had to practically lock the door to keep Goldwyn from meddling with my choreography. Also,
he kept telling me how to shoot the dance numbers" (Lewis, Spring 1991, 29).

On 24 June 1959, the film opened at the Warner Theatre in New York City to
severely contradictory reviews; no two critics appear to have seen the same movie.
The *Saturday Review* (4 July 1959) complained that "Hermes Pan's dances—and
particularly the one he contrived for Sammy Davis Jr. and chorus to the exuberant
'It Ain't Necessarily So'—seem curiously stale and unimaginative, scarcely tapping the talent that is on hand." Although Bosley Crowther of the *New York Times*
(25 June 1959) called it "a stunning, exciting, and moving film, packed with
human emotions and cheerful and mournful melodies . . . [destined] to be as
much a classic on the screen as it is on the stage," spectators seemed to agree with
Arthur J. Weiss, who wrote to the screen editor of the paper, calling the film "the
year's most stupefying bore" (*New York Times*, 12 July 1959). *Porgy and Bess*
earned only half of its costs at the box office and because Goldwyn purchased only
a fifteen-year lease on the rights to the film, showings after 1972 (when the lease
expired) were blocked by the Gershwin estate, which did not approve of the final
product.[1]

Supervising the location filming of the two choreographed musical numbers
for *Porgy and Bess* required Pan to take time off from rehearsing *An Evening with
Fred Astaire*, the television special sponsored by the Chrysler Corporation and
scheduled for live broadcast on 17 October. At the end of August, Hermes joined
Astaire and his new dance partner Barrie Chase, who had already begun rehearsals
in a loft studio situated above a mortuary. When Fred first mentioned doing a
special to Hermes, Pan tried to convince him to use Juliet Prowse as his dance
partner. While he was in Italy, he had seen Juliet Prowse perform in an act she had
created with two Italian dancers, Dante Denti and her fiancé Sergio Fadini.
Because Juliet was a jazz dancer, Hermes felt that she was a better fit for Astaire
than Chase, who was principally a ballet dancer, but Astaire was set on Barrie as
his partner and in spite of the fact that she was often late for rehearsal—an of-
fense that typically led to a dancer's dismissal—she remained Astaire's partner for
five television specials.

Rehearsals for Astaire and Pan typically began at 8:30 a.m., an hour and a half
before the sixteen chorus dancers (eight men, eight women) were scheduled to arrive. Dave Robel once again functioned as Astaire's assistant, and assisting Pan
with the chorus were Pat Denise and Gino Malerba, who had established himself as
a permanent fixture in Pan's life. Chorus rehearsals ordinarily went to 5:00 or 6:00
p.m. with an hour off for lunch, five days a week. Even though Astaire was the producer and star of the show, Pan was clearly in charge of rehearsals, teaching choreography, giving notes and corrections, and often acting as an intermediary between
Astaire and the other dancers. If there was talking to be done, Pan did it. If the
message needed the added resonance of a roar, Gino Malerba did the honors. After
the traditional meet and greet on the first day, rehearsal began on the opening

number of the show; unlike rehearsals for a film, the musical numbers for the television special were always rehearsed in sequence to the accompaniment of piano and drums. If there was a problem with a chorus step, Pan would correct it immediately; if Astaire had a concern, Pan would put the chorus on break or send the dancers into another room with one of the assistants while he and Fred solved the problem. He appreciated that Astaire did not like to be watched while he was working on anything new. A number might be taught in a single day, or spread over several days, during which the chorus might be working on small sections of several routines. In an interview with Peter J. Levinson, Larri Thomas, who danced in the first three television specials, noted, "We would do sixteen bars a day" (Levinson 2009, 267). Hermes found the medium of television difficult and challenging. As he told Arthur Knight:

> [T]he kind of staging that is just fine for movies or in the theatre, with your chorus working in ranks one behind the other, produces a pretty meaningless blur on the TV screen. But I have been finding out things. I saw that the extreme depth of the focus of the television cameras made it possible to create tremendously exciting effects, illusions of space or nearness that could add to the dynamics of the dance. Also, by staggering the arrangement of the dancers—maybe one or two in front, and the rest fanning out behind them—you could make much more meaningful patterns. Not only that, but you could actually fill a stage with relatively few dancers. (Knight 1960, 41)

After six weeks of rehearsal, the cast assembled on 17 October at the NBC Studios in Hollywood to perform Pan and Astaire's first live television broadcast. Following a brief solo for Astaire with a cane during the credits, Hermes begins *An Evening with Fred Astaire* with Fred surrounded by groups of dancers whom he conducts into motion to the accompaniment of David Rose's heavily percussive composition "Svengali." Once each group has been given a specific movement, Astaire conducts the group as a whole, starting and stopping it with a gesture of his cane. The routine calls to mind Bing Crosby's manipulation of the chorus in the "Everybody Step" number in *Blue Skies*. When the music develops into a hot boogie-woogie, the chorus joins with Astaire in a wildly energetic dance.

"Change Partners" from *Carefree* follows as Fred sings, watching Barrie Chase dance with another gentleman. When her partner leaves abruptly, Astaire takes the opportunity to dance with her in a variety of styles before the original partner returns and spirits her away (after Astaire had paid the bill at their table). Astaire's fondness for drumming is explored in the next routine where he dances to the sound of a rhythm section, accenting drum beats with his body and feet. Gradually the number develops into a narrative pantomime in which Astaire creates the illusion of playing and moving a grand piano and cracking the lens of the television camera with an ill-devised golf swing.

After a performance by trumpeter-singer Jonah Jones and his quartet, the nattily attired Astaire appears again in "Man with the Blues," another narrative dance in which he finds himself on the wrong side of town watching a romantic couple dance sensuously. The houses on the street become vertical blinds, opening to reveal the solitary figure of Barrie Chase, who obviously appeals to him. Unexpectedly, she appears on the street, but as Astaire tries to pursue her, other women begin to dance with him. When he finally manages to dance with Barrie, a group of surly looking men in blue jeans surround and taunt him before leaving with each of the women who danced with Astaire earlier. The image of Barrie Chase suddenly appears but disappears immediately as he approaches her, and the number ends as he wanders, dazed and confused, down the street. The producer of the special, Bud Yorkin, told Peter J. Levinson: "That number grew right out of the music. I played a recording of what David [Rose] had done. It motivated Fred. He said, 'Jesus, it's almost like a story. We could do *West Side Story* with it, something like that.' Hermes didn't know what to do with it. I mentioned having seen the *Folies Bergère* in Paris. There was a scene in it with venetian blinds opening and closing. Every time the blinds opened, there was a nude standing there; we couldn't do that, but we did have Barrie Chase. Each time the blinds opened, there was Barrie, and then she started coming after Fred. That's how we started the number" (Levinson 2009, 259–260).[2]

A routine for the chorus, "Old MacDonald's Trip," followed with a country hoedown featuring an athletic solo by Jimmy Huntley, a Spanish Flamenco dance with a stylish solo by Roy Fitzell, and a rock-and-roll routine with a limber-legged gymnastic solo by Bert May. Next came a short patter sequence between Astaire and Jonah Jones during which they each converse using their respective instruments—Astaire's feet and Jonah's trumpet. Jones segued into a rendition of "St. James Infirmary," introducing another narrative dance opening on the image of a bier on which the body of Barrie Chase is laid. Four black-veiled women enter and lament over the body before Astaire appears dancing, gesticulating synchronously with the sound of Jonah's voice and the rhythms of the musical arrangement. Following the lyrics to the song, six crap-shooting pallbearers appear to Astaire through the magic of television, as well as a woman singing and a red-hot jazz trio. Suddenly, as the body of Barrie Chase comes alive, she performs a jazz dance atop the bier before joining Astaire in a unison dance interlaced with elegant ballroom steps and lifts.

Astaire concluded the hour-long special with a medley of songs he had introduced on Broadway or in films, and at just about 6:00 p.m. on the West Coast on 17 October, the live performance of *An Evening with Fred Astaire* was over. It had been sent on a live feed to the East Coast market and taped during the performance for the West Coast airing later that night. There was nothing left for Pan and his dancers to do but party, and party they did at the Persian Room in the Beverly Hills Hotel where the Chrysler Corporation threw an extravagant bash while rave reviews poured in from the East Coast.

Shortly after the New Year, Hermes and Jack Cummings were having dinner at Ciro's, chatting amiably about their successes at M-G-M and enjoying their second bottle of Chianti when the producer asked if Pan would be interested in choreographing his production of Cole Porter's musical *Can-Can* at Twentieth Century-Fox. Cummings added that the film was to star Shirley MacLaine, Frank Sinatra, Maurice Chevalier, and feature Barrie Chase in the role of Claudine (the Gwen Verdon role on Broadway). Hermes accepted the producer's offer on the spot and asked him to contact his representative at MCA to work out the details. Soon after Pan agreed to stage *Can-Can*, Barrie Chase was released from the film for, according to associate producer Saul Chaplin, "she had attained a certain fame from having been Fred Astaire's dancing partner on TV and wanted her part made larger or she wouldn't do the film. The studio refused to accommodate her, and a replacement had to be found. Hermes Pan . . . suggested a girl from South Africa he had worked with in Europe. Her pictures were sent for, and after the decision makers saw them, she was hired. Hermes had made an excellent choice, because she's a marvelous performer—Juliet Prowse" (Chaplin 1994, 166–167).

In March, waiting for *Can-Can* to go into production, Hermes spent two weeks in San Francisco's Golden Gate Park choreographing "Younger than Springtime" for his friends Marge and Gower Champion as part of a television special entitled *America Pauses for Springtime* and scheduled to air at the end of the month. He also signed a contract with Twentieth Century-Fox to choreograph a remake of *The Blue Angel* at $2,000 per week with a four-week guarantee.[3] The film told the familiar story of a German schoolteacher, Professor Rath (Curd Jürgens), who leaves his profession to marry Lola-Lola (May Britt), a cabaret singer. But unlike the ending of the 1930 film, Rath does not go insane and die in his classroom; instead, he is reclaimed by Principal Harter (John Banner) and given the opportunity to return to his previous life.

For this iteration of the story, Hermes produced four musical sequences. The first, "Lola-Lola," composed by Ray Evans and Jay Livingston, was performed by May Britt and six languorous chorus girls seated behind her on the Blue Angel stage. Britt struts and poses throughout the number, offering the spectator a revealing view of the back of her underwear but, except for shaking her derriere, does no dancing. That is left to a single chorus girl who performs a brief and lethargic belly dance. While Pan's choreography is static, the camera work during the number is active, frequently cutting from the stage to the audience, and it soon becomes clear that the focus of the event is not on the performance but on the audience, particularly the effect Lola has on Professor Rath and his students.

Frederick Hollander's "Falling in Love Again" follows, crooned by Lola while assuming various erotic positions with a chair imitating Marlene Dietrich's famous rendition of the song. Again the focus is not on the performance since the camera cuts away for plot action that actually interrupts the singing.

Pan staged a reprise of "Lola-Lola" with May Britt posed on a ladder accompanied by chorus girls, each standing with a leg sexily posed on a stool, unenthusiastically beating on their backsides tambourines with Lola's face on the drum. Britt descends the ladder, struts and poses; the girls sway with their tambourines behind her; and she climbs atop the ladder again, ending the performance exactly where it began. The number is unusual in the film since, unlike earlier routines, the camera does not cut away for reaction shots.

For Mack Gordon and Harry Warren's "I Yi Yi Yi Yi (I Like You Very Much)," Pan presents five chorus girls dressed in bras and feathered skirts waving feathered fans as they strut and sway to the Latin beat. Again the number is interrupted by reaction shots and continues only as a background vocal as the camera moves to the backstage area to find a handsome visitor approaching Lola's dressing room.

The film ends with Lola performing a reprise of "Falling in Love Again," seated sexily in a chair as Professor Rath leaves the Blue Angel to return to his previous life. Pan's work on the film is very sparse and understated, providing rough texture and ambiance rather than "finished" musical numbers. Producer Jack Cummings, who stated that he wanted *The Blue Angel* to be "a little cleaner, with a happier ending" than the original (*New York Times*, 17 May 1959), was thrilled with Pan's contribution. And even the usually self-effacing choreographer was proud of the final product, noting in his studio biography that "in its original version this starred Marlene Dietrich. This version didn't top the original but it was close." Agreeing with Pan, Philip K. Scheuer of the *Los Angeles Times* (28 August 1959) wrote: "The personal drama, in its sexual potency, its pity and depravity, still takes hold. . . . Miss Britt, with her long black-stockinged legs and long blond hair, is an enticing teaser. . . . She is not like Dietrich at all . . . yet the magnetism she exerts is startlingly similar." Bosley Crowther, writing in the *New York Times* (5 September 1959), was not impressed, however, suggesting that Lola "looks and behaves like a normal ballet dancer in a Broadway musical show, not like a slinky sex-pot in a smoky night club in Berlin."

Early in May, while *The Blue Angel* was in production, Hermes Pan attended the Emmy Awards presentation in Hollywood with Gino, Fred Astaire, and much of the cast of *An Evening with Fred Astaire*. It was a glorious night for that company since the show won nine Emmys including "Most Outstanding Single Program of the Year." Pan won the award for "Best Choreography for Television," and Fred Astaire walked away with the award for "Best Single Performance by an Actor," an award that was challenged two days later by Ed Sullivan, who demanded that the ballots be seized and recounted, but no such action was taken by the National Academy of Television Arts and Sciences. At the postawards party, Hermes and Gino danced with Kim Novak and Bea Busch Wilcox, one of the show's dancers who had thrown a party for the cast a few weeks earlier. Bea's party was especially noteworthy for Pan since it was there that he discovered why Astaire had been so adamant in hiring Barrie Chase as his partner. "Fred didn't go to parties. So when he showed up at Bea's with Barrie Chase on his arm, I wondered 'What's going on

May Britt and company in *The Blue Angel* (Courtesy of the author's collection).

here?' Fred danced with everyone at the party but mostly with Barrie, and when I saw him dance with her, I laughed. Suddenly I knew what was going on." Later in the month, Pan finally signed a contract with Jack Cummings for *Can-Can*, at the rate of $1,000 per week during the preparation period between 26 May and 13 June, and a guaranteed eight weeks of employment at $2,000 a week beginning 15 June. In addition, a *Blue Angel* clause stipulated that if Hermes should work on *The Blue Angel* while he was in rehearsal for *Can-Can*, he would receive his full salary of $2,000.

A week after he signed the contract—on Tuesday evening, 2 June—Pan's Cherokee Lane home was invaded by two robbers who broke into his bedroom through a bolted door and ordered him to lie face down on his bed while one of the thieves ransacked the house. After cutting the telephone wires and binding Hermes with his own neckties, the pair escaped with Pan's suitcases filled with his clothing and other personal items. Threatened with violence if he should call the police, Pan fled his home and spent the rest of the night at Gino's apartment in West Hollywood before summoning the courage to report the incident to police at the West Los Angeles police station. Still frightened of possible repercussions, Pan told police that he did not wish to prosecute.[4] Luckily for Pan, the thieves were uninterested in his most valued possessions, his film memorabilia and the Lucite case containing Fred and Ginger's rehearsal shoes (one of Astaire's white bucks and Rogers's satin pumps) presented to him by Astaire with the note, "To Pan—In memory of those thousands of rotten hours in rotten rehearsal halls!" After the robbery, Hermes cemented shards of glass to the top of the wall that

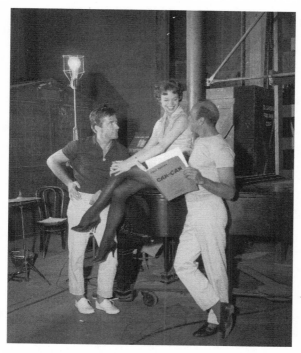

Marc Wilder, Juliet Prowse, and Hermes Pan prepare to rehearse the "Garden of Eden Ballet" (Courtesy of Photofest).

stood in front of his house to protect himself from future burglaries. He was never robbed again.

Two weeks after the robbery, Hermes (assisted by Buddy Bryan and Gino Malerba) began dance rehearsals for *Can-Can* with the infamous "Garden of Eden Ballet," an extended performance number at Pistache's (Shirley MacLaine) Parisian nightclub, the climax of an artists' ball. As originally choreographed by Michael Kidd on Broadway, the ballet was considered quite risqué, and Pan went out of his way to change the concept of the number. Unlike Kidd's sensuous Eden, full of burgeoning sexuality, Pan's paradise is playfully designed as a child's line drawing, with Adam and Eve behaving like a seasoned couple rather than lovers experiencing sexuality for the first time. Working with technical adviser Gwen Verdon who played Eve in the original production, Pan opens his "Garden of Eden" on a rosy dawn with a variety of animals awakening in a kind of naïve ballet bliss, dancing and playing children's games. Eve (Shirley MacLaine) flies in atop a huge butterfly, wearing a flesh-colored leotard covered with spangles and a stylish feathered hat. After she lands, she removes her hat and playfully wakes a bare-chested Adam (Marc Wilder), sporting a large fig leaf over his tights. They engage in a ballet-inspired dance to a brisk waltz arrangement of "I Love Paris," joined briefly by some of the animals, before an apple glowing like a traffic light descends from a twisted wrought-iron tree to the accompaniment of bongo drums. The snake (Juliet Prowse), dressed in a black leotard with spangles, slithers down the tree, winds herself around Adam's body, and presents the apple to Eve. Adam and Eve dance with the apple to the accompaniment of "I Love Paris," this time punctuated by heavily accented jazz phrases that foreshadow the second part of the ballet. Animals appear wondering what all the excitement is about and watch as Eve bites into the apple. When she does, the rosy dawn of the environment becomes a heated yellow; a jazz style takes over the music; and the choreography leaves the realm of ballet and begins to approach the style of Bob Fosse or Jack Cole. After Adam takes a bite, he, Eve, and the snake engage in a unison jazz dance before throwing baskets of apples at the animals, causing them to join in the jazz fest and leading to pandemonium in the animal kingdom. Noticing that Adam has been flirting with the snake, Eve bumps her out of the picture, knocks him out, and drags him off in triumph as the ballet ends. The routine took seven weeks of rehearsal and five days of filming beginning on 4 August 1959.[5] At the end of the month, a syndicated news report presented a verbal snapshot of the production process:

> It had all started seven weeks before on a bare sound stage with the girl dancers rehearsing in blue jeans and Capri pants and with Shirley in a black leotard. A shirt-sleeved pianist let his cigarette ashes drop on the keys. The pianist puffed on his cigarette beside a single electric light bulb dangling from a pole and played the Cole Porter music. Choreographer Hermes Pan worked on the steps with Shirley and the dancers in front of a huge mirror. When the music and steps didn't come out even, red-haired Saul Chaplin was there to adapt Porter's music. The pianist's ashes kept falling on the keys and the dancers pulled leg muscles and winced, and there were chuckles about this being the Garden of Eden in a $6,000,000 musical.
>
> But now the Garden of Eden has blossomed on another stage and you could see where the money is going. Three thousand dollars alone for that fancy apple tree, $33,000 for the complete set. A stage full of costumed dancers, an audience full of people, a hundred technicians and a big Todd-AO camera on a boom swinging above the heads of all. . . . Those sharp-edged brilliants over Shirley's leotard scratched [Adam] every time she slithered down and around his body. Sometimes they drew blood and a standby makeup man was there with a styptic pencil.[6] (*Eureka Humbolt Standard*, 21 August 1959)

In the middle of August, Pan rehearsed and filmed "Maidens Typical of France," a saucy washerwoman routine for Juliet Prowse and ten female chorus dancers in which the chorus mimes doing laundry as Prowse performs an energetic solo ending with a series of chaîné turns. The music turns jazzy for the big finish, and

Prowse and the girls whip the clothes in their baskets like strippers, bump and grind appropriately, and tumble backward into a final pose, with Prowse on the floor holding her legs up to display her petticoats. A brief cancan routine for Juliet and the girls followed on Pan's production schedule, after which three days were devoted to the comic "Apache" number for Shirley MacLaine and an ensemble of male dancers. Pan begins the "Apache" with MacLaine being dragged from a table (she is seated among the patrons) by Dancer No. 1 and thrown to the floor. After their physical and comically aggressive dance, Dancer No. 2 appears and fights with No. 1 over MacLaine who manages to knock him out with a breakaway bottle. No. 1 shoves her across the floor into the arms of Dancer No. 3, but immediately Dancer No. 4 enters and begins a tug of war with No. 3 over the woman, one dancer pulling her legs, the other pulling her arms. After she succeeds in freeing herself by knocking both of their heads against the floor, Dancer No. 1 reappears and lifts her into a dance to the tune of "Allez Vous-en," one of Porter's songs in the Broadway score of *Can-Can* not sung in the film. Suddenly, they find themselves surrounded by the other dancers brandishing knives and No. 1 attempts to fend them off and shield her. A fifth dancer appears, and a fight ensues after which MacLaine is slapped into an anteroom a few steps below the dance floor and her dummy-double is pulled out and thrown from dancer to dancer, ending back in the anteroom. MacLaine reemerges in a dazed condition but manages to fend off another attack from the dancers stabbing Dancer No. 2 in the chest and crawling back to the table where the routine began. Still very much alive, No. 2 follows her to the table and raises his hand as if to stab her. MacLaine screams shrilly; the dancer falls dead at her feet; and the on-screen audience applauds wildly. The "Apache" is quintessential Pan: a narrative dance filled with humor, props, furniture, and most important, movement that organically transforms reality into fantasy.

At the end of August, Pan put the final cancan number into rehearsal before leaving on 2 September to begin work on *Another Evening with Fred Astaire*, a television special scheduled for broadcast on 4 November (he would spend the month of September dividing his time between daytime cancan rehearsals at Twentieth Century-Fox and evening rehearsals with Astaire). Again assisted by Gino Malerba, Pat Denise, and Dave Robel, and following the rehearsal routine of Astaire's first television special, Pan collaborated with Astaire on the choreography for seven numbers. The opening sequence was called "The Afterbeat," introduced by a singing and dancing Astaire who is joined in a syncopated jazz dance, first by the chorus entering in groups through a backdrop of colorful, geometrically designed shapes, and finally by Barrie Chase. In the second number, "That Face," Astaire discovers the face of Barrie Chase on the cover of a fashion magazine and is propelled into a kind of dream fantasy in which he sees her face and body all around him until she finally appears in the flesh and dances an adagio with him, filled with elegantly conceived hip lifts. Drummer Alvin Stoller provides the impetus for the third number, in which Astaire creates a kind of comic narrative dance and pantomime to the rhythmic patterns and accents of the drums. In the routine Astaire plays drunk, pantomimes a baseball pitcher throwing a ball, acts the role of a matador during a bull fight, dances a waltz, and tosses an imaginary partner into the air and is crushed by her when she lands.

"Night Train," a narrative dance about unrequited love, begins with Astaire singing to the accompaniment of Jonah Jones's trumpet. Suddenly, the set of a train station is revealed and the Bill Thompson Singers take over the vocal narrative. Because Pan had only sixteen chorus dancers, he created the illusion of a crowded and busy station by means of nonstop diagonal movement patterns while Astaire sits alone on a central bench anticipating the arrival of his sweetheart. When she arrives, she is met by another man who spirits her away, and the solitary, stationary figure of Astaire, in sharp contrast to the quickly moving ensemble, emphasizes the pathos inherent in his disappointment. The number had originally been staged according to the lyrics of the song: "My sweetie's gone away on the night train." But Pan and Astaire quickly realized that as soon as the "sweetie" got on the train, the number was finished dramatically and no amount of choreography, no matter how well executed, could change that. When it seemed that the number was going to be cut from the show, Pan suddenly realized that the problem was the lyric. If "sweetie" was *returning* on the night train instead of going away, there would be something to build toward. Rewriting the lyric overnight, he slipped it into rehearsal the following day and suddenly the number had a dramatic build that worked.[7]

"My Baby," a word-jazz routine narrated by poet Ken Nordine, provides the background for the next number, a kind of "beat generation" dance for Astaire and Chase against a background of virtually immobile chorus dancers, evidently too "cool" to move (evocative of the chorus in "Frankie and Johnny" from *Meet Me in Las Vegas*). A nod to Astaire's participation in Stanley Kramer's soon-to-be-released film *On the Beach*, "Waltzing Matilda" follows with a swirling chorus dance beginning with couples waltzing in ballroom style and moving through a variety of musical moods and choreographic genres. "Sophisticated Lady" depicts Fred Astaire wearing an Alfred E. Neuman mask and sitting at a bar while Barrie Chase flirts with eight chorus dancers smartly dressed in black tie. To tease them, she ascends a spiral staircase briefly (like Sally Forrest in the "Waterfront Ballet" from *Excuse My Dust*) but after a comic tango with the Alfred E. Neuman character, she tosses the chorus men in a heap, pushes Neuman to the ground, and steps on him in triumph.

Unlike the first Astaire special that was taped during a live performance (the live feed that was sent to the East Coast on the day it was aired), the second special was taped in advance, allowing the show to be recorded in sections and eliminating problems such as quick set or costume changes. Pan approved of the process but worried that it might lead to excessive retakes that would eliminate the sense of spontaneity that he believed was the particular charm of the television medium. Hermes was particularly against tape editing—cutting shots into a completed sequence. "Until just about two weeks before we staged the Astaire show," Pan explained, "editing tape wasn't physically possible. There was always a jump and a wiggle on the screen right after each cut. Then somebody solved the problem, and as a result I think we ended up with two edited close-ups in the entire hour, both in the "Sophisticated Lady" number. I'm still not sure it wasn't a mistake" (Knight 1960, 43).

On Saturday 19 September, Pan took a day off from working with Fred Astaire to drive out to Twentieth Century-Fox to be on hand for a visit from Russian premier Nikita Khrushchev, the first Soviet premier to tour the United States. He had wanted to visit Disneyland, but the State Department felt that was too dangerous a choice and suggested instead a trip to a film studio where the premier could watch the making of a musical (which they felt was the lesser politically volatile choice). Following a luncheon at the Fox studio commissary, Khrushchev and his family were taken to the sound stage where *Can-Can* was in production. After formal introductions, Frank Sinatra explained that the cast would be performing excerpts from two scenes, in the first of which Maurice Chevalier and Louis Jourdan sang "Live and Let Live." Next, Shirley MacLaine speaking in Russian thanked Premier Khrushchev for sending artists such as those from the Bolshoi Ballet to the United States and invited him to watch a performance by American dancers. The *Oakland Tribune* (22 November 1959) described what happened next:

> Then, bang! It came with a wham! The can-can—led first by Juliet Prowse and then the rest of the girls and Shirley. They kicked and twirled, showed off their fronts, their backs, their sides. They dropped to the floor, raised their legs, and went through a series of gyrations Mr. Khrushchev thought belonged to private rather than public demonstration. Mrs. Khrushchev, who had smiled happily at Chevalier's number, frowned in disbelief. Khrushchev tried to maintain the self-possessed air of the man-of-the-world. But even this pretension was demolished by the climax of the dance. Juliet Prowse and Shirley MacLaine assumed stances with their legs spread wide apart. Two young male dancers then slid through their legs, each holding triumphantly aloft a pair of panties. Mr. and Mrs. Khrushchev looked at each other astonished, said nothing.

The following day in San Francisco, at a meeting of American union chiefs at the Mark Hopkins Hotel, Khrushchev sarcastically imitated the cancan he had seen in Hollywood, announcing: "This is a dance in which girls pull up their skirts. You're going to see that. We are not. This is what you call freedom—freedom for the girls to show their backsides. To us it's pornography, the culture of a people who want pornography. It's capitalism that makes girls that way." Certainly, the State Department would have been happier had Khrushchev gone to Disneyland. The next day, the premier's opinion of the dance made headlines all over the world, and Pan woke up to find himself more famous than he ever wanted to be, the man who staged the dance that offended Nikita Khrushchev.

The infamous cancan sequence was filmed in late September and following the taping of the Astaire special in early October, Hermes returned with Gino to the *Can-Can* set where he continued working at $2,000 a week until the beginning of November staging numbers for Frank Sinatra, Maurice Chevalier, and Louis Jourdan. Just as he was finishing up on the film, the television special was aired and received good reviews, though perhaps not the raves that greeted the first special. Nonetheless, the *New York Times* (5 November 1959) found Pan's choreography imaginative and the *Los Angeles Times* (5 November 1959) suggested that the special might win another Emmy for Hermes Pan because he "outdid himself in the choreography—this was probably the best danced show I ever saw—both from the standpoint of Barrie Chase and the kids in the chorus as well as the miraculous Astaire."

With the completion of his duties at Twentieth Century-Fox, Pan left for an extended vacation in New York City, staying at a luxurious penthouse duplex atop the Essex Hotel where he spoke to film critic Arthur Knight about his second exposure to the Todd-AO process. "I never liked to do tricks with the camera," he began, "nor do I like an excessive amount of cutting during a dance routine. With Todd-AO, there is really no need for either of these. You have a screen that is roughly the size and shape of the stage proscenium, and a camera that permits you to get very close to your dancers and yet show them in full figure." He explained, "What I think I like best about this new system is that you can stage a number more or less as you would see it from 'out front.' There is still a good deal of camera movement in the *Can-Can* dances, but it isn't movement for its own sake, or for tricky effects. The camera moves when a dancer moves. . . . On the whole, I'm very pleased with the way the dances for *Can-Can* have come out—and particularly our little 'Adam and Eve' number, with marvelous costumes that parody the animals, and some really fine dancing" (Knight 1960, 40–41).

Back in Los Angeles for the holidays, Pan signed on to choreograph *The Frances Langford Show*, a television special scheduled to be colorcast on 1 May 1960, and he also agreed to help Astaire with the social dance routines in *The Pleasure of His Company*, a nonmusical film at Paramount Pictures in which Astaire portrays "Pogo" Poole, an international playboy who unexpectedly returns to San Francisco for the wedding of his daughter (Debbie Reynolds) to an unsophisticated rancher (Tab Hunter). Pogo's charm manages to stir up trouble between his daughter and her fiancé and leads the husband (Gary Merrill) of his former wife (Lilli Palmer) to believe that Pogo wants to rekindle the old relationship.

Pan choreographed (or, rather, supervised) three social dance events for the film. The first takes place at a party in which Fred Astaire dances and converses with Debbie Reynolds to the music of "Personality" by Jimmy Van Heusen and Johnny Burke. As the dance progresses, another young man cuts in and Astaire ends up dancing with the hostess's mother. The second event happens later at the same party when Astaire dances with Lilli Palmer to the tune of "Lover" by Richard Rodgers and Lorenz Hart. As the dance continues, Astaire sings the song to his dance partner, recalling that the melody used to be "their song." In her memoir *Change Lobsters and Dance*, Lilli Palmer recalled begging the director, George Seaton, to cut the scene because of her fear of stepping on Astaire's feet while they danced. But as every opportunity to film Astaire dancing was golden, Lilli was forced to dance and immediately stepped on Astaire's feet, stopping him dead in his tracks. "I warned you," she said by way of excuse. Lilli recalled that the next time they attempted the routine, "he swept me off, he never allowed me to land at all, and I just hung suspended in his arms, trying to remember my lines while bereft of the support of terra firma" (Palmer 1975, 296–297). The third social dance moment occurs at the wedding celebration, where Astaire dances with Lilli Palmer, again to the tune of "Lover." A Screen Actors Guild strike halted production on 7 March and, although the strike was resolved in early April, Paramount delayed the completion of the film until November.

While Hermes was working on *The Pleasure of His Company*, he choreographed two production numbers—"The Continental" and "Zip-A-Dee-Doo-Dah"—for an episode of *Ford Startime* entitled "Jane Wyman and the Songs That Won Academy Awards," which was broadcast on 15 March and earned Pan much critical praise. The following month, Pan was hired to create the dances for *The George Burns Show*, an NBC television special scheduled to air on 7 June with a guest appearance from Betty Grable who performed "I Refuse to Rock 'n' Roll" from *Meet Me in Las Vegas*. After completing the Burns project, Hermes had time on his hands and according to his sister's diary, he "loafed around his house and garden all day."

As summer approached, Pan agreed to stage a club act for Johnny Mathis, the velvet-voiced ballad singer who, like Astaire in the television specials, wanted to produce his own show. Beginning with an engagement at the Greek Theatre in Hollywood in September, Mathis planned to produce a concert tour throughout the United States including a stop at the Geary Theatre in San Francisco, Mathis's home town. In August, while Hermes was in rehearsal with the act, the *New York Times* (4 August 1960) reported that he was being sought to choreograph a new Broadway musical, *The Count of Ten*, written by William L. Penzner, a Los Angeles real estate operator and producer of low-budget films. Announced as a February 1961 production under the direction of Busby Berkeley, the musical was set in a nightclub owned by a heavyweight boxing champion known as "the Count" because of his natty appearance. It is not known how far Pan allowed himself to be pursued for the project, but *The Count of Ten* never opened on Broadway.

By the middle of August, Hermes was back to doing double duty, choreographing the *Johnny Mathis* show during the day and working with Fred Astaire on his next television special, *Astaire Time*, in the evening. Doing two shows at once became more onerous for Pan than it had been in the past because of the difficulties inadvertently created by Bob Alberti, the musical director hired by Mathis. Alberti, who had been on the road successfully with Paul Anka prior to accepting the job, was a superb pianist but had no experience working with dancers or choreographers. From the outset, the job on the Mathis show seemed to him to be a bad fit, as he remarked in his autobiography *Up the Ladder and Over the Top*:

> At the first rehearsal I found a troupe of male "gypsies," a term used for freelance dancers, that were part of the new Mathis show. There was also a choreographer, Hermes Pan who was renowned for his work with Fred Astaire. This was all new to me, since I'd never been exposed to production shows with an entire cast of participants. I'd been doing okay as a personal conductor and accompanist, but this new challenge loomed larger than life, and to be honest, I was terrified. . . . It didn't take me too many days to realize that I wasn't going to be particularly happy with this venture. We did a few local one-nighters in the western part of the country, and during that time I really got the feeling that this career move was not a positive one. I never bonded with Johnny or anyone else in the organization, nor did I feel that I would ever fit. I wasn't ready to take on the responsibility of conducting a production of the magnitude that they had prepared, and I felt more depressed every day that I worked with the choreographer and the dancers. I didn't know exactly why, but it was a gut feeling. I decided to honor that feeling. (Alberti 2003, 72)

Alberti gave notice and was replaced by Gil Bowers who remained with Mathis through the tour. According to Larry Billman, who was a replacement dancer in the show after the Asian leg of the tour, Pan's work for the show was displayed in five dance numbers performed by eight dancers, four men and four women: the opening with Johnny Mathis, a version of the "Svengali" routine in *An Evening with Fred Astaire*; "The Gal with the Yaller Shoes," from *Meet Me in Las Vegas*, with square dancing and acrobatics; a basketball routine to the tune of "Puttin' on the Ritz," for Mathis and the male dancers with basketballs and hoops; a Latin routine entitled "Felicidades"; and a liltingly romantic finale during which Mathis sang "Tonight" and "Lover" while the dancers whirled around the stage. Billman recalled that "Puttin' on the Ritz" "was one of the toughest numbers I ever did, as—if you hit a crack in the stage floor—the balls would go into the audience and we'd finish bouncing imaginary basketballs. It was great fun, however and the audience enjoyed it." After a successful opening week at the Greek Theatre in Los Angeles, the company moved to San Francisco before opening in Honolulu, Manila, and cities across the country.

For *Astaire Time*, on which Hermes Pan served as associate producer as well as choreographer, an unprecedented deal was struck with the musicians' union to allow the use of prerecorded music. In addition to David Rose and his orchestra, the Count Basie Orchestra was invited on the show and, exciting as it may be to dance to jazz rhythms and brassy horn licks, both Pan and Astaire realized that jazz bands rarely play anything twice the same way and without the exact repetition of accents, melodic phrases, and rhythmic nuances, it would be impossible to set the choreography. The union permitted the use of prerecorded music but stipulated that the musicians had to be present (and therefore paid) when the prerecord was used for rehearsals, a small price to pay for the convenience of having the dance music fixed from the beginning of rehearsals.

Pan began the special with a rendition of the love theme from Tchaikovsky's *Romeo and Juliet Overture*, danced first by eight chorus couples before they are joined by Astaire and Barrie Chase. The music changes to a jazzy arrangement of Grieg's "Anrita's Dance" from *Peer Gynt*, which Hermes staged as a kind of call-and-response dance: when Astaire and Chase move the chorus is motionless behind them; when the chorus dances Astaire and Chase are silent. The number suggests the influence of Bob Fosse on Pan's choreography if only in the flagrant use of Fosse's hand-and-arm-over-the-head pose.

Cole Porter's "Miss Otis Regrets" follows in which Barrie Chase who is seated at a table dressed in a blue-spangled pant dress with a translucent skirt is told by her manservant (Astaire) why Miss Otis is unable to lunch today. Pan staged a comically seductive dance routine that resolves in a playful Latin segment where Astaire and Chase bounce on a fluffy pouf before returning to their original stuffy positions. After a performance of "Not Now, I'll Tell You When" by the Basie Orchestra, Astaire begins a subtle soft-shoe as Basie and the rhythm section play "Sweet Georgia Brown." As Astaire becomes more rhythmic in his dancing, beating accents on the piano with his hands and kicking it with his feet (like the "Piano Dance" in *Let's Dance*), the orchestra enters with wailing brass and Fred comically pantomimes dancing with an unseen partner, developing the routine he began with drummer Alvin Stoller in *Another Evening with Fred Astaire*. As the music gets wilder, so does Astaire's dancing, and after falling to his knees several times in a Jolson-like pose, he ends up on the piano with Count Basie.

Jean Sibelius's popular "Valse Triste" is the accompaniment to a narrative dance Pan designed for Barrie Chase and chorus in which she plays an old woman whose gaze into a mirror recalls her youthful beauty and amorous adventures. As the younger woman, she leaves the confines of her bedroom and joins a colorfully costumed group of dancers in a waltz. She dances with individual men in an elegant ballet-inspired routine that enables her to display precision pointe work, but in the end, the mood becomes somber as a foreboding figure in a dark cape carries her off, presumably to her death. To lighten the mood, Hermes created a number for twelve male chorus dancers, "If We Don't Dance, We Don't Get Paid," for which Pan is also credited as composer and lyricist. The credit is misleading since the number is an almost exact replica of "Le Comparse di Cinecittà (Extras of the Movie Studio)" in *Un Paio d'Ali*, the Italian musical Hermes staged in 1957. The number portrays the various styles of performance required of chorus dancers in films, beginning with a Spanish flamenco, a Russian Cossack dance, a tropical island routine, a gangster jazz ballet, a mambo, cowboy choreography, a tap dance, and an eighteenth-century minuet. Although the order of the dance styles and the musical accompaniment are slightly different than in the original, the number is the single extant recording in English of any of Pan's work on Italian musicals.

A mirror number with twin dancers Jane and Ruth Earl followed, during which Astaire watches Jane rehearse dance combinations in front of what appears to be her reflection in a large mirror. As in the "Bojangles of Harlem" shadow routine from *Swing Time*, the reflection suddenly moves out of sync with the "real" dancer revealing the trick that is being played on the eye. What makes the number especially appealing is the use of two mirror frames, one of which contains an actual mirror. When Jane walks in front of it to speak with Astaire, it is really her reflection that the audience members see, causing them to wonder, like Astaire, if the apparent incongruity witnessed in the other mirror was merely a figment of their imaginations. The question is answered when Fred steps through the first mirror frame discovering Jane's twin Ruth, and the three perform an expertly synchronized dance with the Earl twins mirroring one another throughout.[8]

Singer Joe Williams and the Basie Orchestra follow with a "Blues Medley" accompanying a narrative dance set in a stylized shantytown. Astaire appears as a student on his way to school dancing mournfully with a picture of the girl who broke his heart. After he tears up the photograph, the scene shifts to Barrie Chase, a tart wearing a red scarf and an off-the-shoulder black dress, performing a sexy dance to the tune of "Hallelujah, I Love Her So" in front of a seated figure smoking a cigar and wearing a derby. The music changes to "It's a Lowdown Dirty Shame," and we return briefly to Astaire sweeping up the litter in the street before watching Barrie Chase flirt with the chorus dancers. She and Astaire approach on opposite sides of a fence doing similar dance steps and, to the tune of "Going to Chicago Blues," they do a brief duet during which she flirts and he makes the sign of money, displeasing her to the degree that she berates him physically. The cigar-smoking figure appears with the chorus men, and Astaire attempts to flee over the fence. He is stopped by Chase and to the tune of "Shake, Rattle and Roll" they dance a jitterbugging duet, after which she takes out a gun and fires at him, chasing him around the set. They end up dancing again, having apparently resolved their differences, but the cigar smoker who has been watching from a bench takes out a gun and shoots them both as they fall into one another's arms.

When *Astaire Time* aired on Sunday, 25 September 1960, critics found Astaire's special "slick, smooth, and sharp," but without "the effervescence or style of his earlier two." Pan's work was generally praised, particularly "If We Don't Dance, We Don't Get Paid" and "Valse Triste" of which Jack Gould in the *New York Times* (29 September 1960) wrote, "The concept of Hermes Pan . . . was inventive, and there were some ensemble scenes with an attractive graciousness." If not as successful as *An Evening with Fred Astaire*, the show still managed to win two Emmy Awards for "Outstanding Program Achievement in the Field of Variety" and for "Outstanding Performance in Variety or Musical Performance."

In the fall, Hermes completed his work on *The Pleasure of His Company* at Paramount before returning to television to choreograph *Remember How Great*, scheduled to air on 9 February 1961. Produced by Gil Rodin, who served as production coordinator for *Astaire Time*, and sponsored by Lucky Strike cigarettes, the special featured Jack Benny, Connie Francis, Harry James and his band, Andy Williams, the McGuire Sisters, and Juliet Prowse, for whom Pan devised a narrative dance, "The Saga of Sadie Thompson," that critics called "the best part of the telecast." Once Pan completed his assignment for Juliet Prowse, he spent six weeks designing three production numbers for *The Sounds of America*, an NBC Telephone Hour Special scheduled for telecast on 17 February with an original score by Gordon Jenkins and featuring dancers Gene Nelson, Jacques d'Amboise, and the Earl Twins. Set in Disneyland (the special was originally titled *Sounds of Disneyland*), Pan's production numbers made use of Cinderella's Castle, Main Street, and the old saloon.[9] As Hermes noted in an interview with Charles Witbeck, "If we had sets like that for a movie musical, they'd cost a fortune. Naturally we worked out the dances to fit the sets. I think it's really a good show. It's different. There's no dialogue to speak of and the scenery is fun." Explaining how he came up with his ideas for the Disneyland numbers he noted, "Once I begin to move, things unfold and I get an idea. It's something that just creeps in. That's what worries me. I'm afraid ideas may just creep out sometime and I'll be stuck." When Witbeck remarked how fit Pan appeared, Hermes replied, "You should see me get out of a car. Sometimes I'm so stiff I can hardly move. Then I begin to warm up and I can dance. I don't walk very well, but I can dance. And I think that if I didn't dance I probably couldn't walk" (*Hartford Courant*, 15 February 1961).

By the middle of February 1961, Pan was already at work on the Ross Hunter $4,000,000 film adaptation of *Flower Drum Song*, Rodgers and Hammerstein's 1958 Broadway musical about a mail-order bride, Mei Li (Miyoshi Umeki), who arrives in San Francisco and discovers that her husband-to-be, nightclub owner Sammy Fong (Jack Soo), is uninterested in fulfilling the contract. Instead he attempts to convince the wealthy Wang family to accept Mei Li as the bride of the eldest son Wang Ta (James Shigeta) who happens to be in love with Linda Low (Nancy Kwan), a singer and exotic dancer in Sammy Fong's nightclub, with whom Fong is also enamored. When the Wang family discovers Linda's less than honorable profession they forbid the relationship and Wang Ta turns his affections toward Mei Li who loves him.

In the creation and teaching of the dance numbers, Pan worked from February 1961 well into May, assisted by Jimmy Huntley, one of the soloists in *An Evening with Fred Astaire*; Becky Varno, a dancer in *Another Evening with Fred Astaire*; and his constant companion, Gino Malerba. Pan designed "A Hundred Million Miracles" as a scene in a San Francisco park, in which Miyoshi Umeki, using illustrative hand gestures, captivates a spontaneously created audience that follows her throughout the routine. With "Fan Tan Fannie" Pan introduces the entertainment at the "Celestial Gardens" nightclub as Nancy Kwan and ten chorus girls perform

Pan rehearses Nancy Kwan on the set of "I Enjoy Being a Girl" (Courtesy of Photofest).

a brief cutely seductive number with enough bumps and grinds to render it naughty. Pan staged "The Other Generation" with simple walking movements and realistic gestures when first sung by the older members of the Wang family and then added jaunty steps and stylized gestures satirizing old folks and suggesting children's games when the number is performed by the youngsters. Hermes followed the singing with an impressive jazz dance solo for Patrick Adiarte before the number returns to reality as he accidently pitches a ball through a window.

In "I Enjoy Being a Girl," Pan staged another trompe l'oeil routine with Nancy Kwan dressed in a towel in front of three full-length mirrors creating four images of the singer on the screen as she sings. When the dance break begins, the figures in the mirror become fantasized images of what she might look like wearing a fancy hat, white stole, different colored dresses, or a bikini. When the singing continues, the images sing in harmony with the "real" character and abruptly return to the reality of the initial situation—a girl in a towel seeing her reflection in a triad of mirrors. In "Chop Suey," a number performed at a party celebrating one of the Wangs' becoming a United States citizen, Pan designed a potpourri of American dances beginning with a kind of Chinese square dance, followed by a sweeping ballroom waltz, a spirited Charleston, and finally a rock-and-roll sequence during which Patrick Adiarte performs another virtuosic solo. A "cool" section drawing its inspiration from Bob Fosse drives the number to a jazzy and energetic finish.

"Grant Avenue" made use of a $310,000 set, a facsimile of a three-block portion of San Francisco's Grant Avenue situated in the heart of Chinatown. Visuals of San Francisco's Chinese New Year Parade (with marching bands, floats, and paper dragons) lead to the performance of the number that begins on a float with Nancy Kwan and an ensemble of six men and eight women and later spills out into the street with a unison dance routine combining brassy jazz with Asian-flavored motifs. The dance travels, conspicuously exploring every inch of the huge and expensive set. Another performance number, "Gliding through My Memories," offered Pan the opportunity to stage a burlesque striptease. Beginning with the presentation of scantily clad showgirls with international monikers and colors evocative of their various countries, the number turns into a gimmicky fan dance for Nancy Kwan whose tastefully placed fans slap shut at the flick of a switch. In the *Los Angeles Examiner* (21 May 1961), Neil Rau visited the set as Nancy Kwan was preparing to do the routine on Stage Twenty-Two at Universal Studios:

> The setting is a splashy San Francisco Chinatown nightclub where the cover charge exceeds the covering of the chorines. Nancy is the premier ecdysiast, dressed mainly in three large strategically placed oriental fans. "I didn't know science was a hobby of yours," says director Henry Koster as he greets me with a grin. But I retain my dignity as an explorer on the new frontier of science, and question him about the automated striptease. "It isn't complete automation," he confesses. "The machine is unable to replace entirely the woman-power necessary to get the job done."
>
> He informs me the idea started when he, [Ross] Hunter and dance director Hermes Pan decided a standard fan dance would be "old hat." They called in Orien Ernest, a scholarly individual who invents special effects for motion pictures. And Ernest manufactured three tiny motors the size of a half dollar operated by wires and a battery, that open and close Nancy's fans seemingly by remote control. "It was a routine assignment for me," Ernest says casually when Koster invites him over for further explanation, "but I was stuck for an answer when my wife asked me what kind of day I had at the office."

Designed to demonstrate to the Wang family the inappropriateness of Wang Ta's affection for fan-tan dancer Linda, the number is frequently interrupted by reaction shots.

Wang Ta's other love interest, Helen Chao (Reiko Sato), expresses her feelings in the unrequited love song "Love Look Away" for which Pan devised a dream ballet that begins with her becoming engulfed by the San Francisco fog. She passes a series of mannequins—one wears a wedding gown, another a flowing white dress—and she finds herself wearing the dress and waltzing with Wang Ta to the tune of "You Are Beautiful" as a mannequin wearing skimpy clothes passes by them and Wang Ta follows it off. Suddenly, a dancer with a demonic Chinese mask appears and dances with her followed by three other dancers wearing the same type of mask. The music becomes more percussive developing first into a jazz arrangement of "Love Look Away" and later into a rhythmic bolero during which she is lifted from dancer to dancer and chased to the top of a rock, finally ending up in Wang Ta's arms before sliding back into the fog.

Hermes balanced the nightmarish collision of Eastern and Western cultures in "Love Look Away" with "Sunday," a humorous pantomime ballet depicting Nancy Kwan and Jack Soo's ideal Sunday at home. After beginning the song in a real situation, the couple find themselves in a highly stylized apartment setting in which a maid greets a visiting couple who are immediately served drinks by a servant on roller skates. When the couple goes off to another part of the apartment, two sexy girls appear—evidently the guests of Jack Soo—and Kwan dispenses with them quickly. Another couple passes through the living room: a young man is walking in a seated position supporting a woman leaning back on his chest to the sound of Latin music. A little girl in a cowboy outfit appears and watches an old-fashioned cowboy show on a large-screen television. She shoots at the screen and the black-and-white cowboy and Indian step out of the television and chase the various houseguests in a circle around the girl shooting her gun. A general

"Sunday" performed by, l. to r., Irene Tau, Al Huang, Pat Uyemura, Frank Radcliffe, Jeanne Limyou, Finis Jhung, Patti Leo, Nancy Kwan, Jack Soo, Alice Nishimura, Cherylene Lee, Jack Tygett, and David Toguri (Courtesy of the author's collection).

chase throughout the house follows in which all of the dancers in the number enter and exit through various hallway doors in the manner of the old Mack Sennett comedies, and the ballet ends when Kwan knocks out Jack Soo causing the couple to return to reality.

Flower Drum Song was completed on 21 June 1961 and released in November, at which time Hermes Pan received excellent notices for his work. The *Hollywood Reporter* (8 November 1961) wrote that "Hermes Pan's choreography is witedged at times, as in the 'Fan Tan Fannie' number, and indigenous to the locale and rising out of the pavements, as in the spectacular 'Grant Avenue' number." *Limelight* (9 November 1961) echoed the praise for "Fan Tan Fannie" and "Grant Avenue" and added that "[Nancy Kwan] and Soo also are good in a production number called 'Sunday,' though the choreography of Hermes Pan at this point is not very original. Pan atones for this lack with a top flight bit of terpsichorean staging for Reiko Sato in a number called 'Love Look Away.' " The *Motion Picture Herald* (15 November 1961) concluded, "But more than the tuneful music are the dance numbers, all of which are rollicking, elaborate, lavishly mounted and smashingly successful. The exhibitor may reasonably anticipate that his audience will break into spontaneous and appreciative applause at the conclusion of several of them. . . . The dance numbers without question are the highlights of the picture."

11

Seventy-Five Watusi Witch Doctors

Hermes Pan was introduced to the Twentieth Century-Fox production of *Cleopatra* in the fall of 1959 while he was working on *Can-Can*. Producer Walter Wanger was busy with preproduction for the film at the studio and asked Hermes to prepare Joan Collins for a screen test for the title role. In his spare time, Pan taught the actress the manners and bearing of the legendary pharaoh and, though eventually the screen test was made, Hermes was never apprised of the results. A year and a half later, Pan was again approached by the producer, this time with an offer to choreograph a key processional sequence for the film—Cleopatra's triumphal entry into Rome. Like everyone else in Hollywood, Hermes was aware of the problems that had surrounded the production: the never-ending rewrites; the costly delays caused by the illnesses and vicissitudes of the star, Elizabeth Taylor; and the resignation of its original director, Rouben Mamoulian. But when Wanger revealed that Joseph Mankiewicz, Taylor's director on *Suddenly Last Summer*, had taken over the film and that production had moved from London to the studios of Cinecittà in Rome, Pan's favorite city, Hermes jumped at the opportunity.

On 10 May 1961, Pan worked out an agreement with Wanger in which he would provide choreography for the film at $2,000 a week, guaranteed for no less than fifteen consecutive weeks. In addition, he was guaranteed credit as "Choreography by Hermes Pan" on a separate card, given lodging and traveling expenses (first class if available), and a weekly per diem of $300 for living expenses. Originally stipulating that work would begin on 15 June after the completion of *Flower Drum Song*, the contract was amended to begin a week later. Arthur Park, Pan's representative at MCA, advised him not to sign the agreement immediately, hoping to negotiate for the inclusion of Pan's name on all paid publicity for the film and more important billing than he had heretofore received. When it appeared evident that Twentieth Century-Fox was adamant in its refusal to add Pan's name to publicity and equally clear that Pan was satisfied with his billing, MCA held up the contract no longer and Pan signed it on 8 January 1962, seven months after he began work on the film.

Early in June Pan met with Wanger to discuss Vittorio Nino Novarese's costume designs for Cleopatra's procession into Rome. In a letter to Mankiewicz,

Wanger noted that "Hermes has some very good ideas which I am pretty sure are going to please you tremendously" (Wanger 1963, 81). At the same meeting, the producer turned over to Pan photos and resumes of African-American actors and actresses he wanted to use, types that might be very useful to the choreographer in developing the procession. After spending a week researching Roman pageants and dances, Hermes was back in Wanger's office where he was told to let his imagination run wild: "It was the biggest responsibility in my career," Pan later explained. "They told me to spare no expense, but make it the most spectacular thing ever seen in movies. Well, that was quite a premise! I asked for hundreds of horses, chariots, girls on elephants tossing coins, cobras, pole vaulters, and African warriors. All the elements had to keep moving, like in a ballet, to create a spontaneous excitement. It was a headache, but I think it worked as expected" (Rimoldi 1988, 8).

On 22 June, the day he was scheduled to begin work on *Cleopatra*, Pan was still in Hollywood in a business meeting with Fred Astaire at Choreo Enterprises, Inc., a record company that Pan and Astaire had created in the spring of 1961 in partnership with drummer Jackie Mills and composer Tommy Wolf. Pan appears to have also used his association with Mills and Wolf to hone his skills as a songwriter (the United States Copyright Office shows claims dated May and October 1961 for "Hip Strip," "The Slop," "Ulysses's" and "Fickle Chicle," all with the designation "Music by Hermes Pan, Jackie Mills, and Tommy Wolf"). In addition to releasing a number of jazz albums, Choreo Records (later known as Ava Records) issued the sound tracks of Astaire's three television specials, *Three Evenings with Fred Astaire*, as well as Elmer Bernstein's *To Kill a Mockingbird* and *Walk on the Wild Side*. The singles release of the theme from *Walk on the Wild Side* hit number one on the charts and earned the company a gold record.

When Pan arrived in Rome at the end of June, he was ushered into a penthouse apartment on the Piazza Colonna and provided with a car and chauffeur to drive him to and from the studio and all around Rome. His first order of business upon arrival was meeting with his assistant Wilbert Bradley and casting the women dancers, African warriors, horses, elephants, zebras, and cobras that he had planned to use in the procession. Hermes had wanted to import a Watusi tribe of dancers seven feet tall from Uganda but hired West-Indian dancers instead when negotiations with the African tribe became overly complicated. "I was thanked profusely by the production team for my 'generous artistic concession,'" Pan wrote in "The Mortal Goddesses" segment of his memoir. "Their attitude was astoundingly flattering. It really was like Paradise, I began thinking. Of course I had no idea that big troubles were beginning to brew for the picture" (Pan, Columbia, Kramer 1983, 50a). One of Pan's troubles became evident during rehearsals: the elephants he had cast were temperamental and would not work with the horses. In fact, one of the pachyderms pulled up stakes and started to run mad around the studio. After scouting throughout Europe for trainable elephants, Pan finally settled on a good-natured herd from England that took direction quickly.

Minutes from the Special Meeting of Choreo Enterprises, Inc. (Courtesy of the author's collection).

Before rehearsals began Hermes had mapped out the extended spectacle of Cleopatra's entrance, each part of which was designed to surpass what came before. In Pan's conception the procession begins with a blast of fanfare trumpets from forty trumpeters mounted on matched Arabian stallions that charge into a replica of the Roman Forum through the resplendent, though anachronistic, Arch of Constantine (it had actually been built three centuries later). Eight chariots driven by matching teams of horses follow in a crisscross pattern with an archer standing beside the charioteer. An escort of one hundred bowmen next shoot into the sky golden arrows attached to long colored streamers. These are followed by a troupe of Egyptian dancing girls carrying long poles with more streamers attached, which they manage to shoot into the air as far as thirty feet while they dance. The principal female dancer is bare-chested except for two strategically placed pasties. Through the arch appears a model of the Lighthouse of Alexandria drawn by the royal oxen followed by sixteen donkeys painted as zebras on top of which are dwarfs painted black-and-white tossing baskets of sweets to the crowd. A human pyramid forms, dissolves, and re-forms repeatedly as two elephants bearing four acrobats and two more elephants bearing scantily clothed women

The "Egyptian Dancing Girls" sequence in *Cleopatra* (Courtesy of the author's collection).

appear. As the women throw coins to the populace, one of the elephants carries a woman to Mark Antony, who seductively lifts her off the elephant and deposits her on another. Twelve green-smoke dancers enter through all three openings of the arch. A cobra measuring a hundred feet in length appears behind them accompanied by "Cobra Girls" waving their arms in snakelike motions before seventy-five Watusi witch doctors charge into the forum moving in a cloud of yellow smoke emanating from the tall staffs they carry. Behind them, a golden backdrop of butterfly wings is created by dancers holding fabric in the air while African dancers go into a wild dance to the accompaniment of indigenous percussion instruments. The smoke suddenly becomes red and pole-vaulters dressed as bird men fly over the heads of the Watusi and let drop cascades of multicolored confetti from bombs triggered in their spears. An army of fan dancers appear drawing a huge golden pyramid around which dancers manipulate their fans like wings in a dance of supplication before the pyramid opens, letting two thousand doves fly up to the sky. Roman trumpeters blow a long and ceremonial fanfare answered by Egyptian mounted trumpeters. An Egyptian honor guard appears before the entrance of three hundred gold-covered slaves walking sixteen men abreast in precision cadence pulling a huge black marble Sphinx between the paws of which are seated Cleopatra and her son Caesarion. A group of Nubians painted like marble and appearing at first to be a bas-relief come to life and carry the queen and her son down to the floor of the forum where they bow before Julius Caesar and the

Senate to the cheers of the six thousand spectators on hand, marking the end of the number.[1]

On 4 October, Pan's guaranteed fifteen weeks had run out and the sequence had yet to be filmed. Bad weather, illness, and a variety of other problems (including Elizabeth Taylor's scandalous affair with her costar, Richard Burton) that kept *Cleopatra* in the headlines contributed to the delay. As Pan noted to Ronald L. Davis in 1983, "We rehearsed for four months on that procession with Cleopatra into Rome. I had seventy-five black dancers, seventy-five white dancers, and animals. It was just a nightmare. But I finally just relaxed and enjoyed it because nothing you could do would hurry it up."[2] At the studio Pan continued to work on the physical mannerisms and poses of the characters, particularly Cleopatra's waiting women for whom he designed a short dance when Cleopatra receives Caesar (Rex Harrison) in the first part of the film. In the second half, Pan created an orgiastic bacchanal in which a swarm of nymphs seduce Mark Antony (Richard Burton) with a sensuous, sinewy dance. Even the rehearsals of Pan's smaller projects met with delays because Taylor and Burton were in love, often indisposed and unable to attend. "Sometimes they'd go three or four weeks and not even have to go to the studio. I mean—having a nice apartment in Rome and, of course, enjoying the pool with their friends" (Davis 1983, n.p.). By the third week of November, Pan's contract with Fox was put on an indefinite hiatus so in January 1962, still waiting for his production number to be filmed, Hermes agreed to do the choreography for an Italian television show produced by his friend Gorni Kramer, who had composed the music for *Un Paio d'Ali*. The program *Alta Fedelta* (*High Fidelity*) featured popular Italian singer-dancer Lauretta Masiero and jazz trombonist Mario Pezzotti in an evening similar to the Astaire specials in conception and presentation. When he completed his work for the television show, Pan moved on to choreograph an Italian film, *Canzoni nel mondo* (*Songs of the World*), assisted by Tito LeDuc and Gino Malerba, who had recently returned to Italy. The film starred Gilbert Bécaud, Dean Martin, and Melina Mercouri heading a list of popular European performers. In his studio biography, Hermes noted that "after the nine month session with *Cleopatra* in Italy I had become a pretty good linguist, hence the opportunity to do this particular Italian show."

Finally on 13 April, with thousands of extras on hand to cheer, Cleopatra's entrance between the paws of the Sphinx went before the cameras, nine months after rehearsals began. The rest of the lengthy procession sequence followed on 8 and 9 May. Speaking to Hedda Hopper about the experience Hermes explained: "The dancing girls are French, English, German, Spanish, African and West Indian, with a few Americans. Trying to get girls of exceptional beauty of face and figure who could dance was the main problem. Weather was another as, on several occasions, deluges of rain sent 6,000 extras home and called for time out to repair costumes and settings. The doves [actually pigeons] in the pyramid were shut up so long waiting for the 'take' that when the pyramid opened not a single bird flew out. They'd gone to sleep in the dim interior of the pyramid and I had to station

Hermes Pan preparing Cleopatra's handmaidens to welcome Julius Caesar in *Cleopatra* (Courtesy of the author's collection).

a man in there with a gun and blank cartridges to get them started" (*Los Angeles Times*, 23 April 1963). The man inside the pyramid was Gino Malerba, who emerged covered in droppings from the startled birds!

After eleven months in Rome, Hermes Pan was on his way back to Cherokee Lane at the beginning of June 1962. Hermes, his niece Christa (who had come to visit near the end of the shoot), and a Fiat he had bought in Rome were aboard the Italian liner *Michelangelo* along with Elizabeth Taylor and Richard Burton. Sailing across the Atlantic, the famous couple sought out his companionship and Hermes enjoyed theirs. Pan found Burton witty, urbane, and loquacious, easy to engage in conversation on a myriad of topics. Taylor, the quieter of the two, was no less charming to Hermes, who found her private reticence to be an endearing complement to her public image. In New York, Pan and Christa disembarked and began to drive cross-country to California, but by the time they reached Chicago, the pair were disenchanted with driving and decided to put the car on a train headed for Los Angeles. Almost as soon as they boarded, they once again met up with Taylor and Burton who continued to travel with them (and the car) all the way to Los Angeles. In his memoir, Pan notes that Burton was taken with Christa's eyes, a compliment indeed since Elizabeth Taylor was famous for her beautifully expressive glances.

Hermes recalls that on one occasion, while he and Christa sat across from the couple in the dining car, Burton broached the subject with his companion. "Doesn't she have the most *beautiful* eyes?" he gushed. Taylor looked across the table at the young girl and smiled. "Yes, she does," she replied in a tone that was neither envious nor condescending but designed to put the issue to rest (Pan, Columbia, Kramer 1983, 59a).

"I wish I had saved all the countless memos I got from them during the making of the picture," Pan told Hedda Hopper. "I could have sold them for thousands. They were all puzzling; most explaining why they wouldn't be present and why they couldn't work. I was so disgusted I tore them up and threw them in the wastebasket" (*Los Angeles Times*, 2 September 1965).

Almost immediately upon his return, Hermes was back at work choreographing a new nightclub act for his friend Ann Miller that kept him occupied through the summer months when he wasn't out in Malibu with Father Jim—now Monsignor Jim—and his sister-in-law Dot who had taken a job at Jim's rectory. Monsignor Jim O'Callaghan had become pastor of Our Lady of Malibu in 1960, the church where conductor and arranger Nelson Riddle and his wife worshipped. Monsignor Jim recalled the time when Hermes Pan, Fred Astaire, and Nelson Riddle attended a bossa nova concert in Santa Monica. "After the concert, they came over to my house for some food. They started discussing the tempo of the bossa nova. Fred and Hermes thought it went one way, but Nelson saw it differently. It was quite a discussion. The next day Nelson called me. He realized that Fred and Hermes were right" (Levinson 2001, 216–217).

Much of the fall was spent loafing at home with friends and training his pet toucan, but as winter began, Blake Edwards invited him to choreograph the musical numbers in *The Pink Panther* starring David Niven as Sir Charles Lytton, the famous jewel thief the Phantom, and Peter Sellers as Inspector Jacques Clouseau, the French detective on his trail. The early days of 1963 returned Pan to Cinecittà in Rome where *The Pink Panther* was filming, and in less than a week he staged three social dance sequences (one of which was the twist performed at a costume ball) and "Meglio Stasera (It Had Better Be Tonight)," a Latin, jet-set number sung by Fran Jeffries at a comfortable get-together in front of a fireplace at a ski resort in Cortina. The number begins subtly with the sound of percussion instruments playing a Latin rhythm and a rear view of Fran Jeffries swaying in a tight-fitting black ski outfit. When she turns to sing, she is filmed from the waist up (like the way Pan shot Carmen Miranda) to emphasize shoulder accents, extended arms, and rhythmic hand movements. After a short musical interlude in which Pan gave Jeffries sensuous and sinewy movements, she performs a brief but pulsating samba with two male dancers and leads Clouseau and the other guests to the center of the floor, moving spontaneously to the infectious beat of the music.

When his work with *The Pink Panther* was finished, Pan moved on to choreograph a revival of Garinei and Giovannini's 1958 blockbuster *Buonanotte Bettina* (*Good Night, Betty*) starring Walter Chiari, one of Italy's most popular performers, at the Teatro Nuovo in Milan. Inspired by the outstanding success of Françoise Sagan's novel *Bonjour Tristesse*, the musical tells the story of a shy wife (Delia Scala) who writes a scandalous novel and accidently forgets the manuscript in the backseat of a cab. At a birthday party for her husband (Walter Chiari), one of their friends gives him a book called *Buonanotte Bettina* as a gift, and it turns out that the book is the wife's novel. The husband becomes threatened by the overwhelming success of the book and his wife's sudden celebrity, and he is tempted by another woman who wastes little time in trying to seduce him. In the end, the husband remains faithful and accepts having a famous authoress rather than a shrinking violet for a wife. A bluesy rock-and-roll number, "Super Joe," depicted the husband's idea of his wife's fantasies in a dream ballet performed by Delia Scala and a chorus of macho male dancers. "Com'è bello dormer soli" ("How nice it is to sleep alone"), a rhythmic charm song evoking "Let's Call the Whole Thing Off," was performed by the bickering couple in adjacent rooms. "Papparazzo," a lively patter production number depicting the metamorphosis from shy wife to celebrity, recalled Pan's staging of the "Night Train" sequence in *Another Evening with Fred Astaire*. The seductress performed the Italian equivalent of "I Enjoy Being a Girl," a fashion routine in which she looks into the mirror and fantasizes wearing seductive clothing, and "Simpatico" ("Compatible"), the big ballad of the musical, provided Hermes with the opportunity to design an elegant ballroom dance. Neither innovative nor original, Pan's choreography for *Buonanotte Bettina* gave Italian audiences precisely what they wanted: the look and ambiance of American film musicals of the 1930s and 1940s.

Hermes flew back to California in March to stage Barrie Chase's act at the Congo Room of the Hotel Sahara in Las Vegas with three of Pan's favorite dancers, Buddy Bryan, Bert May, and Christopher Riordan, who noted to Peter Levinson that Hermes "was like Fred [Astaire], working, working, working. Fred was sort of mimicking everything that Hermes did. He came in every day to watch rehearsals. Fred wanted something wonderful to happen for Barrie, even though he was not going to be part of it" (Levinson 2009, 335). After a month of rehearsal, Chase and company opened at the Sahara at the beginning of April and were greeted with a "tremendous welcome" (*Dance Magazine* [May 1963]: 77). Later in the month, in anticipation of the release of *Cleopatra* in June, Hedda Hopper devoted an entire column to Pan's work on the film. "This is the first time choreography has taken on such dimension," he told her. "I've never before had a completely free hand with a pageant which used thousands of people and a limitless budget to stage the fantasy of a lifetime" (*Los Angeles Times*, 23 April 1963). Pan was so pleased with the article that he wrote her the following day:

> Dear Hedda,
> I want to thank you so much for the lovely article you wrote about me. I was indeed pleased and flattered to have the whole column devoted to my work on "Cleo."

With heartfelt thanks,
Sincerely,
Hermes Pan

Pan was less pleased when he saw the finished picture since it chopped up the pageant he so carefully created, cutting out the Lighthouse at Alexandria, the human pyramid, the cobra sequence, the elephant girls, and the dwarfs on zebras—all of the animal spectacle. But he was happy that his work was favorably noticed in the press, even by critics who otherwise disliked the film. While a negative review in London from the *Times* (31 July 1963) argued that "almost alone Mr. Harrison carries the first half—with some slight aid, admittedly, from one or two elaborately staged if unexcitingly shot set-pieces like Cleopatra's triumphal entry into Rome," Justin Gilbert's rave notice in the *New York Mirror* emphasized that "*Cleopatra* is a spectacular, sensuous spectacle. It is enormous. A single scene, wherein Cleopatra enters Rome, perched atop a ten-story float pulled by hundreds of slaves and witnessed by thousands, might well be considered its hallmark" (*Variety*, 19 June 1963). It should perhaps be noted that Bosley Crowther, the *New York Times* film critic, devoted two paragraphs praising Pan's staging but failed to mention his name in the review.

Around the time Hedda Hopper published her column about Pan, Hermes was in negotiations for *My Fair Lady*, a significant event because it was only the second time in his career that Pan actively pursued choreographing a particular film. Getting hired by producer Jack Warner and director George Cukor was no easy task, however, since they were focused on getting a choreographer who was either "hot" at the moment or British for the job. Cukor originally wanted Bob Fosse but he had been signed for a revival of *Pal Joey* and was unavailable. Because of her Tony Award–nominated choreography for *The Music Man*, Onna White was considered as well as the award-winning Agnes de Mille; Miriam Nelson, the choreographer for the *Donna Reed Show*, *Bonanza*, and the *Red Skelton Hour*; and Ernest Flatt, the choreographer for the *Garry Moore Show*. Early in April, Audrey Hepburn, who had been hired to play the role of Eliza Doolittle, wrote to Cukor suggesting Eugene Loring, her choreographer for *Funny Face*, but an interoffice memo at Warner Brothers on 5 April 1963 notes that a deal had been concluded with Pan at $2,000 a week, with a guarantee of fifteen weeks, beginning on 22 April.[3] As the month progressed, a collaboration between Hermes Pan and Lady Vida Hope, the British dance director, was in place until her salary demands ($3,000 a week) and previous commitments removed her from consideration. Sir Frederick Ashton, who had just assumed the directorship of the Royal Ballet in London, was also approached but had to decline because he could not take time away from the ballet company. In May, Tony Charmoli, a television and nightclub choreographer, was also considered but by the beginning of June, Hermes Pan alone was slated as the dance director for *My Fair Lady*, the Alan Jay Lerner–Frederick Loewe musical about Eliza Doolittle, a flower girl transformed into a sophisticated lady by phonetics professor Henry Higgins (Rex Harrison).

Assisted by his friends Becky Varno and Frank Radcliffe, Hermes began dance rehearsals at the end of June in preparation for the start of filming on 12 August. Pan did not want simply to reproduce Hanya Holm's original Broadway choreography for the film, but he also knew that with Alan Jay Lerner adapting his original libretto into the screenplay, Rex Harrison reprising his role as Henry Higgins, and Jack Warner's desire to create a road show film version of the stage show, the opportunities for innovation would be slight. "Cukor let me do anything I wanted to," Pan recalled. "Like the idea on the 'Loverly' number. [The original] was nothing like I did, which I'm glad. Of course, the 'Ascot' had similarity because it was black and white and Cecil Beaton wanted it a certain way . . . so I tried to keep all the movements just ridiculously stuffy. And then I put [in] the idea of the near misses—almost stepping on a train, or the woman and man bending over and almost goosing the woman as she walked away, and little things like that . . . subtle . . . as a running gag. I don't know whether it came across or not" (Davis 1983, n.p.).

Neither Cukor nor Pan was interested in simply re-creating the Broadway musical. "We're trying to use all this wonderful material without letting any of it slip by—and still get a film and not a photographed musical comedy out of it," Cukor explained in an interview with Philip K. Scheuer of the *Los Angeles Times* (6 October 1963). "For instance, some of the things 'Liza talks about, we illustrate. During this 'Just You Wait' song, six red-coated soldiers and a king march Henry Higgins down the steps of his house and shoot him dead." During the same interview, Hermes Pan added another example of cinematic movement. "When 'Liza . . . sings 'I Could Have Danced All Night,' we'll have her dance, shooed on by the housekeeper, all the way up the spiral staircase to her bedroom." Because of the sensitive nature of Eliza's transformation from flower girl to lady, Cukor decided to shoot the film in sequence, an unusual procedure in filmmaking, and because of Rex Harrison's desire to perform his musical numbers "live" as he did them on stage, he did not perform to a prerecorded vocal track. Instead, he was furnished with a concealed microphone and talk-sang the songs as he was being filmed.

The filming of *My Fair Lady* was completed around Christmas 1963, and Pan summarized the effort as "the perfect blend of story, dance and music" (*Pacific Stars and Stripes*, 15 December 1963). Almost a year later, on 21 October 1964, it opened in New York City to rave reviews, with Bosley Crowther calling it a "superlative," rendition of *My Fair Lady*, "the most eloquent and moving that has yet been done. . . . Though it runs for three hours—or close to it—this *My Fair Lady* seems to fly past, like a breeze. Like Eliza's disposition to dancing, it could go on, for all I'd care, all night" (*New York Times*, 22 October 1964). Although enraptured with the film, Crowther again neglected to mention Pan by name in his review even when favorably mentioning the musical numbers. Arthur Knight, however, devotes much of his review to Pan's work in *Dance Magazine* (December 1964):

Hermes Pan, the film's choreographer, has explained that he sought to build characterization, particularly in that earlier part of the picture, through dance movement and gesture—the huddling of the shoulders and the proffering of a bunch of violets no less than the skipping and jigging that Audrey Hepburn does to the tune of "Wouldn't It Be Loverly.". . . Pan's work goes considerably beyond that. "Wouldn't It Be Loverly" affords him the opportunity to stage a street dance with the fruit and flower handlers of Covent Garden clustering about as Audrey Hepburn converts a peddler's wagon into a kind of teeter totter. In "A Little Bit of Luck" and the rollicking "Get Me to the Church on Time," Stanley Holloway recalls the London music halls as he feints a soft-shoe, or high-steps it through a pub. "The Rain in Spain" inspires Miss Hepburn, Rex Harrison, and Wilfred Hyde-White to a gay fandango, well related to Hanya Holm's original, but somehow not as dynamically exciting. . . . "The Ascot Gavotte" and "The Embassy Waltz" are less, not more fully developed choreographically than the stage production, but much more opulently costumed and staged.

In all of this, Pan obviously had the close and sympathetic collaboration of George Cukor, a director of exquisite taste and sensibility. Between them, they keep the film looking and moving marvelously well. What both lack, however, is that ultimate flair for cinematic invention that would have kept this *Fair Lady* on its toes—and might have brought the audience to its feet. . . . The ingredients were there, but not the drive. By clinging too close to the original, the film emerges as tasteful, intelligent, superior—and just a bit stuffy. (Knight 1964, 30–32)

Knight's views seem to be reflected by Cukor in an interview with Gavin Lambert. "My only criticism of what we did [in *My Fair Lady*] is that some of the choreography might have been bolder" (Lambert 1972, 240–241).

The completion of *My Fair Lady* in December 1963 was a milestone in Pan's career. It would be the last "hit" American movie for the choreographer whose career began thirty years before. The end of the year marked a significant change in Hermes's social life as well. His intimate friend Gino Malerba, who had returned to Italy the previous year, had fallen in love with a twenty-year-old English actress named Margaret Lee and married her. Possibly, Gino felt that the attachment to a rising starlet was more promising than that to an aging choreographer. In any case, Pan viewed the break philosophically: "What happens is what is supposed to happen" and continued gardening and educating himself (and his toucan) by learning the names of all the different species of palm trees that grow in California. If there were any angry words between him and Gino, Pan never mentioned them to anyone, nor did he display any negative feelings. In the eyes of his friends and family—many of whom may have been relieved to see Gino out of Pan's life—Hermes seemed to take it all in stride. How he really felt about the loss is as much a shadow as the relationship itself—but one thing is certain: Hermes never entered into such an intimate relationship again.

The family festivities during the Christmas holidays were a welcomed respite for Pan, but immediately after the New Year he proceeded to bury himself in work choreographing "Days of Wine and Roses" for Barrie Chase and Christopher Reardon on *The Hollywood Palace*. When that was done he started rehearsals with Fred Astaire and Barrie Chase on another television special, "Think Pretty," an episode of *Bob Hope Presents the Chrysler Theatre* with a title song composed by Tommy Wolf and original music by John (then billed as Johnny) Williams. In "Think Pretty" Astaire plays the head of a small recording company who plans to record comedian Louis Nye's nightclub act for future release as an album against the wishes of Nye's personal manager (Barrie Chase). The comic winds up in the hospital and Fred decides to record him there, offering 10 percent of the album sales to the hospital for its cooperation. Neither Hermes Pan nor Barrie Chase thought much of the script; only Astaire, who had worked with the writers, seemed to like the material.

Pan collaborated with Astaire on the choreography for three numbers: an old-fashioned tap solo with cane; a mellow ballroom routine for Astaire and Barrie Chase; and an ebullient ensemble Watusi, the bright rock-and-roll dance in which partners stand several feet apart and engage in angular gyrations. In his regular visits to nightclubs and dance halls, Hermes had learned the Watusi from watching the younger generation dance and he enjoyed teaching it to Astaire. He even persuaded him to visit a few night spots to observe it. "I think it's a lot of fun," Fred told syndicated columnist Bob Thomas. "It's not really a dance. It's more of a movement, an expression. . . . The music plays real loud and everybody gets carried away" (*Cumberland Evening Times*, 6 July 1964). The videotaping of "Think Pretty" at Universal Studios during the month of July was filled with practical jokes and high-spirited fun, little of which was in evidence when the show aired in October. The television critics were as unimpressed with the script in their reviews as Pan was in rehearsals. In the *New York Times*, Jack Gould complained, "For a few tantalizing moments of seeing Fred Astaire dance once again, the viewer . . . had to wait a long hour of ridiculous situation comedy. . . . The prospect of seeing [Barrie Chase and Fred Astaire] in light and lilting movement turned out to be nothing but a come-on for routine silliness from Hollywood" (3 October 1964). Modern sources suggest that the show was a pilot for a potential television series, but the critical reception prevented the project from progressing any further.

When his work on "Think Pretty" was finished, Pan moved on to the next Blake Edwards film, *The Great Race*, a turn-of-the-century comedy about an automobile race from New York to Paris. Pan staged another grand waltz sequence and created an extended western saloon routine, "He Shouldn't-a-Hadn't-a Oughtn't-a Swang on Me," composed by Henry Mancini and Johnny Mercer, featuring low-class showgirls decked out in red, white, and blue spangled costumes and Dorothy Provine sitting on a crescent moon suspended in the air.

After *The Great Race*, Pan returned to Rome to choreograph television musicals for his friend Gorni Kramer, remaining there through June 1965 when he and his niece Christa traveled to Positano, a small town on the Amalfi coast that became popular with tourists ever since John Steinbeck wrote about it in *Harper's Bazaar* in 1953.[4] Christa and Hermes returned from Italy in July, and Pan almost immediately went back to work—this time on a television special for Carol Channing for which he composed the words and music for a "Mona Lisa" spoof and choreographed the routine for Channing, Christopher Riordan, and a chorus of fifty male dancers. "It looks like D-Day," Carol quipped. "I've always admired Hermes Pan, ever since I was a little girl" (*New York Times*, 13 February 1966).

Early in September, after completing the "Mona Lisa" routine, Pan was in rehearsal for *The Hollywood Palace*, the first of four episodes Fred Astaire had been invited to host. Pan created two numbers for Astaire: an opening sequence, "Top Hat," in which Astaire's performing contemporary dance styles like the frug, the twist, and the jerk is counterpointed by the go-go dancers that surround him; and "The Cat," a Lalo Schifrin composition accompanied by jazz organist Jimmy Smith. The number depicted a cat trying to kill a fly and took the entire month of September to perfect. Following the broadcast of *The Hollywood Palace* on 2 October 1965, Pan began planning a routine for Astaire and Barrie Chase to be used on Fred's next episode. To the music of a Cy Coleman composition, "Sweet Pussycat," and inspired by the Pygmalion and Galatea myth, Hermes created a narrative dance involving a department store window dresser (Astaire) putting an outfit on a mannequin (Barrie Chase). When suddenly the mannequin comes to life, the couple moves beyond the store window and engages in an elegantly lyrical and sinewy duet. "We rehearsed the Coleman number for three weeks with the famous choreographer, Hermes Pan," Chase explained. "Three weeks for one number seems incredible but Fred is such a perfectionist, he won't settle for anything that has any kind of flaw in it" (*Independent Star News*, 16 January 1966). In addition to the duet, Hermes assisted Astaire with "Let's Call the Whole Thing Off" and "They All Laughed," the two Gershwin numbers with which he opened the show, and choreographed Barrie Chase in the sensuous "Girl from Ipanema." While working on *The Hollywood Palace* dances, Pan took the time to appear as a special guest at the first Christmas Ball at the Regency Room of the Walnut Valley Country Club sponsored by Saint John Vianney Catholic Church in Hacienda Heights, Monsignor Jim's new parish. Jim had told Hermes that the parish was trying to raise money to complete the building of a new church and Hermes responded by organizing a fund-raising dance with a few Catholic Hollywood celebrities in attendance. Fortuitously, Pan's idea was successful and raised enough money to complete the construction of the church.

By the time Fred Astaire and Barrie Chase were telecast on 22 January 1966 dancing to "Pussycat," Pan and dancers Jerry Jackson, John Brascia, and Tybee Afra were in Rome working on a television special with Marcello Mastroianni for Studio Uno, and early in the spring Pan and company were joined by Barrie Chase, who flew out to Rome to dance in a series of television spectaculars.[5] "There are more 'don'ts' connected with Italian TV than you'd ever believe," Chase reported in a syndicated column. "With half of Europe running around practically nude on the beaches, Italian TV won't even permit showing a bare midriff. Also girls cannot wear tight-fitting flesh-colored gowns. Every dance sequence has a censor on the set to see there are no sensuous or suggestive movements. Compared to Italian shows, American TV is as free as the birds" (*Anderson Daily Bulletin*, 6 September 1966).

At the beginning of August when he returned to California, Hermes was hired by producer Desi Arnaz to choreograph the pilot for a Carol Channing television series on CBS designed as a "charming, domestic, believable" sitcom with musical numbers along the lines of the popular "I Love Lucy" series in the 1950s with a musical score by Jerry Herman, the composer of *Hello, Dolly!* Loosely based on the musical *Wonderful Town*, the series planned to explore the plight of a girl who comes to New York City to get on the Broadway stage. When the pilot was done, Pan headed off to Las Vegas to choreograph the $750,000 centennial edition of the *Folies Bergere* at the Tropicana Hotel. Assisted by Jerry Jackson[6] and accompanied by pianist Jim Hendrickson and percussionist Irving Kluger, Pan rehearsed eighteen dancers and sixteen showgirls for six weeks in a variety of lavish production numbers, some with extravagant costumes and many with no costumes at all. Rehearsals generally began late in the morning with a break for dinner, followed by further rehearsal from 8:00 p.m. to around midnight. The male lead dancer in the production, Vassili Sulich, recalled that "Hermes was a charmer and worked fast, but after 5:00 p.m. he had had too many visits to the bar enjoying dry martinis, so Jerry had to take over" (Sulich 2001, 183). Jackson replied that Hermes liked to tipple a bit but always planned time for his wine so that it would never interfere with his work. If Jackson took over rehearsals after five o'clock, it was because he had been scheduled to do so, not because of Pan's incapacity. John L. Scott writing for the *Los Angeles Times* (1 January 1967) recalled seeing Pan in production meetings after midnight completely unimpaired by an overabundance of alcohol and noted Pan's work with dancers Jennifer and Susan Baker, identical twins from England on a complicated Apache number:

> Jennifer and Susan Baker worked out with male lead dancer Vassili Sulich before a few privileged spectators when I observed from the sidelines. Pan was pioneering a wild, comedy-Apache routine for the winsome young women, demonstrating action and patiently correcting errors with the help of Jerry Jackson, assistant chorographer.
>
> The extremely vigorous routines of the Apache number were foreign to the twins although they had appeared in other stage shows, and when Pan called a halt the girls flopped prone on the floor, completely exhausted. But they recovered quickly and soon were ready to continue. During the break I asked Pan how he stayed in good shape physically. He answered by doing a few fancy dance steps.

In December the *Folies Bergere* opened in Las Vegas and Pan returned to Los Angeles to begin preparation for *Finian's Rainbow*, the Warner Brothers–Seven Arts production of the 1947 Broadway hit musical that told the story of Finian McLonergan (Fred Astaire) who moves from Ireland to Rainbow Valley in the fictional state of Missitucky, USA, with his daughter Sharon (Petula Clark) and a pot of gold stolen from a leprechaun named Og (Tommy Steele) which he buries next to Fort Knox in the erroneous belief that it will multiply. Francis Ford Coppola, having just graduated with an MFA in film directing from UCLA, with no experience in directing film musicals and knowing little about choreography, was hired to direct. When he was offered the job, he imagined the production to be substantial, along the lines of *My Fair Lady* or *The Sound of Music*, allowing him to film on location in Kentucky. But after he signed the contract, he was given a budget of $3,500,000 and told that he must film the musical on Warner's back lot and on the same forest set that had been used for an earlier musical film, *Camelot* (the studio had spent a great deal of money on it and wanted to get its money's worth). Pan's assistant choreographer Jerry Jackson noted that studio head Jack Warner would only do *Finian's Rainbow* if Astaire played Finian. "Coppola did not necessarily want Fred because he thought he was old-fashioned, and Francis was into the new thing and new actors. The studio insisted on Fred, and Fred insisted on Pan" (Levinson 2009, 347). Pan was paid his usual weekly salary of $2,000 with a guarantee of twenty weeks' work and began working with Fred on the dances in the spring of 1967.

From the outset, Pan and Coppola did not collaborate well. In his interview with Dan Georgakas, Pan, who rarely made an unkind statement in public about a coworker, had this to say:

A director who was a real pain when we were working on *Finian's Rainbow* was Francis Ford Coppola. He may have been great on *The Godfather*, but he knew very little about dancing and musicals. He would interfere with my work and even with Fred's. Fred is such a gentleman he wanted to try to please, but Coppola and Joe Landon, the producer, actually told me, "Try not to make Astaire be like Astaire." I said, "Who do you want him to be like?" "We want him to be Finian." I said, "He's Astaire and nobody's going to forget that." "No, we don't want Astaire, we want Finian." "Well, you're not going to get Finian," I told him, "you're going to get Astaire." That would never have happened with Louis B. Mayer because they were too aware of what the public wanted. You see, these schoolboys who studied at UCLA think they're geniuses, but there is a lot they don't understand. (Georgakas 1983, 27)

The relationship was strained further when Pan was forced to choreograph dances to be performed on the soft grass and muddy terrain of the *Camelot* forest set. Hermes argued that he could only do what he was hired to do on a proper dance floor and that the *Camelot* set was completely inadequate for musical staging. As Gene D. Phillips concluded, "They reached an impasse. Coppola was not satisfied with Pan's choreography, and Pan contended that it was the best he could do with a principal set that had not even been designed for the present film. He asked to have more rehearsal time, but Coppola could not grant this request since there was no margin in the tight production schedule" (Phillips 2004, 48).

Rehearsals began at the end of May culminating in a 16 June dress rehearsal performance for family and friends accompanied by Francis's father Carmine leading a small combo. On 21 June 1967, Coppola hosted a kickoff press luncheon on the Burbank lot of Warner Brothers Studios, introducing the creative staff to the press and announcing that his method of rehearsing a movie musical as if it were a theatrical performance would make it a "film of performances" (*Variety*, 22 June 1967). Since Coppola had only directed stage musicals in college he knew of no other way to direct the film.

The next week, *Finian's Rainbow* began a twelve-week filming schedule. Jerry Jackson recalled that when Coppola was unhappy with Pan's choreography he would ask him (Jackson) to change it rather than approach Pan directly—so poor was the working relationship between director and choreographer. Michael Goodwin and Naomi Wise suggest that the tension between them may have had less to do with Pan's work and more to do with the challenge he presented to Coppola's authority: "Coppola described Pan as 'a disaster.' That probably means that Pan disagreed with him or insisted that the camera serve the choreography, not vice versa, or asked for more rehearsal time for the numbers" (Goodwin 1989, 79). After the filming of "That Great Come-and-Get-It Day" in which Pan makes his final on-screen appearance shining shoes in a barbershop vignette, his twenty-week guarantee was up and he was released from the film. Since Jackson refused to stay on after Pan left, a young choreographer named Claude Thompson was hired to stage the remaining numbers.

Even before Pan had been released, his work was subverted by Coppola who continually interrupted the choreography with cutaway shots of vignettes that were neither entertaining nor dramatically effective. The director had no choreographic training or experience and staged musical numbers based on concepts that often had no relationship to the sound of the music or the sense of the lyrics. For example, he filmed "Something Sort of Grandish" on a hill with Petula Clark hanging white bed sheets on a clothesline and conceptualized "If This Isn't Love" as a series of children's games. The director's method of staging was little more than playing the music for a dance routine and telling the actors to "move with it" while he directed from behind the camera. The usually meticulously rehearsed Astaire had to be satisfied with a director who gave him directions like "We'll put the camera here; Fred, go over there and do something. Then let's have two girls block in this space" (Phillips 2004, 49).[7]

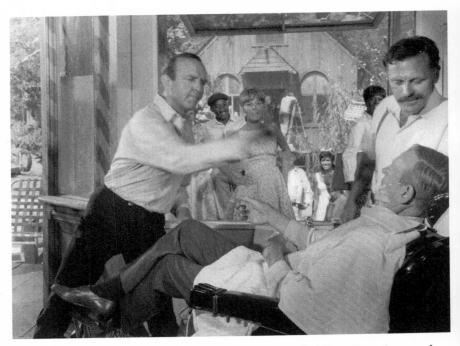

Pan throws shaving cream at Fred Astaire during rehearsal of "That Great Come-and-Get-It Day" (Courtesy of Photofest).

Expecting a hit, Warner Brothers released *Finian's Rainbow* as a two-and-a-half-hour road show picture, expanding the original thirty-five millimeter print to seventy millimeters and in the process cropping the top and bottom of the original frame, losing Fred Astaire's feet when he was dancing. The studio might have saved itself the effort. When the film was released on 1 October 1968, it was a box office failure even in spite of a few good reviews. Writing in *Dance Magazine* (March 1969), however, Robert C. Roman noted that "the material given Fred Astaire to express the whimsy of Finian does little to dispel (as it should have) the sleek, fashionable Astaire of the top hat, white tie, and tails. Fred in worn tweeds or in long red underwear is still using the familiar materials of earlier Astaire film dances. Even when it's an Irish jig or a reel, we're still set to thinking of *Flying Down to Rio*" (94). The review goes on to praise Pan's choreography for Susan's "Rain Dance," though it was actually staged by Claude Thompson. Because all the choreography in the film was attributed to Pan, reviewers praised or blamed him for work that in the final product was not always his. In the *New York Times* (10 October 1968), Renata Adler found little satisfying about the film:

> There is something awfully depressing about seeing *Finian's Rainbow* this year this way—with Fred Astaire looking ancient, far beyond his years,

collapsed and red-eyed; with film work so shoddy that the camera hardly ever includes his feet when he dances and that people who have been sopping wet in one cut are absent-mindedly dry in the next; with nobody even bothering to put the whole cheesy, joyless thing, which is in execrable color—Technicolor, widescreen Panavision—into sync. . . . It is not just that the musical is dated. Something lovely and nostalgic could have been made out of old Missitucky for the generation that grew up on *Finian's Rainbow* and *Brigadoon*. It is that it has been done listlessly and even tastelessly, with quick updating of Negro personalities to match what people who have lived in Beverly Hills too long must imagine modern black sensibilities are. The cast is full of children who act as artificially and insincerely as the whole enterprise directed by Francis Ford Coppola would suggest.

Hermes Pan did enjoy one bright spot during the ordeal of *Finian's Rainbow*. He managed to cast his sister in the noncredited actress-dancer role of Elderly Lovely. As Vasso recorded in her diary, "I did work on *Finians*, had a ball and made over $5,000—then $1,600 in unemployment!"

12

Help Me Dream

Hermes Pan was quick to rebound from *Finian's Rainbow*. He virtually walked off that set into rehearsals for a new Carol Channing special *Carol Channing and 101 Men* in August 1967, and early in September Blake Edwards hired him to choreograph *Darling Lili*, a vehicle for Julie Andrews slated to begin production the following spring. Again assisted by Jerry Jackson, Pan contributed two production numbers to the new Channing special: "Jazz Baby" and an international spectacle that climaxed the evening. Performed in an art deco setting by Channing and a dancing chorus of men in tuxedos, "Jazz Baby" was an ebullient return to the roaring days of the "Charleston" complete with a dancer pretending to drink champagne from one of Carol's high-heeled shoes. The international finale involved Channing moving from country to country and costume to costume, performing a Russian Cossack dance, a Kabuki routine, a German peasant *Ländler*, a Parisian Apache dance (evoking Pan's staging of the "Apache" in *Can-Can*), and a samba in which Channing satirizes Carmen Miranda. For the big finish, Carol is serenaded to the tune of "Hello, Dolly!" in five languages before the entire Air Force Academy Cadet Chorale marches in and croons to her while she struts from cadet to cadet like Dolly Levi, as if performing Gower Champion's original choreography for the number.

Following the taping of the television special, Hermes and Jerry Jackson returned to Las Vegas to stage a second edition of the *Folies Bergere* at the Hotel Tropicana opening in the New Year, after which Pan was signed to choreograph another Irving Berlin musical at Metro-Goldwyn-Mayer, *Say It with Music*. Produced by Blake Edwards and Arthur Freed, the songfest was slated to star Julie Andrews and Fred Astaire, and Berlin was contracted to compose seven new songs. The *Los Angeles Times* (22 January 1968) advertised that the film "will go before the cameras at M-G-M's Culver City Studios in early 1969" but the musical was never made. In an undated interview with Hugh Fordin, Pan suggested that Astaire was not pleased to be working with Julie Andrews, and few shed a tear when a change in studio management led to the cancellation of the picture.

In the spring of 1968, Hermes and Bea Busch began working on the dance routines for *Darling Lili* in preparation for filming in Dublin, Paris, and Brussels in the summer. Set during the First World War, *Darling Lili* cast Julie Andrews as Lili Smith, a popular English singer and German spy who goes to Paris to seduce the American officer Major William Larrabee (Rock Hudson) into revealing military secrets which she passes on to her German superior Kurt von Ruger (Jeremy Kemp) causing French intelligence to suspect Larrabee as a spy. Finding that he has a mistress, a stripper by the name of Crêpe Suzette (Gloria Paul), Lili indicts her as the German agent, but when the major is accused of espionage, Lili reveals her identity to save him.

The music for the film combined a number of First World War favorites with five new songs evoking the period by Henry Mancini and Johnny Mercer. Pan staged the opening number "Whistling Away the Dark," a performance piece for Julie Andrews in a London theatre with simple waltzing movements, and the two songs Julie sings outdoors to convalescing Allied troops, "The Girl in No Man's Land" and "Smile Away Each Rainy Day," with comfortable walking patterns not burdening the star with unnecessary choreography. For a traditional cancan performed at a French nightclub, Pan used eight dancers who managed to recreate the energy and excitement of a similar routine in the film *Can-Can* which had twice the personnel. Hermes staged "I'll Give You Three Guesses," another theatre performance number for Lili, with four male dancers bearing straw hats and ukuleles walking and moving synchronously with her as she sings. A bright soft-shoe dance routine leads to Julie's being passed from man to man and finally lifted on to a functional swing unit that enables her to soar over the orchestra pit, an idiomatic music hall routine—not unlike his choreography for "Be Sweet to Me Kid" in *I Wonder Who's Kissing Her Now*. Pan choreographed "Your Good-Will Ambassador" as a traditional striptease performed by Crêpe Suzette with appropriate bumps and grinds and the suggestion of real nudity as Suzette removes her bra on her exit. Dramatically the routine serves as an essential preamble to the striptease by Lili that follows in which she attempts to let down her hair during a reprise of "I'll Give You Three Guesses" in a scene similar to Cyd Charisse's "My Lucky Charm" routine in *Meet Me in Las Vegas*.

Because of weather problems and scheduling issues that always torment a film on location, Pan's association with *Darling Lili* lasted until 13 December, considerably longer than he had anticipated. A year and a half after it finished shooting, the film was released, and though it managed to earn some positive notices for Pan's choreography and for the performances of the stars, *Darling Lili* failed at the box office. Writing in the *New York Times* (24 July 1970), Vincent Canby explained: "I might also point out that *Darling Lili* is in itself the kind of romantic gesture we're not likely to see again for a very long time. It's the last of the mammoth movie musicals (*Dolly!*, *Paint Your Wagon*) that were inspired by the success of *The Sound of Music* (and each of which cost two or three times as much as Alaska). I doubt that Hollywood, now practically broke and trying to make a connection with the youth market, will ever again indulge itself in this sort of splendidly extravagant, quite frivolous enterprise."

After *Darling Lili*, Hermes Pan decided to retire. He had, he reasoned, enjoyed steady employment since 1933 in an industry that had always been fun—but after thirty-five years and nearly a hundred films, it had gotten harder to find the fun in the work. Hermes acknowledged that the industry was changing. He felt that younger dancers wanted immediate results, not the slow, methodical choreographic process that he believed in, and that choreographers were beginning to impose styles and mannerisms on dancers as if they were merely mannequins rather than creative collaborators. "People used to smile when they danced," he told Dan Georgakas. "Now you often see stark blankness and deliberate ugliness. There's a mechanical exercise rather than movement. How many drops or turns can you do without any sense of inspiration for the music? It's step-step-step violence. Perhaps it's a sign of our times. You see the sex and violence of the cities in dance" (Georgakas 1983, 29).

In retirement all Hermes wanted to do was lie around the pool, dabble in his garden, and travel, so after the holidays Pan left California for Rome and another trip to Iran, again at the invitation of the royal family. In October, while Hermes was in the middle of the Atlantic Ocean returning on the *Christopher Columbus* from his second trip that year to Tehran, he was contacted by Ann Miller in Hollywood: "Hey, Bear [her nickname for him], get yourself off that boat and get back here fast. We're doing a TV commercial." It seemed that humorist-producer Stan Freberg had convinced her to do a "Great American Soup" commercial and she wanted Pan to choreograph. Pan objected, "We don't do commercials," but at Ann's insistence, Hermes hurried back to the West Coast, only to waste a week trying to make contact with Stan Freberg whose working habits were notoriously mercurial. Eventually Pan, Ann, and Stan managed to meet in one place and Freberg's concept for the soup spot began to take shape. The producer built a $25,000 set on which a husband (played by Dave Willock) asks his wife (Ann Miller) what kind of soup she's preparing. Ann throws off her apron and tap dances on five thousand square feet of mirrorlike black tile accompanied by two dozen chorus girls dancing up silver stairs while four thousand varicolored jets of water appear. Next, Ann is seen dancing on top of a giant soup can rising from the floor, singing "Let's face the gumbo and dance," after which she twirls into the arms of her husband who asks ironically, "Emily, why do you have to make such a big production out of everything?"

After a week's rehearsal, the sixty-second number was shot in three days in early November with the scoring session (synchronizing music, vocals, and tap sounds to the visual) left to be done at a later date—or, as Pan complained, when Stan was "in the mood." Freberg, Hermes learned, did not operate according to a planned schedule, but preferred to work according to the "mood of the moment." Evidently, the mood struck him on 10 November when Pan and Miller were suddenly called for a 7:00 p.m. session and Hermes had to cancel a dinner party he was supposed to attend. Meeting in Projection Room A on the Goldwyn Studios lot, Hermes and Ann watched a soundless version of the commercial before adjourning to Sound Stage Eight with the producer to watch the twenty-two-piece orchestra rehearse under the direction of the celebrated jazz arranger Billy May.

Like Ann Miller, Stan Freberg had earned the reputation in Hollywood of always wanting another take, and the soup commercial was no exception. Ann was still singing and tapping to the sound of the orchestra with her image projected on the screen at 9:30 p.m. when Hermes checked his watch. "I don't know how he gets by with it," he said, frustrated with the producer's methods. After a ten-minute break for coffee and sandwiches, more takes followed until 10:30 p.m. when Pan looked at his watch again. Freberg announced, "One more take and then we'll let the band go." At 10:45 p.m. the band was still in the studio and Freberg suggested, "We'll do one more take." At 11:00 p.m., with the band still in attendance, Hermes could restrain himself no longer. "This is incredible. Julie Andrews's biggest number in *Darling Lili* didn't take this long. They scored it in an hour and 15 minutes." At 11:05 p.m. Hermes and Ann were permitted to leave to go and watch *The Dick Cavett Show* since Fred Astaire was his special guest, but Freberg and the band remained in the studio until 2:00 a.m.[1]

Hermes returned to Iran in the fall of 1971 as the guest of the royal family for the 2,500th anniversary of the Persian Empire created by Cyrus the Great. The celebration taking place at the ancient city of Persepolis from 12 to 16 October was intended to be a document of Iran's long history as well as an illustration of modern advances under the leadership of Pan's friend, Mohammad Reza Pahlavi, the shah. An impressive "Tent City" was created at Persepolis consisting of fifty luxury apartments surrounded by Persian tent cloth arranged in a star pattern around a central fountain with a great number of trees planted around them in the desert in an attempt to suggest the appearance of the ancient city. A large "Tent of Honor" was erected for the reception of heads of state as well as a 224-by-80-foot "Banqueting Hall" to house the gala dinner on 14 October celebrating the birthday of the shahbanu, the shah's wife Farah. The celebration was catered by Maxim's of Paris, and the celebrated hotelier Max Blouet came out of retirement to supervise the banquet. Lanvin designed the uniforms for the royal household, Limoges the silverware, Porthault the linen for the celebration, and 250 red Mercedes-Benz limousines carried guests to and from the airport.

Having been a repeated guest of the royal family, Pan was somewhat used to the pomp and splendor, but he wasn't prepared for the dinner menu set before him and the 599 other guests at Farah's birthday party. The five-and-a-half-hour feast began with quails' eggs stuffed with golden Imperial Caspian caviar, champagne, and Château de Saran, followed by mousse of crayfish tails with Nantua sauce and Château Haut-Brion Blanc, 1964. Roast saddle of lamb with truffles was served next accompanied by a Château Lafite Rothschild, 1945, and a palette cleanser of champagne sorbet Moët et Chandon, 1911. Fifty roast peacocks with tail feathers stuffed with foie gras next appeared accompanied by roast quails and a nut and truffle salad served with Musigny Comte de Vogué, 1945. For dessert, a glazed Oporto ring of fresh figs with cream, raspberry champagne sherbet, and port was offered with Dom Pérignon Rosé, 1959, followed by mocha coffee and Prince Eugène cognac. A fireworks display accompanied by Iannis Xenakis's specially commissioned composition for synthesizer, *Persepolis*, brought an end to the evening.

The following day, Hermes joined Emperor Haile Selassie of Ethiopia, King Olav V of Norway, Prince Rainier III and Princess Grace of Monaco, President Tito of Yugoslavia, Chancellor Willy Brandt of West Germany, First Lady Imelda Marcos of the Philippines, and Vice President Spiro Agnew to view 1,724 men of the Iranian military parade in period costumes, representing twenty-five-hundred years of the Iranian Empire. That night, Pan attended a less formal "Persian party," the concluding social event of the celebration, and the following day he accompanied the shah in paying homage to his father Reza Shah Pahlavi at his mausoleum, as the official conclusion of the festivities.

Following the celebration, Pan returned to Rome where he was joined by Vasso and her husband who had been traveling through Europe since the end of September. In the 13 June 1972 entry of her journal, Vasso commented on four months in Europe: "Wow! We got to Greece, met cousins and saw Pop's childhood house. Snooks wants to buy the cousins' beach house in Akrata—HOPE, HOPE SO!" The Pans returned to California in the middle of January 1972, and Hermes quickly forgot about his cousins' beach house, for in February, in spite of his claims of being retired, he accepted a choreographic assignment at Columbia Pictures, Ross Hunter's production of *Lost Horizon*, with a score by the hit songwriting team of Burt Bacharach and Hal David.

In *Lost Horizon*, a revolution during a United Nations peace mission in southern Asia necessitates the evacuation of British and American citizens, including British diplomat Richard Conway (Peter Finch), his newspaperman brother George (Michael York), disenchanted American photojournalist Sally Hughes (Sally Kellerman), American engineer Sam Cornelius (George Kennedy), and Harry Lovett (Bobby Van), a performer separated from his USO troupe. After their plane is forced to make a crash landing on a snowy Tibetan mountain peak, they are guided by Chang (John Gielgud) to Shangri-La, a community unknown to Westerners, hidden in the Valley of the Blue Moon, where Richard falls in love with Catherine (Liv Ullmann), a schoolteacher, and George begins a romance with Maria (Olivia Hussey), a two-hundred-year-old inhabitant of Shangri-La who appears to be only twenty.

By the beginning of June 1972, the cast had assembled at the Twentieth Century-Fox ranch in Malibu, which Ross Hunter filled with bamboo, willow trees, ferns, peach trees, and a schoolroom beside a man-made lake, surrounded by green lawns, grass huts, and practicable wooden playground equipment. In this environment, Hermes Pan and his assistants Bea Busch and Frank Radcliffe rehearsed and filmed "The World Is a Circle" in which Liv Ullmann (dubbed by Diana Lee) teaches class by moving her students around in circles, allowing them to play on a horseless merry-go-round unit and a wooden Ferris wheel before parading them up a grassy hillside evoking images of Julie Andrews in *The Sound of Music*. Although Ullmann was neither a dancer nor a singer, she was comfortable working with Pan. "He was really very sweet," she noted in a syndicated interview. "I think he felt my shyness. I'm sure in the beginning he was sweating but he made me believe I could dance" (*Playground Daily News*, 15 January 1973).

Dancer Bobby Van, who makes only a brief appearance in "The World Is a Circle," is given the opportunity to teach a class on his own with "Question Me an Answer," a number Pan staged with twenty Asian children. After singing the song to his class (with choreography that subtly demonstrated his dancing abilities), Van leads his students in a soft-shoe routine ending with an imagined hat-and-cane kick routine before a spontaneous solo leads him over the railing and into the water, signaling the end of the lesson. Reporter Wayne Warga witnessed the creation of the routine:

> The number was rehearsed with a grabbed two hours here and there for an hours total of well over seven days. It was also prerecorded and a sophisticated sound system is on the outdoor set to play back the music along with some loud taps which sound like bad scratches. Actually, they're cues to keep people in the right place and on the right beat. Happenstance cues. Filming of the sequence—it will require two days of steady filming to finish what will eventually be fewer than four minutes of film—had been anticipated by both cast and crew. Thus, stars who weren't working were nevertheless in attendance. . . . Hermes Pan, the choreographer, and his two serious assistants run through the number for the cameraman and lighting people. Hermes does Van's dance and his assistants dance the parts of ten children each. Then the cast takes over and, sure enough, they love it. Never mind that Van, who is as inexhaustible as dancers come, requires ice packs on his spine between takes. He looks as though he invented it all that second. (*Los Angeles Times*, 2 July 1972)

Hermes completed the number by 13 June when, assisted by his housekeeper Ingrid, he hosted a small dinner party at his home for his family serving Beluga caviar which he brought back from Iran, Swedish pot roast, and tropical fruit. The next day, he returned to *Lost Horizon*, moving to the back lot of the Burbank Studios (a complex shared by Warner Brothers and Columbia Pictures), where the four-acre, $500,000 Shangri-La set had been built on a site previously used for *Camelot* and *Finian's Rainbow*. Next to a six-hundred-foot-long mountain range made of plaster were two forty-foot waterfalls, four glittering pools, an eighty-foot-high lamasery that perhaps owed more to Conrad Hilton in its design than anything Greco-Roman, Byzantine, or Tibetan, and 150 different varieties of vegetation costing $30,000 a week to keep flourishing. When director Charles Jarrott began work on the set for *Lost Horizon*, his first musical and his first film to be made in Hollywood, he told the *Hollywood Reporter* (28 June 1972) that "I think people who are used to working on back lots are bored with it, but being a newcomer to it I'm quite impressed. . . . My only concern was to coordinate the dramatic action with the dancing. [Pan, Ross Hunter, and I] worked together closely and Pan didn't call for any jazzy camera angles because they're not those kinds of numbers. It's nice, too, that one or two of the numbers are dramatic, and I'm able to play them like dramatic scenes. They originally told me when the songs start you can just sit back and relax, but I just can't."

On the back lot, Hermes created a huge outdoor spectacle to celebrate the "Festival of the Family" in Shangri-La with a song called "Living Together, Growing Together" led by James Shigeta (Wang Ta in *Flower Drum Song*) in the role of Brother To-Lenn. A long procession moves down the steps of the lamasery during which a married couple engages in a stylized family dance presenting their swaddled baby to the community. A wild "husband" dance ensues by male dancers in loincloths encircling themselves with orange chiffon sashes and swirling them into the air, not unlike Pan's choreography for Cleopatra's triumphant entry into Rome. In an interior scene, Pan designed "Share the Joy" as a trio for Olivia Hussey and two female dancers providing dinner entertainment for the Westerners. Maximizing

Assistant director Sheldon Schrager, Hermes Pan, and Charles Jarrott on the set of *Lost Horizon* (Courtesy of the Academy of Motion Picture Arts and Sciences).

the capabilities of his nondancing star, Hermes created an Asian-looking routine that emphasized arms, hands, and turns, substituting body shapes for complicated dance steps. The dressing and undressing of the central performer in a large yellow cloak also lent the number an aura of ritual derived from the Japanese Noh tradition. As always, Pan's research into period style and movement was meticulous. Hermes's affection for props led him to choreograph "The Things I Will Not Miss," another number for Hussey with Sally Kellerman, in the library in Shangri-La, allowing the performers to leap over desks, climb up ladders, and rush down a staircase rather than having to struggle with complex choreography. When they did actually dance, they executed simple unison steps and turns with a carefully rehearsed precision, always a hallmark of Pan's choreography.

Hermes completed his work on *Lost Horizon* in August 1972, seven months before the gala Los Angeles premiere at the National Theatre in Westwood on 7 March 1973 to which he escorted Fred Astaire's sister Adele. Neither Pan nor his companion was satisfied with the finished product, an opinion shared by Charles Champlin, critic for the *Los Angeles Times* (7 March 1973), who found little to like in the film, calling it a "flat-footed disappointment, a lost chance" and Pan's dances "cumbersome, unlyrical, and tedious." After the New York City opening a week later, Vincent Canby called *Lost Horizon* "a big, stale marshmallow . . . surprisingly tacky in appearance. When we aren't seeing the magical valley of Shangri-La in long-shot as something painted through trick photography, we see it in close-up as a couple of seedy back lot sets, one of which, the High Lama's palace, looks like Pickfair remodeled as a motel. . . . The most hilarious moments, however, are the original contributions of Hunter, Charles Jarrott, his director, and Hermes Pan, who choreographed some of the great Astaire-Rogers musicals but is out of his element here" (*New York Times*, 15 March 1973). [2]

Four months after *Lost Horizon* opened, Hermes was booked on a train headed east to New York where he planned to board the *Queen Elizabeth II* for another trip across the Atlantic—destination, Rome. In the fall, he traveled again to Iran to attend a film festival which he described in some detail in an undated letter to his niece Michelene:

Dear Michie,

Got your letter shortly after I arrived here last week. I went to the opening of the festival in Tehran at Roudaki opera house. The Empress greeted all the guests one by one as they stood in single file around the large reception room. The picture was "Kamaraski" or something like that[3]—a Canadian film all in French—fairly good.

Tonight I saw "The Optimist" with Peter Sellers (but at the palace). There's a girl in it, Donna Mullane, that looks so much like you when you were about 12 or 13. Be sure to see for yourself. I am not going in to see any more films as there are four movies a week here at the palace, although tomorrow I am going to a dinner party and another on Monday.

Was at the Queen Mother's for dinner the other night and had quite a long talk with the Shah. He asked me why there was so much sex and violence in movies today and said he was sick of seeing the same old things in most every picture he saw—from there we talked on—from Vietnam to Watergate, oil crisis, etc. He's a very interesting man to talk to and puts you at your ease.

The princess is giving a dinner party for the film folk next Tuesday here at the palace and it should be quite a gala affair—the man servants all wear white or blue flannel jackets with the Imperial coat of arms embroidered in black and gold. Every morning I'm served breakfast in my room, usually by an Ethiopian servant named "Barakat"—real black with a big smile.

I just left the princess's suite where she was reclining on a divan like Cleopatra with two servants, one massaging her feet and the other her arms—and others flitting in and out bringing tea and fruit as she chatted and held court with several friends that surrounded her—plus four dogs on her lap and a parrot on the back of the lounge. This is the nightly routine from 10 till about 12.

I'll leave here on the 7th or 8th and will be home sometime before Christmas.

Say hello to everybody and especially to "Jijo"[4] and tell him I'll answer him next time he talks to me!

Love to all
Hermes

Hermes returned to California in time to spend the holidays with his family before again engaging in the Hollywood social scene after the New Year with Ann Miller, Marge Champion, Loretta Young, Princess Shams Pahlavi, and her daughter, Shahrazad (anglicized as Scheherazade). The following year, Hermes was back in Iran, seated at the main table with the shah of Iran and Empress Farah at the wedding of Princess Scheherazade to Howard Burris, an investment broker in Washington, and former member of the Johnson administration.

By 1977 Pan's name had begun to appear less frequently in the society columns as more and more he tended to refrain from celebrity parties, preferring to socialize in the comfort of his home on Cherokee Lane and reminisce about the glory days of movie musicals. His simple daily routine invariably included a phone call to Fred Astaire to discuss whatever happened to catch his eye in the *Los Angeles Times*, a crossword puzzle, gardening, and dinner at the home of his niece who lived close by.[5] After three years of relative obscurity, Pan's solitude was interrupted in the spring of 1980 by director Pupi Avati, who invited him to return to Rome to choreograph *Aiutami a sognare* (*Help Me Dream*) with original music by Riz Ortolani, and starring Mariangela Melato, perhaps best known in America for the role of Raffaella in Lina Wertmüller's *Swept Away*, and Italian-American actor

Princess Scheherazade, her father, Mehrdad Pahlbod, Fred Astaire, Hermes, his niece Michelene, Princess Shams, Monsignor Jim O'Callaghan, and Ann Miller at one of Pan's famous pasta dinner parties (Courtesy of Michelene Laski).

Anthony Franciosa. Set during the Second World War, *Aiutami a sognare* tells the story of Ray (Franciosa), an American pilot whose plane breaks down close to the farmhouse of Francesca (Melato), a middle-aged widow with three young daughters who has recently returned to the Emilia-Romagna countryside to rekindle old friendships. Ray needs a safe place to hide until he can rejoin his military unit, and his presence enables Francesca and her daughters to live out their fantasies about America, its films, its songs, and dances. Since Francesca had concealed the death of her husband from her children by telling them that he is off in America, the girls form an immediate bond with the American who plays the piano and teaches them American songs. In his honor, Francesca's daughters and their neighbors perform "Pennies from Heaven" and "Jeepers Creepers" with choreography adapted from Hollywood musicals, and while the countryside is echoing with the sound of American music, Francesca and Ray begin to fall in love. When the flyer's plane has been repaired, he is forced to rejoin his unit leaving Francesca ennobled by his memory and the fantasies his presence inspired in her and her children. Having spent a lifetime transforming real situations into fantasy, Pan believed that *Aiutami a sognare* would be the capstone of his career and Pupi Avati could imagine no better man for the job:

[Getting Pan] was easy: we contacted his lawyer. Hermes Pan, an ex-
traordinarily delightful human being, gave his ok right away, grasping
the spirit of the film perfectly. The film is an homage to the United
States. For a refined American as Pan—a man who experienced America and helped make it what it is—it was easy to understand my inten-
tion. We started out completely at ease, free from awkwardness.
Instead of the greatest dancers he was used to, I gave him twenty left-
footed extras who had never danced. His job was to communicate
American musicals even to the most provincial of Italian women. . . .
What we wanted to do was see a musical through the eyes of someone
like my mother: a woman who had been sent away from her hometown during the war and dreamt of America looking at the airplanes
in the sky. And Hermes understood this immediately. (Maraldi n.d.,
48–49)[6]

Hermes noted to interviewer Susan Winslow, however, that he never saw the
completed version of the film since he returned to the United States as soon as
the choreography was finished. *Aiutami a sognare* was released in Italy on 26
March 1981 to generally excellent notices. The international critic for *Variety*
(21 March 1981) wrote, "*Help Me Dream* brings out the best of the director's
concerns for his native Emilia-Romagna, warm family structures, and U.S. musical nostalgia in an unusual and very personal picture. The odd mixture of
romantic drama, song and dance makes its box office future a toss-up on native
screens addicted to filmic sitcoms. But [the picture's] story has a built-in appeal
for American audiences and is a sure festival bet. . . . An eminently family picture, *Dream* has the charm of a children's fable, an insistence on basic human
goodness and an overriding conviction about the importance of the family,"
Pan's philosophy in a nutshell!

Choreographing in Rome injected Hermes with another burst of energy for,
upon his return to Hollywood, he participated in a television special, "The American Film Institute Tribute to Fred Astaire," and accepted the National Film Society
Award for lifetime contribution to film. Because of their extensive working relationship and long friendship, Pan asked Fred Astaire to present him the award but
Astaire refused, offering no excuse. Hermes was deeply disappointed but never
mentioned the matter again to Fred. At the ceremony Pan was given the honor by
dancer Ruby Keeler who, having recently suffered a stroke, appeared on stage in a
wheelchair. Hermes was profoundly struck by the irony: someone with whom he
had never worked and did not know well would support him, even in the midst of
an illness, while his collaborator and closest friend would not. As usual, no harsh
words were spoken, but it was clear to Pan's friends and family that Astaire's
behavior was not something that Hermes could shrug off easily even though out
wardly little seemed to change in their relationship. As Richard McKenzie, who
was married to Fred Astaire's daughter Ava, explained:

[Fred] doesn't like to drive at night so I pick him up in front of his house and sometimes Hermes too, and then it's like having dinner with the two men from the Muppet Show. Last week, after they made such a display of "helping" each other out of the car, and in the lift Pan did a time step while Fred suspended himself up on the brass railing inside and kicked his feet in the air, I told them to behave themselves; this was a nice hotel and we had reputations to consider if they hadn't. People are used to celebrities [at the Hotel] L'Ermitage but when the door opened on me shaking my finger at Fred Astaire and Hermes Pan nudging each other like schoolboys, the faces of departed diners waiting for the lift were something to behold. (McKenzie 1998, 243)

McKenzie recalled that on another occasion, after mingling with hippies on Sunset Boulevard, Hermes and Fred appeared at their residence wearing shoulder-length fright wigs, headbands, love beads, and carrying flowers. In spring 1983, Pan was feeding his cat (which he named "Kitty") when he received a call from Fred Astaire asking him to come to his home immediately. Thinking it was some kind of emergency, Hermes rushed over only to find Astaire excitedly watching a videotape. "Just wait till you see this," he said by way of greeting. Pan sat beside him and the two watched Michael Jackson perform "Billie Jean" on *Motown 25: Yesterday, Today, Forever*, which had aired the night before. Impressed by the performance, Pan persuaded Astaire to call Michael Jackson to congratulate him. Hermes explained:

Somehow, Fred tracked [Michael] down. He told him that he was one hell of a dancer. . . . "You really put them on their asses last night. You're an angry dancer. I'm the same way." I got on the line to say hello, and this whisper of a voice answered me. I was surprised, actually, that a person that dances with such anger would have such a soft voice. I told him how much I enjoyed his work, and he was very gracious, very excited to hear from us. For a moment, I believed he thought it was a practical joke. I liked him right away because he seemed so unaffected by show business, and also star struck. He really could not believe that Fred Astaire had called him. (Taraborrelli 2009, 242–243)

Three months later Hermes complained of numbness in his hands and the feeling that something odd was happening to his body, a condition his doctor diagnosed as a transient ischemic attack, or minor stroke. Throughout his life Hermes had never been seriously ill. He complained that the soles of his feet thinned as he got older but found relief in Gucci tennis shoes, which he began to wear on every occasion, anticipating the fad for wearing sneakers with evening clothes. When he injured his back during the filming of *Hit the Deck*, he recovered without any loss of mobility, and even though he had high blood pressure it did not concern him until his doctor reminded him that people with high blood pressure were especially at risk for repeated strokes. Pan quickly recovered from the stroke without paralysis, but the incident forced him to face his mortality and, according to his niece Michelene, he became depressed and quiet. Reminiscing about his old friends managed to cheer him, and early in October with the help of two new friends, Kenyon Kramer and David Patrick Columbia, he completed a prospectus and two chapters of a memoir, "Dancin' in the Movies: A Hollywood Life," a lively and anecdotal survey of his extensive film career.

Certainly, Hermes was in good spirits in November, when he was interviewed by film and television writer Maureen Solomon. "[Fred and I] spent a great deal of time trying to find out how to get into a number gracefully. Many songs would come out of the dialogue, Fred would even speak the first line of the song and before you knew it, you were into music. We experimented with camera movements because we'd taken great pains to figure out the best camera angles and recording of the dances. I didn't influence his style because he was already a star when I was just starting out. People naturally influence each other whether it's unconscious or not. Later on I could see certain moves or attitudes he would never have done before" (*Los Angeles Times*, 20 November 1983). With nearly a hundred films to his credit, most of them without Astaire, Pan's favorite topic was still his work with Fred.

After almost three years of public inactivity, Hermes was again in the limelight on Friday, 18 March 1986 when the Friends of the Joffrey Ballet saluted him at a $100-per-person, black tie, top hat optional, black-and-white champagne ball at the Biltmore Hotel in Los Angeles. It was considered a great coup for Gerald Arpino, the ballet's associate director, to have persuaded the shy and unassuming Pan to be the guest of honor. "I'm uncomfortable in crowds," Hermes confided. Noticing that Pan kept pouring himself glasses of wine because he was nervous about receiving the award, Vasso and her daughters, who attended the event, sought to keep him calm and sober before he made his speech. Also in attendance was Pan's friend David Patrick Columbia, who reported that when Hermes accepted the Joffrey's invitation he invited Fred Astaire to present the award. At eighty-seven, with an inner ear affliction that affected his balance, Astaire refused. Columbia continued:

> [H]e called Pan and said in his characteristic mild grumbling, "I just didn't want to and I hope you understand." . . . Hermes was disappointed, but, for the first time in their half-century relationship, he spoke up. "Well, Fred, as a matter of fact, I *don't* understand." He reminded his old friend of the time an inambulatory Ruby Keeler with whom he'd never worked came through. "Well, I just don't want to," Fred reiterated. Nothing more was said about the matter.

A few minutes after the two men ended their conversation, Fred's second wife Robyn, who like Phyllis Astaire was very fond of Hermes, called to tell him that Fred would be there. It turned out to be a great moment for Pan and for the two men's partnership. More than the award, for Pan it was the gesture, the acknowledgement. Fred in his presentation was brief but succinct. "I'm sorry we won't be rehearsing tomorrow, Pan. Thank you for letting me do this. It gives me a chance to tell him he's good."

Pan was nervous. "I really don't know what to say except that I am very honored that the Joffrey Ballet is giving me this tribute," he said. "Thank you also for the honor of having my longtime friend present me the award. How thankful and flattered I am." (Columbia, June 1991, 850)

Astaire presented Pan with a crystal ball from the Joffrey Friends, laughing, "Put that in your pocket." Emcee Ruta Lee (who was escorted by television host Alex Trebek) announced, "We are here to worship at the shrine of Hermes Pan." Ginger Rogers, who flew in from New York, quipped, "In the nine films I did with Fred, the rehearsals were more fun than anything." And Astaire remarked, "He never got mad. Hermes, have you ever been mad at anything?" Gerald Arpino enthusiastically thanked Hermes, Astaire, and Rogers for their contributions: "I don't think there would be a Joffrey Ballet if not for Fred Astaire, Ginger Rogers and Hermes Pan. They were the innovators." The trio responded by giving Arpino a copy of Daniel Cohen's book, *Musicals*, each autographing the cover picture of Astaire and Rogers dancing "Pick Yourself Up" from *Swing Time*.

On Thursday, 14 May 1987, Hermes Pan lost one of his most cherished friends. Rita Hayworth, who had been suffering from Alzheimer's disease, died in New York at the home of her daughter Princess Yasmin Khan Embiricos. Her body was flown to Los Angeles, and Hermes, along with actors Glenn Ford, Ricardo Montalban, Cesar Romero, Tony Franciosa, and Don Ameche, served as pallbearer at her funeral at the Church of the Good Shepherd. "It was terrible," Hermes sighed, "because her friends began to desert her. They were afraid, you know. One woman said to me, 'I just hate to go over there because I never know what Rita's going to say or do' " (Leaming 1989 346). Never one to desert a friend, Pan experienced Rita's Alzheimer's outbursts firsthand. He recalled inviting her along with Fred and Adele Astaire to dinner at his home. During the meal the conversation turned to Rita's daughter Yasmin and her singing. Adele remarked innocuously, "I wonder where she gets that talent from?" but Rita mistook it as an insult and rose up in her seat, her Latin blood beginning to boil. She said nothing at the time but later in the evening, when she was sitting next to Adele, who had a drink in her hand, she took the drink and threw it in Adele's face, still without saying a word. Fred and Adele left almost immediately, and after they left, Pan asked Rita, "What happened?" She responded with a shrug, and the next day when Pan spoke to her on the telephone, Rita had no memory of the incident.

Hermes recalled another dinner party, this time at Hayworth's home, when he and Ann Miller were her guests. "We had just finished eating when suddenly

The autographed copy of *Musicals* presented to Gerald Arpino (Courtesy of the author's collection).

she said, 'I want you all to get out! Just get out!' And *nothing* had happened! Ann said, 'Oh, what's the matter?' But Rita didn't answer. 'Just get out!' she kept saying. 'Leave me alone!' " Worse still was the evening when Rita threatened Pan and Miller with a butcher knife after they arrived at her house for dinner. Ann Miller recalled that when Rita's Spanish maid answered the doorbell and was told that Ann and Hermes were expected for dinner, she went to get Rita, leaving the guests outside. When Hayworth appeared at the door, she wielded a butcher knife and announced, "I'm not signing any autographs today!" Rita then looked at her old friends and asked in all seriousness, "Who are you?" Miller recalled, "We were terrified. She chased us out with the butcher knife. As we got in the car she was still screaming, 'How dare you invade my private property! I don't see autograph seekers! How dare you! Get out! Get out!' She had no idea who she was screaming at. Then the next day she called me and said, 'Why didn't you come for dinner?' I just didn't know what to make of it. I said to Hermes 'Hermes, something is terribly wrong. Is she an alcoholic?' And Hermes said, 'I don't think so, Annie. I don't think she drinks that much.' We were *very* puzzled" (Leaming 1989, 346–347).[7]

A month after Rita Hayworth passed away, Hermes Pan lost Fred Astaire to pneumonia on 22 June. In accordance with Astaire's final wishes, the funeral two days later at Oakwood Memorial Park was private and without a memorial service. Fred's wife Robyn, Ava and Richard McKenzie, Fred, Jr., and his wife, and Hermes Pan stood silently around the grave as Monsignor Jim O'Callaghan and the rector of All Saints Episcopal Church in Beverly Hills co-officiated the service that included a reading in Hebrew. Though Robyn and Fred, Jr., remained for the interment, Hermes, Monsignor Jim, and the McKenzies chose not to stay, as Ava's husband Richard McKenzie explained, "The rest of us had no wish to see the least earthbound man we knew lowered into the ground" (McKenzie 1998, 314). Instead, they returned to the Hotel L'Ermitage for a personal and gentle wake. At the end of July, Vasso's husband passed away, his ashes scattered over the Pacific Ocean. On almost every day that followed, for the next two years, Hermes would visit his sister, dropping by for lunch and then again for dinner. He wanted her never to have to eat alone.

Pan continued to make infrequent public appearances[8] until the spring of 1990 when he participated in a symposium celebrating the Oscars for dance direction sponsored by the Academy of Motion Picture Arts and Sciences in collaboration with the Museum of Modern Art in New York City. Near the end of April 1990, Hermes boarded the California Zephyr bound for Chicago on his way to the East Coast. On 23 April, at 1:30 p.m. the train jumped the tracks eighty miles south of Des Moines, flipping several of its sixteen cars and injuring 83 of its 394 passengers. Pan was not seriously hurt, but he was in one of the sleeping cars that had been completely overturned, forcing him to break through a window and crawl to safety. Hermes spent the night in Batavia, Iowa, waiting for the track to be cleared and rerouted himself to Manhattan on the next available train. He managed to arrive on time for the event and, not untypically, he never mentioned a word of the accident or any of the difficulties he had in getting across the country (*Hollywood Reporter*, 30 April 1990). At the symposium, Pan refused to address queries that seemed to belittle Ginger Rogers's abilities as a dancer, but he did comment on the celebrated "feud" between her and Fred Astaire: "She's a sweet person," he insisted. "It always makes me mad when people say they didn't get along. The supposed feud over the shedding feathers costume in the "Cheek to Cheek" number from *Top Hat* was the basis of the story. It was just a laugh between Fred and Ginger. Ginger would say 'Feathers,' and Fred would say, 'Feathers! Those damned feathers!' It became a gag. When the press got a hold of it, they tried to make it into a big thing. Sometimes, the press drives me crazy. They always make so much out of nothing. As for Ginger Rogers, she's not a great, great dancer, but she's a good dancer. She was his best partner because the chemistry was right. As one critic said, 'she gave him sex, he gave her class'" (Lewis, Winter 1991, 42).

Over the years, it had become a kind of ritual for Hermes to eat lunch and dinner with his sister or his niece Michelene, who lived two blocks away. On 19 September 1990, Pan did not appear for either meal. When he did not call with an excuse, Michelene sent her son Jimmy to Cherokee Lane to check if anything was amiss. The gate was always locked, and when Hermes didn't answer the bell, Jimmy crawled over the fence to get into the house. He found Hermes lifeless in the living room, the victim of another stroke, with an unfinished crossword puzzle in his lap and a melted pan of oatmeal on the stove. On Saturday, 22 September a funeral mass for Hermes Joseph Pan was celebrated at the Church of the Good Shepherd in Beverly Hills, and although most of his friends and colleagues had already passed on, the church was full with family and dancers wishing to say good-bye. Hermes was laid to rest in block B127 overlooking the main altar in the mausoleum at Holy Cross Cemetery, the final resting place of many of Hollywood's most celebrated Roman Catholic stars.

After Pan's death, tributes came pouring in from around the world and choreographers such as Susan Stroman, Judith Jamison, and Mikhail Baryshnikov lauded Hermes as one of the fathers of American dance—an opinion voiced by George Balanchine early in the 1950s when he invited Pan to choreograph a new work for the New York City Ballet. More surprised than flattered by the request, Hermes asked the famous ballet choreographer why he wanted him to create a work for a company that did not represent his particular métier. Balanchine replied, "I think that you represent the American dance form more than any other choreographer— whatever you do is typical of the American dance."[9] By the end of his life, Hermes Pan had become a legendary figure to fans and students of the Hollywood musical, not a bad end for the boy from Memphis who never had a dance lesson and never intended to be a choreographer. Pan idealistically spent much of his life wondering what he was meant to do and, in the end, he discovered that his was a blessed existence, almost always in the right place at the right time.

Ava Astaire McKenzie recalled the barrels of oysters Hermes used to have flown in to Los Angeles from New Orleans through which they all used to search for pearls, a happy memory from her childhood that expressed Pan's whimsical approach to life. But few stories appear to characterize Hermes's personality and his relationship with Fred Astaire as well as the locked-bathroom incident.

During one of their visits to California, Ava and her husband, Richard, had badgered Hermes into cooking lasagna for them, Fred Astaire, their son Tyler, and his wife, Ann. It was a tradition for Pan to brush his teeth before having dinner but on this occasion, he had inadvertently hit the lock button on the doorknob and locked himself out of the bathroom. Because it seemed urgent for Pan to have access to the bathroom, all of the dinner guests struggled to find ways of unlocking the door, realizing that they had nothing small enough to release the lock. Early in the evening, Richard McKenzie had quietly suggested that a corkscrew might do the trick, but his suggestion went unheeded. After some time had passed—the bathroom door still locked tight—Hermes insisted that everyone sit down to eat because the food was getting cold. On the way to the table, one of the diners suggested that perhaps a corkscrew would unlock the door and this time the suggestion was applauded, and, as McKenzie explained, suddenly "Mr. Pan relaxed in the knowledge that he could brush his teeth *after* dinner. The activity piqued Fred's appetite to such lengths he cleaned his plate, and Pan's ineptitude occupied most of his conversation when we drove him home. They love it when the other does something dumb" (McKenzie 1998, 277).

After his guests had departed and the dinner dishes were washed, Hermes reflected on the comedy that had just been enacted in his bathroom. Replaying in his mind his own irrational frustration, the well-meaning, though futile, attempts of his friends to help, and the ridiculous image of Fred Astaire on his knees, fiddling with the locked door, Pan poured himself a glass of wine, tossed back his head, and laughed. Life was good.

ACKNOWLEDGMENTS

The author extends his heartfelt thanks to everyone who had an anecdote or document to share concerning Hermes Pan, particularly Julie Graham, Performing Arts Special Collections librarian at UCLA, and her associate, Lauren Buisson; Ned Comstock, senior library assistant in the Special Collections of the Cinematic Arts Library at USC; and Jenny Romero, coordinator of Special Collections at the Margaret Herrick Library, all of whom went out of their way to locate rare materials and memorabilia and offered much encouragement for the project. Larry Billman, whose *Film Choreographers and Dance Directors: An Illustrated Biographical Encyclopedia with a History and Filmographies, 1893 through 1995* provided the backbone of early research, provided years of enthusiastic support and answers to seemingly unanswerable questions. Jerry Jackson, one of Pan's assistants, generously took the time to speak about his experiences, as did Hermes's friend and biographer, David Patrick Columbia, whose published and unpublished writings about Hermes Pan are central to the study of the choreographer. Huston Horn, Pan's cousin, provided invaluable information about the family's early days in Tennessee, and Michelene Laski, Hermes's niece, was a wealth of information and kindness, unselfishly sharing memories, photographs, documents, and memorabilia, and without whose contribution this book could not have been written. The author also wishes to thank choreographer Jimmy Hoskins for supplying research material and entertaining anecdotes, David Mills Boynton for reading early drafts of the manuscript and making suggestions, and Jen Rappaport, Anitha Chellamuthu, Amy Whitmer, and Norman Hirschy, his editors at Oxford University Press, who guided the process with considerate and patient hands. Finally, the author wishes to thank Fred Astaire's daughter, Ava Astaire McKenzie, for her kind and enthusiastic support for a book about the second most important dancer in her life.

NOTES

Introduction

1. See Kevin Lewis, "Hermes Pan," in *Dance Pages* 8 n3 (Winter 1991): 26.
2. Robert Viagas, *I'm the Greatest Star: Broadway's Top Musical Legends from 1900 to Today*, 67. See also Kevin Lewis, "Hermes Pan," in *Dance Pages* 8 n3 (Winter 1991): 26–29, 42; Amy Dawes, "Hermes Pan: Quiet 'Giant' of Film Dance," in *Daily Variety* (5 April 1988): 11; Dan Georgakas, "The Man behind Fred and Ginger: An Interview with Hermes Pan," in *Cineaste* 12 n4 (1983): 26–29.
3. *Dance in the Hollywood Musical*, 93.
4. See, for example, Dan Georgakas, "The Man behind Fred and Ginger: An Interview with Hermes Pan," in *Cineaste* 12 n4 (1983): 26–29; David Patrick Columbia, "The Man Who Danced with Fred Astaire," in *The Dancing Times* (May 1991): 759; Arthur Knight, "Hermes Pan—Who Is He?," in *Dance Magazine* (January 1960): 40–43; John Kobal, *People Will Talk*, 621–633; Kevin Lewis, "Hermes Pan," in *Dance Pages* 8 n3 (Winter 1991): 26–29; Svetlana McLee Grody and Dorothy Daniels Lister, *Conversations with Choreographers*, 1–12; Constantine, "Constantine Interviews Hermes Pan," in *Dance Magazine* (June 1945): 6–7; Oscar Rimoldi, "The Great Hollywood Choreographers, Part II: Hermes Pan, Robert Alton and Bobby Connolly," in *Hollywood Studio Magazine* 21 n6 (1988): 7–10, 40; Lenna DeMarco, "In Step with Hermes Pan," in *American Classic Screen Interviews*, edited by John C. Tibbetts and James M. Welsh, 2010 (first published in *American Classic Screen*, May/June 1983): 175–181; Kevin Gough-Yates, "Hermes Pan," in *Film Dope* (April 1994): 30–32.
5. John Kobal, *People Will Talk*, 621.
6. Quotations from David Patrick Columbia are derived from a personal interview with the author dated 14 July 2011.
7. Jerry Jackson's comments are derived from personal interviews with the author dated 11 and 13 July 2011.
8. David Patrick Columbia adds that "Pan lived a very solitary life, and not a very exciting one."
9. Pan's sister, Vasso, kept a diary in which she chronicled many of the details of her brother's life and career. In all the many years they lived together, she never hinted at his same-sex inclinations.
10. Pan's friend David Patrick Columbia argues that Hermes did, indeed, have homosexual relationships and that his closest friends were aware of his orientation as is evidenced in discreet references in private letters addressed to him but again, nothing was ever said in public.
11. See John Cooney, *The American Pope: The Life and Times of Francis Cardinal Spellman*, 152, 412 n. 25.
12. David Patrick Columbia adds that Pan "was not uncomfortable about his sexuality, but he was always uncomfortable about the politics. And with good reason, for, ironically, the Hollywood community was then, even more than now, a very homophobic place to work. It may

have been his prominent position that governed his choices and his discretions, but he was very discrete [*sic*]." See "The Man Who Danced with Fred Astaire," in *The Dancing Times* (June 1991): 849.

Chapter 1

1. The family history of Hermes Pan is derived from the city directories of Memphis and Nashville, Tennessee; conversations with Huston Horn, Pan's cousin, and Michelene Laski, Pan's niece; US census documents; Texas death records; Tennessee birth certificates; contemporary newspaper clippings and photographs; the city website of Aigion, Greece (in Greek); and "Dancin' in the Movies: A Hollywood Life," the unpublished autobiography by Hermes Pan, David Patrick Columbia, and Kenyon Kramer.
2. Although the accepted transliteration from the Greek is Panagiotopoulos, Pantelis's last name was spelled Panagiotopulos on his business card.
3. According to Michelene Laski, her mother Vasso suggested that Sam Clark was discovered later at a gas station in Florida and hired to drive the Panagiotopoulos family to New York City in 1922. In his unfinished autobiography, however, Hermes indicates that Sam worked for his father while he was growing up.

Chapter 2

1. See Lenna DeMarco, "In Step with Hermes Pan," 175–176; Dan Georgakas, "The Man behind Fred and Ginger: An Interview with Hermes Pan," 28; and Arthur Knight, "Hermes Pan: Who Is He?," 41, for further details.
2. Constantine's interview with Hermes Pan in *Dance Magazine* (June 1945): 6 suggests that Pan gave notice at the speakeasy after the very first night, a detail inconsistent with all of the other sources.

Chapter 3

1. The following section is based on "Dancin' in the Movies: A Hollywood Life" by Hermes Pan, David Patrick Columbia, and Kenyon Kramer, as well as Pan's interviews in *Conversations with Choreographers* by Svetlana McLee Grody and Dorothy Daniels Lister; *People Will Talk* by John Kobal; "Hermes Pan" by Kevin Lewis, in *Dance Pages* 8 n3 (Winter 1991): 26–29, 42; "Let's Dance" by Barbara Leaming, in *Memories* (August/September 1990); "Hermes Pan: Quiet 'Giant' of Film Dance" by Amy Dawes, in *Daily Variety* (5 April 1988): 11; "The Man Who Danced with Fred Astaire" by David Patrick Columbia, in *The Dancing Times* (June 1991): 848; "Constantine Interviews Hermes Pan," in *Dance Magazine* (June 1945): 6–7; *It Just Happened*, a film by Robert Kuperberg and Gérard Paquet; and the Ronald L. Davis Oral History Collection, 12 January 1983.

Chapter 4

1. In his autobiography Fred Astaire notes that Mark Sandrich explained the title change from "Divorce" to "Divorcee" as a studio decision. "They thought it was a more attractive-sounding title, centered around a girl. I agreed with them" (Astaire 2000, 198).
2. Pan describes this process in the documentary film *It Just Happened*.
3. This story is derived from Laurence Bergreen's *As Thousands Cheer: The Life of Irving Berlin* 348, and Philip Furia's *America's Songs: The Stories behind the Songs of Broadway, Hollywood and Tin Pan Alley*, 130–131.
4. A news item published 9 February 1936 in the *San Antonio Light* notes that Hermes Pan taught Ginger Rogers her dance routines by drawing chalk marks on the floor.
5. In their autobiographies, Fred Astaire and Ginger Rogers tell the story from their individual points of view. See *Steps in Time: An Autobiography*, 213–215, and *Ginger: My Story*, 180–181.

6. See John Mueller's *Astaire Dancing: The Musical Films* (104, 113) for a full explanation of the number.
7. The following discussions of the creation of numbers for *Swing Time* is based on material in Joe Collura, "He Danced with Fred Astaire: Hermes Pan," *Classic Images* 91 (January 1983): 10–11; Susan Winslow's interview with Hermes Pan, 20 May 1982; the Ronald L. Davis Oral History Collection, 12 January 1983; *Fred Astaire: Putting On His Top Hat*, produced and directed by David Heeley; George J. Ferencz, ed., *The Broadway Sound: The Autobiography and Selected Essays of Robert Russell Bennett*, 159–160; Gerald Bordman, *Jerome Kern: His Life and Music*, 357–361; and Marilyn Ann Moss, *Giant: George Stevens, a Life on Film*, 43–48.
8. According to the American Film Institute, producer Pandro Berman had hoped that legendary ballet master George Balanchine, who choreographed *On Your Toes*, would be involved with the Astaire-Rogers film, but commitments to the School of American Ballet and the Metropolitan Opera House made it impossible for him to leave New York.
9. The first meeting with George Gershwin was one of Pan's favorite stories and has appeared with many variations. See Walter Rimler's *George Gershwin: An Intimate Portrait*, 133; Joan Peyser's *The Memory of All That: The Life of George Gershwin*, 290–291; Ronald L. Davis Oral History Collection, 12 January 1983.
10. The *San Antonio Light* (4 March 1937) also noted that Pan was scheduled to appear as the ballet master in *Shall We Dance*, another assertion unsubstantiated by the production files.
11. See Ginger Rogers, *Ginger: My Story*, 213–215, and Peter J. Levinson, *Puttin' on the Ritz: Fred Astaire and the Fine Art of Panache*, 99.
12. On 7 April, after watching a preview cut of the film, George Gershwin sent a letter to Mark Sandrich with suggestions for changes. Complaining about the African-American singer who begins "Slap That Bass," he continued, "On Fred's first vocal chorus it would be swell if you could go right to the close up of Fred rather than wait until four bars of the chorus has elapsed . . . as with the movement behind Fred it is a little difficult to understand exactly what he is singing about. A very disturbing thing in the two choruses that Fred dances on the floor in this number is the fact that it seems as though the music is holding back his dance and is a fraction of a beat behind his steps all through. . . . Would it be possible to cut in half the interlude between the verse and the chorus?" Gershwin felt that "Beginner's Luck," sounded well (he particularly enjoyed the howling of the dogs at the end of the number) and suggested that it exchange places with "Slap That Bass" in the running order of the show. He felt that "They All Laughed" was one of the best produced numbers in the film even though Ginger seemed slightly off key at the beginning of the verse. He had no comment about "Let's Call the Whole Thing Off," calling it "perfect." He noted that "You Can't Take That Away from Me" was "very effective" but expressed the hope that Sandrich had not forgotten to put in the foghorn notes at the end of the song. Gershwin felt the ballet was overlong and needed new music and a new orchestration and asked that at least one chorus of "Shall We Dance" and the reprise of "Who's Got the Last Laugh Now" be sung by a mixed choir (Letter dated 7 April 1937 in the Mark Sandrich Collection at the Margaret Herrick Library).

    Pan was never made aware of Gershwin's remarks because Sandrich and the studio bosses chose to disregard them. Certainly cost was a factor. Used to the ever-changing dynamic of a live Broadway musical in which running orders and musical arrangement were never frozen until opening night, Gershwin was completely unaware of the expense and time required to make the corrections he suggested. But it is also true that if Gershwin's track record of hits had been as great as Irving Berlin's or Jerome Kern's, his comments would have been more highly regarded.
13. RKO Production Files indicate that Angela Blue assisted Hermes Pan on *A Damsel in Distress*. It is likely that she worked with Joan Fontaine as well.
14. In her memoir, *Tapping into the Force*, Ann Miller names Francis Grant as Pan's assistant. Studio documents, however, list Vasso Pan and Bill Brande.
15. Larry Billman suggests that Joseph Santley was involved with the musical staging for *Radio City Revels* (*Film Choreographers and Dance Directors: An Illustrated Biographical*

Encyclopedia with a History and Filmographies, 1893 through 1995, 481). Since Santley's name does not appear on call sheets for dancers, it is difficult to verify his participation. Perhaps he was involved with staging the sung numbers such as "There's a New Moon over the Old Mill."

16. For the computation of profit and/or loss for the Astaire-Rogers films, see Edward Gallafent, *Astaire and Rogers*, 80–81. Peter J. Levinson in *Puttin' on the Ritz* suggests that the grosses for *Carefree* ($1,731,000) and *The Story of Vernon and Irene Castle* ($1,200,000), though higher than the production costs, produced a negligible profit for the studio.

Chapter 5

1. For example, a story conference memo from Darryl Zanuck dated 11 December 1940 regarding *Moon over Miami* stated, "We want to treat it musically in the manner that we treated *Down Argentine Way*. That is to say, we don't want to make any effort to explain the music or prepare for it. The song numbers can be worked in smoothly, of course, but with whatever musical license we want to take" (Behlmer 46). After years of working to integrate music and dance into the dramatic fabric of a film, Pan found such an aesthetic completely foreign to his way of working.

2. See *Coshocton Tribune*, 8 December 1940, *Big Spring Daily Herald*, 7 January 1941, and *San Antonio Express*, 9 January 1941.

3. See also *Coshocton Tribune*, 8 December 1940, and *Oakland Tribune*, 5 January 1941.

4. Jerry Jackson recalled that the studio often put Hayworth under house arrest to keep her on a diet. On one occasion she crawled out of a window and fled to Pan's house to get food.

5. See, for example, *Waterloo Sunday Courier*, 18 May 1941; *Panama City News-Herald*, 17 August 1941.

6. See Glenn Loney's *Unsung Genius: The Passion of Dancer-Choreographer Jack Cole*, 126–129.

7. For a detailed analysis of the "Chattanooga Choo Choo" routine, see Constance Valis Hill's *Brotherhood in Rhythm: The Jazz Tap Dancing of the Nicholas Brothers*, 162–169 and Donald Bogle's *Dorothy Dandridge: A Biography*, 85–87.

8. In his interview with Ronald L. Davis (1983), Pan notes a series of memos from Zanuck during the making of *Rise and Shine* that read, "Ask Mr. Pan about dance sequences." Story conference notes dated 19 August 1941, for example, state: "At the rally, we will have a reprise of 'Hail to Bolenciewicz.' Here too, we may have a number designed to feature Oakie and twelve girls, which Hermes Pan is working out. Mr. Zanuck does not want the number to run over two and one-half minutes. Before deciding on its inclusion in the picture, Mr. Zanuck would like to have an outline of what Pan wants to do."

9. Script conference notes dated 6 March 1942 describe the insertion of the number into a preexisting scene:

In order to motivate the routine with Pat [Betty Grable] and Hermes Pan, which [director Gregory] Ratoff described, we will change the continuity on page 47, as follows:

As Pat comes running down the stairs, the Dance Director calls out to her to hurry—he wants her to run through a routine. He also picks one of the boys (Hermes Pan) to do the routine with Pat, and the couple start dancing.

Now we play scene 107—Tommy [Victor Mature] enters and asks: "What are they doing that for?" Slap [Phil Silvers] tells him that that's a specialty they're working out for Tommy and Estelle [Cobina Wright, Jr.]. Tommy watches—asks: "Which one is supposed to be me?"

At the end of the number Tommy says, "Estelle will never be able to get that routine." And it leads to the understudy suggestion, etc.

(Mr. Ratoff described the routine as being very intricate. He had in mind that Tommy would react in astonishment at the complicated steps—while, on the other hand, all through the routine, the dance director—or Slap—would keep on telling Tommy: "See? It's very simple.")

10. Studio publicity, dated 22 June 1942, advertised that "Magazines" and "I Like to Be Loved by You," two numbers written by Harry Warren and Mack Gordon, were scheduled to be included in the film. They do not appear in the final print.

11. According to a syndicated news report, by the beginning of 1943 nearly half of Hollywood's male dancing force was in the army. Twentieth Century-Fox producer Lew Schreiber noted the severity of the situation when a friend called him in high spirits to announce, "I've got my picture all cast." "You mean you've got the stars you wanted already?" Lew inquired. "Heck, no! I've got all my chorus men" (*Salt Lake Tribune*, 3 January 1943).

12. Hermes may well have added the name of director H. Bruce Humberstone, who was not particularly skilled in the area of musical staging.

Chapter 6

1. A number entitled "The Bagpiper of Buckingham" was composed for the film by Mack Gordon and Harry Warren but does not appear in the final print. Pan did preproduction work on the song, but it is not known if his choreography was actually filmed.

2. Paul Haakon (1911–1992) had danced in *Champagne, Sec*, directed by Monty Woolley in 1933, and was not completely unknown to Cole Porter. In addition he performed in Rudolf Friml's 1934 operetta *Music Hath Charms*, the 1935 Dietz and Schwartz revue *At Home Abroad*, the 1936 Vernon Duke revue *The Show Is On*, and the 1937 Harold Arlen–E. Y. Harburg musical *Hooray for What!* After *Mexican Hayride*, Haakon choreographed just one more show, a two-performance flop produced by Michael Todd's Midnight Players called *Spook Scandals*. Evidently, Todd enjoyed his work sufficiently to hire him a decade later as a specialty dancer in his film *Around the World in Eighty Days*.

3. Dancer and dance director Kenny Williams appears in a photograph with Betty Grable in costume for the "Once Too Often" number. Although Williams's name does not appear on records for the film, since he had previously worked with Pan on *Iceland* it is possible that he was hired to work with Grable on the apache.

4. Lenna DeMarco explained Pan's concept of "Right Now" in an interview entitled "In Step with Hermes Pan":

    Pan has been known to virtually retrain dancers to get that technically demanding quality of "RIGHT NOW." What Pan refers to here is the often disturbing inability of many technically proficient dancers to "sell" a number; that is, to bring a fire and energy from inside instead of relying solely on technical prowess. Pan feels that technique should be used as an "underskirt" and brought in only to aid in creating a look of spontaneity and excitement. When the movement isn't measured, but felt and responded to at the moment, the dancer creates an emotion that is immediately sensed by the audience. (DeMarco 2010, 180)

    Note the similarity of the concept of "Right Now" to actor-trainer Stanislavski's concept of acting "in the moment."

5. The opening sequence of *Mexican Hayride* was choreographed by Dan Eckley; the "Good-Will Movement" dance was staged by Eckley and Virginia Johnson; and "Girls" and "Abracadabra" were choreographed by Lew Kessler.

6. In *The Nine Lives of Mike Todd*, 143, Art Cohn relates the story with different embellishments.

7. See *Winnipeg Free Press*, 28 March 1944, and *Vidette-Messenger*, 8 April 1944.

8. The studio was ultimately sued by the animation company, High Harman Productions, for breach of contract.

9. Kenny Williams, Pan's assistant on previous films, was also involved with the production. On this occasion he was appropriately cast as Kenny, the dance director of the Diamond Horseshoe.

10. In *Puttin' on the Ritz*, Astaire's biographer Peter J. Levinson argues that the original director of *Blue Skies* died nine days after the film started shooting and that the subsequent director,

Stuart Heisler, sought to replace Paul Draper with Astaire, who demanded that Hermes Pan be hired as choreographer (151). Mark Sandrich died on 4 March 1945, and according to studio records, filming began on 16 July, with Paul Draper's name on cast and call sheets until 31 July. The contract between Twentieth Century-Fox and Paramount for the lending of Pan is dated 18 May while Draper was still very much involved.

11. Exactly how the eight chorus images of Astaire were created is subject to interpretation. In *Astaire Dancing*, John Mueller argues that "every other Astaire in the chorus is identical— that is, two repeated versions of Astaire-as-chorus-member were filmed and duplicated and then these two versions were interleaved" (269–270). In *Puttin' on the Ritz*, however, Peter J. Levinson, on the authority of Bob Thomas's book, *Astaire*, suggests that "Fred insisted on being photographed eight different times dancing the routine" (153).

12. For a complete discussion of all the dances in *Blue Skies*, see John Mueller, *Astaire Dancing: The Musical Films*, 263–273.

13. Ed Hulse gives these figures (149). Ruth Prigozy, Dick Haymes's biographer, argues that the film earned only $2,250,000 (*The Life of Dick Haymes: No More Little White Lies*, 97). In any case, *The Shocking Miss Pilgrim* was not considered a success by anyone involved with the production.

14. See Harrison Carroll's syndicated column, "Behind the Scenes in Hollywood," 21 August 1946 for a firsthand description of one of June Haver's days during the production of *I Wonder Who's Kissing Her Now*.

15. In addition to routines for June Haver and Martha Stewart, Pan created novel staging for Mark Stevens in the Joseph Howard specialty "Honeymoon," with the use of magic lantern projections.

16. See Vi and Bill Benter's article, "The Ancient Greeks Would Have Loved This," in the *Los Angeles Times*, 7 March 1948, G7. The Benters were hired by Hermes to design the interior of the house.

Chapter 7

1. For a further discussion of "Shoes with Wings On," see Ginger Rogers, *Ginger: My Story*, 340–341; Fred Astaire, *Steps in Time: An Autobiography*, 294–295; and John Mueller, *Astaire Dancing: The Musical Films*, 294–295.

2. Madame Barbara Karinska (1886–1983) realized Oleg Cassini's designs for *As the Girls Go*. She designed for George Balanchine in Europe as well as in New York, and, in addition to her work in musicals, won the Oscar for costume design in the 1948 film *Joan of Arc*.

3. "As the Girls Go," words by Harold Adamson, music by Jimmy McHugh. Copyright 1948 (Renewed) WB Music Corp. (ASCAP). All rights reserved. Used by permission.

4. Pan originally voiced these opinions in a syndicated newspaper article, 18 June 1942.

5. On 8 September Mike Todd signed the contract for the Winter Garden enabling it to become a legitimate theatre house once again. For about eighteen months, it had been a movie the-atre under the management of J. Arthur Rank. Todd's move enabled the Shuberts to regain possession of the building as of 1 October.

6. See Art Cohn, *The Nine Lives of Mike Todd*, 225ff.

7. "Lucky in the Rain," words by Harold Adamson, music by Jimmy McHugh. Copyright 1948 (Renewed) WB Music Corp. (ASCAP). All rights reserved. Used by permission.

8. All reviews were published in New York City on 15 November 1948.

Chapter 8

1. Pan's niece, Michelene Reed Laski, challenges Miller's recollections, saying that while there was a big oak tree on the property, she never saw an actual tree house built there. Laski sug-gested that the reference might have been some private joke between her uncle and the dancer.

2. The American Film Institute record for *Let's Dance* suggests Dave Rogel instead of Dave Robel. Since Robel was Astaire's assistant for work during this period, Rogel is likely

misspelling, common in studio records. Peggy Carroll was well known to Pan, having performed in *Bachelor Mother*, *Carefree*, and *The Story of Vernon and Irene Castle*.

3. Pan explained to Kevin Lewis, "You put one leg on the top and the other on the seat of the chair. You push on top and push back on the bottom. It gives you perfect control like being in the middle of a see-saw. As you control the speed, you ride slowly over" ("Hermes Pan," *Dance Pages* 8 n3 [Winter 1991]: 29).

4. See *Los Angeles Times*, 11, 18, and 19 September 1949.

5. There is some confusion about the order in which Hermes worked on *Let's Dance* and *Three Little Words*. In his autobiography, Fred Astaire argues that he filmed *Three Little Words* at M-G-M first because the Paramount film wasn't ready. The fact that it was released before *Let's Dance* also suggests that it was the earlier film. However, studio records, call sheets, and shooting schedules indicate that *Let's Dance* was in production from July through September 1949 and that *Three Little Words* went before the cameras in December, when Betty Hutton was at work on *Annie Get Your Gun*, having replaced Judy Garland in the title role.

6. For a complete description of the dances in *Three Little Words*, see John Mueller, *Astaire Dancing: The Musical Films*, 301–310.

7. Alfred Newman had been the musical director for much of Pan's work at Fox, including *Billy Rose's Diamond Horseshoe*, *Captain from Castile*, *Coney Island*, *I Wonder Who's Kissing Her Now*, *Irish Eyes Are Smiling*, *Moon Over Miami*, *My Gal Sal*, *The Shocking Miss Pilgrim*, *Springtime in the Rockies*, *State Fair*, *Sweet Rosie O'Grady*, *That Lady in Ermine*, *That Night in Rio*, and *Week-End in Havana*.

8. A Fox memo, dated 11 July, suggested that work on the rumba would begin on 1 August after the major scenes of the film had been completed. An earlier document indicated that the work should take no more than ten days, and on 26 August the studio announced that Pan's services had been completed.

9. Vasso's two-year-old son Patrick died on 13 January 1946. Hermes paid for the funeral.

10. For a discussion of "It's Dynamite" as an expression of sexual camp, see Steven Cohan's *Incongruous Entertainment: Camp, Cultural Value, and the MGM Musical*, 136.

11. A *Texas Carnival* production report dated 16 October 1951 notes that Slim's Dream—Water Number (scenes 120–133) had been cut from the film. The sequence represented 199 feet of film and cost $42,390 to shoot.

12. Walton Walker had worked with Hermes on *Springtime in the Rockies*, *Blue Skies*, and *Excuse My Dust*. On *Lovely to Look At*, actor Lawrence Montaigne claims that Walker used his position as Pan's assistant to seduce him, not an unusual event in theatre or film, certainly, but not the sort of thing typically associated with a Hermes Pan show. For specifics, see Lawrence Montaigne, *A Vulcan Odyssey*, 25–26.

Chapter 9

1. See *Los Angeles Times*, 8 November 1953.

2. According to Howard Keel, Kathryn Grayson and he began working on "Wunderbar," but after a couple of hours, she complained of dizziness and Carol Haney was drafted as her dance-in. See Keel, *Only Make Believe: My Life in Show Business*, 151–152.

3. For a detailed account of the dispute, see Roland L. Bessette, *Mario Lanza: Tenor in Exile*, 134–153; Derek Mannering, *Mario Lanza: Singing to the Gods*, 102–118; and Raymond Strait and Terry Robinson, *Lanza: His Tragic Life*, 101–117.

4. M-G-M production department records note that Pan hired Angie Blue and Pat Denise as dance-ins for the production.

5. M-G-M production records (24 January 1955) show that Pan staged several other numbers that were cut from the final print: "Never Trust a Woman," sung by Hannibal in his tent; "I Had a Dream," first sung by Fabius (George Sanders) and later by Fabius and Amytis; and an unspecified dance number for Meta and Varius.

6. Earl Blackwell was responsible for the famous Marilyn Monroe publicity stunt in which she sang "Happy Birthday, Mr. President" to John F. Kennedy in 1962.

7. The American Film Institute adds the names of Jeanne Coyne and Barrie Chase to the list of choreographic assistants.
8. About Pan's working habits, Pan's assistant Jerry Jackson adds that Hermes was methodical but not energetic as a choreographer. He was very relaxed rather than aggressive. It was not that he was unprepared; he would adjust and reconsider as he was working—doing it all in his head. As a result, some dancers felt that he was slow and vague in his instructions.
9. *Variety* (1 May 1957) also reported that closing off city landmarks, such as Telegraph Hill, from tourists and San Franciscans was causing much unrest in the city even though the production had acquired the necessary permissions beforehand. Moreover, wherever a shoot was located, crowds of people would assemble to watch Frank Sinatra, Rita Hayworth, and Kim Novak, causing great distractions for the stars. Frank Sinatra was said to have walked off the set before Easter because of the crowds. If being in San Francisco was not entirely pleasant for the company, the work schedule when they returned to the studio certainly made up for it. Unlike most films that shoot from 9:00 a.m. to 6:00 p.m., *Pal Joey* filmed from noon to 8:00 p.m., allowing the cast and crew to arrive substantially more rested and refreshed than if they had an 8:00 a.m. call. The *Hollywood Reporter* (8 May 1957) quoted Frank Sinatra as saying, "This is for me. Everyone, cast and crew, is much more relaxed. It stands to reason that an actor will give more of himself later in a working day than early in the morning. And anyway, who made the rule that you have to start early?"
10. See "The Man Who Danced with Fred Astaire," *The Dancing Times* (June 1991): 849.
11. In 1958 *Un Paio d'Ali* was released as a film under the title *Come te movi, te fulmino!* (*The way you move, you shine!*), with the original cast and Pan's choreography.

Chapter 10

1. For a fuller discussion of the making of *Porgy and Bess*, see Hollis Alpert, *The Life and Times of* Porgy and Bess: *The Story of an American Classic*, 249–282; A. Scott Berg, *Goldwyn: A Biography*, 478–487; Chris Fujiwara, *The World and Its Double: The Life and Work of Otto Preminger*, 224–229; and Foster Hirsch, *Otto Preminger: The Man Who Would Be King*, 285–302.
2. On another occasion, Yorkin told Levinson, "If you stood back forty or fifty feet, and you watched this man dance, you wouldn't know whether it was Hermes or Fred Astaire. Hermes had every move, he looked like Astaire. He performed like him. Almost every step that Fred made, Hermes would do and turn like Fred would do, and he might embellish or change it" (Levinson 2009, 261).
3. The 6 March contract also stipulated that Pan would work on a remake of *Stage Door*, but that production did not materialize. The contract also included a right of preemption, by which the studio had the right to preempt outside employment after the four-week period. If preemption occurred, the studio would guarantee an additional six weeks of employment for a total of ten weeks guaranteed.
4. See *Los Angeles Examiner*, 4 June 1959.
5. Studio publicity reported that both Shirley MacLaine and Juliet Prowse were acrophobic. As a result, Pan had to ease them into choreography that involved high platforms or flying entrances.
6. For another firsthand account of the filming of "The Garden of Eden Ballet," see Harrison Carroll's column, "Behind the Scenes in Hollywood," 31 August 1959.
7. See *Dance Magazine* (January 1960): 43.
8. Pan had heard about the Earl twins from dancer John Brascia, the Johnny of the "Frankie and Johnny" number in *Meet Me in Las Vegas*, and found them dancing to a juke box in a Hollywood coffeehouse down the street from the American School of Dance, where they took classes from Eugene Loring. Pan immediately took a liking to their work and cast them in the chorus of *Can-Can*, promising to use them whenever he could. In fact, he had wanted to hire them for the second Astaire special but they were too tied up with *Can-Can* to be available for rehearsals.

9. According to publicity, *The Sounds of America* explores the sounds of yesterday, the sounds of the west, the sounds of the river, and the sounds of small-town America (on Disneyland's Main Street), using representative period songs and original material composed by Gordon Jenkins.

Chapter 11

1. See the Stanley K. Schever Collection, USC; *Los Angeles Times*, 23 April 1963; Walter Wanger and Joe Hyams, *My Life with Cleopatra*, 156–158; Monica Silveira Cyrino, *Big Screen Rome*, 141; and Jon Solomon, *The Ancient World and the Cinema*, 74.
2. During the hiatus, Pan went to parties. At the Grand Hotel, where Kirk Douglas and his wife threw a party to celebrate the first anniversary of *Spartacus*, Hermes danced the rumba completely unaware that Elizabeth Taylor's dress had caught on fire (an Italian musician put it out with his bare hands). At the Cinecittà commissary, Pan met President Sukarno of Indonesia and taught him a tap combination.
3. The interoffice memo also notes that the deal was made directly with Hermes Pan, explaining that he did not have an agent. Hermes had been dissatisfied with the way MCA had handled the *Cleopatra* negotiations and left the agency, choosing to handle future work on his own.
4. While in Positano, Hermes and Christa heard mass at the Church of Santa Maria Assunta, famous for its dome made completely of majolica tiles and a thirteenth-century icon of a black Madonna, said to have been stolen from Byzantium by pirates. A connoisseur of fine wines and spirits, Pan was anxious to try an Albertissimo, a local alcoholic drink that is said to be only available in the main harbor of Positano.
5. Barrie Chase is credited on at least two Studio Uno musical specials, one of which, airing in 1968, featured Nancy Sinatra and the Ikettes.
6. Jerry Jackson first met Pan when he worked with him in Rome on Studio Uno.
7. For an extended account of the filming of *Finian's Rainbow*, see Peter J. Levinson, *Puttin' on the Ritz: Fred Astaire and the Fine Art of Panache*, 344–349; John Mueller, *Astaire Dancing: The Musical Films*, 401–407; Gene D. Phillips, *Godfather: The Intimate Francis Ford Coppola*, 47–50; and Michael Schumacher, *Francis Ford Coppola: A Filmmaker's Life*, 52–61.

Chapter 12

1. See *Independent Press-Telegram*, 6 December 1970; *Valley Morning Star*, 20 December 1970; *Cedar Rapids Gazette*, 16 May 1971; and *Anderson Daily-Bulletin*, 22 October 1971.
2. For detailed studies of *Lost Horizon*, see Michael Brocken, *Bacharach: Maestro! The Life of a Pop Genius*, 209–230; Milton Krims, "Lost Horizon Again," in *The Saturday Evening Post* (March–April 1973): 68–69, 118; *Filmfacts* 16 n5 (1973): 119–122.
3. The film was *Kamouraska*, a 1973 Québécois film directed by Claude Jutra.
4. Jijo was Michelene's eight-year-old son, who complained, "Tio didn't answer me when I talked to him." Tio (uncle) was what the children always called Hermes.
5. In 1978, Pan made only one heralded public appearance, escorting Rita Hayworth to a $150-a-person bash at Hugh Hefner's Holmby Hills mansion to raise money to refurbish the landmark Hollywood sign before he sailed back to Italy late in the year. When he returned from Europe in the fall of 1979, he took an active part in a panel discussion about choreography in the movies along with LeRoy Prinz and dancer Eleanor Powell at a program focusing on the Academy Award for Best Dance Direction sponsored by the Academy of Motion Picture Arts and Sciences at its Samuel Goldwyn Theatre on Wilshire Boulevard in Beverly Hills.
6. The interview with Pupi Avati is in Italian. Since the English version provided in Maraldi was painfully literal and sometimes inaccurate, I have provided my own translation.
7. In *If This Was Happiness: A Biography of Rita Hayworth*, Barbara Leaming chronicles the development of Hayworth's Alzheimer's disease and its effect on her relationships. This section is indebted to Leaming and her interviews with Hermes Pan and Ann Miller.

8. Early in 1988, Pan received the second annual Gypsy Award for extraordinary contribution to dance from the Professional Dancers Society at a 12:30 p.m. luncheon in the Blossom Room of the Hollywood Roosevelt Hotel. Three hundred celebrities were on hand to fete him on this occasion, including Ann Miller, Cesar Romero, Cyd Charisse, Juliet Prowse, Marge Champion, and Sammy Davis, Jr., who gave Pan a kiss before he received the award. In April, the French Théâtre National de la Dance et de l'Image began videotaping him for a European television documentary about his career, *It Just Happened,* and in May, Hermes was in Washington, D.C., as a special guest at "A Remembrance of Fred Astaire," the American Film Institute's first annual Preservation Ball. In August Hermes joined Ruby Keeler and Buddy Ebsen onstage at the Samuel Goldwyn Theatre of the Academy of Motion Picture Arts and Sciences to honor the Oscars given for dance direction between the years 1935 and 1937.

9. See Maureen C. Solomon, "Gotta Dance: The Life and Tapping Times of Hermes Pan, Dancemaster to Hollywood's Golden Era" in *Los Angeles Reader* (11 February 1983): 22.

BIBLIOGRAPHY

Primary Sources

MARGARET HERRICK LIBRARY

Alex North Papers, *Cleopatra*: Clippings and Correspondence, 1962–1964, Elmo Williams Papers, Fred MacMurray and June Haver Papers, George Cukor Papers, George Stevens Papers, Mark Sandrich Papers, Metro-Goldwyn-Mayer Wardrobe Department Records, Paramount Pictures Production Records, Paramount Pictures Scripts, *The Hollywood Reporter*, 1930–1981, Core Production and Biographical Files, Hedda Hopper Papers, Samuel Goldwyn Papers, Hermes Pan Studio Biography, Unpublished Interviews: 20 May 1982, conducted by Susan Winslow; 15 June 1982, conducted by George Stevens, Jr.; 12 January 1983, conducted by Ronald L. Davis, Ronald L. Davis Oral History Collection No. 245.

UCLA SPECIAL COLLECTIONS

RKO Production Files, Twentieth Century-Fox Production Files, Twentieth Century-Fox Legal Files.

USC SPECIAL COLLECTIONS

Hugh Fordin Interview with Hermes Pan, n.d., Arthur Freed Collection, M-G-M Production Department Collection, Joe Pasternak Collection, Robert Richardson Collection on Southern California Theatre, The Stanley K. Schever Collection, Studio Press Books, Twentieth Century-Fox Collection, Jack Warner Collection.

PUBLIC RECORDS

California birth and death records; city directories of Memphis and Nashville, Tennessee; city directories of Los Angeles, California; Tennessee birth records; Texas death records; United States census documents.

UNPUBLISHED MANUSCRIPTS

Pan, Hermes, David Patrick Columbia, and Kenyon Kramer. "Dancin' in the Movies: A Hollywood Life." A brief outline of thirteen chapters, and two completed chapters ("Back from Arizona" and "The Mortal Goddesses"). October 12, 1983.
———. "Meeting the Frog Prince." Chapter 7 of a memoir. n.d.
Pan, Vasso. "June Thirteenth." Taken from the Journal of Vasso Pan by Christa Meade. n.d.

FILMS

The Actress (1953)
Aiutami a sognare (1981)
Another Evening with Fred Astaire (1959)
Astaire Time (1960)
Bachelor Mother (1939)
The Barkleys of Broadway (1949)
Becky Sharp (1935)
Blood and Sand (1941)
The Blue Angel (1959)
Blue Skies (1946)
Can-Can (1960)
Captain from Castile (1948)
Carefree (1938)
Carol Channing and 101 Men (1968)
Cleopatra (1963)
Cockeyed Cavaliers (1934)
Coney Island (1943)
A Damsel in Distress (1937)
Dance Crazy in Hollywood (1994)
Darling Lili (1970)
Diamond Horseshoe (1945)
A Dog of Flanders (1935)
An Evening with Fred Astaire (1958)
Excuse My Dust (1951)
Finian's Rainbow (1968)
Flower Drum Song (1961)
Flying Down to Rio (1933)
Follow the Fleet (1936)
Footlight Serenade (1942)
For Heaven's Sake (1950)
Fred Astaire: Putting On His Top Hat (1980)
The Gay Divorcee (1934)
The Great American Broadcast (1941)
The Great Race (1965)
Hangover Square (1945)
Having Wonderful Time (1938)
Hello Frisco, Hello (1942)
Hidden Hollywood: Treasures from the Twentieth Century Fox Vaults (1997)
Hips, Hips, Hooray (1934)
Hit Parade of 1941 (1940)
Hit the Deck (1955)
Iceland (1942)
I Dream Too Much (1935)
In Person (1935)
Irish Eyes Are Smiling (1944)
It Just Happened (1988)
I Wonder Who's Kissing Her Now (1947)
Jupiter's Darling (1955)
Kiss Me Kate (1953)
Let's Dance (1950)
Lost Horizon (1973)
Lovely to Look At (1952)

Mary of Scotland (1936)
Meet Me in Las Vegas (1956)
Moon over Miami (1941)
My Fair Lady (1964)
My Gal Sal (1942)
Never Steal Anything Small (1959)
Old Man Rhythm (1935)
Pal Joey (1957)
The Pink Panther (1963)
Pin Up Girl (1944)
The Pleasure of His Company (1961)
Porgy and Bess (1959)
Quality Street (1937)
Radio City Revels (1938)
Rise and Shine (1941)
Roberta (1935)
Roxie Hart (1942)
Second Chorus (1940)
Shall We Dance (1937)
Silk Stockings (1957)
The Shocking Miss Pilgrim (1947)
Sombrero (1953)
Song of the Islands (1942)
Springtime in the Rockies (1942)
Stage Door (1937)
State Fair (1945)
The Story of Vernon and Irene Castle (1939)
Strictly Dynamite (1934)
The Student Prince (1954)
Sun Valley Serenade (1941)
Sweet Rosie O'Grady (1943)
Swing Time (1936)
Texas Carnival (1951)
That Lady in Ermine (1948)
That Night in Rio (1941)
Three Little Words (1950)
The Toast of New York (1937)
Top Hat (1935)
Vivacious Lady (1938)
Week-End in Havana (1941)
A Woman Rebels (1936)

Secondary Sources

ARTICLES

Barnes, Clive. "Who's Jazzy Now?" *Dance Magazine* 74 n8 (August 2000): 90.
Barrett, Mary Ellin. "West Berlin." *Los Angeles Magazine* 39 n9 (September 1994): 102–107.
Collura, Joe. "He Danced with Fred Astaire: Hermes Pan." *Classic Images* 91 (January 1983): 10–12.
Columbia, David Patrick. "The Man Who Danced with Fred Astaire." *The Dancing Times* (May 1991): 759.
———. "The Man Who Danced with Fred Astaire: Part Two of the Biography of Hermes Pan, including His Early Collaboration with Fred Astaire on the RKO films." *The Dancing Times* (June 1991): 848–850.
Constantine. "Constantine Interviews Hermes Pan." *Dance Magazine* (June 1945): 6–7.

"Dancing with Astaire and Rogers: Their Smooth Steps Take Many Torturous Weeks to Perfect." *Literary Digest* (December 12, 1936): 20–21.

Dawes, Amy. "Hermes Pan: Quiet 'Giant' of Film Dance." *Daily Variety* (5 April 1988): 11.

DeMarco, Lenna. "In Step with Hermes Pan." In *American Classic Screen Interviews*. Edited by John C. Tibbetts and James M. Welsh. Lanham, MD: Scarecrow Press, 2010.

Georgakas, Dan. "The Man behind Fred and Ginger: An Interview with Hermes Pan." *Cineaste* 12 n4 (1983): 26–29.

Gold, Sylviane. "Dance Theater." *Dance Magazine* 77 n5 (May, 2003): 80.

Gough-Yates, Kevin. "Hermes Pan." *Film Dope* 50 (April 1994): 30–32.

Ivry, Benjamin. "Gotta Dance." *American Theatre* 17 n4 (April 2000): 48.

Jarvis, Jeff. "Now Rita Sits in Silence." *People Weekly* (7 November 1983): 112.

"Judith Jamison." *Daily Variety* 294 n5 (5 January 2007): 23.

Knight, Arthur. "Hermes Pan: Who Is He?" *Dance Magazine* (January 1960): 40–43.

———. "My Second-Fare Lady." *Dance Magazine* (December 1964): 30–32.

Leaming, Barbara. "Let's Dance." *Memories* (August/September 1990): 1.

Lewis, Kevin. "Hermes Pan." *Dance Pages* 8 n3 (Winter 1991): 26–29, 42.

———. "More Hermes Pan: Sex Symbols in Rhythm." *Dance Pages* 8 n4 (Spring 1991): 26–29.

McDonald, Neil. "Music, Film and Sound." *Quadrant* 44 n12 (December 2000): 72–75.

Mirault, Don. "Dancing in Guam." *Dance Magazine* 73 n8 (August 1999): 39.

Nielsen, Ray. "Ray's Way: Hermes Pan and My Gal Sal." *Classic Images* 88 (October 1982): 42–43, 50.

Rico, Diana. "Choreography: Hermes Pan." *Interview* 15 n9 (September 1985): 115.

Rimoldi, Oscar. "The Great Hollywood Choreographers, Part II: Hermes Pan, Robert Alton and Bobby Connolly." *Hollywood Studio Magazine* 21 n6 (1988): 7–10, 40.

Rothman, Cliff. "Beyond Mullholland Drive." *Variety* 385 n2 (26 November 2001): A19.

Schaffner, Caroline. "A Tab Show: The Stepchild of Musical Comedy." In *Musical Theatre in America*. Edited by Glenn Loney. Westport, CT: Greenwood Press, 1984.

Skupin, Michael. "A Damsel in Distress." Paper presented at the Houston convention of the Wodehouse Society, October 1999.

Solomon, Maureen C. "Gotta Dance: The Life and Tapping Times of Hermes Pan, Dancemaster to Hollywood's Golden Era." *Los Angeles Reader* (11 February 1983): 11–12, 22.

Sulcas, Roslyn. "From Spark to Sparkle: The Road to Perfection." *Dance Magazine* 81 n1 (January 2007): 210–211.

"What They Meant." *Dance Magazine* 81 n9 (September 2007): 70–74.

BOOKS

Adler, Bill. *Fred Astaire: A Wonderful Life*. New York: Carroll and Graf, 1987.

Alberti, Bob. *Up the Ladder and Over the Top: Memoirs of a Hollywood Studio Musician*. Lexington, KY: Shirbo Books, 2003.

Alpert, Hollis. *The Life and Times of Porgy and Bess: The Story of an American Classic*. New York: Alfred A. Knopf, 1990.

Arceri, Gene. *Rocking Horse: A Personal Biography of Betty Hutton*. Albany, GA: Bearmanor Media 2009.

Astaire, Fred. *Steps in Time: An Autobiography*. 1959. Reprint. New York: Cooper Square Press 2000.

Behlmer, Rudy, ed. *Memo from Darryl F. Zanuck: The Golden Years at Twentieth Century-Fox*. Fore word by Philip Dunne. New York: Grove Press, 1993.

Berg, A. Scott. *Goldwyn: A Biography*. New York: Riverhead Books, 1989.

Bergreen, Laurence. *As Thousands Cheer: The Life of Irving Berlin*. New York: Viking, 1990.

Bessette, Roland L. *Mario Lanza: Tenor in Exile*. Portland, OR: Amadeus Press, 1999.

Billman, Larry. *Film Choreographers and Dance Directors: An Illustrated Biographical Encyclopedia with a History and Filmographies, 1893 through 1995*. Jefferson, NC: McFarland, 1997.

Bogle, Donald. *Dorothy Dandridge: A Biography*. New York: Boulevard Books, 1998.

Bordman, Gerald. *Days to Be Happy, Years to Be Sad: The Life and Music of Vincent Youmans*. New York Oxford University Press, 1982.

————. *Jerome Kern: His Life and Music.* 1980. Reprint. New York: Oxford University Press, 1990.

Brady, Kathleen. *Lucille: The Life of Lucille Ball.* New York: Hyperion, 1994.

Brocken, Michael. *Bacharach: Maestro! The Life of a Pop Genius.* New Malden, Surrey, UK: A Chrome Dreams Publication, 2003.

Brodsky, Jack, and Nathan Weiss. *The Cleopatra Papers: A Private Correspondence.* New York: Simon and Schuster, 1963.

Cassini, Oleg. *In My Own Fashion: An Autobiography.* New York: Simon and Schuster, 1987.

Channing, Carol. *Just Lucky I Guess: A Memoir of Sorts.* New York: Simon and Schuster, 2002.

Chaplin, Saul. *The Golden Age of Movie Musicals and Me.* Norman: University of Oklahoma Press, 1994.

Cohan, Steven. *Incongruous Entertainment: Camp, Cultural Value, and the MGM Musical.* Durham, NC: Duke University Press, 2005.

Cohn, Art. *The Nine Lives of Mike Todd.* London: Hutchinson, 1959.

Connor, Jim. *Ann Miller, Tops in Taps: An Authorized Pictorial History.* With an introduction by Hermes Pan. New York: Franklin Watts, 1981.

Cooney, John. *The American Pope: The Life and Times of Francis Cardinal Spellman.* New York: New York Times Books, 1984. Reprint. New York: Dell, 1986.

Croce, Arlene. *The Fred Astaire & Ginger Rogers Book.* 1972. Reprint. New York: E. P. Dutton, 1987.

Cyrino, Monica Silveira. *Big Screen Rome.* Malden, MA: Wiley-Blackwell, 2005.

Davis, Ronald L. *Hollywood Beauty: Linda Darnell and the American Dream.* Norman: University of Oklahoma Press, 1991.

Delamater, Jerome. *Dance in the Hollywood Musical.* Ann Arbor, MI: UMI Research Press, 1981.

Edwards, Anne. *Katharine Hepburn: A Remarkable Woman.* 1985. Reprint. New York: St. Martin's Griffin, 2000.

Ehrenstein, David. *Open Secret (Gay Hollywood 1928–1998).* New York: William Morrow, 1998.

Epstein, Joseph. *Fred Astaire.* New Haven, CT: Yale University Press, 2008.

Eyman, Scott. *Lion of Hollywood: The Life and Legend of Louis B. Mayer.* New York: Simon and Schuster, 2005.

Fehr, Richard, and Frederick G. Vogel. *Lullabies of Hollywood: Movie Music and the Movie Musical, 1915–1992.* Jefferson, NC: McFarland, 1993.

Ferencz, George J., ed. *The Broadway Sound: The Autobiography and Selected Essays of Robert Russell Bennett.* Rochester, NY: University of Rochester Press, 1999.

————. *Robert Russell Bennett: A Bio-Bibliography.* New York: Greenwood Press, 1990.

Fishgall, Gary. *Gonna Do Great Things: The Life of Sammy Davis, Jr.* New York: Scribner, 2003.

Fontaine, Joan. *No Bed of Roses.* New York: William Morrow, 1978.

Fordin, Hugh. *M-G-M's Greatest Musicals: The Arthur Freed Unit.* 1975. New York: Da Capo Press, 1996.

Frank, Rusty E. *Tap! The Greatest Tap Dance Stars and Their Stories 1900–1955.* 1990. Rev. ed. New York: Da Capo Press, 1994.

Fujiwara, Chris. *The World and Its Double: The Life and Work of Otto Preminger.* New York: Faber and Faber, 2008.

Furia, Philip. *America's Songs: The Stories behind the Songs of Broadway, Hollywood, and Tin Pan Alley.* New York: Routledge, 2006.

————. *Irving Berlin: A Life in Song.* New York: Schirmer Books, 1998.

Gallafent, Edward. *Astaire and Rogers.* New York: Columbia University Press, 2002.

Geist, Kenneth L. *Pictures Will Talk: The Life and Films of Joseph L. Mankiewicz.* New York: Charles Scribner's Sons, 1978.

Giles, Sarah. *Fred Astaire: His Friends Talk.* New York: Doubleday, 1988.

Gil-Montero, Martha. *Brazilian Bombshell: The Biography of Carmen Miranda.* New York: Donald I. Fine, 1989.

Goodwin, Michael, and Naomi Wise. *On The Edge: The Life and Times of Francis Coppola.* New York: William Morrow, 1989.

Gottfried, Martin. *All His Jazz: The Life and Death of Bob Fosse.* New York: Bantam Books, 1990.

————. *George Burns and the Hundred-Year Dash.* New York: Simon and Schuster, 1996.

Green, Benny. *Let's Face the Music: The Golden Age of Popular Song*. London: Pavilion Books, 1989.

Griffin, Mark. *A Hundred or More Hidden Things: The Life and Films of Vincente Minnelli*. Cambridge, MA: Da Capo Press, 2010.

Grody, Svetlana McLee, and Dorothy Daniels Lister. *Conversations with Choreographers*. Portsmouth, NH: Heinemann, 1996.

Grubb, Kevin Boyd. *Razzle Dazzle: The Life and Work of Bob Fosse*. New York: St. Martin's Press, 1989.

Hill, Constance Valis. *Brotherhood in Rhythm: The Jazz Tap Dancing of the Nicholas Brothers*. New York: Cooper Square Press, 2002.

Hirsch, Foster. *Otto Preminger*. New York: Alfred A. Knopf, 2007.

Hirschhorn, Clive. *The Hollywood Musical: Every Hollywood Musical from 1927 to the Present Day*. New York: Crown, 1981.

Hulse, Ed. *The Films of Betty Grable*. Burbank, CA: Riverwood Press, 1996.

Hyam, Hannah. *Fred & Ginger: The Astaire-Rogers Partnership 1934–1938*. Brighton, UK: Pen Press, 2007.

Hyland, William G. *George Gershwin: A New Biography*. Westport, CT: Praeger, 2003.

Irvin, Sam. *Kay Thompson: From Funny Face to Eloise*. New York: Simon and Schuster, 2010.

Jablonski, Edward. *Irving Berlin: American Troubadour*. New York: Henry Holt, 1999.

Keel, Howard, with Joyce Spizer. *Only Make Believe: My Life in Show Business*. Fort Lee, NJ: Barricade Books, 2005.

Kobal, John. *Gotta Sing, Gotta Dance: A History of Movie Musicals*. Rev. ed. London: Spring Books, 1983.

———. *People Will Talk*. New York: Alfred A. Knopf, 1985.

———. *Rita Hayworth: The Time, the Place and the Woman*. New York: W. W. Norton, 1977.

Lambert, Gavin. *On Cukor*. New York: G. P. Putnam's Sons, 1972.

Leaming, Barbara. *If This Was Happiness: A Biography of Rita Hayworth*. New York: Viking, 1989.

Levinson, Peter J. *Puttin' on the Ritz: Fred Astaire and the Fine Art of Panache*. New York: St. Martin's Press, 2009.

———. *September in the Rain: The Life of Nelson Riddle*. New York: Billboard Books, 2001.

Loney, Glenn, ed. *Musical Theatre in America*. Westport, CT: Greenwood Press, 1984.

Loney, Glenn. *Unsung Genius: The Passion of Dancer-Choreographer Jack Cole*. New York: Franklin Watts, 1984a.

Maltin, Leonard. *Movie Crazy*. Milwaukie, OR: M Press, 2008.

Mann, William J. *Behind the Screen: How Gays and Lesbians Shaped Hollywood 1910–1969*. New York: Viking, 2001.

Mannering, Derek. *Mario Lanza: Singing to the Gods*. Jackson: University Press of Mississippi, 2005.

Mantle, Burns. *The Best Plays of 1927–1928*. New York: Dodd, Mead, 1928.

Maraldi, Antonio, ed. *The Cinema of Pupi Avati*. Rome: Cinecittà Holding, n.d.

Marx, Arthur. *Red Skelton*. New York: E. P. Dutton, 1979.

Mast, Gerald. *Can't Help Singin': The American Musical on Stage and Screen*. Woodstock, NY: Overlook Press, 1987.

McBrien, William. *Cole Porter*. New York: Vintage Books, 1998.

McGee, Tom. *Betty Grable: The Girl with the Million Dollar Legs*. Vestal, NY: Vestal Press, 1995.

McGilligan, Patrick. *George Cukor, a Double Life: A Biography of the Gentleman Director*. 1991. Reprint. New York: St. Martin's Griffin, 1997.

McKenzie, Richard. *Turn Left at the Black Cow: One Family's Journey from Beverly Hills to Ireland*. Boulder, CO: Roberts Rinehart, 1998.

Miller, Ann, and Dr. Maxine Asher. *Tapping Into the Force*. Norfolk, VA: Hampton Roads, 1990.

Miller, Ann, with Norma Lee Browning. *Miller's High Life*. Garden City, NY: Doubleday, 1972.

Minnelli, Vincente, with Hector Arce. *I Remember It Well*. Foreword by Alan Jay Lerner. Garden City, NY: Doubleday, 1974. Reprint. Hollywood, CA: Samuel French, 1990.

Montaigne, Lawrence. *A Vulcan Odyssey*. Charleston, SC: BookSurge, 2006.

Morella, Joe, and Edward Z. Epstein. *Paulette: The Adventurous Life of Paulette Goddard*. New York: St. Martin's Press, 1985.

Moss, Marilyn Ann. *Giant: George Stevens, a Life on Film*. Madison: University of Wisconsin Press, 2004.

Mueller, John. *Astaire Dancing: The Musical Films.* New York: Alfred A. Knopf, 1985.

Pahlavi, Ashraf. *Faces in a Mirror: Memoirs from Exile.* Englewood Cliffs, NJ: Prentice-Hall, 1980.

Pahlavi, Farah. *An Enduring Love. Translated from the French by Patricia Clancy.* New York: Miramax Books, 2004.

Palmer, Lili. *Change Lobsters and Dance: An Autobiography.* New York: Macmillan, 1975.

Parrish, James Robert. *Katharine Hepburn: The Untold Story.* New York: Advocate Books, 2005.

Peyser, Joan. *The Memory of All That: The Life of George Gershwin.* New York: Simon and Schuster, 1993. Reprint. Milwaukee, WI: Hal Leonard, 2006.

Phillips, Gene D. *Godfather: The Intimate Francis Ford Coppola.* Lexington: University Press of Kentucky, 2004.

Pollack, Howard. *George Gershwin: His Life and Work.* Berkeley: University of California Press, 2006.

Prigozy, Ruth. *The Life of Dick Haymes: No More Little White Lies.* Jackson: University Press of Mississippi, 2006.

Rimler, Walter. *George Gershwin: An Intimate Portrait.* Urbana: University of Illinois Press, 2009.

Rodgers, Richard. *Musical Stages: An Autobiography.* New York: Random House, 1975.

Rogers, Ginger. *Ginger: My Story.* 1991. Reprint. New York: Harper Entertainment, 2008.

Santopietro, Tom. *Sinatra in Hollywood.* New York: Thomas Dunne Books, 2008.

Schechter, Scott. *Judy Garland: The Day-by-Day Chronicle of a Legend.* 2002. Reprint. Lanham, MD: Taylor Trade, 2006.

Schumacher, Michael. *Francis Ford Coppola: A Filmmaker's Life.* New York: Crown, 1999.

Shilkret, Nathaniel. *Sixty Years in the Music Business.* Edited by Niel Shell and Barbara Shilkret. Lanham, MD: Scarecrow Press, 2005.

Shipton, Alyn. *I Feel a Song Coming On: The Life of Jimmy McHugh.* Urbana: University of Illinois Press, 2009.

Solomon, Jon. *The Ancient World and the Cinema.* New Haven, CT: Yale University Press, 2001.

Strait, Raymond, and Terry Robinson. *Lanza: His Tragic Life.* Englewood Cliffs, NJ: Prentice-Hall, 1980.

Sulich, Vassili. *Vision in the Desert.* San Francisco, CA: Robert D. Reed, 2001.

Taraborrelli, J. Randy. *Michael Jackson: The Magic, the Madness, the Whole Story, 1958–2009.* New York: Grand Central, 2009.

Taylor, John Russell, and Arthur Jackson. *The Hollywood Musical.* New York: McGraw-Hill, 1971.

Thomas, Bob. *Astaire: The Man, the Dancer.* New York: St. Martin's Press, 1984.

Thomas, Tony. *Harry Warren and the Hollywood Musical.* Secaucus, NJ: Citadel Press, 1975.

———. *That's Dancing.* New York: Harry N. Abrams, 1984a.

Todd, Michael, Jr., and Susan McCarthy Todd. *A Valuable Property: The Life Story of Michael Todd.* New York: Arbor House, 1983.

Viagas, Robert. *I'm the Greatest Star: Broadway's Top Musical Legends from 1900 to Today.* Milwaukee, WI: Applause Books, 2009.

Walden, Kelly Sullivan. *I Had the Strangest Dream . . . The Dreamer's Dictionary for the 21st Century.* New York: Grand Central, 2006.

Wanger, Walter, and Joe Hyams. *My Life with Cleopatra.* New York: Bantam Books, 1963.

Williams, Esther, with Digby Diehl. *The Million Dollar Mermaid: An Autobiography.* 1999. Reprint. San Diego, CA: A Harvest Book, 2000.

Youngkin, Stephen D. *The Lost One: A Life of Peter Lorre.* Lexington: University Press of Kentucky, 2005.

Zona, Christine and Chris George. *Gotta Ballroom.* Champaign, IL: Human Kinetics, 2008.

INDEX

(Numbers in *italics* refer to illustrations.)

Abbey of Our Lady of Gethsemani, 133
Ackerman, Don, 72
The Actress, 185
Adamson, Harold, 48, 155, 156, 162, 189
Adiarte, Patrick, 230
Afra, Tybee, 199, 246
"The Afterbeat," 221
Agnew, Spiro, 256
Aigion, 9, 10, 198
Aiutami a sognare (Help Me Dream), 260–262
Alberti, Bob, 225–226
Albertson, Frank, 101
Allan, Elizabeth, 84
Allen, Gracie, 93,
Allez Vous-en," 221
All I Owe Iowa," 143
All of You," 200
Allred, John, 83
Alta Fedelta (High Fidelity), 238
Alton, Robert, 155
Always True to You in My Fashion," 188
Ameche, Don, 106, 107, 110, 111, 265
American Cannes," 162, *162*
The American Film Institute Tribute to Fred
    Astaire," 262
America Pauses for Springtime, 216
Anchors Aweigh, 139
Anderson, Guy, 177
Anderson, Maxwell, 210
Andrews, Dana, 142
Andrews, Julie, 252, 253, 257
Animal Crackers, 26–28, 30, 47
Another Evening with Fred Astaire, 221–223, 227,
    229, 241
Anrita's Dance," 227
Apache," 221, 247, 252
Aquinas, Thomas, 110
Are You Kiddin'?," 122
Arnaz, Desi, 247
Arnold, Edward, 89

Arpino, Gerald, 264, 265, *266*
"Arrivederci Roma," 209
"The Ascot Gavotte," 243, 244
Ashton, Sir Frederick, 242
Astaire, Adele, 7, 32, 86, 193, 259, 265
Astaire, Ava. *See* McKenzie, Ava Astaire
Astaire, Fred, 3, 4, 5, 6, 7, 18, 31, 32, 42, 43,
    44–47, 52–55, *55*, 56, 57–58, *58*, 59,
    60–66, 67, 68–69, *70*, 70–73, 74, 76–81,
    84, 85–87. *87*, 88, 90–91, 92–94, 96,
    97–99, 100–101, 102, 103, *104*, 104–105,
    106, 112, 115, 118, 121, 122, 124, 125,
    128, 129, 132, 135, 141, 144–145, 147,
    148, 152, 154–155, 160, 163, 164, 168,
    169–171, 172, *173*, 174–175, 180, 183,
    186–187, 193, 197–201, 202, 203, 209,
    210, 213–215, 217–218, 221–223, 224–
    225, 226–228, 235, 240, 241, 245, 246,
    248–250, *250*, 252, 255, 259, 260, *261*,
    262–263, 264–265, *266*, 267, 268–269,
    274nn1, 5, 277n10, 278n11, 279n5, 280n2
Astaire, Fred, Jr., 267
Astaire, Phyllis, 90, 129, 167, 193, 264
Astaire, Robyn, 264, 267
Astaire Time, 225, 226–228, 229
As the Girls Go, 155–158, *158*, 159–166
"As the Girls Go," 156–157, 159
"At Last," 115
Aubert, Lenore, 148
Aunt Betty, 14, *17*, 212
Aunt Lucy Godfather, 17
Avati, Pupi, 260–262
Avery, Bettye, 108

Bacharach, Burt, 256
Bachelor Mother, 101, 102, 278–279n2
"The Back Bay Polka," 146
Bainbridge, Dorothy ("Dot"), 19, *19*, 21, 22, 23, 25,
    28, 33, 40, 53, 66–67, 102, 115, 130, 240
Bainter, Fay, 142

Baker, Jennifer, 247
Baker, Josephine, 205
Baker, Kenny, 94, 95, 105
Baker, Susan, 247
Balanchine, George, 268, 275n8, 278n2
Ball, Ernest R., 137–138
Ball, Lucille, 57, 59, 83–84, 92
Banda da Lua, 108, 116
"The Band Played Out of Tune," 94
The Band Wagon, 183
Banner, John, 216
Bara, Theda, 16, 17, 31, 76
The Barkleys of Broadway, 154–155
"The Baron Is in Conference," 107–108
Barrymore, John, 37
Barrymore, Lionel, 37, 76
Barto, Betty Lou, 160, *161*
Baryshnikov, Mikhail, 268
Bay, Howard, 155, 159, 164
Beaton, Cecil, 243
"Beautiful Coney Island," 125
"Beautiful Lady," 185
Bécaud, Gilbert, 238
Becky Sharp, 62–63, 84
Beery, Wallace, 37
"Belles of Broadway" ("On the Gay White Way"),
    120
Belmonte, Hernán, 205
"Beloved," 184
"Be My Little Baby Bumblebee," 137
Bender, Dawn, 185
Bennett, Joan, 176–177
Bennett, Robert Russell, 79
Benny, Jack, 229
Berkeley, Busby, 41, 42, 43, 45, 49, 57, 66, 74, 89,
    97, 117, 140, 141, 157, 225
Berle, Milton, 94, 113, 117
Berlin, Irving, 21, 48, 60, 61, 63, 70, 86, 97, 143,
    163, 252
Berlin Painter, 135
Berman, Pandro S., 48, 49, 54, 77, 86, 88, 97
Bernstein, Elmer, 235
Berube, Al, 38
"Bessie in a Bustle," 138, *138*, 164
"Be Sweet to Me Kid," 148, 253
"Bewitched, Bothered, and Bewildered," 203, 205
"The Big Bad Wolf Was Dead," 49, 50
"Billie Jean," 263
Billman, Larry, 42, 106, 226, 275n15
Billy Rose's Diamond Horseshoe, 139–141, 279n7
Biroc, Joseph, 54, *55*
Bixby, Joseph, 101
"Black Bottom" (dance), 18, 22, 119
Black Bottom (region), 14, 22, 36
The Black Crook, 90
"Black Hula," 119
Blackwell, Earl, 197, 279n6
Blaine, Vivian, 142, 143
Blondell, Joan, 155, 157, 176, 177

Blood and Sand, 109, 122
Blore, Eric, *66*, 84
Blossom Time, 21, 25
Blouet, Max, 255
The Blue Angel, 216–218, *218*
Blue, Angela ("Angie"), 55, 93, 106, 107, 110, 111,
    118, 122, 124, 125, 128, 130, 140, 143,
    144, 146, 147, 152, 154, 176, 188, 191,
    199
Blue Skies, 143–145, 214, 277n10, 278n12,
    279n12
"Blues Medley," 228
Blyth, Ann, 188, *189*
Bob Hope Presents the Chrysler Theatre, 245
Le Boeuf sur le Toit, 23
Bogart, Humphrey, 89
"Bojangles of Harlem," 77, 79–80, *80*, 81, 84, 88,
    89, 122, 141, 144, 228
Bolton, Guy, 30
Bombo, 21
Bond, Brenda, 32
Bondi, Beulah, 96
Borne, Hal, 45, 52, 53, 57, 62, 70, *70*, 71, 76, 79,
    80, 81, 85, 86, 90, 92, 93, 97, 101, 103, 170
Bowman, Patricia, 139
Boyer, Charles, 152
Boyle, John, 30
Bradley, Wilbert, 235
Brandt, Willy, 256
Brascia, John, 195–196, 246, 280n8
Breen, Joseph Ignatius, 48
Brennan, Walter, 89, 117, 118, 134
Brent, Earl K., 179
"Brighten Up and Be a Little Sunbeam," 159, *160*,
    166
Britt, May, 216–217, *218*
Brocca, Valerio, 206
Brock, Lou, 41, 42, 43
Broderick, Helen, 84, 94
Brodszky, Nicholas, 184, 195
The Brown Sisters, 95
Brown, Sperry, 130
"Brush Up Your Shakespeare," 187, 188
Bryan, Buddy, 219, 241
Bryan, William Jennings, 11
Bullock, Walter, 105
Buloff, Joseph, 199
Buonanotte Bettina (Good Night, Betty), 240–241
Burke, Johnny, 224
Burns, Bob, 94
Burns, George, 93, 225
Burris, Howard, 260
Burton, Richard, 5, 238, 239, 240
Burton, Val, 49
Busch, Bea, 217, 252, 256
"By the Sea," 125

Cagney, James, 174, 209, 210–211
Cahn, Sammy, 195

Callahan, Bill, 129, 157, 159, 160, 162, 163, *163*, 166
Callaway, Cleveland, 13, *14*
Calloway, Harriet, 95
Camelot, 248, 249, 257
El Camino Real de la Cruz, 171–172
Canby, Vincent, 253, 259
Can-Can, 181, 216, 218, 219–221, 223–224, 234, 252, 253, 280n8
"Can-Can," 223–224
Cansino, Carmina, 157
"Can't Stop Talking," 170
Canzoni nel mondo (Songs of the World), 238
Capra, Frank, 75
Captain from Castile, 149–150, 279n7
Carborundum, 123
Carefree, 92, 96, 97–99, 101, 150, 200, 214, 276n16, 278–279n2
Carey, Macdonald, 172, 177, 178
Caribbean Cruise. See *Week-End in Havana*
"The Carioca," 43–44, 45–46, 47, 50, 63, 68, 95, 98, 160
Carley, Millie, 13, *14*
The Carnival Story. See *Texas Carnival*
Carol Channing and 101 Men, 252
Carotenuto, Mario, 206
"Carrie Marry Harry," 141, 145
Carroll, Harrison, 120, 182, 193
Carroll, Peggy, 169, 191, 278–279n2
Carruthers, Stephen, 101
Cassini, Oleg, 155, 161, 162
Castle, Irene, 100, 101
Castle, Nick, 106
"Castle Walk," 100, 101
"The Cat," 246
Caulfield, Joan, 144
"Central Two, Two, Oh, Oh," 117–118
Champion, Gower, 121, 179, 180, 181, 191, 216
Champion, Marge, 179, 180, 181, 191, 216, 260, 282n8
"Change Partners," 96, 98, 214
"Changing My Tune," 146, 203
Channing, Carol, 246, 247, 252
Chaplin, Saul, 182, 186, 216, 220
Charisse, Cyd, 182–183, 195–196, 198, 200, 282n8
"Charleston," 18, 21, 22, 23, 57, 119, 230, 252
Charley Ballet, 206, *208*, 209
Charmoli, Tony, 242
Chase, Barrie, 199, 210, 213–215, 216, 217–218, 221–222, 224, 227–228, 241, 245, 246, 280n8, 281n5
"Chattanooga Choo Choo," 115, 276n7
"Cheek to Cheek," 63, *64*, 65, 76, 267
Chevalier, Maurice, 216, 223, 224
Chiari, Walter, 240–241
"Chica Chica Boom Chic," 107
Chicago, 120
"Chop Suey," 230–231

Choreo Enterprises, Inc., 235, *236*
Christian, Linda, 150, 175
Church of Santa Maria Assunta, 281n4
Church of the Good Shepherd, 59, 112, 142, 168, 265, 268
Church, Violet, 117
Cinecittà Studios, 206, 234, 240, 281n2
Circus Club, 23, 29
Circus Queen Murder, 40
"Ciribiribin," 193
Civic League, 67
"Clap Yo' Hands," 197–198
"Clap Your Hands" 179
Clark, Bobby, 129, 137, 147, 155, 157, 159, *160*, 162, *162*
Clark, Petula, 248, 249
Clark, Sam, 17, 18, *18*, 19, 20, 21, 22, 33, 274n3
Cleopatra (1917), 16
Cleopatra (1963), 234, 235–237, *237*, 238–239, *239*, 241–242, 281n3
Cockeyed Cavaliers, 47, 49–50
Cohen, Daniel, 265
Cole, Jack, 5, 112, 199, 220
Collins, Harvey, 162
Collins, Joan, 234
Columbia, David Patrick, 4, 5, 6, 7, 14, 19, 22, 26, 87, 106, 110, 167, 209, 264, 273nn6, 8, 10, 12
Columbia Pictures, 40, 57, 144, 201, 256, 257
"Com'è bello dormer soli" ("How nice it is to sleep alone"), 241
"Comes the Revolution, Baby," 65
"Come On, Papa," 174
"Come Tell Me What's Your Answer, Yes or No," 121
Condos Brothers, 111, 112, 131, 132
Coney Island, 92, 125–126, *126*, 127, 128, 164, 279n7
Connolly, Bobby, 76, 89, 97
Conrad, Con, 52
Considine, Millie, 197
Constantine, 38, 60, 113, 183, 191
"The Continental," 54, 55, *55*, 56, 57, 63, 98, 225
"Cooking Up a Show," 140, 141
Coons, Robin, 17, 66, 100
Cooper, Merian C., 43, 48
Coppola, Carmine, 249
Coppola, Francis Ford, 248–249, 251
Cordoba, Pedro de, 172
Cotton Club, 22, 36
Count Basie Orchestra, 226, 227, 228
The Count of Ten, 225
"A Couple of Song and Dance Men," 145
Coyne, Jeanne, 186, 280n7
Crain, Jeanne, 134, 142
Crawford, Joan, 37, 89, 90
Cregar, Laird, 141
Croce, Arlene, 43, 46, 47, 53, 54
Cromer, Bob, 72

Crooker, Earle, 25
Crosby, Bing, 76, 144, 145
Crowther, Bosley, 213, 217, 242, 243
Cugat, Xavier, 158
Cukor, George, 242, 243, 244
Cummings, Irving, 120
Cummings, Jack, 172, 181, 216, 217, 218
Cummings, Robert, 110, 111, 176, 177
Cushman's Garden of Glorious Girls, 38, 42, 91, 159
Cushman, Hazel, 38
Cushman, Wilbur, 38, 39, 40
Cyrus the Great, 255

Dahl, Arlene, 172
Dailey, Dan, 195, 196
d'Amboise, Jacques, 229
Damone, Vic, 191, 192
A Damsel in Distress, 92–94, 97, 106, 141, 179, 188, 193, 275n13
Dance Crazy in Hollywood, 39, 57, 132
"Dance It Off," 118
"Dancin' in the Movies: A Hollywood Life," 4, 16, 29, 35, 45, 55, 102, 105, 235, 239–240, 264
Dandridge, Dorothy, 113, 115
Dare, Danny, 105
Darling Lili, 252–253, 254, 255
Darnell, Linda, 5, 109, 117, 118, 141, 197
Daughters of the American Revolution, 11
Davis, Bette, 75
David, Hal, 256
Davis, Ronald L., 39, 46, 70, 144, 172, 238, 276n8
Davis, Sammy, Jr., 195, 212, 213, 282n8
Day, Dennis, 175
Day, Richard, 114
"Days of Wine and Roses," 245
"Deep in My Heart," 189
"Deep in the Heart of Texas," 179
DeHaven, Gloria, 175
Delamater, Jerome, 4, 164
Del Rio, Dolores, 43, 45
Delroy, Irene, 31, 32
de Mille, Agnes, 163, 166, 242
"Demon Rum," 146
Denise, Pat, 195, 199, 213, 221, 279n4
Denti, Dante, 213
"Devil's Funhouse," 193
The Devil's Hornpipe. See Never Steal Anything Small
Dexter, Joan, 143
Diamond, "Legs," 23
The Dick Cavett Show, 255
The Dick Van Dyke Show, 48
Dietrich, Marlene, 216–217
"Dig It," 103, 104
"Dilly Dally," 49–50
Disney, Walt, 75–76, 96, 97, 139, 154
Dixon, Harland, 32
Dobbs, George, 122

A Dog of Flanders, 59–60
Donnelly, Ruth, 118
"Do Nothing 'Til You Hear From Me," 177
"Don't Carry Tales Out of School," 131
"Don't Mention Love to Me," 68
Douglas, Kirk, 281n2
"Down on Ami Ami Oni Oni Island," 119
Down to Their Last Yacht, 49, 50, 53
Draper, Paul, 144, 277–278n10
Dream Wife, 184
Dresser, Paul, 120
Dukas, Paul, 154
Dumont, Margaret, 140
Dunne, Irene, 62, 152
Duquette, Tony, 181
Durante, Jimmy, 48

Earl, Jane, 228, 229, 280n8
Earl, Ruth, 228, 229, 280n8
Ebsen, Buddy, 282n8
Edens, Roger, 198
Edison Follies, 22
Edwards, Blake, 240, 245, 252
Eggers, Lillian, 108
Eliscu, Edward, 43
Ellison, Ben, 36
Ellison, James, 96
Eltinge, Julian, 40
"The Embassy Waltz," 244
Embiricos, Princess Yasmin Khan, 205, 265
Emmy Awards, 217, 228
Ernest, Orien, 231
"Euripides Rock and Blues," 208
Eutrophia Company, 13
Evans and Evans, 93
Evans, Harvey, 201
Evans, Ray, 216
An Evening with Fred Astaire, 211–212, 213–215, 217, 226, 228, 229
"Everybody Step," 145, 214
Excuse My Dust, 177–178, 187, 222, 279n12
"Extras of the Movie Studio," 208, 227

Fadini, Sergio, 213
Fain, Sammy, 48
Fairbanks, Douglas, Jr., 94, 152
"Falling in Love Again," 216, 217
Fanchon, 106, 125, 127, 128, 130
"Fancy Free," 63, 64
"Fan Tan Fannie," 229–230, 233
Fantasia, 154
A Farewell to Arms, 206
Farmer, Frances, 89
Farrell, Glenda, 41
"Fated to Be Mated," 200–201
"Father's Day," 160, 163
Faye, Alice, 106, 110, 115, 116, 127
"Felicidades," 226

Felix, Seymour, 89, 106
"Fickle Chicle," 235
Fields, Dorothy, 67, 68, 76, 129, 142, 155, 177, 178
Fields, Herbert, 129, 142, 155
Finch, Peter, 256
Findlay, Hal, 36, 37, 42, 47, 48, 67, 79, 85
Finian's Rainbow, 92, 248–250, *250*, 251, 252, 257, 281n7
Fitzell, Roy, 215
Fitzgerald, Harry, 67
Flatt, Ernest, 242
Fleisman, Dorothy, 72
Flippen, J. C., 26
Flower Drum Song, 229–230, *230*, 231–232, *232*, 233, 234, 258
Flying Down to Rio, 42, 43, 44, 45–47, 92, 250
"Flying Down to Rio," 43, 44, 45
Folies Bergère, 247, 248, 252
Follow the Fleet, 70, *70*, 71–74, 84, 193
Fonda, Henry, 67, 76, 91
Fontaine, Joan, 92–93, 275n13
Footlight Serenade, 121–123
Ford, George, 101
Ford, Glenn, 265
Fordin, Hugh, 200, 252
Ford Startime ("Jane Wyman and the Songs that Won Academy Awards"), 225
For Heaven's Sake, 176–177
Forrest, Sally, 177–178, 184–185, 222
"For You, For Me, Forevermore," 146
Fosse, Bob, 5, 186–187, 220, 227, 231, 242
Foster, Gae, 132
Four Ink Spots, 110
Fox Studios, 16, 34
Fra Angelico, 151
The Frances Langford Show, 224
Franciosa, Anthony, 261, 265
Francis, Connie, 229
Francis, Kay, 89
"Frankie and Johnny," 195–197, 222, 280n8
Die Frau im Hermelin, 152
Frawley, Paul, 31
Freberg, Stan, 254–255
Freed, Arthur, 183, 252
Freeland, Thornton, 45
Friedman, Charles, 116
Friganza, Trixie, 30
Friml, Rudolf, 21
Froman, Jane, 94, 95
"From This Moment On," 186–187
Funny Face (film), 197–198, 242
Funny Face (musical play), 7, 64, 86
Furness, Betty, 211

Gable, Clark, 147
"The Gal with the Yaller Shoes," 196, 226
Garrabrant, W. A., 99–100

Garbo, Greta, 37
"Garden of Eden Ballet," 181, *219*, 219–220, 280n6
Garinei, Pietro, 206, 240
Garland, Joe, 208
Garland, Judy, 154–155, 279n5
Gaxton, William, 139, 140, 141
The Gay Divorce (musical play), 52, 56
The Gay Divorcee (film), 51, 52, 53–54, *55*, 55–56, 57, 60
Gelsey, Erwin, 43
Gennaro, Peter, 211
Gensler, Lewis, 65
Georgakas, Dan, 12, 22, 52, 248, 254
The George Burns Show, 225
George White Scandals, 21
Gershwin, George, 86, 87, 89, 92, 93, 146, 163, 213, 246, 275nn9, 12
Gershwin, Ira, 86, 89, 92, 93, 139, 146, 213, 246
"Get Me to the Church on Time," 244
"Get Thee Behind Me, Clayton," 117
"Get Thee Behind Me, Satan," 63
Giovannini, Sandro, 206, 240
"Girl from Ipanema," 246
"The Girl in No Man's Land," 253
"The Girl on the Magazine Cover," 100
"Give My Regards to Broadway," 110
"Gliding through My Memories," 231
"The Glow Worm," 148
Goddard, Paulette, 103–104, *104*, 134
"Going to Chicago Blues," 228
"Goin' to the County Fair," 128, 143
"Goin' Steady," 178
Goldwyn, Samuel, 193, 211–212, 213, 281n5, 282n8
Goldwyn Studios, 50, 144, 254
Golestan Palace, 4, 168
Gonzales, James, 123
"Good Bye My Lady Love," 147
The Good Old Summertime. See Top Speed
Gordon, Mack, 52, 106, 110, 113, 115, 118, 123, 124, 128, 130, 138, 139, 217, 277nn10, 1
Gottfried, Martin, 186–187
Gould, Dave, 41, 42, 43–44, 45, 47, 49, 50, 52, 53, 54, 55, 57, 63, 68, 74, 76, 89, 97, 99, 157
Grable, Betty, 56, 108, 109, 110, 111, 112, 118, 119, 121, 122, 124–126, *126*, 128–129, 130–131, *131*, 132, 139–141, 145, 146, 151–152, 193, 225, 276n9, 277n3
Grand Hotel, 37
"Grant Avenue," 231, 233
Grant, Cary, 89, 184
Grayson, Kathryn, 179, 181, 188, 279n2
The Great American Broadcast, 110
"The Great American Broadcast," 110
"Great American Soup," 254
"Great Big Town," 202
The Great Race, 245, 246

The Great Ziegfeld, 89, 126
Greco, José, 182
Greek Revolution of 1821, 9
Green, Johnny, 195
Greenwood, Charlotte, 95, 110, 111, 125, 134
Grimaldi, Princess Grace, 256
Grody, Svetlana McLee, 30, 39, 57, 93, 107, 142
Guinan, Texas, 26
Gunn, Blackwell, 82
"Guys and Dolls," 156

Haakon, Paul, 129, 277n2
Hadley, Reed, 101
Haile Selassie (emperor of Ethiopia), 256
"Hail to Bolenciewicz," 117, 276n8
Haley, Jack, 111
"Hallelujah," 192, 211
"Hallelujah, I Love Her So," 228
Hammerstein, Oscar II, 142, 143, 229
Hanemann, H. W., 43
Haney, Carol, 186, 187, 188, 279n2
Hangover Square, 141, 142
Happy, 7, 25, 26
Harbach, Otto, 57
Harrison, Rex, 238, 242, 243, 244
Hartley, Bunny, 108
Hart, Lorenz, 85, 201, 225
Hart, William S., 16
Harvey, John, 130
Harvey, Stephen, 111
Harwood, John, 30
Haver, June, 111, 134, 137, 138, *138*, 147, 148,
    175, 278n15
"Have You Seen Joe?," 141
Having Wonderful Time, 94, 97
Havoc, June, 127, 129
"Hawaiian War Chant," 119, 184
Haymes, Dick, 137, 139, 141, 142, 146, 278n13
Hayworth, Rita, 5, 109, 120, 121, 147, 175, 181,
    201, 202, 203, *203*, *204*, 265–266, 267,
    276n4, 280n9, 281nn5, 7
"Heat Wave," 144–145
Heflin, Van, 84
"Heigh Ho," 97
"Hell Hath No Fury," 196
Hello, Dolly!, 121, 247
"Hello, Dolly!," 121, 252
Hello Frisco, Hello, 127, 128
"Hello! Hello! Who's Your Lady Friend?" 101
Hello, My Baby. See *I Wonder Who's Kissing Her Now*
"Hello! Ma Baby," 148
"Helping Our Neighbors," 210
Henderson, Charles, 141
Henderson, Fletcher, 22
Hendrickson, Jim, 274
Henie, Sonja, 113, 114–115, 123, 131
Hepburn, Audrey, 197, 242, 244
Hepburn, Katharine, 5, 56, 68, 74, 84, 85, 91

Herbert, Victor, 11
Herman, Jerry, 156, 247
Hermes, 135
"He Shouldn't-a-Hadn't-a Oughtn't-a Swang on
    Me," 245
Hetzler, William, 60
"High Hat," 64
Hilliard, Harriet, 70
Hilton, Conrad, 197, 257
Hips, Hips, Hooray, 45, 47–48
"Hip Strip," 235
"Hit Parade," 61, 68–69
Hit Parade of 1941, 105
Hit the Deck, 191–194, 202, 211, 263
Hoctor, Harriet, 85, 90
"Hoe Down the Bayou," 103, 104–105
"Holiday in the Country," 160
Hollander, Frederick, 151, 216
The Hollywood Palace, 245, 246
Hollywood Republican Committee, 168
Holm, Hanya, 243, 244
"Homemade Calypso," 208
"Hooray for Captain Spaulding," 26–27
Hope, Bob, 206
Hope, Lady Vida, 242
Hopper, Hedda, 126, 174, 175, 238, 240, 241, 242
Horn, Claude, 34–35
Horseless Carriage. See *Excuse My Dust*
Horton, Edward Everett, 56, 124, 125
"Hot and Bothered," 32
"Hot Pattata," 48
Howard, Joseph E., 147
"How'd You Like to Spoon with Me," 148
Hoy, Bruce, 197
Huang, Al, 232
Hudson, Rock, 206, 253
Huffman, J. C., 23–24
Humberstone, H. Bruce, 132, 277n12
Hume, Cyril, 43
Hume, David, 110
"A Hundred Million Miracles," 229
Hunter, Ross, 229, 231, 256, 258, 259
Hunter, Tab, 224
Huntley, Jim (Jimmy), 215, 229
Hussey, Olivia, 256, 258–259
Huston, Charles Henry, 11, 15, 19, 21, 34–35
Huston, Edmonia Elizabeth Phillips, 11, 15, 17
Huston, Lillian, 12, 15, 34
Huston, Mary Aljeanne, *See* Panagiotopoulos,
    Mary
Hutton, Betty, 169–170, 279n5

Iceland, 123–124, 277n3
"I Could Have Danced All Night," 243
"I Could Write a Book," 203, 204
"I'd Rather Lead a Band," 71, 193
I Dream Too Much, 67, 71
"I Dream Too Much," 71

"I Enjoy Being a Girl," 230, *230*, 241
"If This Be Slavery," 191
"If This Isn't Love," 249
"If We Don't Dance We Don't Get Paid," 227–228
"I Got Love," 67
"I Have a Dream," 189–190
"I Haven't Got a Thing to Wear," 210
"I Heard the Birdies Sing," 122
Ikettes, 281n5
"I Know That You Know," 193
"I Know Why," 115
"I'll Be Hard to Handle," 58, *58*, 59, 180
"I'll Be Marching to a Love Song," 122, 132
I'll Get By, 175
"I'll Give You Three Guesses," 253
"I'll See You in C-U-B-A," 145
"I Love Lucy," 247
"I Love Paris," 219–220
"I Love You," 129
Imagine Us. See *Pin Up Girl*
"I'm Making a Play for You," 118
"I'm Putting All My Eggs in One Basket," 71–72
"I'm Putty in Your Hands," 48
"I'm Sorry, I Want a Ferrari," 210–211
"In Acapulco," 141
"In My Harem," 125
In My Own Fashion, 161
In Person, 67–68, 72
"In the Birdhouse at the Zoo," 61
"In the Mood," 208
"I Refuse to Rock'n' Roll," 196, 225
Irish Eyes Are Smiling, 134, 137–138, *138*, 139, 164, 279n7
Irvin, Sam, 198
"Isn't This a Lovely Day," 61, 63, 64
"Is That Good," 111–112
"It Ain't Necessarily So," 212, 213
"Italian Lesson," 206–207
"It All Depends on Thee," 118
It Just Happened, 23, 282n8
"It's a Grand Night for Singing," 143
"It's a Lowdown Dirty Shame," 228
"It's Always a Beautiful Day," 152
"It's Dynamite," 178–179, 279n10
"It's Fun to Be in Love," 196
"It's More Fun than a Picnic," 160, *161*
"It's Not in the Cards," 76–77
"It's Today," 156
"It's Tulip Time in Holland," 127
"It Takes a Woman to Take a Man," 160
"It Takes Love to Make a Home," 211
"I Used to Be Color Blind," 98–99
"I've Got a New Lease on Life," 68
"I've Got the President's Ear," 162
I Wonder Who's Kissing Her Now, 147–149, 253, 278n14, 279n7
"I Wonder Who's Kissing Her Now," 148
"I Won't Dance," 59, 180

I Won't Dance. See *Swing Time*
"I Yi Yi Yi Yi (I Like You Very Much)," 217

Jackson, Dale, 38
Jackson, Jerry, 5, 6, 7–8, 209, 246, 247, 248, 249, 252, 276n4, 280n8, 281n6
Jackson, Michael, 263
James, Claire, 117
James, Harry, 124, 175, 229
Jamison, Judith, 268
"Jane Wyman and the Songs That Won Academy Awards," 225
Janis, Beverly, 162
Jarrott, Charles, 257–258, *258*, 159
Jason, Lee, 41, 43
Jason, Rick, 182
Jason, Will, 49
"Jazz Baby," 252
"Jeepers Creepers," 261
Jeffries, Fran, 240
Jenkins, Gordon, 229, 281n9
Jessel, George, 89, 96
Jhung, Finis, *232*
"Jimmy Dean," 7
Joffrey Ballet, 264–265
Johnny Mathis show, 225–226
"Join the Navy/Harbor of Heart," 192
Jolson, Al, 21, 227
Jones, Edna Mae, 117
Jones, Jonah, 215
Jones, Shirley, 210
Jordan, Dorothy, 43
Jourdan, Louis, 223, 224
Jupiter's Darling, 189–191, 193, 201
Jürgens, Curd, 216
"Just You Wait," 243

Kahal, Irving, 48
Kahlo, Frida, 134
Kahn, Gus, 43
Kalmar, Bert, 26, 30, 31, 47, 172
Kant, Immanuel, 110
"Kare-Free-Kamp," 94
Karinska, Barbara, 156, 278n2
Kaufman, George S., 26, 91
Kay, Beatrice, 139, 140, 141
Kaye, Sammy, 123
Keavy, Hubbard, 61
Keeler, Ruby, 262, 264, 282n8
Keel, Howard, 178, 179, 181, 187, 188, 190, 279n2
"Keeping Myself for You," 192
"Keep on Doing What You're Doing," 47, 48
"Keep Your Undershirt On," 32
Kellerman, Sally, 256, 259
Kelly, Gene, 139
Kelly, Grace. See Grimaldi, Princess Grace
Kemp, Jeremy, 253
Kennedy, Edgar, 71–72

Kennedy, George, 256
Kennedy, John F., 279n6
Kennedy, Phyllis, 91–92
Kern, Jerome, 21, 57, 67, 76, 77, 79–80, 86, 147, 163
Kerr, Deborah, 184
Khan, Prince Aly, 175, 181
Khan, Princess Yasmin. *See* Embiricos, Princess Yasmin Khan
Khrushchev, Nikita, 223–224
Kidd, Michael, 5, 7–8, 183, 219
Kilgallen, Dorothy, 143
"Killarney," 119
"The Kindergarten Conga," 112
Kingsley, Dorothy, 189–190
Kiss Me Kate, 185, 186–188, 192, 201
"A Kiss or Two," 192
"The Kiss Polka," 113–114, 115, 123
Kluger, Irving, 247
Knickerbocker, Cholly, 155
Knight, Arthur, 32, 214, 224, 243–244,
Kobal, John, 4, 30, 46, 61, 79, 86, 90, 109, 112
Kosloff, Maurice, 40, 102
Koster, Henry, 231
Kramer, Gorni, 206, 238, 246
Kramer, Kenyon, 4, 264
Kuperberg, Robert, 23
Kwan, Nancy, 229, 230, *230*, 231, 232, *232*, 233

La Cava, Gregory, 92
"Lady from the Bayou," 193–194
Lady Be Good!, 86
Lady in Ermine. See That Lady in Ermine
Lady in the Dark, 121
"Lady Is a Tramp," 203
Lake, Florence, 83
Lambert, Eddie, 41
Lambert, Gavin, 244
Lambert, Sammy, 137
"The Lambeth Walk," 124
Lamont, Sonny, 65, 101
Lamour, Dorothy, 108
"Land on Your Feet," 122
Lane, Abbe, 158
Lane, Burton, 48, 189
Langford, Frances, 105, 224
La Nore, De, 82
Lanza, Mario, 183–184, 188
Laski, Michelene, 4, 38, 115, 142, 167, 178, 182, 194, 205–206, 208, 209, 259, *261*, 264, 267–268, 274n3, 278n1
Lawrence, Vincent, 25
Leaming, Barbara, 18, 22, 171, 281n7
LeBaron, William, 132
LeDuc, Tito, 238
Lee, Cherylene, *232*
Lee, Diana, 256
Lee, Dorothy, 47, 49

Lee, Gypsy Rose, 129
Leeds, Thelma, 90
Lee, Kathryn, 159, 160, 163, *163*, 166
Lee, Margaret, 244
Lee, Ruta, 265
Lee, Sammy, 74, 97
Legion of Decency, 48
Lehár, Franz, 130
Leo, Patti, *232*
Lerner, Alan Jay, 242, 243
LeRoy, Mervyn, 41
Les Girls, 199
"Let's Begin," 59
"Let's Call the Whole Thing Off," 88, 127, 206–207, 241, 246
Let's Dance, 85, 169–171, 227, 278n2, 279n5
"Let's Face the Music and Dance," 73
"Let's K-nock K-nees," 56
"Let the Rest of the World Go By," 138
"Let Yourself Go," 71, 72
Levant, Oscar, 68
Levinson, Peter J., 169, 200, 214, 215, 241, 276n16, 277n10, 278n11, 280n2, 281n7
Lewis, Frank, 53
Lewis, Kevin, 115, 169, 205, 212, 279n3
Lewis, Maebelle, 51
Lewis, Monica, 178
Lewis, Russell, 62
Lewis, Ted, 37
"The Life of an Elephant," 191
A Life of Her Own, 175
Limyou, Jeanne, *232*
"A Little Bit of Luck," 244
Little Mother. See Bachelor Mother
"Live and Let Live," 223
Livingston, Jay, 216
"Living Together, Growing Together," 258
Lloyd, Harold, 89
Lockhart, Gene, 172
Loesser, Frank, 156, 158, 169
"Lola-Lola," 216, 217
Loman, Hal, 212
Loney, Glenn, 112
"Loo Loo," 191, 192, 193
"Lorelei Brown," 178
Loring, Eugene, 195, 197, 198–199, 242, 280n8
Lorre, Peter, 199
Losee, Harry, 85, 86, 90
Lost Horizon, 256–259, 281n2
"Love Look Away," 231–232, 233
Lovely to Look At, 179–181, 205, 279n12
"Lovely to Look At," 76, 181
"Lover," 225, 226
"Lover's Knot," 123–124
Love Song. See I Dream Too Much
Loewe, Frederick, 242
Loy, Myrna, 76
Lubitsch, Ernst, 41, 151, 152, 153, 212

"Lucky Bird," 192

Lucky Day, 36, 42

"Lucky in the Rain," 160, 163, *163*

"Lullaby of Broadway," 76

Lundigan, William, 175

McCrea, Joel, 43

McGee, Tom, 132

McGuire Sisters, 229

McHugh, Jimmy, 155, 156

McKenzie, Ava Astaire, 262, 267, 268

McKenzie, Richard, 262–263, 267, 268–269

McKinley, William, 11

MacLaine, Shirley, 216, 219, 221, 223, 280n5

McNally, Stephen, 172

Magidson, Herb, 52, 94

"Maidens Typical of France," 220–221

Maiden Voyage. See *Melody Cruise*

Malerba, Gino, 209, 211, 213, 217, 219, 221, 224, 229, 238, 239, 244

Maltin, Leonard, 54

Mamoulian, Rouben, 62, 109, 200, 210, 211, 212, 234

Mancini, Henry, 245, 253

Manhattan Ballet, 139

Mankiewicz, Joseph, 234

Manners, David, 84

Mann, William J., 6

The Man Who Danced with Fred Astaire, 4

"Man with the Blues," 215

Maples, Virginia, 117

Marcos, Imelda, 256

Martin, Dean, 238

Martin, Tony, 191, 192

Mary of Scotland, 74–75

Marx, Chico, 26, 27, 28

Marx, Groucho, 26, 27, 28

Marx, Zeppo, 102

Mason, Jack, 24

Mason, Melissa, 95

Masiero, Lauretta, 238

Massine, Léonide, 85

Mastroianni, Marcello, 246

Mathis, Johnny, 225, 226

Mature, Victor, 118, 120, 121, 122, 123, 276n9

"Maxixe," 100

May, Bert, 215, 241

May, Billy, 255

Mayer, Louis B., 172, 195, 248

Meade, Charles, 103, 267

Meade, Christa, 178, 239, 240, 246, 281n4

Meade, Mary Anne, 142, 178, 205, 206, 209

Meade, Michelene. *See* Laski, Michelene

Meade, Patrick, 142, 279n9

Meade, Rock, 178

"Me and My Fella," 121

"Me and the Ghost Upstairs," 103, 105

"Meeting the Frog Prince," 55, 97, 133, 135

Meet Me in Las Vegas, 194, 195–197, 253, 280n8

"Meglio Stasera (It Had Better Be Tonight)," 240

Melato, Mariangela, 260

Melody Cruise, 41, 42, 43, 47

"Memphis Glide," 67

Menjou, Adolphe, 76

"Men of Clayton," 117

Mercer, Johnny, 65, 103, 245, 253

Mercouri, Melina, 238

Meredith, Burgess, 103

"Merry Widow Waltz," 130

Merton, John, 148

Meskill, Jack, 96

Metaxa, George, 76

Meth, Max, 159

Metro-Goldwyn-Mayer, 4, 37, 139, 147, 154, 155, 172, 174, 175, 177, 178, 179, 185, 188, 191, 194, 195, 197, 201, 216, 252, 279nn5, 4, 5

Mexican Hayride, 129, 136–137, 142, 277nn2, 5

Mexican Village. See *Sombrero*

Miami. See *Moon Over Miami*

Miehle, John, 83

Milland, Ray, 175

Miller, Ann, 5, 92, 94, 95, 96–97, 105, 108, 113, 141, 167–168, 178–179, 180, 181, 186, 187–188, 191, 192, 193–194, 197, 240, 254–255, 260, *261*, 265–266, 275n14, 281n7, 282n8

Miller, Glenn, 113

Mills, Jackie, 235

Minevich, Borrah, and His Harmonica Rascals, 105

"Ming Toy," 171

Minnelli, Vincente, 88, 181

Miranda, Carmen, 106, 107, 108, 115, 116, 124, 125, 240, 252

"Miss Lulu from Louisville," 126

"Miss Otis Regrets," 227

"Mr. and Mrs. Hoofer at Home," 172, *173*, 187

Mr. Wonderful, 212

Mix, Tom, 16

Monaco, James V., 130, 138

"Mona Lisa," 246

Monroe, Marilyn, 279n6

Montalban, Ricardo, 265

Montevecchi, Liliane, 195

Montgomery, George, 119, 125

Moon Over Miami, 110–113, 121, 131, 276n1, 279n7

Moore, McElbert, 25

Moore, Victor, 76, 77, *77*, 84, 94

Morales, Antonia, 149, 150

"The More I See You," 141

Morey, Vincent, 139

Morgan, Frank, 89

"The Mortal Goddesses," 16, 102, 115, 150, 235

Motown 25: Yesterday, Today, Forever, 263

Mowbray, Alan, 149

Index

Mueller, John, 45, 66, 145, 169, 174, 200, 278nn11, 12, 279n6, 281n7
Mullane, Donna, 259
Munshin, Jules, 199
Murphy, George, 89, 117–118, 168, 172
Murray Anderson's Almanac, 30
Murray, John T., 41
Murray, Jules, 36
Murray, Roseanne, 108
Museo Gregoriano Etrusco Vaticano, 135
Musicals (Cohen), 265, 266
"Music Makes Me," 44
The Music Man, 211, 242
"My Album of Memories," 138
"My Baby," 222
My Fair Lady, 92, 242, 243, 244, 248
"My First Impression of You," 94
My Gal Sal, 120–121, 279n7
"My Gal Sal," 121
"My Heart Tells Me," 207
"My Lucky Charm," 196, 253
My Maryland, 24, *24*, 25, 26, 30

Naish, J. Carrol, 172
"The Nango," 115–116
"A Needle in the Haystack," 53
Nelidov, Prince, *28, 29*
Nelson, Gene, 148, 229
Nelson, Miriam, 242
Neuman, Alfred E., 222
"Never Gonna Dance," 77, 78–79
Never Steal Anything Small, 209, 210–211
"Never Steal Anything Small," 210
"Nevertheless," 174
Newman, Alfred, 177, 279n7
Newman, Lionel, 141
"A Nickel's Worth of Jive," 140
Nicholas Brothers, 110, 113, 115, 132
Nichols, Nichelle, 212
Nielsen, Ray, 120
"Night and Day," 52, 53, 98
"The Night Is Filled with Music," 99
"Night Train," 222, 241
"Nighty Night," 94
Nilsson, Norma Jean, 185
Nine O'Clock Revue, 40, 41, 42
Nishimura, Alice, *232*
Niven, David, 7, 90–91, 101, 147, 193, 240
Nixon, Marian, 48
Nordine, Ken, 222
Norton, Elliott, 161
Norton, Pearlie May, 106
"Not Now, I'll Tell You When," 227
Novak, Kim, 201–202, 204, 205, 217, 280n9
Novarese, Vittorio Nino, 234
Nye, Louis, 245

Oakie, Jack, 89, 94, 110, 117, 118, 127

Oakland, Vivien, 41
"O'Brien Has Gone Hawaiian," 119
O'Callaghan, Father (Monsignor) Jim, 59, 99, 102, 130, 133, 139, 175, 176, 211, 240, 267
Ocean Restaurant, 13, 19, 20
O'Driscoll, Martha, 39, 76
"Oh, I Can't Sit Down," 212
"Oh, Me! Oh, My! Oh, You!," 48
"Oh Them Dudes," 169–170
Oklahoma!, 143, 148, 162
"Oklahoma!," 143
Olav V (king of Norway), 256
"Old MacDonald's Trip," 215
Old Man Rhythm, 65, 66, 67, 101
"Old Man Rhythm," 65, 67, 68
Oliveira, Aloysio, 116
"O Me, O Mi-Ami," 111
"Once Too Often," 130, *131*
"One More You," 178
One Touch of Venus, 6
"One, Two, Three," 146
"On the Banks of the Wabash," 121
On Your Toes, 85, 275n8
"Ooh, La, La," 90
"Ooh! What I'll Do (to That Wild Hungarian)," 152
"Orchids in the Moonlight," 45, 47
Order of the Little Sisters of the Poor, 35
"Organ Number," 59
Ortolani, Riz, 260
"The Other Generation," 230
"Our State Fair," 142–143
"Out of Sight, Out of Mind," 68
Out of This World, 186
Overdorff, I. C., 99–100
Owens, Harry, 118

The Packard Hour, 87
Padlocks of 1927, 26
Padlocks of 1928, 26
"Padua Street Song," 187
Pahlavi, Farah (empress of Iran), 255, 259, 260
Pahlavi, Mohammad Rezā (shah of Iran), 4, 168, 175, 187, 255, 256, 260
Pahlbod, Mehrdad, *261*
Pahlbod, Princess Shams Pahlavi, 168, 175, 197–198, 260, *261*
Pahlbod, Shahrazad (Scheherazade), 260, *261*
Paige, Janis, 198, 199, 200
Un Paio d'Ali (*A Pair of Wings*), 205, 206–207, *207*, *208*, 208–209, 227, 238, 280n11
"A Pair of Wings," 207
Pal Joey, 201–204, *204*, 205, 242, 280n9
Palmer, Lilli, 224–225
Panagiotopoulos, Alkis, 9, 12, 20, 21–22
Panagiotopoulos, Andreas, 9
Panagiotopoulos, Pantelis, 9, *10*, 10–14, 15, *16*, 19–20, 21
Panagiotopoulos, Spyros, 9

"Pan American Conga," 105
"Pan American Jubilee," 125
Pan-Jose, 91, 99, 102, 108, 109, 115
"Panorama," 150–151, 167
Pan (Panagiotopoulos), Aljeanne, 19, *19*, 25, 29,
    33, 40, 115, 130
Pan (Panagiotopoulos), Dorothy ("Dot"). *See*
    Bainbridge, Dorothy ("Dot")
Pan (Panagiotopoulos), Hermes Joseph ("Snooks")
    awards, 4, 38, 97, 217, 224, 228
    birth, 13
    burglary, 218
    career
        at Columbia Pictures, 40, 57, 144, 201, 256, 257
        at Goldwyn Studios, 254
        at M-G-M, 4, 139, 147, 154, 155, 172, 174,
            175, 177, 178, 179, 185, 188, 191, 194,
            195, 197, 201, 216, 252, 279nn5, 4, 5
        at Paramount Pictures, 143, 144, 145, 168,
            197, 224, 225, 229, 277–278n10, 279n5
        at Republic Pictures, 105
        at RKO, 4, 7, 35, 36, 41, 42, 43, 44, 45, 46, 48,
            49, 52, 53, 56, 57, 59, 62, 63, 64, 66, 67,
            69, 72, 73, 74, 76, 81, 82, 83, 86, 87, 88,
            91, 92, 93, 95, 98, 100, 101, 102, 106, 118,
            121, 127, 154, 180, 207, 210
        at Twentieth Century-Fox, 105, 106, 113,
            116, 119, 120, 121, 126, 127, 129, 130,
            136, 139, 143, 145, 147, 153, 154, 175,
            176, 207, 216, 221, 223, 224, 234, 256,
            277–278n10, 279nn7, 8
        at Universal-International Pictures, 209–211
        at Warner Brothers, 174, 242, 248, 249, 257
        in clubs, 184, 197, 225–226, 240, 241, 247,
            252
        in television, 213–215, 216, 221–223,
            224, 225–228, 229, 238, 245–247, 252,
            254–255, 262
        in theatre, 23–32, 36, 37, 38–39, 40–41,
            50–51, 155–166, 206–207, *207, 208*,
            208–209, 225, 240–241
    Catholicism, 6, 26, 35, 48, 133, 165, 168,
        171–172, 197, 246
    dance training, 14–15, 17–18, 22, 30–31
    death, 268
    Diego Rivera portrait, 134–136
    education, 4, 18, 20
    homosexuality, 6, 108, 209, 273nn9, 10
    illnesses, 194, 263–264
    lawsuit, 99–100
    personality, 3–8, 29, 60, 76, 82–83, 97, 100,
        102, 109–111, 129–130, 132–133, 136,
        142, 167–168, 201, 206, 244–245, 267
    political opinions, 108, 168
    relationships
        with Fred Astaire, 18, 31, 32, 44–45, 46, 52,
            53–55, *55*, 57–58, *58*, 60, 61–62,
            63–66, 68–69, *70*, 71–72, 73, 77–81, 84,

85, *87*, 87, 90, 92–94, 97–98, 103–104,
    104, 105, 129, 144, 154, 169–171, 172,
    174–175, 193,
    197–198, 199–201, 213–215,
    217–218, 221–223, 224–228, 235, 245,
    246, 248, *250*, 262–263, 264–265, 267
with Theda Bara, 16
with Eric Blore, *66*
with Angela Blue, 55, 93, 106, 107, 110, 111,
    118, 122, 124, 125, 128, 130, 140, 143,
    144, 146, 147, 152, 154, 176, 188, 191,
    199
with Cyd Charisse, 182–183, 195–196, 200
with chorus dancers, *64*, 66, 72, *80*, 81, *81*,
    82, *82*, 83, 100, 108, 123, 157–158, *158*
with Joan Dexter, 143
with George Gershwin, 86–87
with Dave Gould, 43–45, 47, 49, 50, 52, 53,
    54, 55, 74, 76, 89, 97, 99, 157
with Betty Grable, 56, 108, 109, 110, 111,
    112, 113, 119, 122–123, 124–125, 126,
    126, 128–129, 130–131, *131*, 139–141,
    145, 146, 152, 225, 276n9
with Elizabeth Hatfield, 194
with Sonja Henie, 114–115, 123
with June Haver, 111, 134, 137, 138, *138*,
    147, 148, 175
with Rita Hayworth, 5, 109, 120, 121,
    147, 175, 181, 201, 202, 203, *203*, *204*,
    265–266, 267, 276n4, 281n5
with Katharine Hepburn, 56, 74, 84, 85
with Hedda Hopper, 175–176, 238–240,
    241–242
with Betty Hutton, 169–170
with Nikita Khrushchev, 223–224
with Gino Malerba, 209, 211, 213, 217, 219,
    221, 224, 229, 238, 239, 244
with Ann Miller, 5, 92, 94, 95, 96–97, 105,
    108, 113, 141, 167–168, 178–179, 180,
    181, 186, 187–188, 191, 192, 193–194,
    197, 240, 254–255, 260, *261*, 265–266,
    282n8
with Monsignor Jim O'Callaghan, 59, 99, 102,
    130, 133, 139, 175, 176, 211, 240, 267
with Mary Pan (mother), 4, 6, 14, 15, *16*, 19,
    20, 21, 22, 26, 29, 33, 34, 39, 40, 91, 102,
    103, 108, 109
with Panos Pan (brother), 13, *15*, *16*, 21, 25,
    26
with Pantelis Panagiotopoulos (father), 15,
    15, *16*, 20
with Vasso Pan (sister), 7, 13, 15, *16*, 17–18,
    21, 22–23, 25, 26, 33, 34, 37–38, 40, 55,
    59, 66–67, *69*, 75, 76, 94, 97, 102, 103,
    115, 124, 130, 178, 194, 251, 256, 264,
    273n9
with Princess Shams Pahlavi, 168, 175,
    197–198, 260, *261*

Pan (Panagiotopoulos) (*continued*)
    with Diego Rivera, 134–136
    with Ginger Rogers, 31, 67–68, *70*, 72, 73,
        78, 78–79, 83–84, 88, 89, 95–96, 101, 119,
        130, 155, 167, 168, 265, 267
    with Lana Turner, 150, 175
    residences, *13*, *15*, 16, 21, 23, 28, 34, 35, 37, 40,
        49, 74, *75*, 91, 99, 102, 108, 109, 115, 124,
        150–151, 167
    work habits, 22, 53, 77–78, 83, 102, 108, 115,
        117, 123, 127, 149, 156, 178, 180–181,
        182–183, 189–190, 205, 224, 238, 240,
        243, 254, 257–258
Pan (Panagiotopoulos), Mary, 4, 6, 11, 12, *12*, 14,
    15, *16*, 19, 20, 21, 22, 26, 29, 33, 34, 39,
    40, 91, 102, 103, 108, 109
Pan (Panagiotopoulos), Panos ("Bubber"), 12, 13,
    15, *16*, 19, 21, 25, 26
Pan (Panagiotopoulos), Vasso ("Ditty"), 4, 7, 12,
    13, 15, *16*, 17, 18, *19*, 21, 22, 23, 25, 26,
    28, 33, 34–35, 37, 38, 40, 41, 44, 53, 55,
    59, 66, 67, *69*, 75, *75*, 76, 94, 97, 102, 103,
    115, 124, 130, 178, 194, 197, 251, 256,
    264, 267, 273n9, 274n3, 275n14
Papa's in the Cradle. See *Old Man Rhythm*
"Papparazzo," 241
Paramount Studios, 143, 144, 145, 168, 197, 224,
    225, 229, 277–278n10, 279n5
"Paris Loves Lovers," 200
Park, Arthur, 234
Parrish, Helen, 60
Passport to Life. See *Sun Valley Serenade*
Patrick, Janice, *208*, 209
Paul, Gloria, 253
Le Pavillon, 3
Payne, John, 110, 113, 115, 116, 121, 122, 123,
    124, 125, 127
P. Brous and Company, 11, 13
"Pennies from Heaven," 261
Penzner, William L., 225
Perkins, Anthony, 185
Persepolis, 256
"Personality," 224
Peters, Jean, 149, 150
Pezzotti, Mario, 238
Phillips, Edmonia Elizabeth (Betty). See Huston,
    Edmonia Elizabeth Phillips
"Piano Dance," 170–171, 227
"Piccolino," 63, 65, 68, 69, 164
"Pick Yourself Up," 77–78, 265
Piedra, Ernesto, 116
The Pink Lady, 185
The Pink Panther, 240
Pin Up Girl, 129, 130–131, *131*, 132, 139, 193
"Pin Up Girl," 131
"Play Me an Old Fashioned Melody," 140
The Pleasure of His Company, 224–225, 229
"A Poem Set to Music," 124–125

Polglase, Van Nest, 45, 88, 94
Polychroniadi, 9
Pons, Lily, 67, 71
"The Pool, and the School of Life," 207
Porgy and Bess, 211, 212–213, 280n1
Porter, Cole, 3, 52, 56, 129, 136, 137, 185, 186,
    188, 198, 200, 201, 216, 220, 221, 227,
    277n2
Powell, Eleanor, 281n5
Powell, Jane, 191, 192, 193
Power, Tyrone, 5, 109, 149, 150, 175
Preminger, Otto, 153, 212, 213
"Pretty Baby," 125
"A Pretty Girl Is Like a Melody" 126
Prinz, LeRoy, 30, 32, 36, 74, 76, 97, 99–100, 157,
    281n5
Professional Dancers Society, 282n8
Provine, Dorothy, 245
Prowse, Juliet, 209, 213, 216, *219*, 220–221, 223,
    229, 280n5, 282n8
Purdom, Edmund, 188, *189*
Purdom, Tita, 197
Purple, Aunt Mamie, 75
"Put Me to the Test," 93, 188
"Puttin' on the Ritz," 144, 226
"Put Your Arms around Me, Honey," 125
"Put Your Heart into Your Feet and Dance," 92

Quality Street, 85
"Question Me an Answer," 257
Quinn, Anthony, 109

Radcliffe, Frank, 167, 210, *232*, 243, 256
Radin, Oscar, 24
Radio City Revels, 94–95, 101, 275n15
"Rain Dance," 250
Rainer, Luise, 102
Rainger, Ralph, 111, 117, 121
Rainier III (prince of Monaco), 256
"The Rain in Spain," 244
RKO Studios, 4, 7, 35, 36, 41, 42, 43, 44, 45, 46,
    48, 49, 52, 53, 56, 57, 59, 62, 63, 64, 66,
    67, 69, 72, 73, 74, 76, 81, 82, 83, 86, 87,
    88, 91, 92, 93, 95, 98, 100, 101, 102, 106,
    118, 121, 127, 154, 180, 207, 210
Rall, Tommy, 186, 187, 188
Ralli, Giovanna, 206, 207
Randall, Carl, 53
Randolph, Roy, 76
Rascel, Renato, 206, 207, 209
Raset, Val "Mickey," 50, 120, 127
Rau, Neil, 231
Raye, Martha, 131, 132
Raymond, Gene, 43, 45, 191
Razaf, Andy, 208
"Rebola Bola," 116
"Red Robins, Bob Whites and Bluebirds," 131–132
Reis, Irving G., 154

Remember How Great, 229
Renee, Leon, 36
Renee, Otis, 36
Republic Pictures, 105
Revel, Harry, 52
Reynolds, Debbie, 191, 192, 193, 224
Rhodes, Erik, 76
Richards, Cully, 50
Richardson, Bill, 165
Rich, Irene, 157, 161
Riddle, Nelson, 240
Riordan, Christopher, 241, 246
Rise and Shine, 117–118
"The Ritz Roll and Rock," 201
Rivera, Diego, 134–135, 136
Road to Rio. See That Night in Rio
The Robber Barons. See The Toast of New York
Robbins, Jerome, 166, 211
Robel, Dave, 100, 143, 144, 154, 169, 191, 199,
    213, 221, 278n2
Roberta, 57–58, *58*, 59, 62, 70, 71, 179
Robert Mitchell Boy Choir, 128–129
Robin, Leo, 111, 117, 121, 151
Robinson, Bill "Bojangles," 36
Robinson, Dewey, 148
"Rock, Rock, Rock!," 159–160, 166
Rodgers, Richard, 21, 85, 142, 143, 201, 225, 229
Rodin, Gil, 229
Rogers, Buddy, 65
Rogers, Ginger, 4, 5, 31, 32, 33, 43, 45, 46, 47, 48,
    52, 53, 55, *55*, 56, 57, 58, 59, 60, 61, 62,
    63, 65, 66, 67, 68, 70, *70*, 71, 72, 73, 74,
    76, 77, 78, *78*, 79, 81, 83–84, 85, 86, 88,
    89, 91, 92, 94, 95–96, 97, 98, 99, 100, 101,
    102, 103, 104, 109, 112, 118, 119–120,
    121, 124–125, 128, 130, 148, 152,
    154–155, 163, 167, 168, 180, 198, 259,
    265, 267, 274nn4, 5, 275n8, 276n16
Rogers, Lela, 31, 83
Roger Wagner Chorale, 172
Rohe, Vera-Ellen Westmeier. *See* Vera-Ellen
Roman Catholicism, 6, 26, 35, 48, 50, 133, 168,
    172, 197, 246, 268
Romberg, Sigmund, 21, 23, 142
Romeo and Juliet Overture, 177, 227
Romero, Alex, 187, 188
Romero, Cesar, 89, 110, 115, 116, 124, 125, 152,
    265, 282n8
Roos, William, 155, 164
Rosamond, Marian, 108
Rose, David, 179, 215, 226
Rose, Edward W., 99–100
Roth, Lillian, 26
Roulien, Raul, 43, 45
Roxie Hart, 119–120
Royal Wedding, 174–175
Rubin, Eddie, *70*, 83
Ruby, Harry, 26, 30, 31, 32, 47, 172

Ruddigore, 152
"Run Little Raindrop, Run," 124
Running Wild, 21
Runyon, Damon, 137
Ryskind, Morrie, 26

St. Denis, Ruth, 85
"St. James Infirmary," 215
St. John, Betta, 184, 189
Saint John Vianney Catholic Church, 246
"The Saga of Sadie Thompson," 229
Sampson, Harold, 29, *29*, 99
Sanctos, Virginia, 169
Sandrich, Mark, 41–42, 45, 47, 48, 49, 54, 55, 56,
    60, 69, 84, 85, *87*, 88, 90, 98, 106, 274n1,
    275n12, 277–278n10
San Juan, Olga, 144, 145
Santell, Alfred, 97
Santopietro, Tom, 205
Sato, Reiko, 231–232, 233
Savo, Jimmy, 30
Sawyer, Geneva, 106, 109, 113, 122, 123, 134
Say It with Music, 252
"Say, Young Man of Manhattan," 65
Scala, Delia, 241
Schaffner, Caroline, 37
Schallert, Edwin S., 50, 84
Schary, Dore, 195
Schrager, Sheldon, *258*
Schwartz, Arthur, 177, 277n2
Scott, Allan, 60
Scott, Mary, 117
Scott, Randolph, 7, 70, 90, 193
Seaton, George, 225
Second Chorus, 103–104, *104*, 105, 179
Self, Bill, 7
Sellers, Peter, 240
Selznick, David O., 41–42, 43
Serra, Fra Junipero, 171–172
Sersen, Fred, 141
"The Sgargamella," 207
Shall We Dance, 85–87, *87*, 88, 90, 91, 92, 95, 127,
    206, 275n10
"Shall We Dance," 275n12
Shah of Iran. *See* Pahlavi, Mohammad Rezā
"Shake, Rattle and Roll," 228
Shapiro, Ted, 96
"Share the Joy," 258–259
Shawn, Ted, 85
Sherwood, Gregg, 158
Shigeta, James, 229, 258
Shilkret, Nathaniel, 75, 77, 90
Shim Sham Revue, 50–51, 120
The Shocking Miss Pilgrim, 146, 147, 203, 278n13,
    279n7
"Shoes with Wings On," 154, 155
Shubert, Lee, 164
Shubert Organization, 23, 26, 36

Index

Sidney, George, 187, 189, 201
Silk Stockings, 198–201
Silvers, Phil, 125, 276n9
Simmons, Jean, 185
"Simpatico" ("Compatible"), 241
Sinatra, Frank, 201, 202, *204*, 205, 216, 223, 224, 280n9
Sinatra, Nancy, 281n5
"Since They Turned Loch Lomond into Swing," 98
Six Hits and a Miss, 105
Skelton, Red, 172, 174, 177, 178, 179, 181, 242
"Slap That Bass," 87, *87*, 88, 89, 275n12
Slate Brothers, 196
"Sleepy Time Down South," 36
"The Slop," 235
Smaroff, Gregory, 35
"Smile Away Each Rainy Day," 253
Smiles, 65
Smith, Roger, 210
"Smoke Gets in Your Eyes," 59, 108
Snow White and the Seven Dwarfs, 97
"Solitary Seminole," 112–113
Solomon, Maureen C., 3, 23, 31, 39, 264
Sombrero, 182–183
"Something Sort of Grandish," 249
"Sometimes I'm Happy," 193
Sondergaard, Gale, 89
Sondheim, Stephen, 121, 160
Song of the Islands, 118–119, 120, 184
Song of the South, 210
Sonneveld, Wim, 198
Soo, Jack, 229, 232, *232*, 233
"Sophisticated Lady," 222, 223
"The Sorcerer's Apprentice," 154
So This Is Harris, 41
The Sound of Music, 248, 253, 257
The Sounds of America, 229, 281n9
Sounds of Disneyland. See *The Sounds of America*
"Speak Your Heart," 95
Spellman, Francis Joseph Cardinal, 6
Spivak, Charlie, 130
Springtime in the Rockies, 124–125, 279nn7, 12
Stage Door, 91–92, 280n3
Stardusters, 131
Star Trek, 212
State Fair, 142–143, 146, 203, 210, 279n7
Steele, Tommy, 248
Steinbeck, John, 246
Steiner, Max, 45
Stepping Toes. see *Shall We Dance*
Stept, Sam H., 94
"Stereophonic Sound," 199–200
Stevens, George, 77, 78–79, 80, 81, 85, 94, 95, 97
Stevens, Mark, 147, 278n15
Stewart, James, 95–96
Stewart, Martha, 148–149, 278n15
"Stiff Upper Lip," 93–94
Stoller, Alvin, 221–222, 227

"The Story of the Very Merry Widow," 130, 132
The Story of Vernon and Irene Castle, 100–101, 276n16, 278–279n2
Stratton, Chet, 91
Strictly Dynamite (RKO), 48–49
Strictly Dynamite (Twentieth Century-Fox). See *Footlight Serenade*
Stroman, Susan, 268
"Strut Miss Lizzie," 137–138
The Student Prince, 183–184, 188–189, *189*, 197
Studio Uno, 246, 281nn5, 6
Styne, Jule, 105
Suddenly Last Summer, 234
Sukarno (president of Indonesia), 281n2
Sulgrave, Arthur, 139
Sulich, Vassili, 247
Sullivan, Alice, 132
Sullivan, Arthur, 152, 206
Sullivan, Ed, 217
Sullivan, Jo, 158
"Sunday," 232, *232*, 233
Sunday in the Park with George, 121
Sun Valley Serenade, 113–115, 122, 185
"Super Joe," 241
"Svengali," 214, 226
Swanson, Gloria, 31
"Sweet Georgia Brown," 227
"Sweet Pussycat," 246
Sweet Rosie O'Grady, 128–129, 207
"Sweet Rosie O'Grady," 128–129
Swept Away, 260
Swift, Kay, 146
"Swingin' in the Corn," 95
"Swing Low, Sweet Rhythm," 105
Swing Time, 76–77, 77, 78, *78*, 79–80, *80*, 81, *81*, 82, *82*, 83, 84, 89, 91, 122, 144, 228, 265, 275n7

"The Table Dance," 52, 53
Tadj ol-Molouk, Queen Mother of Iran, 168, 197
"Taking a Shine to You," 95
Talbot, Jean, 41
Tamblyn, Russ, 191, 192, 193, 202
Tamed. See *In Person*
Taylor, Dwight, 60
Taylor, Elizabeth, 5, 234, 238, 239–240
"Temptation," 176
"The Temptation Waltz," 90
Tennessee Centennial and International Exposition, 10–11
"Test Solo," 174
Texas Carnival, 178–179, 279n11
Texas Centennial Exposition, 83–84
"Texas Tommy," 100
"That Face," 221
"That Great Come-and-Get-It Day," 249, *250*
That Lady in Ermine, 151–153, 212, 279n7
That Night in Rio, 106–108, 111, 207, 279n7

"That's for Children," 178
"That's For Me," 143
"That Terrific Rainbow," 202
Theodores, 50
"There's Danger in a Dance," 126, *126*, 164
"There's No Getting Away from You," 160
"There's No Tune like a Show Tune," 156
"There's Something about Midnight," 152
"There Will Never Be Another You," 123
Thew, Harvey, 43
"They All Laughed," 88, 246, 275n12
"Things Are Looking Up," 93
"The Things I Will Not Miss," 259
"Thinking of You," 174
"Think Pretty," 245
"This Is It," 131
"This Is the Moment," 152
Thomas, Bob, 245
Thomas, Frankie, 60
Thomas, Larri, 214
Thomas, Tony, 170, 183
Thompson, C. C., 67
Thompson, Claude, 249, 250
Thompson, Harrison, 113
The Three Caballeros, 139
Three Evenings with Fred Astaire, 235
Three Hierarchs Greek Orthodox Church, 143
Three Little Words, 172–173, *173*, 174, 187, 200, 279nn5, 6
"Tiger Rag," 170
Till the Clouds Roll By, 147
Tito, Josip Broz (president of Yugoslavia), 256
The Toast of New York, 89–90, 137
Tobias, Charles, 94
Todd-AO Process, 212, 220, 224
Todd, Mike, 137, 142, 155–156, 157, 158, 161, 162, 164, 165, 277n6
Todd, Mike, Jr., 136, 155, 156
Todd, Thelma, 49, 50
Toguri, David, *232*
To Kill a Mockingbird, 235
Tom, Dick, or Harry," 187–188
Tone, Franchot, 85, 89, 90
Tonight," 226
Too Bad," 199
Too Darn Hot," 187, 191
Toomey, Regis, 172
Top Hat, 60–64, *64*, 65–66, *66*, 69, *69*, 70, 71, 72, 74, 84, 164, 198, 267
Top Hat," 246
Top Hat, White Tie, and Tails," 63, 64, 72
Top Speed, 30–32, 33, 36, 47
The Touch of Your Hand," 59, 181
Tour of the Town," 146
Treacher, Arthur, 91
Trebek, Alex, 265
Tunnel of Love," 170
Turner, Lana, 5, 150, 175, *176*

"I 12 Solisti," 206, 209
Twentieth Century-Fox, 4, 105, 106, 113, 116, 119, 120, 121, 126, 127, 129, 130, 136, 139, 143, 145, 147, 153, 154, 175, 176, 207, 216, 221, 223, 224, 234, 256, 277n11, 277–278n10, 279nn7, 8
2,500th anniversary of the Persian Empire, 255–256
Twenty-Second Regiment Band, 11
Tygett, Jack, *232*

Uitti, Betty, 199
Ullmann, Liv, 256–257
"Ulysses's," 235
Umeki, Miyoshi, 229
Ungern-Sternberg, Baron Yuri, *28*, 29
Universal-International Pictures, 209–211
Up in Central Park, 142

"Valse Triste," 227, 228
Van, Bobby, 186, 256, 257
Vanderbilt, Alfred, 89
Van Heusen, Jimmy, 224
Varno, Becky, 229, 243
Velez, Lupe, 48, 91
Vera-Ellen, 172, *173*, 174
Verdon, Gwen, 120, 216, 219
Vivacious Lady, 92, 95–96, 101

"Wabash Rag," 17
"Wait 'Til the Sun Shines, Nellie," 126
"Waiting at the Church," 128
Walden, Kelly Sullivan, 17
Walker, Vernon, 81
Walker, Walton, 191, 195, 205, 279n12
Walk on the Wild Side, 235
Walsh, Mary Joyce, 108
Walters, Chuck, 155
"Waltz in Swing Time," 77, 79
Wanger, Walter, 234–235
Ward-Belmont School for Women, 19
Warga, Wayne, 257
Warner Brothers Studios, 41, 174, 242, 248, 249, 250, 257
Warner, Jack, 242, 248
Warren, Harry, 106, 110, 113, 115, 123, 124, 128, 139, 140, 178, 277nn10, 1
Washington, Booker T., 11
Watch Your Step. See *Shall We Dance*
"Waterfront Ballet," 177, 178, 187, 222
Waters, Ethel, 36
Watson, Betty Jane, 162
"The Way You Look Tonight," 89
Webb, Clifton, 176–177
Webb, Roy, 49, 84
Webster, Paul Francis, 184
Week-End in Havana, 115–116, 279n7
Weekend in Las Vegas. See *Meet Me in Las Vegas*

"A Weekend in the Country," 160
Weill, Kurt, 139
"Welcome to the Diamond Horseshoe," 140
"Welcome Song," 146
Wells, George, 189
Welles, Rebecca, 205
"We Open in Venice," 188
Wertmüller, Lina, 206, 260
West, Buster, 95
The West Point Story, 174
West Side Story, 211
"What a Crisis," 152
"What Can I Do for You," 111
"What Do I Care for a Dame?," 204
"What's the Use of Dreaming," 148
Wheeler and Woolsey, 47, 48, 49, 50
Wheeler, Bert. See Wheeler and Woolsey
When Irish Eyes Are Smiling. See *Irish Eyes Are Smiling*
"When Irish Eyes Are Smiling," 138
"Where Did You Get That Girl?," 174
Where Do We Go from Here?, 139
"Where Is the Life That Late I Led?," 188
The Whirl of Life, 100
"Whistling Away the Dark," 253
White, Onna, 211, 242
Whitney, Jock, 7
"Who Am I?," 105
"Why Can't You Behave?," 187
"Why Fight the Feeling," 170
Wiere Brothers, 110
Wilcox, Bea Busch. See Busch, Bea
Wilder, Marc, 219, *219*
Williams, Andy, 229
Williams, Cara, 196, 210–211
Williams, Esther, 178, 179, 189–190
Williams, Joe, 228
Williams, John, 245
Williams, Kay, 185
Williams, Kenny, 123, 138, 277nn3, 9
Williams, Mary, 13, *14*

Willock, Dave, 254
Winninger, Charles, 142
Winslow, Susan, 78, 262
Wintner, Rudy, 38
"The Wishing Waltz," 128
Witbeck, Charles, 208, 229
The Wizard of Oz, 111
Wolf, Tommy, 235, 245
Woolsey, Robert. See Wheeler and Woolsey
A Woman Rebels, 84
Wonderful Town, 247
"The World Is a Circle," 256–257
"Wouldn't It Be Loverly," 243, 244
"Would You Like to Be the Love of My Life," 103, 104
Wrubel, Allie, 210
"Wunderbar," 188, 279n2

Xenakis, Iannis, 256

"The Yam," 98, 150, 175
"Yama Yama Man," 101
"Yankee Doodle Hayride," 132
Years Ago. See *The Actress*
"Yesterdays," 181
Yorkin, Bud, 215, 280n2
York, Michael, 256
"You'll Be Reminded of Me," 96
You Made Me Love You. See *The Barkleys of Broadway*
Youmans, Vincent, 21, 43
"You Mustn't Kick it Around," 204
"Younger than Springtime," 216
"Your Good-Will Ambassador," 253
"You Started Something," 111

Zanuck, Darryl, 105–106, 114, 117, 118, 276nn1, 8
Zarabanda, 149
Ziegfeld, Florenz, Jr., 35, 66, 141
Ziegfeld Follies, 21, 157
"Zip," 202
"Zip-A-Dee-Doo-Dah," 210, 225

Printed in the USA/Agawam, MA
May 6, 2014